CW00821447

Fighter Command
Air Combat Claims
1939-45

Volume Two

200149928

This book is dedicated to the fighter aircrew of
Fighter Command, Second Tactical Air Force
and the intruder crews of
No.100 (Bomber Support) Group

Fighter Command
Air Combat Claims
1939-45
by
John Foreman

Red Kite

First published 2005 by
Red Kite
PO Box 223, Walton-on-Thames,
Surrey, KT12 3YQ
England

© John Foreman 2005

All Rights Reserved.
No part of this publication
may be reproduced, stored
in any form of retrieval
system, or transmitted
in any form or by any
means without prior
permission in writing
from the publishers.

Typeset in Great Britain by
A.C.E.Services,
Radlett, Herts, WD7 8LU

Printed by Cromwell Press

ISBN 0-9546201-5-1

WEST SUSSEX LIBRARIES	
20/0149928	
H J	06/12/2005
940.544941	£19.95

CONTENTS

The Legend of the Fighter Pilot

"At first, pilots of the opposing nations would pass each other in the air and wave at each other. Then someone took a pistol with them, and ruined a perfectly good thing".
- General Charles 'Chuck' Yeager

Throughout recorded history, civilisation has required its military heroes. The concept of 'hand-to-hand' and 'face-to-face' individual combat has held a perhaps over-romanticised fascination for many. This scenario has been manifested in the Gladiators of ancient Rome, the Arthurian knights, the gunfighters of the old West and, in more recent times, the fighter pilots. All of these manifestions of single combat have, to a large degree, been over-dramaticised and 'over-chivalrised' by novels and films until the truth has been totally swamped by the legend. However, in the beginnings of combat aviation there does seem to have been a degree of chivalry – but this did not last long.

The early military aircraft of the First World War were too fragile to carry weapons and the air war over France was a gentlemanly affair. *"We were there to lend a little tone to what would otherwise have been a vulgar brawl"*, as one pilot put it. By 1916 however the aircraft were faster, more powerful and well armed and the 'gentlemanly affair' had evolved into bloody carnage, with sixty or more fighter aircraft, known then as 'scouts' wheeling and turning in deadly meleés over the trenches, the machine-guns turning the highly flammable aircraft into potential torches. From this was born the legend of the fighter pilot and the concept of the 'ace' was born. A pilot who had downed five opponents was admitted to that fairly exclusive circle, but precisely when and how the term originated is unclear. What is certain is that the standing of a pilot was marked by his combat successes and this was carried forward into the Second World War.

Although I confess to having been fascinated by the subject and have been privileged to have met many British, German and American fighter pilots, I also feel strongly that the highly successful deeds of the few have overshadowed the tireless courage of the many, who were not fortunate enough to have the opportunity to engage the enemy so often; it is worth considering why this was.

The real 'shooting war' started in 1940 and culminated in the huge struggle over southern England that has gone down in history as the Battle of Britain. Rightly described as our 'Finest Hour' by Winston Churchill, the campaign has thrown up an interesting fact; roughly one-third of all RAF aces achieved most, if not all, of their combat successes during this period and the reason for this is clear. Outnumbered, and fighting over their own soil, they faced a determined and skilful enemy coming at them in large numbers and thus there was no shortage of targets – assuming that the ground control organisation was effective, and it usually was. In 1941, all this changed. The German invasion of Russia stripped the Germans of their forces in the west as the RAF went on the offensive. Now it was the *Luftwaffe* that was outnumbered, but with a significant advantage. The range of the British daylight bomber formations was necessarily tied to that of their short-range escorts, covering a fairly limited area over western France. Within that area there was little of strategic importance that required air defence at all costs, unlike the situation in 1940 where the RAF was forced to defend strategic targets. The Germans could pick their fights and did so carefully, only engaging the RAF under the most favourable tactical conditions and in relatively small formations. Therefore the opportunities for combat were. For the RAF, vastly reduced. Certainly, squadron, flight and section commanders, leading their pilots into battle, had opportunities, but those following could often only watch as their opponents power-dived to safety. There was also the question of temperament and sheer natural ability. As Lynn Garrison, ex-403 Squadron, once remarked, *"In every squadron there were perhaps four or five pilots who exuded confidence. They knew that they were going out to shoot. The rest knew sub-consciously that they would make up the numbers, mill about, and get shot at"*. Perhaps over-stated, it does bear at least an element of truth. Any scrutiny of squadron claims will reveal that the same names appear, time after time. These men were truly the hunters. There have been many books written about the great pilots such as Johnnie Johnson, Douglas Bader, Ginger Lacey and Bob Tuck. It is to all of the others, the 'ordinary Joes' who never became aces, milled about, got shot at and, above all, those who were frightened but still went, that this book is respectfully dedicated.

John Foreman

Notes

This book is about fighter claims, not combat victories, or actual 'shoot downs', for the two are very different; to confuse claims with victories would be a mistake. The business of air fighting was and is fast and deadly and the pilot could seldom be certain of what he saw. Claims are what pilots thought they saw, but were not necessarily what actually happened and are explained by the term 'over-claiming'. This happened all the time, even with the use of cine cameras as supporting evidence. The 'norm' as researched by my friend Chris Shores, was an average of three claims to two actual 'shoot downs' and this ratio held for all air forces in World War II. The over-claim rate was higher in 1940 – 41 around 5:1, but reduced later, evening up the average.

Format of the Tables

The format is simple, runs in chronological order and contains the following details:-

1)   Date

2)   Squadron, arranged in ascending order. Where a unit appears more than once on a particular day it indicates that combats occurred on different sorties.

3)   Aircraft Type, abbreviated as

Spit	Spitfire
Hurr	Hurricane
Glad	Gladiator
Blen	Blenheim
Beau	Beaufighter
Whir	Whirlwind
Mosq	Mosquito
Havc	Havoc
Typh	Typhoon
Must	Mustang

4)   Organisation eg FC (Fighter Command) AC (Army Co-operation).

5)   Pilot's Name

6) **Claim**: There were, at this stage of the war, three classifications:

a)   Destroyed. (Dest.) Where an aircraft was seen to crash, to be on fire, or where the pilot/crew was seen to parachute from the aircraft.

b)   Probably Destroyed (Prob.dest). Where the aircraft was not seen to crash but was so badly damaged that, in the opinion of the claiming pilot, it could not have reached safety

c)   Damaged – self explanatory.

7) **Location**: taken from either the Combat Report or the general area noted in Fighter Command Combats and Casualties. One anomaly has come to light regarding 'shared' claims. In some cases, pilots' combat reports claim an aircraft destroyed, probably destroyed or damaged, but make no mention of other pilots present. Indeed, in one instance, three pilots from the same unit, in the same formation and attacking a lone German aircraft, all make the same claim for the aircraft, none mentioning the presence of the others. Where this has occurred I have tried to rectify this in the listings.

8) **Time**. Where possible, times have taken from Combat Reports. However, for many reasons, the author was unable to do this. One reason is that so many of these vital documents were stolen from Public Record Office by an alleged historian to, 'protect them from the morons who were supposed to be looking after them'. Since so many of the documents were never recovered - indeed, the author has even seen original Combat Reports being offered for sale – this rings a little hollow. The convicted thief not only brought shame on himself, but has done irreparable harm to the efforts of the many honest researchers and to our military history in general. In many other cases, the time stated is noted thus: 1030~, indicating that it is an approximate time taken from the take-off and landing times given in FCC & C. Even in the Combat Reports, times are often approximate i.e. 1540 – 1555 and again an approximate time has been inserted. These 'guesstimates' are necessarily my own.

Sources

Some claims featured here do not appear on official listings; they could be spurious, or could be claims that were submitted but disallowed. Some claims are actually 'shares' but are not so indicated in the official documentation. Any mistakes are necessarily my own, but I would say that this work is intended as a basis for research and should be viewed as such.

The principal sources at the National Archives, Kew (Public Record Office) were:-

> Fighter Command Combats and Casualties.
>
> 2nd Tactical Air Force Combats and Casualties.
>
> Squadron Operation Record Books.
>
> Personal Combat Reports.

Published works that were especially helpful were:
> *Aces High* by Chris Shores and Clive Williams
> *RAF Victory Listings* by Frank Olynyk
> *The Typhoon and Tempest Story* by Chris Shores and Chris Thomas

Acknowledgements

I owe grateful thanks to Simon Parry, my publisher, for his was the idea behind this work and he also supplied many photographs. Also to Chris Goss, Mark Postlethwaite, Chris Shores and Frank Olynyk for photographs and information. To Nick Pace of LloydsTSB for his continued faith in my work and his financial support and finally, but by no means least, to my wife Pam, who has never understood my obsession with fighter aviation but, like marvellous wives everywhere, still puts up with it.

Chapter One

Winter Pause 1941

1st January - 12th March 1941

The situation at the beginning of 1941 was in a state of flux. The daylight phase of the Battle of Britain was over and the German night raids, heavy in December, were slackening in intensity. The British day and night fighter aircrew believed that the *Luftwaffe* was now a spent force, but nothing was further from the truth. Certainly, the Germans had been mauled by Fighter Command - but not to the extent that the British aircrew assumed. The actual situation was that many of the German units had been withdrawn to Germany to rest and re-fit and the *Luftwaffe* aircrews, particularly the day fighter pilots, firmly believed that, in the spring, the massive daylight assault would continue. This was also a mistake. In reality, the German attacks would start again, but only by night, while the RAF would commence a policy of 'leaning forward into France'. This latter took the form of the *Circus*, a small force of bombers with heavy fighter escort intended to draw the *Luftwaffe* fighters to battle and destroy both aircraft and pilots in the air. These were precisely the *Luftwaffe* tactics in 1940 and, realistically, there was no reason to suppose that the RAF would be any more successful than their opponents had been.

January 1941

1st January 1941

111 Sqn Hurr FC	S/L Ldr A.J.Biggar	Ju88 prob.dest	Off Montrose	u/k
	F/L J.A.Walker	- shared -		
	F/O M.Kellett	- shared -		

2nd January 1941

79 Sqn Hurr FC	Sgt L.A.Parr	Ju88 prob.dest	S Pembrey	1345~
	Sgt H.K.Hughes	- shared -		
234 Sqn Spit FC	P/O K.S.Dewhurst	Ju88 damaged	Off Dodman Point	1000~

The extremely severe of winter of 1940/41 is amply shown by this photo of a 263 Squadron Whirlwind at Exeter, being serviced by undoubtedly cold and miserable ground staff (ww2images.com)

*At Coltishall, pilots of 257 Squadron don
their parachutes before a scramble. This
obviously 'staged' photo taken on 4th
January shows Squadron Leader Bob
Tuck's Hurricane DT-A. Note the line of
white swastikas beneath the cockpit.
(ww2images.com)*

2/3rd January 1941

23 Sqn Blen FC P/O P.S.B.Ensor	He111 prob.dest	Vereul	u/k

3/4th January 1941

604 Sqn Beau FC F/L J.Cunningham	He111 prob.dest	Near Lyme Regis	1915

4th January 1941

65 Sqn Spit FC F/O B.E.Finucane	Bf110 destroyed	15m S Selsey	0950
152 Sqn Spit FC P/O E.S.Marrs*	Do17 destroyed	SW The Shambles	1400

* Shared with Portland AA sites

4/5th January 1941

87 Sqn Hurr FC F/O D.G.Smallwood	E/A damaged	Near Bristol	u/k

7th January 1941

421 Flt Spit FC F/L B.Drake F/O J.J.O'Meara	Ju88 damaged - shared -	Near Dover	1200
421 Flt Spit FC F/L B.Drake	Ju88 damaged	Near Hawkinge	1400

9/10th January 1941

264 Sqn Deft FC Sgt P.Endersby	Ju88 damaged	Beachy Head	2359

10th January 1941

41 Sqn Spit FC Sgt A.C.Baker	Bf109 prob.dest	Off Griz Nez	1245
145 Sqn Hurr FC P/O P.Dunning-White Sgt G.M.Turnbull	Ju88 damaged - shared -	35m S Littlehampton	1345
249 Sqn Hurr FC W/C F.V.Beamish	Bf109 damaged	Near Mardyck	1300~
Sgt M.K.Maciejowski	Bf109E destroyed	Near Guines	1300~
W/C F.V.Beamish	Bf109 destroyed	Channel	1300~

11/12th January 1941

65 Sqn Spit FC F/L T.Smart	Ju88 destroyed	Near south coast	u/k

Left: 263 Squadron Whirlwind pilots Flight Lieutenant T.P.Pugh, Squadron Leader J.G.Munro and Flying Officer D.A.Crooks on 13th January, probably at Exeter. (ww2images.com). Right: the controversial Brendan Finucane of 65 Squadron claimed a Bf110 destroyed on 4th January.

12th January 1941

3 Sqn	Hurr FC	F/L A.E.Berry		Do17 destroyed	Fair Isle	1140
263 Sqn	Whir FC	P/O D.Stein		Ju88 damaged	Off Cornwall	0000~

12/13th January 1941

604 Sqn	Beau FC	F/L J.Cunningham		He111 damaged	Off Beachy Head	0430

15th January 1941

616 Sqn	Spit FC	F/O H.S.L.Dundas		Do17 damaged	40m E N Coates	1420
		P/O J.E.Johnson		- shared -		

15/16th January 1941

151 Sqn	Deft FC	F/L D.A.P.McMullen		Ju88 prob.dest	Off Cromer	2318
151 Sqn	Deft FC	F/L K.H.Blair		Ju88 prob.dest	Kings Lynn	2343
151 Sqn	Hurr FC	P/O R.P.Stevens		Do17 destroyed	Harts Wood	0136
151 Sqn	Hurr FC	P/O R.P.Stevens		He111 destroyed	Holehaven	0520

16th January 1941

32 Sqn	Hurr FC	F/O J.P.Falkowski		He111 destroyed	Near Shoreham	1940

16/17th January 1941

23 Sqn	Blen FC	F/L D.A.Willans		Do17 damaged	Off orfordness	0100

17th January 1941

3 Sqn	Hurr FC	F/L A.E..Berry		He111 destroyed	Fair Isle	1102
504 Sqn	Hurr FC	Sgt C.Haw		He111 damaged	S Bolt Head	u/k
		Sgt B.H.Hirst		- shared -		

17/18th January 1941

| 23 Sqn | Blen FC | F/L D.A.Willans | He111 destroyed | Poix | u/k |

19th January 1941

| 65 Sqn | Spit FC | F/L B.E.Finucane | Ju88 destroyed | Channel | u/k |
| | | Sgt H.Orchard | - shared - | | |

22nd January 1941

41 Sqn	Spit FC	P/O E.P.Wells	He111 damaged	Bradwell Bay	0950
64 Sqn	Spit FC	S/L J.A.Rankin	Ju88 prob.dest	Off Calais	1215
		P/O J.H.Rowden	- shared -		
		P/O A.R.Tidman	- shared -		
91 Sqn	Spit FC	P/O P.L.Parrott	Ju88 destroyed	Dover-Folkestone	1125
91 Sqn	Spit FC	F/O J.J.O'Meara	Ju88 damaged	Near Dover	1155
242 Sqn	Hurr FC	S/L D.R.S.Bader	Ju88 destroyed	Off Gt Yarmouth	u/k
		F/O L.E.Edmond	- shared -		
		F/O N.D.Cryderman	- shared -		
303 Sqn	Hurr FC	S/L W.Lapkowski	Bf109 damaged	Near Calais*	u/k
		Sgt W.Strembosz	Bf109 damaged	Near Calais*	u/k

Probably by strafing

23rd January 1941

| 92 Sqn | Spit FC | Sgt R.E.Fokes | Bf110 damaged | E Manston | 1100 |
| | | Sgt D.E.Lloyd | - shared - | | |

1st February 1941

| 222 Sqn | Spit FC | F/O B.Van Mentz | Ju88 prob.dest | E Yarmouth | 1215 |

2nd February 1941

1 Sqn	Hurr FC	F/S K.Kuttelwascher	Bf109 damaged	Off Boulogne	1400~
		F/O N.P.W.Hancock	Bf109 damaged	Off Boulogne	1400~
74 Sqn	Spit FC	Sgt A.H.Smith	Bf109 prob.dest	Off Boulogne	1400
		Sgt A.D.Payne	Bf109 destroyed	5m NW Boulogne	1405
		S/L A.G.Malan	Bf109 destroyed	Boulogne	1410
91 Sqn	Spit FC	F/O J.J.O'Meara	Do17 damaged	Off Dover	1535
222 Sqn	Spit FC	F/O B.Van Mentz	He111 damaged	Off Lowestoft	1605
601 Sqn	Hurr FC	S/L W.W.Straight	Bf109 destroyed	Off Boulogne	1400~

3rd February 1941

| 92 Sqn | Spit FC | P/O A.C.Bartley | He111 destroyed | Outer Estuary | a.m. |

85 Squadron had fought throughout the Battle of Britain and had become a designated night fighter unit. Left: Flying Officers W.F.Carnaby, J.E.Marshall, Squadron Leader Peter Townsend DFC and Pilot Officer Howitt prepare for night fighting operations by wearing dark glasses. Right: Flight Lieutenant Geoffrey 'Sammy' Allard receives a DFC and Bar to his DFM from King George VI. Both photos taken at Debden. (ww2images.com)

4th February 1941

91 Sqn	Spit	FC	F/S D.A.S.McKay	Bf109 destroyed	Channel	1440
			F/S D.A.S.McKay	Bf109 damaged	Channel	1440
249 Sqn	Hurr	FC	S/L R.A.Barton	Bf110 destroyed	Kentish Knock LV	p.m.
			S/L R.A.Barton	Bf110 destroyed	Kentish Knock LV	p.m.
			Sgt G.C.C.Palliser	- shared -		
257 Sqn	Hurr	FC	Sgt L.D.Barnes	Do17 destroyed	Off Lowestoft	0930
			Sgt V.Brejcha	- shared -		

4/5th February 1941

85 Sqn	Hurr	FC	P/O P.W.Arbon	Ju88 damaged	SE Debden	night
151 Sqn	Deft	FC	Sgt H.G.Bodien	Do17 destroyed	Welson	2140

5th February 1941

65 Sqn	Spit	FC	F/L B.E.Finucane	Bf109 destroyed	nr Wizernes	p.m.
74 Sqn	Spit	FC	S/L A.G.Malan	Do215 damaged	1m S Dover	1350
			P/O W.Armstrong	- shared -		
			F/L J.C.Freeborn	- shared -		
			P/O P.Chesters	- shared -		
92 Sqn	Spit	FC	P/O R.H.Fokes	Ju87 destroyed	Manston	a.m.
			P/O C.H.Saunders	- shared -		
			Sgt H.Bowen-Morris	- shared -		
			Sgt Ream	- shared -		

611 Sqn	Spit	FC	P/O B.Heath	Bf109 destroyed	French coast		p.m.
			P/O W.GT.G.D.Smith	Bf109 prob.dest	French coast		p.m.
			Sgt A.Gilligin	- shared -			

8th February 1941

234 Sqn	Spit	FC	P/O E.B.Mortimer-Rose	Ju88 damaged	S Warmwell		u/k
242 Sqn	Hurr	FC	F/L P.S.Turner	Do17 destroyed	Off Clacton		1700~
			P/O D.E.Crowley-Milling	- shared -			
			P/O L.E.Cryderman	- shared -			
263 Sqn	Whir	FC	P/O K.A.G.Graham	Ar196 destroyed	Off Dodman Point		0920

9th February 1941

64 Sqn	Spit	FC	S/L J.E.Rankin	Ju88 destroyed	Off Mersea Islamd		1025
			P/O J.H.Rowden	- shared -			
			Sgt T.W.Savage	- shared -			

9/10th February 1941

151 Sqn	Hurr	FC	Sgt A.D.Wagner	E/A damaged	Near Birmingham		0330~

10th February 1941

249 Sqn	Hurr	FC	Sgt M.M.Maciejowski	Bf109E destroyed	Off Dunkirk		1300~
			Sgt S.Brzeski	Bf109E destroyed	Off Dunkirk		1300~

10/11th February 1941

255 Sqn	Deft	FC	P/O R.M.Trousdale	He111 prob.dest	E Spurn Head		2258
255 Sqn	Deft	FC	P/O R.M.D.Hall	He111 prob.dest	E Humber Mouth		2314

11th February 1941

234 Sqn	Spit	FC	P/O E.B.Mortimer-Rose	Ju88 damaged	Off St Eval		1720

13th February 1941

91 Sqn	Spit	FC	Sgt D.A.S.McKay	Bf109 damaged	Dover		1300
111 Sqn	Hurr	FC	P/O D.H.Gage	He111 damaged	Off Aberdeen		1830
609 Sqn	Spit	FC	P/O T.Nowierski	Ju88 damaged	Mid-Channel		1705

14th February 1941

66 Sqn	Spit	FC	P/O J.H.T.Pickering	Bf109 damaged	Dover-Hawkinge		1125
92 Sqn	Spit	FC	F/S D.A.S.McKay	Bf109 destroyed	Cap Griz Nez		1210~
111 Sqn	Hurr	FC	P/O M.Kellett	Ju88 damaged	Off Aberdeen		1830

15th February 1941

71 Sqn	Hurr	FC	P/O V.C.Keough	Do17 damaged	Off Skegness		u/k
			P/O N.Morantz	- shared -			
222 Sqn	Spit	FC	S/L R.C.Love	He111 destroyed	Near Corton		1745
			P/O B.P.Klee	- shared -			

16

Manston, 5th February 1941: Sergeant Ream, Pilot Officer Ronnie Fokes, Segeant Hugh Bowen-Morris and Pilot Officer Cecil Saunders of 92 Squadron inspect the wreckage of a 9./St.G. 1 Ju87B, which Fokes blew up with cannon fire on the airfield perimeter. (ww2images.com)

234 Sqn Spit FC	P/O M.C.B.Boddington	Ju88 damaged	S Plymouth	1705
	Sgt J.F.Armitage	- shared -		
242 Sqn Hurr FC	P/O D.E.Crowley-Milling	Ju88 damaged	Off Aldeburgh	1050

15/16th February 1941

604 Sqn Beau FC	F/L J.Cunningham	He111 destroyed	Totnes	1916

16th February 1941

302 Sqn Hurr FC	P/O E.R.Pilch	Ju88 destroyed	Off Bognor Regis	1210
	Sgt M.Wedzik	- shared -		

17th February 1941

222 Sqn Spit FC	S/L R.C.Love	Do17 damaged	Marham	1240
	Sgt J.Christie	- shared -		
222 Sqn Spit FC	Sgt D.L.Ferraby	Ju88 destroyed	E Cromer	1411
	Sgt P.O.Davis	- shared -		
222 Sqn Spit FC	S/L R.C.Love	Ju88 destroyed	E Yarmouth	1515
	Sgt R.G.Marland	- shared -		

17/18th February 1941

219 Sqn Beau FC	S/L J.H.Little	Do17 destroyed	Bray	1955

20th February 1941

611 Sqn Spit FC	Sgt N.G.Townsend	Bf109 damaged	Wissant	a.m.

21st February 1941

111 Sqn	Hurr FC	P/O M.Kellett	Ju88 damaged	Dyce	1143
		Sgt O.Hruby	- shared -		

22nd February 1941

74 Sqn	Spit FC	P/O E.W.G.Churches	Bf110 destroyed	30-35m E Margate	1125
		Sgt N.Morrison	- shared -		
111 Sqn	Hurr FC	P/O G.S.P.Baine	He115 prob.dest	Off Peterhead	1053
		P/O A.H.Gregory	- shared -		

25th February 1941

611 Sqn	Spit FC	S/L E.A.Bitmead	Bf109 destroyed	Off Dunkirk	1430
		F/L D.H.Watkins	Bf109 destroyed	Off Dunkirk	1430
SF Hch	Spit FC	G/C H.Broadhurst	Bf109 destroyed	Off Dunkirk	1430
		G/C H.Broadhurst	Bf109 prob.dest	Off Dunkirk	1430

25/26th February 1941

23 Sqn	Blen FC	P/O J.Brown	He111 destroyed	Merwe	2345~
85 Sqn	Hurr FC	S/L P.W.Townsend	Do17 destroyed	Sudbury	2125

26th February 1941

242 Sqn	Hurr FC	Sgt E.A.Redfern	Bf110 damaged	W Orfordness	1350
610 Sqn	Spit FC	Sgt F.C.Horner	Bf109 prob.dest	Off Dungeness	2030

26/27th February 1941

23 Sqn	Blen FC	P/O A.J.Love	E/A damaged	Merville	2245~
		P/O A.J.Love	E/A damaged	Bethune	2245~
219 Sqn	Beau FC	P/O A.J.Hodgkinson	He111 damaged	Tangmere	2100~
604 Sqn	Beau FC	S/L C.H.Anderson	Ju88 damaged	Middle Wallop	2100~

28th February 1941

611 Sqn	Spit FC	S/L E.A.Bitmead	Do215 prob.dest	E Crouch estuary	1230
		P/O J.R.G.Sutton	- shared -		
		Sgt W.G.G.D.Smith	- shared -		

1st March 1941

74 Sqn	Spit FC	P/O R.L.Spurdle	Bf109 destroyed	Griz Nez-Boulogne	1620
		P/O R.L.Spurdle	Bf109 destroyed	Griz Nez-Boulogne	1620
		P/O R.L.Spurdle	Bf109 damaged	7-10m SE Margate	1630~
		Sgt J.N.Glendinning	Bf109 destroyed	Griz Nez	1620
145 Sqn	Spit FC	F/O M.A.Newling	Ju88 destroyed	Off St Catherines Pt	1915
		F/O D.H.Clarke	- shared -		
		Sgt F.J.Twitchett	- shared -		
263 Sqn	Whir FC	P/O P.G.Thornton-Brown	Ju88 damaged	S Scilly Isles	1105

18

222 Squadron was very active along the East Anglian coast in the early months of 1941. On 15th February Squadron Leader R.C.Love shared the destruction of an He111 with Pilot Officer B.P.Klee and, in two separate fights on 17th, claimed a Do17 damaged and a Ju88 destroyed. l-r; Sqn Ldr R.C.Love, Fg Off Davies, Flt Lt B.Van Mentz, Plt Off Carpenter and Plt Off Stewart. Brian Van Mentz, who would gain at leat seven confirmed successes, was killed on 16th April 1941 in the bombing of the 'Ferry Inn' near Coltishall. (ww2images.com)

2nd March 1941

257 Sqn	Hurr FC	S/L R.R.S.Tuck	Do17Z destroyed	Off Cromer		1635
3 Sqn	Hurr FC	P/O D.B.Robertson P/O Gabb	FW200 damaged - shared -	E Sumburgh		1435

3rd March 1941

54 Sqn	Spit FC	P/O A.R.McL.Campbell	Bf109 destroyed	Near Brenzett		1600

3/4th March 1941

23 Sqn	Blen FC	P/O P.S.B.Ensor	He111 destroyed	Merville		2245~
23 Sqn	Blen FC	F/L B.R.O'B.Hoare	He111 prob.dest	Near Lille		2359~

4th March 1941

74 Sqn	Spit FC	F/L J.C.Freeborn P/O H.R.G.Poulton	Do215 damaged - shared -	15m N Dunkirk		0745
152 Sqn	Spit FC	P/O Rowlands P/O R.W.C.Miller Sgt J.A.Short	Ju88 damaged* - shared - - shared -	S St Catherines Pt		1110

* Also shared with 302 Squadron.

253 Sqn	Hurr FC	F/O A.H.Corkett	Ju88 damaged	Orkneys		1435

19

			P/O Crowther	- shared -		
			P/O D.S.Yapp	- shared -		
302 Sqn	Hurr	FC	F/L J.Kowalski	Ju88 damaged*	S St Catherines Pt	1110
			Sgt A.Lysek	- shared -		
			P/O J.Malinski	- shared -		

* Also shared with 152 Squadron.

4/5th March 1941

604 Sqn	Beau	FC	S/L C.H.Anderson	He111 destroyed	Swanage	2130~

5th March 1941

54 Sqn	Spit	FC	P/O J.Stokoe	Bf109 destroyed	15m SW Boulogne	1400
			P/O H.N.D.Bailey	Bf109 prob.dest	10m SE Calais	1400
			P/O H.S.Sewell	Bf109 prob.dest	Near Calais	1400
			P/O C.Colebrook	Bf109 prob.dest	S Le Touquet	1400
263 Sqn	Whir	FC	P/O H.H.Kitchener	Ju88 damaged	S Lands End	0954
610 Sqn	Spit	FC	Sgt V.D.Page	Bf109 prob.dest	Boulogne	1400
			Sgt F.C.Horner	Bf109 damaged	Boulogne	1400
			Sgt P.W.Townsend	Bf109 prob.dest.	Boulogne	1400
611 Sqn	Spit	FC	Sgt N.G.Townsend	Bf109 prob.dest	Boulogne	1400
SF Hch	Spit	FC	G/C H.Broadhurst	Bf109 prob.dest	Boulogne	1400
			G/C H.Broadhurst	Bf109 damaged	Boulogne	1400

6th March 1941

91 Sqn	Spit	FC	F/L R.A.Lee-Knight	Do17 damaged	S Dover	1130
91 Sqn	Spit	FC	Sgt D.A.S.McKay	Do17 destroyed	S Folkestone	1625

7th March 1941

255 Sqn	Deft	FC	F/L A.A.Ballantyne	He111 damaged	Humber	1525

8th March 1941

222 Sqn	Spit	FC	P/O B.P.Klee	Ju88 destroyed	Off Gt Yarmouth	1100~
			Sgt R.G.Marland	- shared -		
266 Sqn	Spit	FC	F/O F.P.Ferris	Ju88 destroyed	E Skegness	1013
			Sgt J.E.Van Schaick	- shared -		

8/9th March 1941

23 Sqn	Blen	FC	P/O A.Gawith	He111 damaged	Beauvais	2135
			P/O A.Gawith	Do17 damaged	Beauvais	2135

10th March 1941

145 Sqn	Hurr	FC	F/L R.W.Bungey	Ju88 damaged	SW Selsey	1115
			F/O B.De Hemptinne	- shared -		
			P/O K.C.Gundrey	- shared -		

Group Captain Harry Broadhurst, station commander at Hornchurch, continued to fly on combat sorties until mid-1942. A very controversial figure, he was instrumental in refining close air support in the Middle East which, in turn, was a vital factor in the eventual invasion of France in 1944. On 5th March he claimed a 'probable' and a 'damaged'. Far right: John Glendinning of 74 Squadron, who claimed his fourth victory on 1st March. He was killed in combat with Major Werner Molders of JG 51 on 12th. (ww2images.com)

10/11th March 1941

79 Sqn	Hurr FC	F/L R.W.Denison	Ju88 destroyed	Deeping St James	2300
219 Sqn	Beau FC	W/C T.Pike	He111 prob.dest	Guildford-Horsham	2030~
219 Sqn	Beau FC	Sgt R.E.B.Sargent	He111 prob.dest	Newhaven	2145~

11th March 1941

234 Sqn	Spit FC	S/L M.V.Blake	Bf110 destroyed	SW Portland	1740
		F/L E.B.Mortimer-Rose	- shared -		
		P/O E.W.Wootton	- shared -		
263 Sqn	Whir FC	P/O H.H.Kitchener	Ju88 damaged	Off Lands End	1707

11/12th March 1941

610 Sqn	Spit FC	S/L J.Ellis	He111 destroyed	Selsey Bill	0035

12th March 1941

91 Sqn	Spit FC	P/O G.Fisher	Bf109 destroyed	Dungeness	1730~
		P/O G.Fisher	Bf109 destroyed	Dungeness	1730~

Chapter Two

The End of the Blitz
12th March - 15th June 1941

During February and early March, the *Luftwaffe* bomber units had been returning to the Channel coast from Germany and on the night of 12th March the *Blitz* reopened. At this time the British fighter defences relied heavily upon the Defiant squadrons. These aircraft had proved woefully lacking in performance in daylight operations, but proved to be surprisingly effective by night, although the lack of speed was a great handicap. On conditions of bright moonlight a 'Fighter Night' was declared and single seat fighter squadrons were also widely employed for point defence. Finally, the fast powerful Beaufighter was now reaching squadrons in greater numbers and this AI-equipped aircraft, with its massive armament, was to prove a potent weapon against the night bomber and would demonstrate this ability early in April. The night raids culminated in a massive raid on London on the night of the 10th May and the *Blitz*, in truth the final phase of the Battle of Britain, ended on the night of the 16th. By day, the tentative *Circus* operations were continuing, but the escorting fighter pilots were finding the German defences tougher than expected.

12/13th March 1941

151 Sqn	Deft	FC	Sgt R.J.McNair	He111 destroyed	Widnes	2210
151 Sqn	Hurr	FC	P/O R.P.Stevens	Ju88 prob.dest	Orfordness	0230~
255 Sqn	Deft	FC	F/L J.G.Sanders	He111 prob.dest	Kirton-in-Lindsay	0045
264 Sqn	Deft	FC	F/L D.A.P.Hughes	He111 destroyed	Ockley	2100~
264 Sqn	Deft	FC	F/O T.D.Welsh	He111 destroyed	Off Hastings	2345~
307 Sqn	Hurr	FC	Sgt K.Jankowiak	He111 damaged	Ruthin	2200
604 Sqn	Beau	FC	Sgt J.A.Wright	E/A prob.dest	S England	2105
604 Sqn	Beau	FC	F/O K.I.Geddes	Ju88 destroyed	Warminster	2145~
604 Sqn	Beau	FC	F/L J.Cunningham	Ju88 damaged	Middle Wallop	2305

13th March 1941

91 Sqn	Spit	FC	F/L R.H.Holland	Bf109 destroyed	Folkestone	0705
			Sgt A.W.P.Spears	Bf109 destroyed	Folkestone	0705
92 Sqn	Spit	FC	F/L A.R.Wright	Bf109 damaged	South coast	1700~
			F/L A.R.Wright	Bf109 damaged	South coast	1700~
302 Sqn	Hurr	FC	P/O W.S.Krol	Ju88 destroyed	Worthing	1640
			P/O M.Neyder	- shared -		
			P/O B.Bernas	- shared -		
504 Sqn	Hurr	FC	F/L A.H.Rook	Ju88 destroyed	Mid-Channel	p.m.
			Sgt D.Haywood	- shared -		
610 Sqn	Spit	FC	Sgt F.C.Horner	Bf109 prob.dest	N Calais	1450
			Sgt N.D.Warden	Bf109 prob.dest	N Calais	1450

13/14th March 1941

29 Sqn	Beau FC	P/O J.R.D.Braham	Do17 destroyed	N Wells	2145	
29 Sqn	Beau FC	W/C S.C.Widdows	Ju88 destroyed	Louth	0335~	
72 Sqn	Spit FC	F/L D.F.B.Sheen	Ju88 destroyed	N Acklington	2215~	
219 Sqn	Beau FC	P/O A.J.Hodgkinson	Do17 destroyed	Winchester	2040	
219 Sqn	Beau FC	S/L J.H.Little	E/A destroyed	Needles	2245	
		S/L J.H.Little	E/A damaged	Needles	2248	
219 Sqn	Beau FC	Sgt J.A.Clandillon	He111 destroyed	Shipley	2235	
255 Sqn	Deft FC	P/O M.F.Wynne-Wilson	Do17 damaged	Hull	0030~	
264 Sqn	Deft FC	Sgt C.G.Hilken	He111 damaged	South coast	2100~	
307 Sqn	Deft FC	P/O M.Lewandowski	He111 prob.dest	W Liverpool	0050	
600 Sqn	Beau FC	F/L G.A.Denby	He111 destroyed	Dunure	2225	
604 Sqn	Beau FC	F/L P.C.F.Lawton	Ju88 destroyed	Off Portland	u/k	
604 Sqn	Beau FC	F/O R.A.Chisholm	He111 destroyed	Near Portland	0230~	
604 Sqn	Beau FC	F/L S.H.Skinner	He111 damaged	South coast	2320~	

14th March 1941

152 Sqn	Spit FC	P/O W.D.Williams	Ju88 damaged	SSW Selsey Bill	1815	
		Sgt E.H.Marsh	- shared -			
312 Sqn	Hurr FC	F/L A.M.Dawbarn	Ju88 destroyed	25m SW Bardsey Is	1127	
		Sgt J.Stehlik	- shared -			
610 Sqn	Spit FC	S/L J.Ellis	Ju88 damaged	Channel	0810~	
		P/O J.E.I.Grey	- shared -			
		Sgt N.D.Warden	- shared -			

14/15th March 1941

23 Sqn	Blen FC	S/L E.J.Gracie	Do17 prob.dest	Merville	0300~	
29 Sqn	Beau FC	F/L G.P.Gibson	He111 destroyed	Skegness	2150~	
219 Sqn	Beau FC	F/L J.G.Topham	E/A destroyed	S Beachy Head	2340~	
604 Sqn	Beau FC	F/O K.I.Geddes	Ju88 destroyed	Falfield	2140	

15th March 1941

615 Sqn	Hurr FC	Adj H.G.Lafont	Bf109 prob.dest	Dungeness	1620	

15/16th March 1941

96 Sqn	Hurr FC	F/O V.V.S.Verity	He111 destroyed	Cranage	2300~	
219 Sqn	Beau FC	W/C T.Pike	He111 destroyed	S Bognor Regis	2150~	

16/17th March 1941

604 Sqn	Beau FC	F/O K.I.Geddes	He111 damaged	Studland Bay	2150	

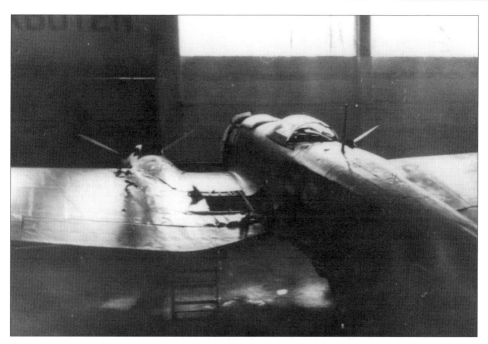

Sometimes they got back... G1+GS, an He111 of III./KG 55 pictured at Le Bourget after a night fighter attack. Three men from Feldwebel Schloms' crew were wounded. (ww2images.com)

Sometimes they didn't.... Oberfeldwebel Karl Singler's He111 G1+OP of II./KG 55, shot down at Widnes by Sergeant R.J.McNair of 151 Squadron on the night of 12/13th March 1941 (ww2images.com)

17th March 1941

111 Sqn	Hurr FC	F/L J.A.Walker	Ju88 damaged	NW Aberdeen	1515

18th March 1941

74 Sqn	Spit FC	P/O E.W.G.Churches	Bf109 destroyed	SW Folkestone	1335
222 Sqn	Spit FC	F/L B.Van Mentz P/O B.P.Klee	Bf110 destroyed - shared -	E Sheringham	1418

19th March 1941

257 Sqn	Hurr FC	S/L R.R.S.Tuck	Do17 destroyed	Cromer Knoll	0825
609 Sqn	Spit FC	P/O A.K.Ogilvie	Bf109 damaged	S Dungeness	1830
610 Sqn	Spit FC	Sgt W.J.Payne	Bf109 destroyed	S Dungeness	1620

19/20th March 1941

257 Sqn	Hurr FC	F/L H.P.Blatchford	Ju88 prob.dest	Southwold	1935

23rd March 1941

238 Sqn	Hurr FC	F/L E.J.Morris Sgt F.A.Bernard	Ju88 destroyed - shared -	Poling	1230
234 Sqn	Spit FC	F/L E.B.Mortimer-Rose P/O R.S.Masters Sgt H.B.Shepherd	Ju88 damaged - shared - - shared -	nr Isle of Wight	1530
41 Sqn	Spit FC	P/O R.S.Draper Sgt T.W.R.Healey	FW200 damaged - shared -	Off Whitby	1430

24th March 1941

1 Sqn	Hurr FC	F/O J.E.Demozay	Bf109 destroyed	SE Hastings	1510~
91 Sqn	Spit FC	F/L R.H.Holland	Bf109 prob.dest	Deal	1520~
74 Sqn	Spit FC	P/O R.L.Spurdle Sgt W.P.Dales	Ju88 prob.dest - shared -	7-8m SE Ramsgate	1525
79 Sqn	Hurr FC	F/O D.G.Clift	He111 damaged	Off The Mumbles	p.m.
111 Sqn	Hurr FC	Sgt O.Kucera	Ju88 damaged	S Montrose	1120
605 Sqn	Hurr FC	F/O R.W.Forster	He111 damaged	SE Felixstowe	0700~

25th March 1941

74 Sqn	Spit FC	P/O R.L.Spurdle Sgt W.P.Dales	Do215 damaged - shared -	2m SE Ramsgate	1140
605 Sqn	Hurr FC	Sgt E.W.Wright	Bf110 damaged	E Orfordness	1645

26th March 1941

308 Sqn	Hurr FC	P/O W.Bozek Sgt J.Kremski P/O F.Surma	Ju88 damaged - shared - - shared -	2m E Kenilworth	1200
605 Sqn	Hurr FC	F/O D.N.Forde P/O P.D.Thompson	Do17 destroyed - shared -	SE Orfordness	0906

Gathering of 'Eagles': 71 Squadron, the first of the American Eagle Squadrons, was operational at Kirton-in-Lindsay. Here, a group of American pilots line up for the camera including 2nd from right; Gus Daymond, 6th from right; 'Red' Tobin, and 7th from right 'Andy' Mamedoff. (ww2images.com)

27th March 1941

74 Sqn	Spit	FC	S/L P.A.Wood	Bf109 damaged	8m E Dungeness	1100
310 Sqn	Hurr	FC	S/L J.Latimer P/O J.Limlicka	Ju88 damaged - shared -	30m E Gt Yarmouth	0830
616 Sqn	Spit	FC	F/L C.H.MacFie	Bf110 damaged	Littlehampton	1400

28th March 1941

257 Sqn	Hurr	FC	F/L P.P.Hanks F/O McIntyre	He111 prob.dest - shared -	Off Happisburgh	1340
302 Sqn	Hurr	FC	P/O S.H.Lapka P/O W.Kaminsky Sgt A.Lysek	Ju88 destroyed - shared - - shared -	15m S Beachy Head	1235

30th March 1941

41 Sqn	Spit	FC	F/L A.D.J.Lovell	Ju88 destroyed	Hillsborough	1517
91 Sqn	Spit	FC	Sgt D.A.S.McKay	Bf109 destroyed	Off Dunkirk	1810

31st March 1941

91 Sqn	Spit	FC	Sgt J.Mann	Bf109 destroyed	Off Boulogne	0935~

1st April 1941

41 Sqn	Spit	FC	F/L A.D.J.Lovell Sgt W.Palmer	He111 damaged - shared -	Seaham Harbour	1605
79 Sqn	Hurr	FC	F/L G.D.L.Haysom	He111 destroyed	W St Davids Head	1605
242 Sqn	Hurr	FC	F/O N.D.Edmond P/O D.E.Crowley-Milling	Ju88 damaged - shared -	Off Harwich	1720
242 Sqn	Hurr	FC	S/L W.P.F.Treacey P/O R.D.Grassick	Ju88 destroyed - shared -	Lowestoft	1725
247 Sqn	Hurr	FC	Sgt J.V.Renvoise	FW200 damaged	Near St Eval	2015
263 Sqn	Whir	FC	S/L A.H.Donaldson	Do215 damaged	N Predannack	
316 Sqn	Hurr	FC	P/O A.K.Gabszewicz P/O B.Anders	He111 destroyed - shared -	Nr Milford Haven	1805

2nd April 1941

79 Sqn	Hurr	FC	S/L J.H.Heyworth	He111 prob.dest	Linney Head	1250
234 Sqn	Spit	FC	F/L E.B.Mortimer-Rose	Ju88 prob.dest	Near Warmwell	0730
504 Sqn	Hurr	FC	F/L P.T.Parsons	He111 destroyed	S Budleigh Salterton	0730

3rd April 1941

242 Sqn	Hurr	FC	S/L W.P.F.Treacey	Bf110 damaged	Off Orfordness	0700
504 Sqn	Hurr	FC	S/L A.H..Rook P/O H.N.Hunt	He111 destroyed - shared -	Portreath	1725
610 Sqn	Spit	FC	F/L S.C.Norris Sgt J.E.W.Ballard	Ju88 destroyed - shared -	S Beachy Head	0657

3/4th April 1941

604 Sqn	Beau	FC	F/L J.Cunningham	He111 destroyed	Middle Wallop	0050

4th April 1941

91 Sqn	Spit	FC	P/O D.H.Gage	Ju88 damaged	Channel	1710
222 Sqn	Spit	FC	F/L E.H.Thomas Sgt H.N.D.Ramsay	Ju88 prob.dest - shared -	NE Cromer	1640

4/5th April 1941

79 Sqn	Hurr	FC	F/O L.T.Bryant-Fenn F/O G.D.L.Haysom	He111 damaged - shared -	Linney Head	2031
604 Sqn	Beau	FC	F/L P.C.F.Lawton	He111 prob.dest	Near Frome	u/k
604 Sqn	Beau	FC	F/L E.D.Crew	He111 destroyed	Weston-Super-Mare	2225
604 Sqn	Beau	FC	F/L J.R.Watson	He111 destroyed	Shaftesbury	2225

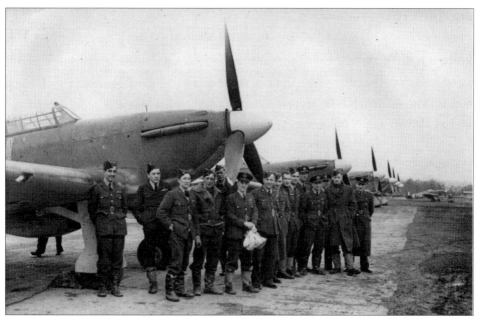

249 Squadron at North.Weald in April: L-R; Mills, May(?), Palliser, Davidson, A.G.Lewis, R.A. 'Butch' Barton (CO), Lomar (Adj), Crossey, Pat Wells, Wynne, Thompson, Cassidy, Woolmer (IO), Tom Neil, unknown, with their Hurricanes. (ww2images.com)

6th April 1941

74 Sqn	Spit	FC	P/O R.L.Spurdle	Bf110 prob.dest	Near St Omer	1700
			F/L A.C.Bartley	Bf109 damaged	St Omer	1700
263 Sqn	Whir	FC	F/O B.Howe	He111 damaged	SE Lizard Point	1305
			P/O Tooth	- shared -		

7th April 1941

74 Sqn	Spit	FC	P/O J.Rogowski	Bf109 destroyed	3m NE Griz Nez	1000
			P/O J.Howard	Bf109 damaged	5m NW St Inglevert	1000
222 Sqn	Spit	FC	Sgt R.G.Marland	Do17 destroyed	ESE Lowestoft	0935

7/8th April 1941

87 Sqn	Hurr	FC	F/L D.H.Ward	E/A destroyed	Branscombe	2145
219 Sqn	Beau	FC	F/O A.J.Hodgkinson	He111 destroyed	Off Worthing	0137
245 Sqn	Hurr	FC	S/L J.W.C.Simpson	He111 destroyed	Off Belfast	0137
256 Sqn	Deft	FC	F/L D.R.West	Ju88 destroyed	Ribble estuary	0001
604 Sqn	Beau	FC	F/L J.Cunningham	He111 destroyed	Middle Wallop	2145

8th April 1941

1 Sqn	Hurr FC	F/S K.Kuttelwascher	Bf109 destroyed	Channel		dawn

8/9th April 1941

151 Sqn	Hurr FC	P/O R.P.Stevens	He111 destroyed	Wellesbourne	0115
		P/O R.P.Stevens	He111 destroyed	Desford	0145
151 Sqn	Deft FC	Sgt A.D.Wagner	He111 destroyed	Coventry	0145~
		Sgt A.D.Wagner	He111 damaged	Coventry	0145~
151 Sqn	Deft FC	F/L D.A.P.McMullen	He111 destroyed	E Coventry	0140
151 Sqn	Deft FC	F/L D.F.W.Darling	He111 destroyed	Windsor Great Park	0230
264 Sqn	Deft FC	F/O D.A.P.Hughes	He111 prob.dest	SE Biggin Hill	0015
264 Sqn	Deft FC	S/L A.T.D.Sanders	He111 destroyed	Hitchin	2212
266 Sqn	Spit FC	S/L P.G.Jameson	He111 destroyed	Wittering	0145
310 Sqn	Hurr FC	S/L J.Latimer	Ju88 prob.dest	E Coventry	0100
604 Sqn	Beau FC	F/L E.D.Crew	He111 damaged	Sopley	0101
604 Sqn	Beau FC	Sgt P.F.Jackson	He111 damaged	Middle Wallop	0200

9th April 1941

3 Sqn	Hurr FC	F/O J.Lonsdale	Do215 damaged	E Lowestoft	1030
32 Sqn	Hurr FC	Sgt A.W.Gear	He111 damaged	S Portland	0640
54 Sqn	Spit FC	P/O N.G.Baxter	Bf109 destroyed	10m E Ramsgate	1800
64 Sqn	Spit FC	F/L J.J.O'Meara	He59 destroyed	Dunkirk-Ostend	1035
		P/O J.H.Rowden	Bf109 prob.dest	Dunkirk-Ostend	1035
		S/L J.E.Rankin	Bf109 damaged	Dunkirk-Ostend	1035
79 Sqn	Hurr FC	S/L J.H.Heyworth	He111 destroyed	W St Davids Head	0950
257 Sqn	Hurr FC	P/O Johnson	Bf110 damaged	E Southwold	1530
		P/O McCracken	- shared -		
316 Sqn	Hurr FC	F/O T.Sawicz	He111 destroyed	3m W St Annes Hd	0950
611 Sqn	Spit FC	S/L E.A.Bitmead	Bf109 destroyed	Gravelines	1210

9/10th April 1941

25 Sqn	Beau FC	Sgt S.Bennett	Ju88 destroyed	Cottesmore	2210
85 Sqn	Havc FC	W/C P.W.Townsend	Ju88 prob.dest	Near Brentwood	2305
85 Sqn	Havc FC	F/L J.E.Marshall	He111 damaged	Debden	0200
85 Sqn	Havc FC	F/O G.L.Howitt	Ju88 destroyed	Whitwell	0200
93 Sqn	Havc FC	F/L P.Burke	E/A prob.dest	SE Portland	2146
141 Sqn	Deft FC	P/O Stevens	He111 destroyed	Biggin Hill	2350
151 Sqn	Deft FC	F/L D.A.P.McMullen*	Ju88 destroyed	nr Bramcote	2235

* Shared with AA Command.

30

Above: Busbridge Surrey the wreckage of G1+DN lies amongst the trees that claimed the lives of three of the four crew when it crashed after being shot down by Sergeants Thorn and Barker of 264 Sqn. Right: The following morning Ted Thorn and Fred Barker celebrate their victory with groundcrew. (ww2images.com)

151 Sqn	Deft	FC	H.G.Sgt Bodien	He111 destroyed	Birmingham	0145
255 Sqn	Deft	FC	Sgt Staples	He111 prob.dest	Birmingham	0005
255 Sqn	Deft	FC	Sgt J.Craig	E/A damaged	S Kirton-in-Lindsay	0041
257 Sqn	Hurr	FC	S/L R.R.S.Tuck	Ju88 destroyed	Lowestoft	u/k
264 Sqn	Deft	FC	F/S E.R.Thorn	He111 destroyed	Brooklands	2355
264 Sqn	Deft	FC	F/L D.H.Hughes	He111 destroyed	Near Isle of Wight	0115
266 Sqn	Spit	FC	F/L D.L.Armitage	He111 prob.dest	Near Birmingham	0200
604 Sqn	Beau	FC	F/O R.A.Chisholm	He111 destroyed	Cranbourne	2105
604 Sqn	Beau	FC	F/L J.Cunningham	He111 destroyed	Bournemouth	2115
604 Sqn	Beau	FC	F/L J.Cunningham	He111 damaged	Middle Wallop	u/k
604 Sqn	Beau	FC	F/O C.L.Gomm	Ju88 damaged	Middle Wallop	0120
604 Sqn	Beau	FC	F/O R.A.Chisholm	He111 destroyed	Boscombe	0217

31

10th April 1941

41 Sqn	Spit FC	Sgt G.W.Swanwick Sgt A.A.Glen	He111 damaged - shared -	N Flamborough Hd	1920
72 Sqn	Spit FC	Sgt L.M.Lack Sgt W.Gregson	Ju88 prob.dest - shared -	Farne Island	1925
72 Sqn	Spit FC	Sgt A.J.Casey Sgt D.J.Prytherch	Ju88 destroyed - shared -	Alnmouth	1940
74 Sqn	Spit FC	P/O P.Chesters	Bf109 destroyed	St Nicholas-at-Wade	1700
312 Sqn	Hurr FC	Sgt J.Truhlar	Bf110 damaged	SW Aberdeen	1425

10/11th April 1941

85 Sqn	Havc FC	W/C P.W.Townsend	Ju88 damaged	Bury St Edmunds	0145
85 Sqn	Havc FC	P/O G.L.Howitt	Ju88 destroyed	East Anglia	0150
87 Sqn	Hurr FC	P/O R.M.S.Rayner	He111 damaged	E Bristol	0155
87 Sqn	Hurr FC	P/O G.L.Roscoe	E/A damaged	Gloucester	2355
93 Sqn	Harr FC	F/L D.Hayley-Bell	E/A prob.dest	S St Albans Head	2139
151 Sqn	Hurr FC	P/O R.P.Stevens	Ju88 destroyed	Murcott	2305
151 Sqn	Hurr FC	P/O R.P.Stevens	Ju88 destroyed	Kettering-Thrapston	0250
219 Sqn	Beau FC	P/O A.J.Hodgkinson	He111 prob.dest	Tangmere	0020
256 Sqn	Deft FC	F/L E.C.Deansley	He111 destroyed	Edge Hill	2235
264 Sqn	Deft FC	F/L E.G.Barwell	He111 destroyed	N Seaford	2200
264 Sqn	Deft FC	F/O E.G.Barwell	He111 prob.dest	S Tangmere	0315
604 Sqn	Beau FC	F/L G.O.Budd	He111 destroyed	Isle of Wight	2328
		F/L G.O.Budd	He111 destroyed	N Bournemouth	2335
		F/L G.O.Budd	He111 destroyed	N Bournemouth	2335
604 Sqn	Beau FC	F/L J.R.Watson	Ju88 destroyed	Sopley	0145
		F/L J.R.Watson	He111 destroyed	Sopley	u/k
604 Sqn	Beau FC	F/L P.C.F.Lawton	Ju88 destroyed	Sopley	0300

11th April 1941

91 Sqn	Spit FC	Sgt D.A.S.McKay	Bf109 destroyed	S Dover	1230~
		Sgt J.Gillies	Bf109 destroyed	Near Dover	1230~
92 Sqn	Spit FC	S/L J.E.Rankin F/L C.B.F.Kingcombe Sgt T.R.Gaskell Sgt Miller	He115 destroyed - shared - - shared - - shared -	French coast	1300

11/12th April 1941

87 Sqn	Hurr FC	P/O E.G.Musgrove	He111 prob.dest	Colerne	0120
307 Sqn	Deft FC	Sgt K.Jankowiak	He111 destroyed	Lydlinch	0135

Left: Oberfeldwebel Heinz Schwiering of I./KG 55 was lost with his crew on 7/8th April, shot down off Worthing by Arthur Hodgkinson of 219 Squadron. Right. Oberfeldwebel Heinz Sollner's crew was luckier. They baled out when their 3./KG 55 Heinkel was shot down at Roes Rest Farm Desford Leics, by Richard Stevens of 151 Squadron. (ww2images.com)

604 Sqn	Beau FC	S/L J.Cunningham	He111 prob.dest	60m S Isle of Wight	2300
		S/L J.Cunningham	He111 destroyed	Bournemouth	0135
604 Sqn	Beau FC	S/L R.A.Chisholm	He111 destroyed	Off Southborne	0140
		S/L R.A.Chisholm	Ju88 prob.dest	South coast	0200
604 Sqn	Beau FC	Sgt E.R.L.Poole	Ju88 damaged	Middle Wallop	0200

12th April 1941

601 Sqn	Hurr FC	Sgt F.Mares	Bf109 destroyed	Hazebrouck	1310

13th April 1941

152 Sqn	Spit FC	S/L R.E.P.Brooker Sgt J.A.Short	He111 destroyed - shared -	S Falmouth	1114
242 Sqn	Hurr FC	P/O F.E.Fayolle	Bf110 destroyed	E Harwich	1159

14th April 1941

247 Sqn	Hurr FC	F/L D.G.Smallwood	He111 damaged	S Falmouth	0758

15th April 1941

65 Sqn	Spit FC	F/L B.E.Finucane	Bf109 destroyed	Mid Channel	1700
610 Sqn	Spit FC	P/O J.K.Ross Sgt R.W.Richardson	Ju88 destroyed - shared -	Off St Catherines Pt	1840
615 Sqn	Hurr FC	F/L P.W.Dunning-White	Bf109 destroyed	Dover	1200

15/16th April 1941

23 Sqn	Blen FC	P/O K.Matthews	E/A damaged	Carpiquet AD	u/k

219 Sqn	Beau FC	Sgt O.A.Dupee	He111 destroyed	Durrington	0240
307 Sqn	Deft FC	F/O M.Lewandowski	He111 damaged	Bradford-on-Avon	0120
604 Sqn	Beau FC	F/L C.L.Gomm	He111 destroyed	Exminster	2245
		F/L C.L.Gomm	He111 destroyed	SE Lymington	0230
604 Sqn	Beau FC	S/L J.Cunningham	He111 destroyed	Southampton	0200
		S/L J.Cunningham	He111 destroyed	Near Lymington	0235
		S/L J.Cunningham	He111 destroyed	Off Portland	0240

16th April 1941

56 Sqn	Hurr FC	P/O T.F.Guest Sgt G.V.Hoyle	Bf110 prob.dest - shared -	NE Martlesham	0715
601 Sqn	Hurr FC	S/L J.A.O'Neill	Bf109 destroyed	Off Dungeness	1720

16/17th April 1941

85 Sqn	Havc FC	Sgt T.C.E.Berkeley	Ju88 damaged	Cheshunt	0145
219 Sqn	Beau FC	F/L A.J.Dotteridge	E/A destroyed	Wimbledon	2134
219 Sqn	Beau FC	W/C T.Pike	He111 destroyed	Guildford	0135
		W/C T.Pike	He111 destroyed	Wormley	0230

17th April 1941

54 Sqn	Spit FC	S/L R.F.Boyd	Bf110 destroyed	20-30m E Ramsgate	1100
		F/O E.F.J.Charles	Bf110 destroyed	20-30m E Ramsgate	1100

19th April 1941

74 Sqn	Spit FC	Sgt A.D.Payne	Bf109 damaged	3m S Dover	1800

19/20th April 1941

151 Sqn	Hurr FC	P/O R.P.Stevens	He111 destroyed	London	0430

20th April 1941

54 Sqn	Spit FC	P/O J.Stokoe	Bf110 destroyed	10m SE Clacton	1745
303 Sqn	Spit FC	P/O J.K.M.Daszewski	Bf109 prob.dest	Le Touquet	1100
		P/O W.Lokuciewski	Bf109 destroyed	Le Touquet	1100
		Sgt J.Palak	Ju88 damaged	Le Touquet	1100

21st April 1941

1 Sqn	Hurr FC	Sgt J.Prihoda	Bf109 prob.dest	Canterbury-Channel	1915
		F/L C.J.E.Robinson	Bf109 damaged	Canterbury-Channel	1915
222 Sqn	Spit FC	S/L R.C.Love	Ju88 damaged	E Yarmouth	0830

21/22nd April 1941

23 Sqn	Blen FC	F/L B.R.O'B.Hoare	E/A destroyed	St Leger	2330~

On the night oif 15th April, John Cunningham of 604 Squadron claimed the first RAF nightfighter 'triple' by claiming three He111s destroyed - his 8th - 10th confirmed victories. A month later on 7th May HM King George VI visited Middle Wallop and Cunningham, having added to his score on May 3rd, claimed another victory that same night. (ww2images.com)

22nd April 1941

610 Sqn Spit FC Sgt W.J.Payne   Ju88 destroyed E Bognor Regis   0840

23/24th April 1941

29 Sqn Beau FC F/L G.P.Gibson   Do17 damaged   E Boston   0100~

24th April 1941

3 Sqn   Hurr FC Sgt J.T.Shaw   Ju88 destroyed* 20m E Clacton   0645
                  Sgt J.G.Douglas   - shared -
* Also shared with 54 Squadron.

3 Sqn   Hurr FC Sgt W.M.Gardiner Do17 damaged   Southwold   1025

54 Sqn   Spit FC P/O H.N.D.Bailey Ju88 destroyed* 20m E Clacton   0645
* Shared with 3 Squadron.

92 Sqn   Spit FC S/L J.E.Rankin   Bf109 destroyed Dungeness   0902
                  F/L J.B.H.Brunier - shared -

24/25th April 1941

85 Sqn   Havc FC S/L V.J.Wheeler   He111 damaged   Bury St Edmunds-
                                                    Stradishall   2200~

604 Sqn Beau FC F/O E.D.Crew   He111 damaged   Isle of Wight   2239

25th April 1941

610 Sqn	Spit	FC	S/L H.de C.A.Woodhouse P/O J.R.Stoop	Ju88 destroyed - shared -	S Brighton	0725

26th April 1941

92 Sqn	Spit	FC	P/O R.H.Fokes	Bf109 destroyed	Kent - Channel	1335

26/27th April 1941

25 Sqn	Beau	FC	F/L J.F.Inkster	E/A prob.dest	Wells	0120
85 Sqn	Havc	FC	F/O D.Evans	He111 damaged	Felixstowe	2135

27th April 1941

222 Sqn	Spit	FC	Sgt J.H.B.Burgess Sgt D.L.Ferraby	Ju88 damaged - shared -	E Yarmouth	0707
91 Sqn	Spit	FC	P/O P.P.C.Barthropp	Do17 damaged	Dungeness	0845

27/28th April 1941

93 Sqn	Havc	FC	Sgt V.H.L.Linthune	E/A prob.dest	Start Point	2335
219 Sqn	Beau	FC	P/O D.O.Hobbis	E/A destroyed		2230
257 Sqn	Hurr	FC	S/L R.R.S.Tuck	Ju88 damaged		2050
604 Sqn	Beau	FC	F/O E.D.Crew	He111 destroyed	Lyme Regis	2300

28th April 1941

3 Sqn	Hurr	FC	P/O J.K.Russell Sgt R.T.Brewin	Ju88 damaged - shared -	Deal - Griz Nez	1205
72 Sqn	Spit	FC	P/O E.W.P.Bocock Sgt B.Collyer	Ju88 damaged - shared -	E Berwick	1544
74 Sqn	Spit	FC	E.A.Sgt Mould	Bf109 damaged	3m W Calais	1110
91 Sqn	Spit	FC	F/O J.S.Hart Sgt J.K.Down	Ju88 damaged - shared -	Dover Straits	1015

29th April 1941

74 Sqn	Spit	FC	Unnamed pilot	Bf109 damaged	Dungeness	1615

29/30th April 1941

23 Sqn	Havc	FC	Sgt J.B.Raffels	Bf110 destroyed	Rosieres	0035
93 Sqn	Havc	FC	F/L McLennahan	E/A destroyed	Dartmouth	u/k
604 Sqn	Beau	FC	F/O R.A.Chisholm	He111 destroyed	Off shore South of Middle Wallop	2359

30th April 1941

72 Sqn	Spit	FC	C.L.Sgt Harrison Sgt J.White	Ju88 damaged - shared -	E Farne Island	1500

Left: Jamie Rankin, took command of 92 Squadron in late February. He 'shared' a Bf109 on 24th April when he and Flight Lieutenant J.B.H.Brunier brought down a 2./JG 52 Bf109 near Dungeness. Right: Rankin demonstrates QJ-S R6923 for the benefit of press photgraphers. Rankin would reach the wartime rank of Air Commodore with at least 17 confirmed victories. (ww2 images.com)

1/2nd May 1941

93 Sqn	Havc FC	F/S Way	E/A prob.dest	Channel	u/k
219 Sqn	Beau FC	P/O A.J.Hodgkinson	He111 destroyed	S Shoreham	2245
		P/O A.J.Hodgkinson	He111 damaged	S Shoreham	2255
604 Sqn	Beau FC	F/O I.K.S.Joll	He111 damaged	Sopley	2300

2/3rd May 1941

151 Sqn	Deft FC	F/L G.A.T.Edmiston	Ju88 destroyed	Upper Sheringham	0330
604 Sqn	Beau FC	F/L G.O.Budd	Ju88 destroyed	SE Ibsley	2230

3/4th May 1941

23 Sqn	Havc FC	Sgt J.B.Raffels	Ju88 destroyed	Evreux	0320~
		Sgt J.B.Raffels	E/A prob.dest	Evreux	0320~
23 Sqn	Havc FC	P/O P.S.B.Ensor	Ju88 destroyed	Le Bourget	0017
		P/O P.S.B.Ensor	He111 prob.dest	Le Bourget	0017
23 Sqn	Havc FC	F/L B.R.O'B.Hoare	Ju88 damaged	Near Lille	u/k
		F/L B.R.O'B.Hoare	He111 damaged	Near Lille	u/k
25 Sqn	Beau FC	Sgt A.M.Hill	He111 destroyed	Breedon-on-the-Hill	0050~
29 Sqn	Beau FC	F/L G.P.Gibson	He111 destroyed	N Bognor	2250
85 Sqn	Havc FC	P/O J.A.Hemmingway	He111 damaged	Dunwich	2215~

85 Sqn	Havc FC	F/L J.E.Marshall	He111 damaged	Halesworth	2250
96 Sqn	Deft FC	P/O V.V.S.Verity	Ju88 damaged	Cheshire	2345
151 Sqn	Deft FC	Sgt H.G.Bodien	He111 destroyed	Sharrington	0100~
219 Sqn	Beau FC	F/L A.J.Dotteridge	He111 destroyed	Sidlesham	2235
219 Sqn	Beau FC	W/C T.Pike	He111 destroyed	Tangmere	2250~
		W/C T.Pike	E/A prob.dest	Tangmere	2250~
256 Sqn	Deft FC	F/L E.C.Deanesly	Do17 destroyed	North Wales	2350~
		F/L E.C.Deanesly	Ju88 destroyed	Cheshire	2350~
600 Sqn	Beau FC	F/L R.S.Woodward	Ju88 destroyed	Shepton Mallett	0115~
604 Sqn	Beau FC	S/L J.Cunningham	He111 destroyed	Corton Denham	2245
604 Sqn	Beau FC	F/L H.Speke	He111 destroyed	Crowcombe	0100

4th May 1941

601 Sqn	Hurr FC	Sgt Fearns	Bf109 damaged	Near Deal	1250

4/5th May 1941

23 Sqn	Havc FC	F/O P.S.B.Ensor	He111 prob.dest	Caen	0445~
		F/O P.S.B.Ensor	He111 damaged	Caen	0445~
		F/O P.S.B.Ensor	E/A damaged	Caen	0445~
25 Sqn	Beau FC	W/C D.F.W.Atcherley	Ju88 destroyed	Eastergate, Lincs	2245
25 Sqn	Beau FC	Sgt K.B.Hollowell	Ju88 destroyed	N Bradford	0010~
		Sgt K.B.Hollowell	Ju88 prob.dest	N Bradford	0010~
25 Sqn	Beau FC	S/L H.P.Pleasance	E/A damaged	Nr Aldeburgh	u/k
255 Sqn	Deft FC	S/L R.L.Smith	Ju88 destroyed	N Mablethorpe	0200~
600 Sqn	Beau FC	S/L C.A,Pritchard	He111 damaged	French coast	0450~
604 Sqn	Beau FC	Sgt R.G.Reeves	Ju88 damaged	Sopley	0430
604 Sqn	Beau FC	P/O P.F.Jackson	Ju88 prob.dest	Wool, Dorset	0130~

5th May 1941

91 Sqn	Spit FC	F/L R.A.Lee-Knight	Bf109 destroyed	Beachy Head	1320
145 Sqn	Spit FC	F/O J.H.M.Offenberg	He60 destroyed	Pointe de Barfleur	1540~
		F/O J.H.M.Offenberg	Bf109 prob.dest	Pointe de Barfleur	1540~
616 Sqn	Spit FC	F/O L.H.Casson	Ju88 damaged	S Tangmere	0750~
		F/O R.Marples	- shared -		

5/6th May 1941

23 Sqn	Havc FC	P/O S.S.Duff	He111 destroyed	Vitry-en-Artois	u/k
25 Sqn	Beau FC	Sgt S.V.Holloway	E/A damaged	Watton	0325~
43 Sqn	Hurr FC	S/L T.F.Dalton-Morgan	Ju88 destroyed	Anstruther	0001
43 Sqn	Hurr FC	S/L T.F.Dalton-Morgan	E/A destroyed	Fife Ness	0140

David Atcherley commanded 25 Squadron in 1941 and claimed three victories bwteen May and July. Injured in a crash in August. he saw no further action, but rose to attain the rank of Air Commodore in 1944. on 4/5th May he claimed his first victory,shooting down a Ju88 of 8./KG 1 at Eastergate.
(ww2images.com)

85 Sqn	Havc	FC	P/O J.A.Hemmingway	He111 damaged	Near Mildenhall	2359
85 Sqn	Havc	FC	F/O V.R.Snell	Ju88 damaged	Off Clacton	0200
141 Sqn	Deft	FC	P/O A.D.Meredith	He111 destroyed	Cresswell	0035~
			P/O A.D.Meredith	He111 destroyed	Largs	0035~
141 Sqn	Deft	FC	F/L D.F.Wilson	He111 damaged	Glasgow	u/k
245 Sqn	Hurr	FC	S/L J.W.C.Simpson	Ju88 destroyed	Ardglass	0120~
604 Sqn	Beau	FC	F/O I.K.S.Joll	Ju88 destroyed	Chawleigh	0025

6th May 1941

54 Sqn	Spit	FC	P/O J.Stokoe	Bf109 damaged	Dover	1320
54 Sqn	Spit	FC	S/L F.S.Stapleton	Bf109 prob.dest	Off Dover	1330
72 Sqn	Spit	FC	P/O Gregory Sgt W.Gregson	Ju88 damaged - shared -	E Seaham	u/k
601 Sqn	Hurr	FC	Sgt J.Manak	Bf109 destroyed	French coast	1240

6/7th May 1941

23 Sqn	Havc	FC	F/L B.R.O'B.Hoare	E/A prob.dest	Villacoublay	0415~
29 Sqn	Beau	FC	W/C S.C.Widdows	Ju88 damaged	Beachy Head	0155~
43 Sqn	Hurr	FC	S/L T.F.Dalton-Morgan	Ju88 destroyed	Forth	0135~
79 Sqn	Hurr	FC	F/L J.H.Heyworth	E/A destroyed	Off Welsh coast	u/k

85 Sqn	Havc FC	S/L V.J.Wheeler	He111 prob.dest	Felixstowe	0010~
96 Sqn	Deft FC	F/O V.V.S.Verity	He111 destroyed	Morpeth	2359~
		F/O V.V.S.Verity	Ju88 damaged	Liverpool	2359~
96 Sqn	Deft FC	Sgt A.E.Scott	Ju88 prob.dest	Liverpool	0055~
141 Sqn	Deft FC	F/L D.F.Wilson	He111 destroyed	Glasgow	0110
		F/L D.F.Wilson	He111 destroyed	Glasgow	0142
141 Sqn	Deft FC	P/O R.L.F.Day	Ju88 destroyed	E Seaham	0230~
151 Sqn	Deft FC	S/L E.C.Wolfe	Ju88 destroyed	Clydebank	0230~
600 Sqn	Beau FC	S/L C.A.Pritchard	He111 destroyed	Yeovil	0350~
602 Sqn	Spit FC	Sgt W.L.Brown	He111 damaged	Prestwick	0205
604 Sqn	Beau FC	P/O P.F.Jackson	He111 destroyed	Portland	2320~
604 Sqn	Beau FC	W/C C.Appleton	He111 damaged	Southern England	u/k

7th May 1941

43 Sqn	Hurr FC	F/L D.A.R.G.L.Du Vivier P/O C.Mize	Ju88 destroyed - shared -	Tay estuary	1605
43 Sqn	Hurr FC	P/O M.C.C.Cotton Sgt F.W.Lister	Ju88 destroyed - shared -	N St Abbs Head	1855
64 Sqn	Spit FC	Sgt C.P.Stone	Bf109 destroyed	North Foreland	0845~
74 Sqn	Spit FC	P/O R.J.E.Boulding	Bf109 prob.dest	Margate	1035
		P/O R.J.E.Boulding	Bf109 damaged	Margate	1035
		P/O W.J.Sandman	Bf109 damaged	Broadstairs	1045
		P/O H.R.G..Poulton	Bf109 destroyed	10-15m E Margate	1045
91 Sqn	Spit FC	P/O A.G.Donahue	Bf109 destroyed	NW Calais	0650~
		P/O A.G.Donahue	Bf109 damaged	NW Calais	0650~
91 Sqn	Spit FC	P/O R.L.Spurdle	Bf109 prob.dest	Margate	0845~
91 Sqn	Spit FC	Sgt A.Gavan	Bf109 damaged	W Lympne	1600~
609 Sqn	Spit FC	S/L M.Lister-Robinson	Bf109 damaged	Calais	1650
611 Sqn	Spit FC	F/O T.D.Williams	Bf109 destroyed	Off Deal	0645~
		W.M.Sgt Gilmour	Bf109 destroyed	Off Deal	0645~
		F/L T.F.A.Buys	Bf109 damaged	Off Ramsgate	0645~
611 Sqn	Spit FC	P/O J.F.Reeves	Bf109 destroyed	Deal	0700~
611 Sqn	Spit FC	Sgt B.R.M.Burnham	Bf109 destroyed	French coast	1200~

7/8th May 1941

23 Sqn	Havc FC	F/O P.S.B.Ensor	He111 destroyed	Brussels	0345~
25 Sqn	Beau FC	P/O D.W.Thompson	Do17 destroyed	Carrington	0035
25 Sqn	Beau FC	P/O M.J.Herrick	Ju88 prob.dest	Near Grantham	0315~
25 Sqn	Beau FC	S/L H.P.Pleasance	Do17 destroyed	The Wash	0120~

High Fliers. Left: Tom Dalton-Morgan was credited with at least 7 victories during 1940 and 6 more in 1941, all with 43 Squadron. He is believed to have claimed 21 victories with the USAAF 4th Fighter Group in 1944 to bring his total to 35, rather than 14. Right: Tommy Rigler of 609 Squadron claimed two Messerschmitts during his first-ever combat on 8th May. He would increase his score to 8 by the close of hostillities.

87 Sqn	Hurr FC	S/L I.R.Gleed	Do17 destroyed	Near St Albans Hd	2330
96 Sqn	Deft FC	Sgt A.E.Scott	He111 damaged	W Crewe	0100
96 Sqn	Deft FC	F/O V.V.S.Verity	Ju88 destroyed	Wrexham-Chester	0215~
		F/O V.V.S.Verity	Ju88 prob.dest	Leek North	0215~
96 Sqn	Deft FC	Sgt G.S.Taylor	He111 destroyed	Tarporley	0120
		Sgt G.S.Taylor	Do17 prob.dest	SW Crewe	0120
96 Sqn	Deft FC	Sgt R.J.McNair	Ju88 destroyed	W Crewe	0215~
		Sgt R.J.McNair	Ju88 damaged	Leek North-Chester	0215~
151 Sqn	Hurr FC	P/O R.P.Stevens	He111 destroyed	Hull	0210~
		P/O R.P.Stevens	He111 destroyed	Hull	0210~
255 Sqn	Deft FC	Sgt J.Craig	E/A damaged	W Goole	2344
255 Sqn	Deft FC	Sgt P.L.Johnson	He111 destroyed	Gainsborough	0015
		Sgt P.L.Johnson	He111 damaged	W Gainsborough	0015
255 Sqn	Deft FC	P/O P.A.Dale	Do17 damaged	Hull	0130~
256 Sqn	Deft FC	Sgt J.McDonald	He111 damaged	N Liverpool	0140~
256 Sqn	Deft FC	P/O P.L.Caldwell	He111 damaged	W Manchester	0145~
256 Sqn	Deft FC	Sgt J.P.Olney	Ju88 damaged	N Squires Gate	0150~
256 Sqn	Deft FC	F/L E.C.Deanesly	He111 destroyed	SE Manchester	0120

256 Sqn	Deft	FC	S/L G.H.Gatheral	Ju88 damaged	Birkenhead	0110
256 Sqn	Deft	FC	P/O D.Toone	He111 destroyed	Liverpool Docks	0130
256 Sqn	Deft	FC	F/L D.R.West	He111 destroyed	Liverpool	0140
257 Sqn	Hurr	FC	F/L P.P.Hanks	Ju88 destroyed	Lowestoft	2220
264 Sqn	Deft	FC	P/O E.G.Curtice	He111 destroyed	Lille	0340~
			P/O E.G.Curtice	He111 damaged	Lille	0340~
264 Sqn	Deft	FC	P/O A.Grey	He111 destroyed	Lille	0350~
			P/O A.Grey	He111 damaged	Lille	0350~
			P/O A.Grey	He111 damaged	Lille	0350~
600 Sqn	Beau	FC	P/O G.L.Howden	He111 destroyed	Weston-Super-Mare	0005~
600 Sqn	Beau	FC	F/O R.S.Woodward	He111 destroyed	Freshwater, IoW	0250~
604 Sqn	Beau	FC	S/L J.Cunningham	He111 destroyed	Weston Zoyland	2330
604 Sqn	Beau	FC	Sgt J.A.Wright	He111 destroyed	Needles	0410
615 Sqn	Hurr	FC	F/L G.S.K.Haywood	E/A damaged	Menai Straits	0110~

8th May 1941

74 Sqn	Spit	FC	P/O W.Armstrong	Bf109 destroyed	5-6m S Dungeness	1530
92 Sqn	Spit	FC	P/O T.S.Wade	Bf109 destroyed	Folkestone	1730~
			Sgt H.Bowen-Morris	Bf109 destroyed	Folkestone	1730~
302 Sqn	Hurr	FC	F/O Z.Kinel	Bf109 destroyed	Tenterden	1215
			F/O W.S.Krol	Bf109 destroyed	Tenterden	1215
			Sgt M.Rytka	Bf109 prob.dest	Tenterden	1215
302 Sqn	Hurr	FC	Sgt E.J.A.Nowakiewicz	Bf109 destroyed	5m NE Dover	1300
302 Sqn	Hurr	FC	P/O Z.Wroblewski	Bf109 prob.dest	Dymchurch	1900
609 Sqn	Spit	FC	S/L M.Lister-Robinson	Bf109 destroyed	Channel	1740~
			S/L M.Lister-Robinson	Bf109 destroyed	Channel	1740~
			F/L J.Curchin	Bf109 destroyed	Channel	1740~
			F/L J.Curchin Sgt J.A.Hughes-Rees	Bf109 destroyed - shared -	Channel	1740~
			Sgt T.C.Rigler	Bf109 destroyed	Channel	1740~
			Sgt T.C.Rigler	Bf109 destroyed	Channel	1740~
			Sgt R.T.D.Mercer	Bf109 prob.dest	Channel	1740~
			Sgt A.G.Palmer	Bf109 prob.dest	Channel	1740~
610 Sqn	Spit	FC	Sgt G.Mains	Bf109 destroyed	Dover Straits	1200
			Sgt G.Mains	Bf109 prob.dest	Dover Straits	1200
Tang Wg	Spit	FC	W/C D.R.S.Bader	Bf109 prob.dest	Dover Straits	1200

Left: Harold 'Flash' Pleasance of 25 Squadron scored his first confirmed victory on 7/8th May by destroying a Ju88C night intruder of I./NJG 2 near Skegness. Right: The diminutive Ian 'Widge' Gleed, CO of 87 Squadron claimed his tenth victory on the same night. He is pictured on the right, with 'Roddy Rayner'. Unlike Pleasance, Gleed did not survive the war, being killed in action over Tunisia in 1943.

8/9th May 1941

25 Sqn	Beau FC	S/L H.P.Pleasance	Do17 destroyed	N Wells	0250~
25 Sqn	Beau FC	P/O D.W.Thompson	E/A damaged	Grantham	0410~
25 Sqn	Beau FC	Sgt S.V.Holloway	Ju88 damaged	Grantham	0145~
29 Sqn	Beau FC	F/L V.C.Lovell	Ju88 destroyed	Malden	0030~
29 Sqn	Beau FC	F/O J.R.D.Braham	He111 destroyed	Wimbledon	0005
85 Sqn	Havc FC	S/L V.J.Wheeler	Ju88 damaged	45m NE Cromer	0010~
255 Sqn	Deft FC	P/O M.F.Wynne-Wilson	He111 destroyed	Patrington	0125~
255 Sqn	Deft FC	F/L R.M.Trousdale	He111 destroyed	Spurn Head	0200~
		F/L R.M.Trousdale	He111 destroyed	SW Patrington	0200~
255 Sqn	Deft FC	P/O J.D.Wright	Ju88 destroyed	30m E Hull	0200~
255 Sqn	Hurr FC	S/L R.L.Smith	He111 destroyed	4m E Hull	0230~
255 Sqn	Hurr FC	P/O H.G.S.Wyrill	He111 destroyed	Sunk Island	0250~
264 Sqn	Deft FC	P/O M.H.Young	Bf110 destroyed	Merville	0400~
266 Sqn	Spit FC	P/O A.H.Humphrey	He111 destroyed	Derby	0110
266 Sqn	Spit FC	S/L P.G.Jameson	He111 destroyed	Derby	0100~
600 Sqn	Beau FC	F/L G.A.Denby	Ju88 damaged	Watchet	0050~

9th May 1941

92 Sqn	Spit	FC	P/O T.S.Wade	Bf109 destroyed	off Dungeness	u/k
			Sgt H.Bowen-Morris	Bf109 destroyed	Eastwell Park	u/k
609 Sqn	Spit	FC	P/O S.J.Hill	Bf109 damaged	Dungeness	1800~

9/10th May 1941

25 Sqn	Beau	FC	P/O A.J.Picknett	He111 destroyed	The Wash	0230
41 Sqn	Spit	FC	S/L P.E.Meagher	Ju88 destroyed	Whitby	0015
219 Sqn	Beau	FC	P/O A.J.Hodgkinson	Ju88 destroyed	Selsey Bill	0011
604 Sqn	Beau	FC	F/O E.D.Crew	E/A damaged	Lyme Bay	u/k
604 Sqn	Beau	FC	F/L H.Speke	He111 damaged		u/k

10th May 1941

43 Sqn	Hurr	FC	F/L D.A.R.G.L.Du Vivier	Ju88 destroyed	S Edinburgh	1250~
			P/O A.B.Hutchinson	- shared -		
302 Sqn	Hurr	FC	P/O M.Neyder	Bf109 damaged	Maidstone	1920

10/11th May 1941

1 Sqn	Hurr	FC	Sgt J.D.Dygryn-Ligoticky	He111 destroyed	S Kenley	0150~
1 Sqn	Hurr	FC	S/L R.E.P.Brooker	He111 destroyed	London	0030~
			F/O J.E.Demozay	He111 destroyed	Lea Marshes	0030~
1 Sqn	Hurr	FC	F/L C.T.M.P.De Scitivaux	He111 destroyed	Chelmsford	0135~
1 Sqn	Hurr	FC	Sgt B.Kratkorucky	E/A destroyed	Channel	u/k
1 Sqn	Hurr	FC	Sgt J.D.Dygryn-Ligoticky	Ju88 damaged	Redhill	0210~
1 Sqn	Hurr	FC	F/L C.J.E.Robinson	He111 damaged	W Redhill	0320~
1 Sqn	Hurr	FC	P/O W.Raymond	He111 destroyed	S Kenley	0025~
1 Sqn	Hurr	FC	P/O K.C.Jackman	He111 destroyed	S Redhill	0300~
1 Sqn	Hurr	FC	Sgt J.D.Dygryn-Ligoticky	Ju88 prob.dest	S Hastings	0340~
3 Sqn	Hurr	FC	Sgt J.T.Shaw	He111 prob.dest	London	2341
3 Sqn	Hurr	FC	S/L J.W.M.Aitken	Ju88 damaged	Romford	0215~
23 Sqn	Havc	FC	F/L B.R.O'B.Hoare	E/A damaged	Ostend	0230~
23 Sqn	Havc	FC	F/O P.S.B.Ensor	Ju88 destroyed	Beauvais	0330~
29 Sqn	Beau	FC	P/O A.Grant	Ju88 damaged	Channel	0050~
29 Sqn	Beau	FC	P/O Grout	He111 destroyed	Channel	0050~
41 Sqn	Spit	FC	P/O G.H.Ranger	He111 destroyed	W Scarborough	0204
74 Sqn	Spit	FC	P/O R.J.E.Boulding	He111 destroyed	Near Maidstone	2355
85 Sqn	Havc	FC	F/L G.L.Raphael	He111 destroyed	Chelmsford	0140~
85 Sqn	Havc	FC	F/O W.F.Carnaby	Ju88 prob.dest	Hunsdon	0400~
85 Sqn	Havc	FC	P/O Barnard	He111 damaged	Bradwell Bay	0240~

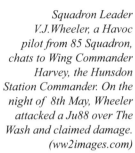

Squadron Leader V.J.Wheeler, a Havoc pilot from 85 Squadron, chats to Wing Commander Harvey, the Hunsdon Station Commander. On the night of 8th May, Wheeler attacked a Ju88 over The Wash and claimed damage. (ww2images.com)

85 Sqn	Havc	FC	F/O D.Evans	He111 destroyed	Thames estuary	0340
151 Sqn	Deft	FC	Sgt J.C.Copeland	He111 destroyed	Gravesend	0330~
151 Sqn	Deft	FC	F/L D.A.P.McMullen	He111 destroyed	Tunbridge Wells	0320~
151 Sqn	Hurr	FC	P/O R.P.Stevens	He111 destroyed	S London	0330
			P/O R.P.Stevens	He111 prob.dest	S London	0350
151 Sqn	Hurr	FC	P/O I.S.Smith	He111 prob.dest	W Southend	0425~
219 Sqn	Beau	FC	F/L A.J.Dotteridge	He111 prob.dest	Guildford	2345~
			F/L A.J.Dotteridge	He111 damaged	Guildford	2345~
219 Sqn	Beau	FC	W/C T.Pike	He111 destroyed	Cranleigh	0100~
242 Sqn	Hurr	FC	F/O F.E.Fayolle	He111 destroyed	Epping	2350~
242 Sqn	Hurr	FC	F/O R.D.Grassick	He111 prob.dest	SW Guildford	0135~
264 Sqn	Deft	FC	F/L L.R.Stephenson	He111 destroyed	Beachy Head	0210~
264 Sqn	Deft	FC	S/L A.T.D.Sanders	He111 destroyed	Wickham	0200~
264 Sqn	Deft	FC	P/O E.G.Curtice	Do17 destroyed	Merville	0330~
266 Sqn	Spit	FC	P/O A.H.Humphrey	He111 destroyed	Dutch coast	0240~
			P/O A.H.Humphrey	He111 destroyed	Dutch coast	0240~
266 Sqn	Spit	FC	S/L P.G.Jameson	He111 destroyed	Romford	0350~
306 Sqn	Hurr	FC	F/O W.Nowak	He111 destroyed	Beachy Head	0115
306 Sqn	Hurr	FC	F/O G.K.Ranoszek	Ju88 damaged	NE London	0230~
610 Sqn	Spit	FC	Sgt N.D.Warden	Ju88 damaged	Guildford	0125~
			W/O C.O.J.Pegge	He111 damaged	Guildford	0125~

11th May 1941

54 Sqn	Spit	FC	P/O H.S.Sewell	Bf109F destroyed	Mid Channel S Dover	2135
91 Sqn	Spit	FC	Sgt D.A.S.McKay	Bf109 destroyed	Lympne	2220~
			F/L R.H.Holland	Bf109 damaged	Lympne	2220~
234 Sqn	Spit	FC	S/L M.V.Blake	Bf109 destroyed	Lulworth-Portland	2020
			Sgt R.T.Martin	Bf109 destroyed	Lulworth-Portland	2020

11/12th May 1941

25 Sqn	Beau	FC	P/O D.W.Thompson	He111 damaged	E West Raynham	0255~
25 Sqn	Beau	FC	S/L H.P.Pleasance	He111 damaged	Digby	0250~
79 Sqn	Hurr	FC	P/O L.T.Bryant-Fenn	He111 prob.dest	Pembroke Dock	1050~
257 Sqn	Hurr	FC	S/L R.R.S.Tuck	Ju88 destroyed	Sheringham	0030~
			S/L R.R.S.Tuck	Ju88 destroyed	Sheringham	0030~
257 Sqn	Hurr	FC	F/L H.P.Blatchford	He111 destroyed	Sheringham	0030~
307 Sqn	Deft	FC	Sgt J.Malinowski	He111 destroyed	Dawlish	0335~

12/13th May 1941

610 Sqn	Spit	FC	Sgt W.J.Payne	Ju88 destroyed	S Brighton	2240~

13th May 1941

245 Sqn	Hurr	FC	S/L J.W.C.Simpson	Do17 destroyed	NW Strand River, Eire	1735~
402 Sqn	Hurr	FC	F/O E.E.E.Morrow	Ju88 damaged	3m E Mablethorpe	0940

14th May 1941

222 Sqn	Spit	FC	P/O G.G.A.Davis	Ju88 destroyed	E Mundesley	1800~
222 Sqn	Spit	FC	F/L E.H.Thomas P/O W.A.Laurie	Ju88 damaged - shared -	SE Yarmouth	1900
222 Sqn	Spit	FC	F/O H.N.D.Ramsay Sgt R.S.Riches	Ju88 damaged - shared -	Off Mundesley	1805
615 Sqn	Hurr	FC	Sgt R.M.Hamilton Sgt A.D.Roberts	Ju88 damaged - shared -	Convoy	1825~

15th May 1941

71 Sqn	Hurr	FC	P/O J.K.Alexander	Bf109 prob.dest	N Calais	2100
303 Sqn	Spit	FC	F/L J.Jankiewicz Sgt G.Giermer	Ju52 destroyed - shared -	Near Aire	1245
303 Sqn	Spit	FC	P/O B.Drobinski Sgt M.Belc	Ju52 damaged - shared -	Near St Inglevert	1310~
310 Sqn	Hurr	FC	F/L P.B.G.Davies	Do17 destroyed	Off Thamesmouth	1245

*Leroy Du Vivier was a former officer in the Belgian
Air Force (Aeronautique Militaire) and, after
the disastrous campaign in France, escaped to
England. He fought through the Battle of Britain
with 43 and 229 Squadrons and then returned to
43, becoming a flight commander in April 1941.
He later rose to command the squadron as the
first non-British Commonwealth pilot to lead an
RAF unit. On May 10th he shared the claimed
destruction of a Ju88 over the River Tay estuary -
believed to have been from 2.(F)/ObdL that crashed
at Workum on return.
(ww2images.com)*

16th May 1941

1 Sqn	Hurr FC	Sgt J.D.Dygryn-Ligoticky	Bf109 prob.dest	Dover Straits	1320
91 Sqn	Spit FC	F/L J.J.Le Roux	Bf109 damaged	S Folkestone	1430
		Sgt J.E.Cooper	Bf109 damaged	S Folkestone	1430
601 Sqn	Hurr FC	Sgt T.A.McCann	Bf109 destroyed	S Dover	1505
		Sgt F.Mares	- shared -		
609 Sqn	Spit FC	P/O A.K.Ogilvie	Bf109 destroyed	Canterbury-Dover	1615
		P/O S.J.Hill	Bf109 destroyed	Canterbury-Dover	1615

16/17th May 1941

25 Sqn	Beau FC	Sgt K.B.Hollowell	He111 destroyed	W Cromer	0315
151 Sqn	Deft FC	P/O G.A.T.Edmiston	Do17 damaged	Birmingham	0350~
		P/O G.A.T.Edmiston	He111 damaged	Birmingham	0350~
219 Sqn	Beau FC	P/O A.J.Hodgkinson	He111 destroyed	Worthing	0002
600 Sqn	Beau FC	F/L A.D.McN.Boyd	Ju88 destroyed	NW Honiton	0012
FIU	Beau FC	F/O C.A.A.G.Clark	Ju88 prob.dest	Ford	0313

17th May 1941

BH Wg	Spit FC	W/C A.G.Malan	Bf109 prob.dest	8-10m E Dover	1250
		W/C A.G.Malan	Bf109 damaged	8-10m E Dover	1250
616 Sqn	Spit FC	F/O H.S.L.Dundas	Bf109 destroyed	Off Shoreham	1635

18th May 1941

72 Sqn	Spit	FC	Sgt C.L.Harrison Sgt W.J.Rosser	Do17 damaged - shared -	SE Alnwick	1600~
91 Sqn	Spit	FC	F/L R.A.Lee-Knight	Bf109 destroyed	Dungeness	0625~
			F/O R.L.Spurdle	Bf109 destroyed	Dungeness	0625~

19th May 1941

87 Sqn	Hurr	FC	P/O I.J.Badger	He114 destroyed	Near Scilly Isles	2107
234 Sqn	Spit	FC	P/O A.S.Harker Sgt Barker	Bf109 damaged - shared -	S Portland	1150
234 Sqn	Spit	FC	F/L E.B.Mortimer-Rose	Bf109 destroyed	SW Portland	1310
			F/L E.B.Mortimer-Rose	Bf109 destroyed	SW Portland	1310
			P/O E.W.Wootten	Bf109 destroyed	SW Portland	1310
			P/O E.W.Wootten	Bf109 destroyed	SW Portland	1310
			P/O G.T.Baynham	Bf109 destroyed	SW Portland	1310

21st May 1941

1 Sqn	Hurr	FC	Sgt B.Kratkorucky	Bf109 destroyed	Channel	1745~
			F/S K.Kuttlewascher	Bf109 destroyed	Channel	1745~
			S/L R.E.P.Brooker	Bf109 damaged	Channel	1745~
			F/O A.Velebnovsky	Bf109 damaged	Channel	1745~
			P/O W.Raymond	Bf109 damaged	Channel	1745~
			Sgt J.D.Dygryn-Ligoticky	Bf109 damaged	Channel	1745~
56 Sqn	Hurr	FC	S/L E.E.P.Gibbs	Bf109 damaged	St Omer	1800~
302 Sqn	Hurr	FC	P/O Z.Wroblewski P/O M.Rytka	Bf109 destroyed Bf109F destroyed	Near St Pol Bethune	1735 1735
609 Sqn	Spit	FC	P/O J.D.Bisdee P/O V.M.M.Ortmans	Bf109 destroyed - shared -	10m off Deal-Ramsgate	1800~
			Sgt J.A.Hughes-Rees	Bf109 damaged	Channel	1800~
BH Wg	Spit	FC	W/C A.G.Malan	Bf109 damaged	1m E Goodwin Sands	1800

22nd May 1941

601 Sqn	Hurr	FC	P/O D.B.Ogilvie Sgt E.Malczewski	Ju52 prob.dest - shared -	E Ambleteuse	u/k
			P/O D.B.Ogilvie	Bf109 destroyed	E Ambleteuse	u/k

24th May 1941

87 Sqn	Hurr	FC	S/L I.R.Gleed Sgt L.A.Thorogood	Do17 damaged - shared -	Scilly Isles	0730

Left: Keith Oglivie of 609 Squadron relaxes with a good book. On 16th May he claimed his third confirmed victory against Bf109s. Right: Archie Boyd of 600 Squadron claimed his first victory that same night - the first for 609 Squadron.(ww2images.com)

25th May 1941

1 Sqn	Hurr FC	F/O J.E.Demozay	Bf110 destroyed	Near Calais	1630
222 Sqn	Spit FC	P/O R.M.D.Hall Sgt D.R.Higgin	Ju88 damaged - shared -	Off Sheringham	0815
601 Sqn	Hurr FC	Sgt N.Taylor	Bf109 destroyed	Calais	0730
		Sgt N.Taylor	Bf109 destroyed	Calais	0730
601 Sqn	Hurr FC	P/O D.B.Ogilvie	Bf109 damaged	Off Dover	1505
		P/O D.B.Ogilvie	Bf109 damaged	Off Dover	1505

25/26th May 1941

604 Sqn	Beau FC	W/C C.Appleton	He111 damaged	6m S St Catherine's Pt	u/k

26th May 1941

74 Sqn	Spit FC	F/O H.C.Baker	Bf109 destroyed	Dover Straits	1610

27/28th May 1941

66 Sqn	Spit FC	P/O P.Olver P/O J.H.T.Pickering	He111 destroyed - shared -	St Ives Bay	2230
		P/O P.Olver P/O J.H.T.Pickering	He111 prob.dest - shared -	St Ives Bay	2230
152 Sqn	Spit FC	P/O C.S.Cox	He111 destroyed	St Ives Bay	2300

28th May 1941

43 Sqn	Hurr FC	F/L D.A.R.G.L.Du Vivier	Ju88 destroyed	Riccarton	1415
87 Sqn	Hurr FC	S/L I.R.Gleed	Ju88 prob.dest	E Scilly Isles	1930
603 Sqn	Spit FC	F/L F.D.S.Scott-Malden	Bf109 prob.dest	Near Calais	1920~
		F/L F.D.S.Scott-Malden	Bf109 damaged	Near Calais	1920~

611 Sqn	Spit	FC	Sgt W.G.G.D.Smith	Bf109 prob.dest	Canterbury - coast	a.m.
611 Sqn	Spit	FC	Sgt W.G.G.D.Smith	Bf109 prob.dest	Le Touquet	1920~
611 Sqn	Spit	FC	F/L S.T.Meares	Bf109 destroyed	Le Touquet	1920~
			S/L F.S.Stapleton	Bf109 prob.dest	Le Touquet	1920~
			P/O P.S.C.Pollard	- shared -		
			Sgt A.C.Leigh	- shared -		
			P/O Watson	- shared -		

28/29th May 1941

604 Sqn	Beau	FC	W/C C.Appleton	He111 destroyed	Buckley	u/k

29th May 1941

245 Sqn	Hurr	FC	Sgt G.E.Hill	Do17 prob.dest	Near Dublin	0923
			Sgt L.Srom	- shared -		

31st May/1st June 1941

219 Sqn	Beau	FC	S/L E.L.Colbeck-Welch	Ju88 destroyed	Off Llandudno	0240
604 Sqn	Beau	FC	F/L C.L.Gomm	He111 destroyed	Tarrant Gunville	0115
604 Sqn	Beau	FC	S/L J.Cunningham	He111 destroyed	Cranborne	0248

1st June 1941

234 Sqn	Spit	FC	F/L R.F.T.Doe	Ju88 damaged	Off Lands End	a.m.
			Sgt Stevens	- shared -		

1/2nd June 1941

219 Sqn	Beau	FC	W/C D.V.Ivins	Ju88 destroyed	Sidlesham	2355
219 Sqn	Beau	FC	P/O D.O.Hobbis	Ju88 destroyed	Off Shoreham	2359
96 Sqn	Deft	FC	S/L R.J.Burns	Ju88 damaged	Wirral	0145

2nd June 1941

601 Sqn	Hurr	FC	Sgt J.Manak	Bf109 destroyed	SW Boulogne	1920
			F/L G.F.Gregory	Bf109 damaged	SW Boulogne	1920

2/3rd June 1941

317 Sqn	Hurr	FC	P/O P.Niemec	Ju88 destroyed	5m ENE Tyne	2229
			Sgt T.Baranowski	- shared -		
485 Sqn	Spit	FC	P/O G.H.Francis	Ju88 damaged	25m E Hornsea	2228
			Sgt H.L.Thomas	- shared -		
485 Sqn	Spit	FC	S/L M.W.B.Knight	Ju88 destroyed	30m E Hornsea	2224

3rd June 1941

66 Sqn	Spit	FC	F/L H.R.Allen	He111 damaged	Off St Agnes Head	u/k

One-way ticket: The wreckage of G1+GR, an He111 from 7./KG 55, lies on the South Downs near Sompting, Sussex. Leutnant Helmut Pichler's crew had been unlucky enough to have met a 219 Squadron Beaufighter on the night of 16th May. There were no survivors and Arthur Hodgkinson had achieved his sixth confirmed victory. (ww2images.com)

4th June 1941

32 Sqn	Hurr FC	F/O Garner	He111 destroyed	SE Wexford	1100
		F/L J.Rose	He111 damaged	SE Wexford	1100
		F/L J.Rose	Do17 damaged	SE Wexford	1110
91 Sqn	Spit FC	P/O P.P.C.Barthropp	Bf109 prob.dest	Near Boulogne	2200~
		P/O A.J.Andrews	Bf109 prob.dest	Near Boulogne	2200~
		Sgt J.K.Down	Bf109 damaged	Near Boulogne	2200~
92 Sqn	Spit FC	Sgt W.J.Payne	Bf109 damaged	15m S Dungeness	1718
145 Sqn	Hurr FC	F/O D.H.Clarke	Ju87 destroyed	Le Havre	1200~
303 Sqn	Spit FC	P/O B.Klosin	Bf109 destroyed	Off Dover	1740
		S/L W.Lapkowski	Bf109 damaged	Off Dover	1740
609 Sqn	Spit FC	P/O V.V.M.Ortmans	Bf109 destroyed	Off Dover	2010
		Sgt T.C.Rigler	Bf109 destroyed	Off Dover	2010
		Sgt T.C.Rigler S/L M.Lister-Robinson	Bf109 damaged - shared -	Off Dover	2010
611 Sqn	Spit FC	F/L T.F.A.Buys	Bf109 destroyed	Off Folkestone	1800

4/5th June 1941

25 Sqn	Beau FC	Sgt K.B.Hollowell	He111 destroyed	Wash	0145
25 Sqn	Beau FC	Sgt H.A.H.Gigney	He111 destroyed	S Reston	0200
604 Sqn	Beau FC	P/O K I Geddes	He111 destroyed	Isle of Wight	0200

5th June 1941

257 Sqn	Hurr FC	Sgt S.Stulir Sgt Garner	He111 damaged - shared -	St Catherines Pt	0826

6/7th June 1941

604 Sqn	Beau FC	F/O I.K.S.Joll	He111 damaged	Off Portland	0024

51

7th June 1941

54 Sqn	Spit	FC	P/O J.Stokoe	Bf109 prob.dest	S Calais	1300
			P/O K.M.Jones	- shared -		

8/9th June 1941

43 Sqn	Hurr	FC	S/L T.F.Dalton-Morgan	Ju88 destroyed	Off St Abbs Head	0010

9th June 1941

74 Sqn	Spit	FC	P/O W.J.Sandman	Bf109 prob.dest	Dover	1445
			P/O W.J.Sandman	Bf109 damaged	Dover	1445
91 Sqn	Spit	FC	P/O P.P.C.Barthropp	Bf109 destroyed	Off Dover	1405
91 Sqn	Spit	FC	Sgt J.E.Cooper	Bf109 damaged	Near Hythe	1430

10th June 1941

32 Sqn	Hurr	FC	Sgt F.A.Bernard	He111 destroyed	Off Pembroke	1045

11th June 1941

74 Sqn	Spit	FC	F/O D.C.Carlson	Bf109 prob.dest	Off Dunkirk	1710
258 Sqn	Hurr	FC	P/O W.T.Everist	Bf109 destroyed	W St Inglevert	1330~
			P/O B.A.McAllister	- shared -		
609 Sqn	Spit	FC	P/O J.D.Bisdee	Bf109 damaged	Off Dunkirk	1710

11/12th June 1941

85 Sqn	Havc	FC	P/O G.L.Howitt	Ju88 damaged	Foulness	0300
604 Sqn	Beau	FC	F/L G.O.Budd	He111 damaged	Salisbury	0305

12th June 1941

92 Sqn	Spit	FC	S/L J.E.Rankin	Bf109 destroyed	SE Dover	1535~

12/13th June 1941

242 Sqn	Hurr	FC	S/L W.Whitney-Straight	Bf110 destroyed	Merville	0030~

13th June 1941

601 Sqn	Hurr	FC	Sgt N.Taylor	Bf109 destroyed	Off Dover	1610~
			Sgt N.Taylor	Bf109 destroyed	Off Dover	1610~
			Sgt N.Taylor	Bf109 damaged	Off Dover	1610~

13/14th June 1941

25 Sqn	Beau	FC	S/L H.P.Pleasance	Ju88 destroyed	Narborough	0030
25 Sqn	Beau	FC	P/O D.W.Thompson	Ju88 destroyed	Terrington	0100
85 Sqn	Havc	FC	F/L G.L.Raphael	He111 prob.dest	Lower Halstow	0115
			F/L G.L.Raphael	He111 destroyed	Sheerness	0200
151 Sqn	Hurr	FC	P/O R.P.Stevens	He111 destroyed	Sheerness	0200

452 Squadron at Kirton-in-Lindsay. L-R; Paul Makin, Ken Cox, Arch Stuart, Brendan Finucane, Ian Milne, Jim Hanigan, Fred McCann, Ray Thorold-Smith, Bob Bungey, Don Willis, Alex Roberts, Don Lewis, Graham Douglas, Andy Costello, Keith Truscott and Dick Gazzard. (ww2images.com)

219 Sqn	Beau FC	F/L J.G.Topham	He111 destroyed	Guestling	0015
219 Sqn	Beau FC	P/O D.O.Hobbis	E/A destroyed	S Hove	0105
604 Sqn	Beau FC	S/L G.O.Budd	He111 damaged	SSE Selsey Bill	0114
04 Sqn	Beau FC	S/L G.O.Budd	He111 damaged	SSE Selsey Bill	0114

14th June 1941

92 Sqn	Spit FC	S/L J.E.Rankin	Bf109 destroyed	Marquise	0723
		Adj X.De Montbron	Bf109 damaged	Marquise	0723
603 Sqn	Spit FC	S/L F.M.Smith	Bf109 damaged	Ostend-Gravelines	0750
		F/L F.D.S.Scott-Malden	Bf109 damaged	Ostend-Gravelines	0750
		F/O H.A.R.Prowse	Bf109 damaged	Ostend-Gravelines	0750
		F/O W.A.Douglas	Bf109 damaged	Ostend-Gravelines	0750
		F/O W.A.Douglas	Bf109 damaged	Ostend-Gravelines	0750

14/15th June 1941

604 Sqn	Beau FC	F/O K.I.Geddes	He111 destroyed	Sturminster Newton	0055

15/16th June 1941

219 Sqn	Beau FC	W/C T.Pike	He111 destroyed	Brighton-Worthing	0023
604 Sqn	Beau FC	F/L J.R.Watson	E/A prob.dest	SW Selsey	0100

Left: Richard Stevens of 151 Squadron was arguably the most successful RAF fighter pilot during the Blitz. On 13th June he claimed his eleventh victim, an He111 of I./KG 28, off Sheerness. Right: On 14th June Adjutant X de Montbron, a Free French pilot from 92 Squadron, claimed a Bf109 damaged over Marquise.

Chapter Three

Non-Stop Offensive
16th June - 26th September 1941

British intelligence had detected that the Germans were beginning to transfer units to the east and, through *Ultra* intercepts, were fully aware of the impending assault upon the Soviet Union. The improving weather now allowed more *Circus* operations to be undertaken. These would be stepped up in size and intensity from mid-June, when the German eastern campaign began, with the intention of helping the Russians by forcing the *Luftwaffe* to retain units in the west. This did not happen. However the *Luftwaffe*, now heavily outnumbered, held an advantage denied to the RAF in the summer of 1940. This was the fact that the tiny bombing forces employed lacked the capacity to inflict any serious damage and that there were no targets within the range of RAF fighter escorts that were of any real strategic importance. Thus the *Luftwaffe* fighter pilots could 'pick their fights', attacking only from positions of tactical superiority and the RAF suffered accordingly.

16th June 1941

1 Sqn	Hurr FC	P/O R.N.G.Allen	He59 destroyed	S Dungeness	1730~
		F/L C.F.Gray	- shared -		
		P/O V.A.Kopecky	Bf109 destroyed	S Dungeness	1730~
		Sgt J.Novak	Bf109 destroyed	S Dungeness	1730~
		Sgt J.Prihoda	Bf109 destroyed	S Dungeness	1730~
74 Sqn	Spit FC	S/L J.C.Mungo-Park	Bf109 destroyed	NE Le Touquet	1630
		S/L J.C.Mungo-Park	Bf109 destroyed	NE Le Touquet	1630
		Sgt C.Stuart	Bf109 destroyed	Off Boulogne	1630
		P/O W.J.Sandman	Bf109 prob.dest	NE Le Touquet	1630
		Sgt R.W.York	Bf109 prob.dest	Hardelot	1630
91 Sqn	Spit FC	Sgt W.W.Connolly	Bf109 damaged	8m S Folkestone	1730
92 Sqn	Spit FC	Sgt H.Bowen-Morris	Bf109 destroyed	Le Touquet	1630~
		P/O T.S.Wade	Bf109 destroyed	Le Touquet	1630~
		F/L C.B.F.Kingcombe	Bf109 prob.dest	Le Touquet	1630~
		S/L J.Rankin	Bf109 prob.dest	Le Touquet	1630~
258 Sqn	Hurr FC	F/L C.V.Campbell	Bf109 destroyed	Boulogne	1630~
		P/O G.M.Marshall	Bf109 destroyed	Boulogne	1630~
		P/O H.Dobbyn	Bf109 destroyed	Boulogne	1630~
		F/L C.R.Bush	Bf109 prob.dest	Boulogne	1630~
		P/O G.M.Marshall	Bf109 damaged	Boulogne	1630~
		P/O B.A.McAllister	Bf109 damaged	Boulogne	1630~
306 Sqn	Hurr FC	P/O K.Rutkowski	Bf109 damaged	S Boulogne	1630
		P/O V.W.Berg	Bf109 prob.dest	Dover Straits	0915
601 Sqn	Hurr FC	Sgt N.Taylor	Bf109 damaged	Dover Straits	0915

16/17th June 1941

68 Sqn	Beau FC	F/L J.F.Pain	He111 destroyed	Bratton	0150
604 Sqn	Beau FC	P/O D.M.Gossland	He111 destroyed	Maiden Bradley	0123

17th June 1941

54 Sqn	Spit FC	F/L V.G.Gardner	Bf109 destroyed	Near Griz Nez	1940
		F/O E.F.J.Charles	Bf109 prob.dest	Griz Nez	1935
		Sgt G.H.Fenton	Bf109 prob.dest	Griz Nez-Calais	1930
92 Sqn	Spit FC	F/L A.R.Wright	Bf109 prob.dest	Bethune	1945~
		Sgt W.J.Payne	Bf109 damaged	Boulogne-Le Touquet	1945~
		Sgt W.J.Payne	Bf109 damaged	Boulogne-Le Touquet	1945~
234 Sqn	Spit FC	F/L E.B.Mortimer-Rose Sgt H.B.Shepherd	Bf109 destroyed	3-5m NW Cherbourg - shared -	1720
242 Sqn	Hurr FC	P/O R.D.Grassick	Bf109 destroyed	Near Boulogne	1945~
		P/O J.Bryks	Bf109 destroyed	Near Boulogne	1945~
		P/O J.Bryks	Bf109 destroyed	Near Boulogne	1945~
		Sgt E.A.Redfern	Bf109 prob.dest	Near Boulogne	1945~
		S/L W.Whitney-Straight	Bf109 prob.dest	Near Boulogne	1945~
		F/L C.T.M.PDe Scitivaux	Bf109 damaged	Near Boulogne	1945~
		P/O R.D.Grassick	Bf109 damaged	Near Boulogne	1945~
		Sgt K.M.Hicks	Bf109 damaged	Near Boulogne	1945~
		F/L M.J.Loudon	Bf109 damaged	Near Boulogne	1945~
		F/L M.J.Loudon	Bf109 damaged	Near Boulogne	1945~
		P/O E.Richardson	Bf109 damaged	Near Boulogne	1945~
		P/O E.Richardson	Bf109 damaged	Near Boulogne	1945~
303 Sqn	Spit FC	P/O W.Kolaczkowski	Bf109 prob.dest	Off Griz Nez	1955
		F/O W.Strembosz	Bf109 prob.dest	Off Griz Nez	1955
306 Sqn	Hurr FC	Sgt J.Jeka	Bf109 destroyed	Near St Omer	1945
		Sgt J.Kosmowski	Bf109 destroyed	Mid-Channel	2000
		F/L J.K.J.Slonski-Ostoja	Bf109 destroyed	Aire	1937
		Sgt J.Kosmowski	Bf109 damaged	Bethune	1940
609 Sqn	Spit FC	P/O J.D.Bisdee	Bf109 destroyed	Nr Le Touquet	1945~
		P/O F.X.E.De Spirlet	Bf109 destroyed	Le Touquet-Channel	1945~
		F/O A.K.Ogilvie	Bf109 destroyed	Le Touquet-Channel	1945~
610 Sqn	Spit FC	F/L R.A.Lee-Knight	Bf109 destroyed	8m SSW Griz Nez	2035
BH Wg	Spit FC	W/C A.G. Malan	Bf109 destroyed	5m NW Bethune	1935
SF Hch	Spit FC	G/C H.Broadhurst	Bf109 destroyed	Off Griz Nez	2010
		G/C H.Broadhurst	Bf109 damaged	Dungeness-Griz Nez	2010

Above: 152 Squadron 1941. (Chris Goss)

Right: Pilot Officer Pocock of 72 Squadron expresses his faith in ultimate victory - or (more likely) his opinion of the photographer! (ww2images.com)

17/18th June 1941

25 Sqn	Beau FC	W/C D.F.W.Atcherley	Ju88 destroyed	Off Sheringham	0153

18th June 1941

92 Sqn	Spit FC	S/L J.Rankin	Bf109 destroyed	Near Calais	1830~
303 Sqn	Spit FC	P/O B.Drobinski	Bf109 destroyed	St Inglevert	1830
		P/O B.Drobinski	Bf109 destroyed	St Inglevert	1830
		S/L W.Lapkowski	Bf109 destroyed	St Inglevert	1830
		F/O W.Lokuciewski	Bf109 destroyed	St Inglevert	1830
312 Sqn	Hurr FC	Sgt O.Kucera	Bf109 prob.dest	Mid-Channel	1830~
609 Sqn	Spit FC	P/O S.J.Hill	Bf109 prob.dest	Off Dover	1830~
610 Sqn	Spit FC	Sgt E.W.Merriman	Bf109 destroyed	20m S Dungeness	1830~
611 Sqn	Spit FC	Sgt B.W.Feely	Bf109 destroyed	Calais	1830~
		P/O W.G.G.D.Smith	Bf109 destroyed	Calais	1830~
		S/L F.S.Stapleton	Bf109 destroyed	Gravelines-Calais	1830~
		Sgt A.C.Leigh	Bf109 destroyed	Calais	1830~
		Sgt N.G.Townsend	Bf109E destroyed	Calais	1830~
		Sgt A.C.Leigh	Bf109 prob.dest	Calais	1830~
		P/O P.S.C.Pollard	Bf109 prob.dest	Calais	1830~
		Sgt N.G.Townsend	Bf109 prob.dest	Calais	1830~

19th June 1941

611 Sqn	Spit FC	F/O T.D.Williams	Bf109 destroyed	Off Etaples	2000~
		Sgt W.M.Gilmour	Bf109 damaged	Channel	2000~
		F/L C.H.MacFie	Bf109 damaged	Near Le Havre	1800~

Left: Adolf Galland, Kommodore of JG26, was shot down twice on June 21st. On the first occasion his victor was Boleslaw 'Ghandi' Drobinski (right) who, many years later, was delighted to learn the identity of his illustrious opponent from the author. (B.Drobinski)

20th June 1941

66 Sqn	Spit	FC	F/L H.R.Allen	Bf109 destroyed	30m S Plymouth	1120
			F/L H.R.Allen	Bf109 destroyed	25m S Bolt Head	1120
			Sgt W.S.Large	- shared -		

20/21st June 1941

151 Sqn	Hurr	FC	P/O R.P.Stevens	E/A damaged	Off Winterton	0200

21st June 1941

1 Sqn	Hurr	FC	S/L R.E.P.Brooker	Bf109 destroyed	Boulogne	1640~
			Sgt B.G.Collyns	Bf109 destroyed	6m W Boulogne	1640~
			Sgt J.F.Plasil	Bf109 destroyed	Boulogne	1640~
			P/O R.Marcinkus	Bf109 destroyed	Boulogne	1640~
			P/O V.A.Kopecky	Bf109E prob.dest	Off Boulogne	1640~
			Sgt J.Prihoda	Bf109 prob.dest	Off Boulogne	1640~
			Sgt J.Prihoda	Bf109 prob.dest	Off Boulogne	1640~
54 Sqn	Spit	FC	P/O J.Stokoe	Bf109 damaged	St Omer-Gravelines	1235
54 Sqn	Spit	FC	F/O E.F.J.Charles	Bf109 destroyed	Dungeness-Griz Nez	1645-
74 Sqn	Spit	FC	F/L D.C.Carlson	Bf109 destroyed	10-15m E Ramsgate	1300
			Sgt J.E.Cole	Bf109 destroyed	Mid-Channel	1300
			Sgt E.A.Mould	Bf109 prob.dest	10m E Ramsgate	1300
74 Sqn	Spit	FC	F/L D.C.Carlson	Bf109 prob.dest	8m SW Boulogne	1635
92 Sqn	Spit	FC	S/L J.Rankin	Bf109 destroyed	Mid-Channel	1245~

Left: The great Adolph 'Sailor' Malan, who led 74 Squadron during 1940 and became one of the original Wing Leaders in March 1941. On 21st June, leading the Biggin Hill Spitfires, he claimed two Bf109s destroyed, his 17th and 18th 'confirmed' - in addition to five 'shares'. Right: Two New Zealander brothers pose with a Hurricane. They are the Clouston brothers, right is Squadron Leader W.G.Clouston a Battle of Britain ace, who commanded 258 Squadron during the summer of 1941. (ww2images.com)

92 Sqn	Spit	FC	Sgt G W.Aston	Bf109 destroyed	Near Boulogne	1640~
			Sgt R.E.Havercroft	Bf109 damaged	Near Boulogne	1640~
			P/O T.S.Wade	Bf109 destroyed	Near Boulogne	1640~
145 Sqn	Spit	FC	F/O J.Machacek*	Bf109 destroyed	Bridge, Kent	1300

* Shared with 616 Squadron.

145 Sqn	Spit	FC	Sgt R.J.C.Grant	Bf109 destroyed	Le Touquet	1640~
242 Sqn	Hurr	FC	S/L W.W.Straight*	Bf109 destroyed	nr St Omer	1235~

* Shared with a Blenheim crew.

			Lt H.O.Mehre	Bf109 damaged	Near St Omer	1235~
257 Sqn	Hurr	FC	S/L R.R.S.Tuck	Bf109 destroyed	Off The Hague	1715
			S/L R.R.S.Tuck	Bf109 destroyed	Off The Hague	1715
			S/L R.R.S.Tuck	Bf109 damaged	Off The Hague	1715
303 Sqn	Spit	FC	P/O B.Drobinski	Bf109 destroyed	Near Calais	1235
306 Sqn	Hurr	FC	Sgt J.Kosmowski	Bf109 destroyed	Near St Omer	1235
603 Sqn	Spit	FC	Sgt W.J.Jackman	Bf109 destroyed	Near St Omer	1235~
			Sgt W.J.Jackman	Bf109 damaged	Near St Omer	1235~
			F/L G.K.Gilroy	Bf109 damaged	Near St Omer	1235~
			F/L F.D.S.Scott-Malden	Bf109 damaged	Near St Omer	1235~
609 Sqn	Spit	FC	F/O A.K.Ogilvie	Bf109 destroyed	Hardelot	1640~
			F/O W.A.Douglas	Bf109 destroyed	10-15m SW Calais	1640~

			Sgt R.J.Boyd	Bf109 destroyed	4m NE Le Touquet	1640~
			Sgt C.Ortmans	Bf109 damaged	Hardelot	1640~
610 Sqn	Spit	FC	F/L R.A.Lee-Knight	Bf109 destroyed	Griz Nez-Calais	1245~
			F/L R.A.Lee-Knight	Bf109 damaged	Griz Nez-Calais	1245~
610 Sqn	Spit	FC	P/O J.R.Scott	Bf109 destroyed	Le Touquet	1640~
611 Sqn	Spit	FC	F/L S.T.Meares	Bf109 damaged	Gravelines	1245~
			Sgt D.E.Fair	Bf109 damaged	Gravelines	1245~
616 Sqn	Spit	FC	S/L H.F.Burton*	Bf109 destroyed	Bridge, Kent	1300~

* Shared with 145 Squadron.

BH Wg	Spit	FC	W/C A.G.Malan	Bf109 destroyed	Just inland Boulogne	1635
			W/C A.G.Malan	Bf109 destroyed	Off Le Touquet	1635
Ntht Wg	Spit	FC	W/C J.A.Kent	Bf109 destroyed	6m W St Omer	1235
Tang Wg	Spit	FC	W/C D.R.S.Bader	Bf109 destroyed	SW Boulogne	1640~
SF Hch	Spit	FC	G/C H.Broadhurst	Bf109 destroyed	St Omer	1245~
			G/C H.Broadhurst	Bf109 destroyed	Calais/Marck	1245~

21/22nd June 1941

25 Sqn	Beau	FC	F/O M.J.Herrick	Ju88 destroyed	Deeping-St-James	0025
151 Sqn	Deft	FC	P/O G.A.T.Edmiston	Ju88 destroyed	Off Cromer 2355	
219 Sqn	Beau	FC	P/O A.J.Hodgkinson	He111 destroyed	S Portsmout	0035

22nd June 1941

54 Sqn	Spit	FC	S/L R.F.Boyd	Bf109 prob.dest	Near Hazebrouck	1610
			Sgt J.W.Panter	Bf109 prob.dest	Hazebrouck-Gravelines	1615
			P/O V.D.Page	Bf109 destroyed	10m S Gravelines	1625
			P/O R.Powling	Bf109 destroyed	10m S Gravelines	1625
74 Sqn	Spit	FC	P/O E.A.Mould	Bf109 damaged	10m SW Dunkirk	1610
			P/O W.J.Sandman	Bf109 destroyed	Bergues	1610
			P/O W.J.Sandman	Bf109 destroyed	Bergues	1615
92 Sqn	Spit	FC	Sgt W.J.Payne	Bf109 damaged	Dunkirk	1615~
145 Sqn	Spit	FC	Sgt J.G.L.Robillard	Bf109 destroyed	Port Philippe	1615~
242 Sqn	Hurr	FC	F/O J.E.Demozay	Bf109 destroyed	N Calais	1615~
			F/O J.E.Demozay	Bf109 destroyed	N Calais	1615~
303 Sqn	Spit	FC	P/O B.Drobinski	Bf109 destroyed	Hazebrouck-coast	1610
			P/O M.Feric	Bf109 destroyed	Hazebrouck-coast	1610
			F/L J.Jankiewicz	Bf109 destroyed	Hazebrouck-coast	1610
			S/L W.Lapkowski	Bf109 destroyed	Hazebrouck-coast	1610
			S/L W.Lapkowski	Bf109 destroyed	Hazebrouck-coast	1610

			F/O W.Lokuciewski	Bf109 destroyed	Hazebrouck-coast	1610
			F/L J.Jankiewicz	Bf109 prob.dest	Hazebrouck-coast	1610
			F/O W.Lokuciewski	Bf109 prob.dest	Hazebrouck-coast	1610
601 Sqn	Hurr	FC	P/O D.B.Ogilvie	Do17 damaged	Near Dunkirk	0440
609 Sqn	Spit	FC	F/O J.D.Bisdee	Bf109 destroyed	Calais-Gravelines	1615~
			P/O J.H.M.Offenberg	Bf109 destroyed	E Gravelines	1615~
			Sgt T.C.Rigler	Bf109 destroyed	Calais-Gravelines	1615~
			Sgt T.C.Rigler	Bf109 destroyed	Calais-Gravelines	1615~
			Sgt T.C.Rigler	Bf109 destroyed	Gravelines	1615~
610 Sqn	Spit	FC	S/L K.Holden	Bf109 destroyed	Hazebrouck	1615~
			P/O F.C.Horner	Bf109 destroyed	Hazebrouck	1615~
			Sgt W.Raine	Bf109 destroyed	Hazebrouck	1615~
611 Sqn	Spit	FC	P/O W.N.C.Salmond	Bf109 destroyed	Hazebrouck area	1615~
			P/O W.N.C.Salmond	Bf109 destroyed	Hazebrouck area	1615~
			Sgt W.M.Gilmour	Bf109 destroyed	St Omer	1615~
			F/L T.F.A.Buys	Bf109 destroyed	St Omer	1615~
			F/L S.T.Meares	Bf109 destroyed	St Omer	1615~
			P/O W.G.G.D.Smith	Bf109 destroyed	St Omer	1615~
			F/O P.S.C.Pollard	Bf109 destroyed	St Omer	1615~
			F/L T.F.A.Buys	Bf109 prob.dest	St Omer	1615~
			Sgt A.C.Leigh	Bf109 prob.dest	10m E St Omer	1615~
			Sgt B.W.Feely	Bf109 damaged	St Omer	1615~
			Sgt W.M.Gilmour	Bf109 damaged	St Omer	1615~
			F/L S.T.Meares	Bf109 damaged	St Omer	1615~
616 Sqn	Spit	FC	F/O L.H.Casson	Bf109 destroyed	Off Gravelines	1615~
			Sgt D.W.Beedham	Bf109 destroyed	Off Gravelines	1615~
			P/O R.Marples	Bf109 destroyed	NW Hazebrouck	1615~
BH Wg	Spit	FC	W/C A.G.Malan	Bf109 destroyed	Calais-Gravelines	u/k

23rd June 1941

19 Sqn	Spit	FC	S/L R.G.Dutton	Bf109 damaged	N Hardelot	1345
			P/O G.W.Scott	Bf109 damaged	Le Touquet	1345
92 Sqn	Spit	FC	P/O P.L.I.Archer	Bf109 destroyed	SE Boulogne	1330~
			Sgt D.E.Kingaby	Bf109 destroyed	SE Boulogne	1330~
			S/L J.Rankin	Bf109 destroyed	SE Boulogne	1330~
			S/L J.Rankin	Bf109 destroyed	SE Boulogne	1330~
			P/O N.F.Duke	Bf109 prob.dest	SE Boulogne	1330~

92 Sqn	Spit	FC	P/O J.Dougall	Bf109 destroyed	Hardelot	2030~
			F/O T.S.Wade	Bf109 prob.dest	Hardelot	2030~
			Sgt J.Le Cheminant	Bf109 damaged	Hardelot	2030~
242 Sqn	Hurr	FC	F/L F.H.De La Bouchere	Bf109 destroyed	Near Desvres	2030~
			F/O J.E.Demozay	Bf109 destroyed	Near Desvres	2030~
			F/L R.D.Grassick	Bf109 prob.dest	Near Desvres	2030~
			F/L R.D.Grassick	Bf109 damaged	Near Desvres	2030~
			Sgt E.A.Redfern	Bf109 damaged	Near Desvres	2030~
266 Sqn	Spit	FC	P/O H.Cook	Bf109 prob.dest	Off Le Touquet	1330~
303 Sqn	Spit	FC	P/O B.M.Gladych	Bf109 destroyed	Choques	1315
			P/O B.M.Gladych	Bf109 prob.dest	Choques	1315
303 Sqn	Spit	FC	Sgt M.Adamek	Bf109 destroyed	Near Desvres	2030
			Sgt M.Adamek	Bf109 destroyed	Near Desvres	2030
			P/O J.Bondar	Bf109 prob.dest	Near Desvres	2030
			P/O B.M.Gladych	Bf109 destroyed	Near Desvres	2030
			P/O B.M.Gladych	Bf109 destroyed	Near Desvres	2030
			P/O B.M.Gladych	Bf109 destroyed	Near Desvres	2030
			Sgt M.Wojciechowski	Bf109 destroyed	Near Desvres	2030
			Sgt K.Wunsche	Bf109 destroyed	Near Desvres	2030
			P/O W.Strembosz	Bf109 destroyed	Near Desvres	2030
			Sgt J.Szlagowski	Bf109 prob.dest	Near Desvres	2030
611 Sqn	Spit	FC	Sgt W.M.Gilmour	Bf109 destroyed	Near Etaples	1330~
611 Sqn	Spit	FC	F/L T.F.A.Buys	Bf109 destroyed	Hardelot	2030~
BH Wg	Spit	FC	W/C A.G.Malan	Bf109 destroyed	SE Boulogne	2025
			W/C A.G.Malan	Bf109 destroyed	SE Boulogne	2025
Witt Wg	Spit	FC	W/C P.G.Jameson	Bf109 destroyed	Off Le Touquet	1330~

23/24th June

29 Sqn	Beau	FC	F/O J.R.D.Braham	He111 prob.dest	Thames estuary	0115
85 Sqn	Havc	FC	P/O E.N.Bunting	He111 prob.dest	Bury St Edmunds	0145
85 Sqn	Havc	FC	S/L G.L.Raphael	Ju88 destroyed	Near Bawdsey	0220~

24th June 1941

54 Sqn	Spit	FC	F/O E.F.J.Charles	Bf109 destroyed	Griz Nez-Calais	2050
			Sgt H.Knight	Bf109 destroyed	Griz Nez-N Calais	2050
			P/O J.Stokoe	Bf109 destroyed	N Gravelines	2058
			P/O H.S.Sewell	Bf109 destroyed	N Gravelines	2100

The Czechs of 310 Squadron were heavily involved in the cross-Channel operations of 1941. "A" Flight are shown here at the Martlesham Heath dispersal (l to r) Sergeant J.Skirka, Flight Lieutenant P.Davies, Flying Officer B.Kimlicka, Squadron Leader F.Weber (CO), Intelligence officer, Flying Officer DE.Nezbeda and Sergeant M.Jiroudek (Z.Hurt).

74 Sqn	Spit	FC	P/O H.R.G.Poulton	Bf109 prob.dest	Gravelines	2110
			Sgt A.F.Wilson	Bf109 damaged	S Gravelines	2115
92 Sqn	Spit	FC	Sgt W.J.Payne	Bf109 destroyed	Gravelines	2050~
			Sgt W.J.Payne	Bf109 destroyed	Gravelines	2050~
222 Sqn	Spit	FC	F/L G.G.A.Davies	Bf109 damaged	Off Ramsgate	2050~
303 Sqn	Spit	FC	S/L W.Lapkowski	Bf109 destroyed	Gravelines	2045
			Sgt M.Belc	Bf109 destroyed	Gravelines	2045
306 Sqn	Hurr	FC	Sgt W.Jasinski	Bf109 prob.dest	S Gravelines	2048
603 Sqn	Spit	FC	P/O C.A.Newman	Bf109 destroyed	Near Gravelines	2050~
609 Sqn	Spit	FC	Sgt T.C.Rigler	Bf109 prob.dest	Near Calais	2050~
			Sgt T.C.Rigler	Bf109 damaged	Near Calais	2050~
			P/O J.D.Bisdee	Bf109 prob.dest	Near Calais	2050~
			Sgt R.J.Boyd	Bf109 prob.dest	Near Calais	2050~
611 Sqn	Spit	FC	F/L R.E.Gardner	Bf109 prob.dest	Near Gravelines	2050~
BH Wg	Spit	FC	W/C A.G.Malan	Bf109 destroyed	Off Gravelines	2045
SF Hch	Spit	FC	G/C H.Broadhurst	Bf109 damaged	Off Gravelines	2050~
			G/C H.Broadhurst	Bf109 damaged	Off Gravelines	2050~

24/25th June 1941

25 Sqn	Beau	FC	P/O D.W.Thompson	He111 destroyed	Wallington	0200
96 Sqn	Deft	FC	Sgt R.Smithson	He111 damaged	Anglesey	0230~
255 Sqn	Deft	FC	Sgt P.S.Kendall	He111 destroyed	15m NE Flambro' Hd	0105

25th June 1941

54 Sqn	Spit	FC	Sgt H.A.Aitken	Bf109 destroyed	Gravelines	1215
			F/L R.Mottram	Bf109 destroyed	Gravelines	1215
66 Sqn	Spit	FC	S/L A.S.Forbes	He111 destroyed	Off Bolt Head	dawn
			Sgt W.J.Corbin	- shared -		
92 Sqn	Spit	FC	F/L A.R.Wright	Bf109 destroyed	St.Omer-Gravelines	1245
			P/O N.F.Duke	Bf109 destroyed	Off Dunkirk	1245
92 Sqn	Spit	FC	Sgt W.J.Payne	Bf109 destroyed	10m from Gravelines	1630~
111 Sqn	Spit	FC	Sgt T.R.Caldwell	Ju88 destroyed	Near Montrose	1840
			Sgt J.R.H.Elphick	- shared -		
145 Sqn	Spit	FC	F/L C.I.R.Arthur	Bf109 destroyed	Le Touquet	1630~
			Sgt R.J.C.Grant	Bf109 destroyed	Le Touquet	1630~
303 Sqn	Spit	FC	F/O A.Wroblewski	Bf109 destroyed	E Dunkirk	1230
			P/O B.Drobinski	Bf109 destroyed	5-7m E Gravelines	1230
303 Sqn	Spit	FC	F/L T.Arentowicz	Bf109 damaged	Near St Omer	1630
610 Sqn	Spit	FC	F/L D.E.Crowley-Milling	Bf109 prob.dest	Hazebrouck	1230~
			P/O J.R.Scott	Bf109 destroyed	Gravelines	1230~
610 Sqn	Spit	FC	W/C J.W.M.Aitken	Bf109 destroyed	Le Touquet	1630~
			S/L K.Holden	Bf109 damaged	Near St Omer	1630~
			P/O F.C.Horner	Bf109 destroyed	Near St Omer	1630~
			Sgt W.Raine	Bf109 prob.dest	Near St Omer	1630~
616 Sqn	Spit	FC	F/O H.S.L.Dundas	Bf109 damaged	10m N Dunkirk	1230~
			Sgt J.G.West*	Bf109 destroyed	Gravelines-Dunkirk	1230~

* Shared with Tangmere Wing.

			F/O R.Marples	Bf109 damaged	5m off Dunkirk	1230~
BH Wg	Spit	FC	W/C A.G.Malan	Bf109 destroyed	St.Omer-Gravelines	1245
Tang Wg	Spit	FC	W/C D.R.S.Bader	Bf109 destroyed	Boulogne area	1230~
			W/C D.R.S.Bader*	Bf109 destroyed	Gravelines-Dunkirk	1230~

* Shared with 616 Squadron.

			W/C D.R.S.Bader	Bf109 destroyed	St Omer	1630~
SF Hch	Spit	FC	G/C H.Broadhurst	Bf109 prob.dest	Gravelines	1215
			G/C H.Broadhurst	Bf109 prob.dest	Gravelines	1215

25/26th June 1941

25 Sqn	Beau	FC	P/O A.J.Hodgkinson	He111 destroyed	Off Selsey Bill	0300~
604 Sqn	Beau	FC	Sgt J.F.Luing	He111 damaged	Bournemouth	0130
FIU	Beau	FC	F/L G.Ashfield	He111 destroyed	Off Shoreham	0330

Roy Mottram had served with distinction with 92 Squadron during 1940, making some eight claims before being wounded in combat. Posted to 54 Squadron in June 1941, he claimed a Bf109 destroyed on 25th, a 'probable' next day and another on 8th July. On 31st August he failed to return from a mission and is believed to have fallen to Leutnant Jakob Augustin of 8./JG 2. (Ken Mottram)

26th June 1941

54 Sqn	Spit	FC	S/L R.F.Boyd	Bf109 destroyed	15-20m NE Graveline	1200~
			F/L R.Mottram	Bf109 prob.dest	N Gravelines	1200~
92 Sqn	Spit	FC	S/L J.Rankin	Bf109 destroyed	S Gravelines	1200~
			F/L A.R.Wright	Bf109 destroyed	Dunkirk	1200~
			Sgt R.E.Havercroft	Bf109 destroyed	Gravelines	1200~
			P/O G.H.A.Wellum	Bf109 damaged	Gravelines	1200~
			Sgt W.J.Payne	Bf109 damaged	Gravelines	1200~
145 Sqn	Spit	FC	Sgt W.J.Johnson	Bf109 destroyed	Off Gravelines	1200~
402 Sqn	Hurr	FC	Sgt G.D.Robertson	Ju88 damaged	15m E Lowestoft	0520
603 Sqn	Spit	FC	F/O P.J.Delorme	Bf109 damaged	Dunkirk-Gravelines	1200~
			P/O H.A.R.Prowse	Bf109 damaged	Dunkirk-Gravelines	1200~
610 Sqn	Spit	FC	P/O F.A.O.Gaze	Bf109 destroyed	Gravelines	1200~
			S/L K.Holden	Bf109 damaged	Gravelines	1200~
			F/L R.A.Lee-Knight	Bf109 damaged	Dunkirk	1200~
611 Sqn	Spit	FC	Sgt D.E.Fair	Bf109 destroyed	Dunkirk-Gravelines	1200~
			P/O W.G.G.D.Smith	Bf109 destroyed	Dunkirk-Gravelines	1200~
			F/O J.R.G.Sutton	Bf109 prob.dest	Dunkirk-Gravelines	1200~
			F/O J.R.G.Sutton	Bf109 damaged	Dunkirk-Gravelines	1200~
			F/O T.D.Williams	Bf109 prob.dest	2m SE Dunkirk	1200~
616 Sqn	Spit	FC	P/O J.E.Johnson	Bf109 destroyed	Over Gravelines	1200
			F/O L.H.Casson	Bf109 damaged	Gravelines	1200
BH Wg	Spit	FC	W/C A.G.Malan	Bf109 prob.dest	Gravelines	1200~

Left: Edward 'Jack' Charles of 54 Squadron claimed his third confirmed victory on 27th June. He survived the war having risen to Wing Commander, leading the Middle Wallop and then the Perranporth Wings. His final score was at least fifteen. Right: Ralph 'Titch' Havercroft of 92 Squadron was another survivor, making his final claim on 26th June. He later became a test pilot and then a staff officer before retiring in 1963. (Ken Mottram)

27th June 1941

1 Sqn	Hurr	FC	F/S K.Kuttelwascher	Bf109 destroyed	Griz Nez-Boulogne	2200~
19 Sqn	Spit	FC	Sgt J.Kosina	Bf109 damaged	St Omer	1700~
19 Sqn	Spit	FC	F/L W.J.Lawson	Bf109 destroyed	10m E St Omer	2200~
			Sgt D.G.S.R.Cox	Bf109 destroyed	Near St Omer	2200~
			F/L W.J.Lawson	Bf109 prob.dest	6m NW Gravelines	2200~
			P/O A.F.Vokes	Bf109 damaged	Near St Omer	2200~
			F/S S.Plzak	Bf109 damaged	Near St Omer	2200~
54 Sqn	Spit	FC	F/O E.F.J.Charles	Bf109 destroyed	Lille	2200
64 Sqn	Spit	FC	Sgt J.W.Slade Sgt C.Thomas	He115 prob.dest - shared -	6m E Bell Rock	2340
74 Sqn	Spit	FC	F/L C.H.Saunders	Bf109 prob.dest	Near Lille	2200
111 Sqn	Spit	FC	Sgt W.J.Archibald P/O J.A.Timmis	Ju88 damaged - shared -	Off Montrose	1751
145 Sqn	Spit	FC	F/L M.A.Newling	Bf109 prob.dest	Lille	2200~
266 Sqn	Spit	FC	Sgt R.F.Lewis	Bf109 destroyed	St Omer	1700~
303 Sqn	Spit	FC	P/O J.E.L.Zumbach	Bf109 damaged	Lille	2200~
306 Sqn	Hurr	FC	Sgt J.Jeka	Bf109 damaged	20m S Gravelines	2200~

Left: On 28th June, Wladyslaw Drecki of 303 Squadron claimed two Bf109s destroyed before he was obliged to bale out into the Channel. (Wojtek Matusiak) (Right) Gustav 'Mickey' Sprick of JG 26 was killed in action on 28th, believed by 'Mike' Drecki. At the time of his death he was credited with 31 victories and he held the coveted Ritterkreuz. (ww2images.com)

609 Sqn	Spit	FC	F/L P.H.M.Richey	Bf109 damaged	S Dunkirk	2200~
615 Sqn	Hurr	FC	F/L G.S.K.Haywood	Ju88 damaged	20m W Holyhead	1540
			P/O C.D.Strickland	- shared -		

28th June 1941

145 Sqn	Spit	FC	F/O J.Machacek	Bf109 prob.dest	Near Cassel	0845~
303 Sqn	Spit	FC	Sgt M.Belc	Bf109 destroyed	On Commines A/D	0845
			P/O W.M.Drecki	Bf109 destroyed	near Commines	0845
			P/O W.M.Drecki	Bf109 destroyed	Near French coast	0850
308 Sqn	Spit	FC	Sgt W.Majchryzyk	Bf109 destroyed	Near Hazebrouck	0845
			P/O S.Wielgus	Bf109 destroyed	Near Hazebrouck	0845
BH Wg	Spit	FC	W/C A.G.Malan	Bf109 destroyed	Gravelines-Calais	0845~

28/29th June 1941

151 Sqn	Hurr	FC	P/O R.P.Stevens	Ju88 destroyed	Off Happisburgh	2340~

30th June 1941

54 Sqn	Spit	FC	F/O E.F.J.Charles	Bf109 destroyed	10m S Gravelines	1900
65 Sqn	Spit	FC	P/O D.C.Mitchell	Bf109 destroyed	Channel	1900~

145 Sqn Spit FC	F/L C.I.R.Arthur P/O J.St Pierre	Bf109 destroyed - shared -	Near Le Touquet	1845~
306 Sqn Hurr FC	P/O Z.Langhamer	Bf109 damaged	Gravelines	1845
603 Sqn Spit FC	F/O H.A.R.Prowse	Bf109 destroyed	Near Gravelines	1900~
609 Sqn Spit FC	Sgt J.A.Hughes-Rees	Bf109 destroyed	Near St Omer	1845~
	S/L M.Lister-Robinson	Bf109 damaged	Near St Omer	1845~
	F/L P.H.M.Richey P/O R.F.F.G.Malengrau	Bf109 prob.dest - shared -	St Omer-Lens	1845~
	P/O V.M.M.Ortmans	Bf109 destroyed	Lille	1845~
	F/L P.H.M.Richey	Bf109 destroyed	Foret de Nieppes	1845~
BH Wg Spit FC	W/C A.G.Malan	Bf109 destroyed	NW Lens	1845~

2nd July 1941

71 Sqn Hurr FC	S/L H.de la.C.Woodhouse	Bf109 destroyed	Lille-Gravelines	1205
	S/L H.de la.C.Woodhouse	Bf109 damaged	W Lille	1230
	P/O V.R.Bono	Bf109 damaged	W Lille	1230
	P/O R.L.Mannix	Bf109 prob.dest	W Lille	1235
	P/O W.R.Dunn	Bf109 destroyed	W Lille	1235
	P/O G.A.Daymond	Bf109 destroyed	W Lille	1240
74 Sqn Spit FC	Sgt W.G.Lockhart Biggin Hill Wing	Bf109 destroyed - shared -	Near Lille	1240
92 Sqn Spit FC	Sgt A.Pietrasiak	Bf109 destroyed	Off Dunirk	1245~
	Sgt D.E.Lloyd	Bf109 destroyed	N France	1245~
	F/S D.E.Kingaby	Bf109 destroyed	Off Gravelines	1245~
	F/S D.E.Kingaby	Bf109 destroyed	Off Gravelines	1245~
145 Sqn Spit FC	Sgt J.G.L.Robillard	Bf109 destroyed	Lille area	1245~
	Sgt J.G.L.Robillard	Bf109 destroyed	Lille area	1245~

Note: Larry Robillard FTR and reported his claims after evading and returning to the UK.

303 Sqn Spit FC	F/L W.Kolaczkowski	Bf109 destroyed	Lille-Mid Channel	1245
	F/O J.E.L.Zumbach	Bf109 destroyed	Lille-Mid Channel	1245
	F/O J.E.L.Zumbach	Bf109 prob.dest	Lille-Mid Channel	1245
	P/O M.Lipinski	Bf109 damaged	Lille-Mid Channel	1245
308 Sqn Spit FC	P/O W.Bozek	Bf109 destroyed	Lille-French coast	1245
	P/O B.Kudrewicz	Bf109 destroyed	Lille-French coast	1245
	S/L M.Pisarek	Bf109 destroyed	Lille-French coast	1245
	Sgt S.Widlarz	Bf109 destroyed	Lille-French coast	1245
	Sgt S.Zielinski	Bf109 destroyed	Lille-coast	1245
	Sgt J.Zielinski	Bf109 destroyed	Lille-French coast	1245
	Sgt S.Krzyzagorski	Bf109 prob.dest	Lille-French coast	1245

			Sgt S.Widlarz	Bf109 prob.dest	Lille-French coast	1245
			P/O B.Kudrewicz	Bf109 damaged	Lille-French coast	1245
610 Sqn	Spit	FC	Sgt G.Mains	Bf109 destroyed	N France	1245~
610 Sqn	Spit	FC	W/C J.W.M.Aitken*	Bf109 destroyed	Le Touquet	1245~
			P/O F.A.O.Gaze	Bf109 damaged	N France	1245~

Note: Max Aitken, OC 68 Squadron, was flying as 'guest' with 610 Squadron.

616 Sqn	Spit	FC	P/O P.W.E.Heppell	Bf109 destroyed	N France	1245~
			Sgt A.Smith	Bf109 destroyed	Lille area	1245~
			Sgt A.Smith	Bf109 damaged	Lille area	1245~
BH Wg	Spit	FC	W/C A.G.Malan	Bf109 destroyed	Near Lille	1240

* *Shared with 74 Squadron.*

Tang Wg	Spit	FC	W/C D.R.S.Bader	Bf109 destroyed	WSW Lille	1245~
			W/C D.R.S.Bader	Bf109 damaged	WSW Lille	1245~

2/3 July 1941

85 Sqn	Havc	FC	P/O P.W.Arbon	He111 prob.dest	30m SE Clacton	0140
151 Sqn	Hurr	FC	P/O R.P.Stevens	Ju88 destroyed	Off East coast	0300~

3rd July 1941

74 Sqn	Spit	FC	P/O H.R.G.Poulton	Bf109 destroyed	Near Hazebrouck	1130
			F/L D.C.Carlson	Bf109 destroyed	Near Hazebrouck	1135
92 Sqn	Spit	FC	F/S D.E.Kingaby	Bf109 prob.dest	St Omer area	1130~
266 Sqn	Spit	FC	P/O R.G.V.Barraclough	Bf109 destroyed	Hazebrouck	1600~
			S/L T.B.de la P.Beresford	Bf109 destroyed	Hazebrouck	1600~
			Sgt J.E.Van Schaick	Bf109 prob.dest	Hazebrouck	1600~
			Sgt C.J.L.Whiteford	Bf109 prob.dest	Hazebrouck	1600~
			P/O A.J.F.Allen-White	Bf109 damaged	Hazebrouck	1600~
			S/L T.B.de la P.Beresford	Bf109 damaged	Hazebrouck	1600~
			Sgt C.J.L.Whiteford	Bf109 damaged	Hazebrouck	1600~
303 Sqn	Spit	FC	P/O B.Drobinski	Bf109 destroyed	Near St Omer	1600
312 Sqn	Hurr	FC	Sgt O.Kucera	Bf109 destroyed	Hazebrouck	1600
603 Sqn	Spit	FC	Sgt W.J.Jackman	Bf109 destroyed	Channel	1130~
			P/O P.J.Delorme	Bf109 prob.dest	Hazebrouck	1130~
			P/O J.A.R.Falconer	Bf109 prob.dest	Hazebrouck	1130~
			F/O H.A.R.Prowse	Bf109 prob.dest	Hazebrouck	1130~
609 Sqn	Spit	FC	S/L M.Lister-Robinson	Bf109 destroyed	Hazebrouck	1130~
			P/O Y.G.A.F.Du Monceau	Bf109 damaged	N St Omer	1200~
609 Sqn	Spit	FC	S/L M.Lister-Robinson	Bf109 destroyed	Hazebrouck	1600~
			P/O V.M.M.Ortmans	Bf109 damaged	Hazebrouck	1600~

610 Sqn	Spit	FC	F/L R.A.Lee-Knight	Bf109 destroyed	SW Lille		1130~
			F/L R.A.Lee-Knight	Bf109 damaged	SW Lille		1130~
			Sgt E.W.Merriman*	Hs126 prob.dest	Hazebrouck		1130~

* *Shared with 616 Squadron.*

			P/O J.R.Stoop	Bf109 destroyed	Hazebrouck		1130~
616 Sqn	Spit	FC	Sgt R.D.Bowen*	Hs126 prob.dest	Hazebrouck		1130~

* *Shared with 610 Squadron.* — shared -

616 Sqn	Spit	FC	Sgt D.W.Beedham	Bf109 prob.dest	Hazebrouck		1600~
BH Wg	Spit	FC	W/C A.G.Malan	Bf109 damaged	St Omer-Hazebrouck	1200~
Ntht Wg	Spit	FC	W/C J.A.Kent	Bf109 destroyed	Calais		1600
SF Hch	Spit	FC	G/C H.Broadhurst	Bf109 destroyed	Hazebrouck		1130~
SF Hch	Spit	FC	G/C H.Broadhurst	Bf109 prob.dest	Hazebrouck		1130~

4th July 1941

54 Sqn	Spit	FC	P/O V.D.Page	Bf109 destroyed	Near Bethune	1530
			Sgt P.McDougall-Black	Bf109E destroyed	Near Bethune	1535
			F/O H.N.D.Bailey	Bf109 destroyed	Near Bethune	1535
			F/O E.F.J.Charles	Bf109 destroyed	Near Bethune	1530
			P/O J.S.Harris	Bf109 destroyed	Near Bethune	1540
			F/O E.F.J.Charles	Bf109 prob.dest	Near Bethune	1530
71 Sqn	Hurr	FC	P/O K.S.Taylor	Bf109 damaged	Near Bethune	1525
74 Sqn	Spit	FC	S/L S.T.Meares	Bf109 damaged	Gravelines	1530~
92 Sqn	Spit	FC	Sgt A.Pietrasiak	Bf109 destroyed	Choques-Gravelines	1530~
			Sgt A.Pietrasiak*	Bf109 destroyed	Choques-Gravelines	1530~

* *Shared with Biggin Hill Wing.* — shared -

242 Sqn	Hurr	FC	F/O R.F.Hamlyn	Bf109 destroyed	Gravelines area	1530~
			F/L M.J.Loudon	Bf109 destroyed	Gravelines	1530~
			Lt H.O.Mehre	Bf109 destroyed	Gravelines area	1530~
			S/L N.Orton	Bf109 prob.dest	Bethune-St Omer	1530~
			P/O K M.Hicks	Bf109 prob.dest	Gravelines area	1530~
			2/Lt E.Hagan	Bf109 damaged	Gravelines area	1530~
			P/O K M.Hicks	Bf109 damaged	Gravelines area	1530~
603 Sqn	Spit	FC	P/O P.J.Delorme	Bf109 destroyed	N France	1530~
609 Sqn	Spit	FC	S/L M.Lister-Robinson	Bf109 damaged	Bethune	1530~
			F/L P.H.M.Richey	Bf109 damaged	Gravelines	1530~
			F/L P.H.M.Richey	Bf109 damaged	Choques	1530~
611 Sqn	Spit	FC	Sgt W.M.Gilmour	Bf109 destroyed	St Omer	1530~
			Sgt A.C.Leigh	Bf109 prob.dest	St Omer area	1530~

Left: On 3rd July, the Luftwaffe lost a great fighter pilot and leader when Major Wilhelm Balthasar, Kommodore of JG 2, fell in combat. Like the loss of Sprick on 28th June, the Luftwaffe reported that his demise was due to wing failure. However, Squadron Leader Mike Lister-Robinson of 609 Squadron reported that a Bf109F lost a wing due to his cannon fire. He is pictured far right, together with John Bisdee and Paul Richey of 609 Squadron, and 'Dicky' Barwell, the station commander. (ww2images.com)

			Sgt A.C.Leigh	Bf109 damaged	St Omer area	1530~
616 Sqn	Spit	FC	P/O J.E.Johnson	Bf109 damaged	5m S Gravelines	1530
			Sgt J.A.A.Morton	Bf109 damaged	Gravelines area	1530~
BH Wg	Spit	FC	W/C A.G.Malan	Bf109 destroyed	Gravelines area	1530~
			W/C A.G.Malan	Bf109 destroyed	Choques-Gravelines	1530~

* Shared with 92 Squadron.

			W/C A.G.Malan	Bf109 damaged	Choques-Gravelines	1500
Hch Wg	Spit	FC	W/C F.S.Stapleton	Bf109 damaged	St Omer	1530~
NW Wg	Hurr	FC	W/C R.G.Kellett	Bf109 damaged	Gravelines	1530~
Tang Wg	Spit	FC	W/C D.R.S.Bader	Bf109 destroyed	5m S Gravelines	1530~
SF BH	Spit	FC	G/C P.R.Barwell	Bf109 prob.dest	Gravelines	1530~
			G/C P.R.Barwell	Bf109 damaged	Gravelines area	1530~
SF Hch	Spit	FC	G/C H.Broadhurst	Bf109 destroyed	Bethune	1530~
			G/C H.Broadhurst	Bf109 destroyed	Bethune area	1530~

4/5th July 1941

25 Sqn	Beau	FC	W/C D.F.W.Atcherley	Ju88 destroyed	25m E Wells, Norfolk	0300
604 Sqn	Beau	FC	F/L H.P.F.Patten	He111 destroyed	Radstock, Soms	0107
604 Sqn	Beau	FC	F/O I.K.S.Joll	He111 destroyed	Oakford, Devon	0339

5th July 1941

74 Sqn	Spit	FC	S/L S.T.Meares	Bf109 damaged	Lille	1300
145 Sqn	Spit	FC	F/O J.Machacek	Bf109 prob.dest	Lille	1315~
			F/O J.Machacek	Bf109 damaged	Lille	1315~

312 Sqn	Hurr FC	F/S V.Smolik	Bf109 prob.dest	Lille	1314
485 Sqn	Spit FC	F/L E.P.Wells	Bf109 destroyed	Lille	1308
		F/L E.P.Wells	Bf109 destroyed	E Gravelines	1315
610 Sqn	Spit FC	Sgt G.Mains	Bf109 destroyed	Lille	1315~
611 Sqn	Spit FC	P/O J.F.Reeves	Bf109 destroyed	Lille	1315~
BH Wg	Spit FC	W/C A.G.Malan	Bf109 damaged	Near Lille	1315~

5/6th July 1941

151 Sqn	Hurr FC	F/O R.P.Stevens	Ju88 destroyed	Sherington	0308

6th July 1941

71 Sqn	Hurr FC	P/O G.A.Daymond	Bf109 destroyed	W Lille	1448
		F/L G.C.Peterson	Bf109 prob.dest	W Lille	1428
		P/O W.R.Dunn*	Bf109 prob.dest	Merville	1430

* Shared with 306 Squadron.

74 Sqn	Spit FC	Sgt W.G.Lockhart	Bf109 destroyed	NE France	1500~
		Sgt W.G.Lockhart	Bf109 destroyed	NE France	1500~
222 Sqn	Spit FC	S/L C.A.Wood	Bf109 damaged	NE France	1500~
242 Sqn	Hurr FC	F/L B.Duperier	Bf109 prob.dest	near Lille	1500~
		Lt H.O.Mehre	Bf109 damaged	near Lille	1500~
303 Sqn	Spit FC	Sgt M.Belza (shared)	Bf109 prob.dest	Ourville	0945
		P/O B.Drobinski	(shared)		
		F/L J.Jankiewicz	(shared)		
306 Sqn	Hurr FC	P/O L.Jaugsch*	Bf109 prob.dest	Merville	1430

* Shared with 71 Squadron.

603 Sqn	Spit FC	Sgt G.W.Tabor	Bf109 prob.dest	NE France	1500~
610 Sqn	Spit FC	S/L K.Holden	Bf109 destroyed	S Lille	1500~
		S/L K.Holden	Bf109 destroyed	S Lille	1500~
		P/O F.A.O.Gaze	- shared -		
611 Sqn	Spit FC	F/L E.S.Lock	Bf109 destroyed	NE St Omer	1500~
		Sgt W.M.Gilmour	Bf109 destroyed	Lille	1500~
		Sgt W.M.Gilmour	Bf109 prob.dest	Lille	1500~
616 Sqn	Spit FC	P/O J.E.Johnson	Bf109 destroyed	S Dunkirk	1500
		Sgt A.Smith	Bf109 prob.dest	Lille area	1500~
		Sgt D.W.Beedham	Bf109 damaged	Dunkirk area	1500~
BH Wg	Spit FC	W/C A.G.Malan	Bf109 destroyed	Gravelines	1500~
Ntht Wg	Spit FC	W/C T.H.Rolski	Bf109 destroyed	SW Lille	1433
		W/C T.H.Rolski	Bf109 prob.dest	SW Lille	1436
		W/C T.H.Rolski	Bf109 damaged	SW Lille	1437
Tang Wg	Spit FC	W/C D.R.S.Bader	Bf109 destroyed	S Dunkirk	1500~

In July 1941, Bomber Command attempted to entice more German fighters into the air by sending Short Stirlings out on escorted missions. Here, a 15 Squadron aircraft farmates with its Hurricane close escorts. (ww2images.com)

6/7th July 1941

29 Sqn	Beau FC	F/L J.R.D.Braham	Ju88 destroyed	Thames estuary	0110
29 Sqn	Beau FC	S/L G.P.Gibson	He111 destroyed	Thames estuary	0140
247 Sqn	Hurr FC	F/O K.W.Mackenzie	Ju88 destroyed	Western Channel	0120~

7th July 1941

74 Sqn	Spit FC	Sgt G.F.Trott	Bf109 destroyed	Lille area	1040~
		F/L D.C.Carlson	Bf109 damaged	Near Candas	1040
		Sgt G.F.Trott	Bf109 damaged	Lille area	1040~
92 Sqn	Spit FC	P/O P.L.I.Archer	Bf109 destroyed	Near Lille	1015~
		P/O P.L.I.Archer	Bf109 destroyed	Near Lille	1015~
308 Sqn	Spit FC	Sgt T.Hegenbarth	Bf109 destroyed	Chocques to coast	1525
		Sgt J.Kremski	Bf109 destroyed	Chocques to coast	1525
		P/O W.Rettinger	Bf109 destroyed	Chocques to coast	1525
		F/O F.F.Szyszka	Bf109 prob.dest	Chocques to coast	1525
603 Sqn	Spit FC	P/O P.J.Delorme	Bf109 destroyed	NE France	1015~
609 Sqn	Spit FC	F/O J.H.M.Offenberg	Bf109 destroyed	Off Le Touquet	1015~
SF Hch	Spit FC	G/C H.Broadhurst	Bf109 destroyed	Gravelines	0950
		G/C H.Broadhurst	Bf109 destroyed	Gravelines	0950
		G/C H.Broadhurst	Bf109 prob.dest	Gravelines	0950

7/8th July 1941

3 Sqn	Hurr FC	Sgt J.T.Shaw	Do17 prob.dest	Off Dunkirk	0225~
118 Sqn	Spit FC	S/L F.J.Howell	He111 destroyed	10m S Worthing	0120

73

501 Sqn	Spit	FC	S/L A.H.Boyd	Ju88 destroyed	S Portsmouth	0245~
604 Sqn	Beau	FC	F/L H.Speke	He111 destroyed	S Swanage	0150~
			F/L H.Speke	He111 destroyed	N Swanage	0150~
604 Sqn	Beau	FC	F/L E.D.Crew	Ju88 destroyed	Southampton	0230~
			F/L E.D.Crew	He111 destroyed	Southampton	0230~
FIU	Beau	FC	W/C D.R.Evans	He111 destroyed	S Selsey Bill	0245~

8th July 1941

54 Sqn	Spit	FC	Sgt H.Knight	Bf109 destroyed	Lille	0630
			F/O E.F.J.Charles Sgt G.H.Fenton	Bf109 destroyed - shared	Lille	0630
			F/L R.Mottram	Bf109 damaged	Lille	0630
			F/S F.Richards	Bf109 damaged	Lille	0630
54 Sqn	Spit	FC	S/L R.F.Boyd	Bf109 destroyed	Lille	1530
			S/L R.F.Boyd	Bf109 damaged	Lille	1530
65 Sqn	Spit	FC	F/L T.Smart	Bf109 destroyed	S Mardyck	1530~
			Sgt A.H.Johnson	Bf109 destroyed	S Mardyck	1530~
			Sgt A.H.Johnson	Bf109 prob.dest	S Mardyck	1530~
92 Sqn	Spit	FC	Sgt A.Pietrasiak	Bf109 destroyed	Off Gravelines	0630~
			S/L J.Rankin	Bf109 prob.dest	near St Omer	0630~
			P/O G.H.A.Wellum	Bf109 prob.dest	St Omer - Mardyck	0630~
242 Sqn	Hurr	FC	Sgt E.A.Redfern	Bf109 damaged	NE France	1530~
258 Sqn	Hurr	FC	P/O D.J.T.Sharpe	Bf109 damaged	NE France	0630~
303 Sqn	Spit	FC	Sgt W.Giermer	Bf109 destroyed	Lille-Dunkirk	1600
308 Sqn	Spit	FC	F/O F.F.Szyszka	Bf109 destroyed	Near Lille	1530
312 Sqn	Hurr	FC	F/S V.Smolik	Bf109 destroyed	Lens-Bruay	0628
			Sgt J.Stehlik	Bf109 damaged	Lens-Bruay	0632
603 Sqn	Spit	FC	Sgt B.H.Wood	Bf109 destroyed	Lens area	0630~
			F/L G.K.Gilroy	Bf109 damaged	Lens area	0630~
			F/L F.D.S.Scott-Malden	Bf109 damaged	Lens	0630~
603 Sqn	Spit	FC	Sgt G.W.Tabor	Bf109 destroyed	NE France	1530~
			Sgt G.W.Tabor	Bf109 destroyed	NE France	1530~
609 Sqn	Spit	FC	Sgt J.A.Hughes-Rees	Bf109 destroyed	Target area	0630~
			Sgt J.A.Hughes-Rees	Bf109 prob.dest	Target area	0630~
			S/L M.Lister-Robinson	Bf109 damaged	S Gravelines	0630~
610 Sqn	Spit	FC	Sgt E.W.Merriman	Bf109 destroyed	S Portsmouth	1215~
			Sgt E.W.Merriman	Bf109 prob.dest	S Portsmouth	1215~
610 Sqn	Spit	FC	F/L R.A.Lee-Knight	Bf109 destroyed	5m N Lille	1530~

During the summer of 1941, the Tangmere Wing became known as 'Bader's Bus Company', as demonstrated here by Pilot Officer 'Johnnie' Johnson. (ww2images.com)

611 Sqn	Spit	FC	F/L E.S.Lock	Bf109 destroyed	St Omer	0630~
			P/O W.G.G.D.Smith	Bf109 destroyed	St Omer	0630~
			Sgt N.G.Townsend	Bf109 destroyed	St Omer area	0630~
611 Sqn	Spit	FC	F/O P.G.Dexter	Bf109 destroyed	S Dunkirk	1530~
			Sgt D.E.Fair	Bf109 destroyed	Lille-Dunkirk	1530~
			F/O P.G.Dexter	Bf109 prob.dest	S Dunkirk	1530~
			Sgt W.M.Gilmour	Bf109 prob.dest	N Lille	1530~
Dux Wg	Spit	FC	W/C R.R.S.Tuck	Bf109 destroyed	5m W Lille	1530~
Hch Wg	Spit	FC	W/C F.S.Stapleton	Bf109 destroyed	St Omer	0630~

8/9th July 1941

96 Sqn	Deft	FC	P/O E.G.Grubb	Ju88 damaged	Birmingham	0253
96 Sqn	Deft	FC	F/O V.V.S.Verity	He111 damaged	SW Litchfield	0143
257 Sqn	Hurr	FC	F/L F.J.Soper	Ju88 destroyed	N Happisburgh	0053
600 Sqn	Beau	FC	F/O R.S.Woodward	He111 prob.dest	near Abergavenny	0220
604 Sqn	Beau	FC	F/O K.I.Geddes	Ju88 destroyed	Ibsley	u/k
604 Sqn	Beau	FC	F/L R.A.Chisholm	He111 destroyed	E Exeter	0400~
			F/L R.A.Chisholm	He111 damaged	E Exeter	0400~
604 Sqn	Beau	FC	W/C C.H.Anderson	He111 destroyed	S St Albans	0050~
604 Sqn	Beau	FC	W/C C.Appleton	He111 destroyed	S St Albans	u/k
604 Sqn	Beau	FC	F/L H.Speke	He111 destroyed	S Lulworth	0304

75

9th July 1941

54 Sqn	Spit	FC	S/L M.V.Blake	Bf109 destroyed	Cherbourg area	1230~
			S/L M.V.Blake	Bf109 destroyed	Cherbourg area	1230~
			S/L R.F.Boyd	Bf109 destroyed	10m N Gravelines	1230~
			F/O E.F.J.Charles	Bf109 destroyed	Near St Omer	1345
92 Sqn	Spit	FC	S/L J.Rankin	Bf109 destroyed	Bethune-hardelot	1400~
			P/O P.L.I.Archer	Bf109 destroyed	near Bethune	1400~
			Sgt A.Pietrasiak	Bf109 destroyed	near Bethune	1400~
			Sgt A.Pietrasiak	Bf109 destroyed	near Bethune	1400~
			P/O G.H.A.Wellum	Bf109 destroyed	near Bethune	1400~
			S/L J.Rankin	Bf109 prob.dest	Bethune-Hardelot	1400~
			Sgt G.C.Waldern	Bf109 damaged	near Bethune	1400~
			Sgt C.N.Wawn	Bf109 damaged	near Bethune	1400~
222 Sqn	Spit	FC	P/O R.G.Marland	Bf109 destroyed	Off Boulogne	1700~
			P/O R.G.Marland	Bf109 damaged	Off Boulogne	1700~
			P/O R.G.Marland	Bf109 damaged	Off Boulogne	1700~
308 Sqn	Spit	FC	F/O S.Wielgus	Bf109 destroyed	St Omer	1400
312 Sqn	Hurr	FC	F/S O.Kucera	Bf109 destroyed	20m off France	1412
			Sgt Z.Zavoral	Bf109 destroyed	Hucqeliers-Fruges	1349
			S/L A.Vasatko	Bf109 prob.dest	N Montreuil	1412
			S/L A.Vasatko	Bf109 damaged	N Montreuil	1412
609 Sqn	Spit	FC	F/L J.D.Bisdee	Bf109 destroyed	Off Le Touquet	1400~
611 Sqn	Spit	FC	F/O J.R.G.Sutton	Bf109E destroyed	NE France	1400~
			Sgt A.B.Summers	Bf109 damaged	NE France	1400~
616 Sqn	Spit	FC	S/L E.E.P.Gibbs	Bf109 destroyed	Mazingarbe	1400~
			S/L E.E.P.Gibbs	Bf109 prob.dest	Mazingarbe	1400~
			Sgt A.Smith	Bf109 damaged	Lille area	1400~
Tang Wg	Spit	FC	W/C D.R.S.Bader	Bf109 prob.dest	E Le Touquet	1400~
			W/C D.R.S.Bader	Bf109 damaged	E Boulogne	1400~

9/10th July 1941

604 Sqn	Beau	FC	S/L S.H.Skinner	Ju88 destroyed	30m SE I o Wight	0140

10th July 1941

54 Sqn	Spit	FC	Sgt P.McDougall-Black	Bf109F destroyed	Gravelines-Lille	1230
			Sgt P.McDougall-Black	Bf109E destroyed	Gravelines-Lille	1230
234 Sqn	Spit	FC	S/L M.V.Blake	Bf109 destroyed	Cherbourg	1230~
			S/L M.V.Blake	Bf109 destroyed	Cherbourg	1230~

On 10th July Hauptmann Rolf Pingel (right), Kommandeur of II./JG 26, pursued a Stirling across the Channel towards Dover. Hit by return fire, he was then engaged by a 306 Squadron Spitfire flown by Jan Smigielski (left), who forced Pingel to belly-land his Bf109F at St. Margarets Bay, the first F-model to be captured. Pingel impressed his interrogators with his manner and bearing and the interrogation file (K-file) describes him as "the best type of German officer". (Wojtek Matusiak - Smigielski)

		S/L M.V.Blake	Bf109 prob.dest	Cherbourg	1230~
306 Sqn	Spit FC	Sgt J.Smigielski	Bf109 destroyed	St Margarets Bay	1040
312 Sqn	Hurr FC	F/S J.Stehlik	Bf109 prob.dest	NW Gravelines	1306
317 Sqn	Hurr FC	F/L H.Szczesny	Bf109 destroyed	Le Havre harbour	1245
		Sgt S.Brzeski	- shared -		
		S/L S.Brzezina	Bf109 destroyed	Le Havre	1240
		Sgt J.Malinowski	Bf109 damaged	1-2m N Le Havre	1225
501 Sqn	Spit FC	S/L A.H.Boyd	Bf109 damaged	Cherbourg area	1230~
		F/L J.H.Lacey	Bf109 destroyed	5m NE Cherbourg	1230~
609 Sqn	Spit FC	S/L M.Lister-Robinson	Bf109 destroyed	Hardelot	1230~
		F/L P.H.M.Richey	Bf109 damaged	S St Omer	1230~
610 Sqn	Spit FC	S/L K.Holden	Bf109 destroyed	Cherbourg area	1230~
611 Sqn	Spit FC	F/L J.C.F.Hayter	Bf109 destroyed	Cherbourg area	1230~
		P/O J.F.Reeves	Bf109 destroyed	Cherbourg area	1230~
616 Sqn	Spit FC	F/L H.S.L.Dundas	Bf109 destroyed	Calais area	1230~
		Sgt J.G.West	Bf109 destroyed	Cherbourg area	1230~
		P/O P.W.E.Heppell	Bf109 damaged	Cherbourg area	1230~
Tang Wg	Spit FC	W/C D.R.S.Bader	Bf109 destroyed	Calais	1230~
		W/C D.R.S.Bader	Bf109 prob.dest	Bethune	1230~

10/11th July 1941

41 Sqn	Spit	FC	P/O G.H.Ranger	He111 destroyed	W Scarborough	0159
43 Sqn	Hurr	FC	S/L T.F.Dalton-Morgan	He111 destroyed	20m ENE Bell Rock	0400
255 Sqn	Deft	FC	Sgt J.C.Cox	He111 damaged	N Hull	0203

11th July 1941

17 Sqn	Hurr	FC	F/L J.K.Ross Sgt S.Clark	Ju88 destroyed - shared -	80m E Aldeburgh	1930~
92 Sqn	Spit	FC	F/O J.W.Lund	Bf109 destroyed	Calais area	1500~
			Sgt A.Pietrasiak	Bf109 destroyed	Calais area	1500~
			Sgt D.E.Kingaby	Bf109 prob.dest	Calais area	1500~
			Sgt D.E.Kingaby	Bf109 prob.dest	Calais area	1500~
303 Sqn	Spit	FC	F/O W.Lokuciewski	Bf109 prob.dest	S St Valery-en-Caux	1130
452 Sqn	Spit	FC	F/L B.E.Finucane	Bf109 destroyed	5m W Lille	1500
609 Sqn	Spit	FC	S/L M.Lister-Robinson	Bf109 destroyed	Near Cassel	1500~
			Sgt W.J.Jackman	Bf109 destroyed	NE France	1630~
			Sgt R.J.Boyd	Bf109 destroyed	36m SE Dunkirk	1500~
			P/O E.Seghers	Bf109 destroyed	Near Cassel	1500~
			P/O Y.G.A.F.Du Monceau	Bf109 prob.dest	8-10m E Dunkirk	1500~
			F/L P.H.M.Richey	Bf109 prob.dest	Near Cassel	1500~
			Sgt R.J.Boyd	Bf109 damaged	36m SE Dunkirk	1500~
			Sgt K.W.Bramble	Bf109 damaged	Near Cassel	1500~
			F/L P.H.M.Richey	Bf109 damaged	Near Cassel	1500~
			F/L P.H.M.Richey	Bf109 damaged	Near Cassel	1500~
610 Sqn	Spit	FC	Sgt J.E.I.Grey	Bf109 damaged	NE France	u/k
			Sgt E.W.Merriman	Bf109 prob.dest	NE France	u/k
SF BH	Spit	FC	G/C P.R.Barwell	Bf109 destroyed	Cassel area	1500~
			G/C P.R.Barwell	Bf109 damaged	Cassel area	1500~

12th July 1941

303 Sqn	Spit	FC	Sgt M.Adamek	Bf109 destroyed	St Omer-coast	1015
308 Sqn	Spit	FC	F/O J.Szyszka	Bf109 destroyed	St Omer-Hardelot	1030
			Sgt S.Zielinski	Bf109 destroyed	St Omer-Hardelot	1030
603 Sqn	Spit	FC	Sgt W.J.Jackman	Bf109 destroyed	St Omer area	1100~
			Sgt D.J.Prytherch	Bf109 prob.dest	St Omer area	1100~
			P/O P.J.Delorme	Bf109 damaged	St Omer area	1100~
			F/L G.K.Gilroy	Bf109 damaged	St Omer area	1100~
			Sgt W.J.Jackman	Bf109 damaged	St Omer area	1030~
			F/L F.D.S.Scott-Malden	Bf109 damaged	St Omer	1100~

609 Squadron of Malan's Biggin Hill Wing was heavily involved on the 1941 summer offensive. (l - r) Standing; Bob Boyd, Bauduoin de Hemptinne, Peter MacKenzie, Paul Richey, John Bisdee, Jean 'Pyker' Offenberg and Jimmy Baraldi. Sitting; Vicki Ortmans, Tommy Rigler, Keith Ogilvie and Bob Wilmet. Paul Richey and Bob Boyd were successful on 11th July. (ww2images.com)

609 Sqn	Spit	FC	S/L M.Lister-Robinson	Bf109 destroyed	S Griz Nez	1500~
616 Sqn	Spit	FC	P/O P.W.E.Heppell	Bf109 damaged	S Dunkirk	1020~
			Sgt A.Smith	Bf109 prob.dest	S Dunkirk	1020~
Hch Wg	Spit	FC	W/C F.S.Stapleton	Bf109 damaged	St Omer	1023
Tang Wg	Spit	FC	W/C D.R.S.Bader	Bf109 destroyed	S Dunkirk	1020~
			W/C D.R.S.Bader	Bf109 damaged	S Dunkirk	1020~
			W/C D.R.S.Bader	Bf109 damaged	S Dunkirk	1020~
			W/C D.R.S.Bader	Bf109 damaged	S Dunkirk	1020~

13/14th July 1941

85 Sqn	Havc	FC	P/O G.L.Howitt	He111 destroyed	Off Thames estuary	0230~
85 Sqn	Havc	FC	S/L G.L.Raphael	He111 destroyed	25m Ray Sand	0050

14th July 1941

54 Sqn	Spit	FC	P/O H.S.Sewell	Bf109 destroyed	Near Le Touquet	1100
145 Sqn	Spit	FC	S/L P.S.Turner	Bf109 damaged	E Dunkirk	1045~
234 Sqn	Spit	FC	S/L E.B.Mortimer-Rose	Bf109 destroyed	Cherbourg	0805
			S/L E.B.Mortimer-Rose	Bf109 damaged	3m N Cherbourg	0805
			P/O E.W.Wootten	Bf109 destroyed	Cherbourg	0805

316 Sqn	Hurr	FC	W/O W.Klawe	He111 prob.dest	1.5m NW Lynton	1415
317 Sqn	Hurr	FC	Sgt S.Brzeski	Ju88 destroyed	18m S Tenby	1620
			F/L H.Szczesny	- shared -		
501 Sqn	Spit	FC	F/L J.H.Lacey	Bf109 damaged	Cherbourg	0804
602 Sqn	Spit	FC	S/L P.E.Meagher	Bf109 destroyed	5m SW Boulogne	1045~
603 Sqn	Spit	FC	Sgt W.J.Archibald	Bf109 damaged	NE France	1100~
609 Sqn	Spit	FC	S/L M.Lister-Robinson	Bf109 destroyed	Le Touquet area	1045~
611 Sqn	Spit	FC	F/L E.S.Lock	Bf109 destroyed	near Le Touquet	1100~
616 Sqn	Spit	FC	P/O J.E.Johnson	Bf109 destroyed	Over Fanquembergues	1030
			Sgt A.Smith	Bf109 damaged	S Dunkirk	1030~

16th July 1941

91 Sqn	Spit	FC	F/L J.E.Demozay	Bf109 prob.dest	7m SE Dover	1600
222 Sqn	Spit	FC	Sgt P.O.Davies	Do17Z damaged	Dover Straits	1430~
			Sgt T.A.Dossett	- shared -		
234 Sqn	Spit	FC	P/O R.S.Masters	Do215 destroyed	S Portland	1110

17th July 1941

54 Sqn	Spit	FC	S/L R.F.Boyd	Bf109 destroyed	Hardelot	1700
118 Sqn	Spit	FC	P/O D.Fulford	Bf109 prob.dest	20m S Swanage	1645
234 Sqn	Spit	FC	P/O G.T.Baynham	Bf109 destroyed	40m S Portland	1645
			P/O G.T.Baynham	Bf109 destroyed	40m S Portland	1645
			P/O G.T.Baynham	Bf109 destroyed	25m S Portland	1645
			P/O R.S.Masters	Bf109 destroyed	40m S Portland	1645
308 Sqn	Spit	FC	S/L M.Pisarek	Bf109 destroyed	St Omer-Gravelines	2055
			P/O W.Rettinger	Bf109 destroyed	St Omer-Gravelines	2055
			Sgt T.Schiele	Bf109 destroyed	St Omer-Gravelines	2055
			Sgt S.Widlarz	Bf109 prob.dest	St Omer-Gravelines	2055
			Sgt S.Widlarz	Bf109 prob.dest	St Omer-Gravelines	2055
501 Sqn	Spit	FC	F/L J.H.Lacey	He59 destroyed	10m S Portland	2030~
610 Sqn	Spit	FC	P/O F.A.O.Gaze	Bf109 destroyed	Hardelot	2000~
611 Sqn	Spit	FC	P/O R.E.Gardner	Bf109 destroyed	Le Touquet	1700~

18th July 1941

87 Sqn	Hurr	FC	F/O G.L.Roscoe	He111 destroyed	15m SSW Scillies	1845
			Sgt A.H.Thom	- shared -		
152 Sqn	Spit	FC	F/O E.S.Marrs	He111 destroyed	20m WSW Scillies	1640
			Sgt E.H.Marsh	- shared -		

Philip Heppell, known as 'Nip', joined 616 in time for the 1941 summer offensive and became another protege of Douglas Bader. After receiving a DFC, he later went to Malta, landing one of the first Spitfires to reach the island. His final unit was 118 Squadron in the UK, where he led long-range Mustang escorts to Bomber Command heavies. He received a bar to his DFC and left the RAF after the close of hostilities. He died in 1987. On 21st July he flew two missions, claiming a Bf109 'probable' on the first and sharing another 'probable' with Pilot Officer J.E."Johnnie" Johnson on the second. (J.E.Johnson)

19th July 1941

54 Sqn	Spit	FC	P/O H.S.Sewell	Bf109 destroyed	Near Calais	1500
			P/O H.S.Sewell	Bf109 prob.dest	Near Calais	1500
71 Sqn	Hurr	FC	P/O V.R.Bono	Bf109 prob.dest	W Lille	1410
92 Sqn	Spit	FC	Sgt J.C.Carpenter	Bf109 prob.dest	Dunkirk	1500~
222 Sqn	Spit	FC	Sgt K.E.Lewis	Bf109 damaged	Dunkirk	1445~
609 Sqn	Spit	FC	F/O J.H.M.Offenberg	Bf109 damaged	Dunkirk	1500~
610 Sqn	Spit	FC	Sgt W.Raine	Bf109 prob.dest	Dunkirk	1500~
611 Sqn	Spit	FC	P/O W.G.G.D.Smith	Bf109 prob.dest	Lille	1415~
616 Sqn	Spit	FC	F/L L.H.Casson	Bf109 prob.dest	Dunkirk	1500~
			F/O H.S.L.Dundas*	Bf109 destroyed	Lille area	1500~

* Shared with Tangmere Wing.

Tang Wg	Spit	FC	W/C D.R.S.Bader*	Bf109 destroyed	W Lille	1500~

* Shared with 616 Squadron.

Tang Wg	Spit	FC	W/C D.R.S.Bader	Bf109 destroyed	Dunkirk	1500~
			W/C D.R.S.Bader	Bf109 destroyed	Dunkirk	1500~

20th July 1941

54 Sqn	Spit	FC	F/O E.F.J.Charles	Bf109 destroyed	Le Touquet	1930
222 Sqn	Spit	FC	Sgt D.L.Ferraby	Bf109 damaged	Off Etaples	1600~
Ntht Wg	Spit	FC	W/C J.A.Kent	Bf109 destroyed	1/2-1m off Gravelines	1215

21st July 1941

19 Sqn	Spit	FC	Sgt S.F.Brooker	Bf109 damaged	Near Montreuil	2040
			Sgt H.W.Charnock	Bf109 destroyed	5m N Montreuil	2050
			F/L W.Cunningham	Bf109 damaged	Montreuil	2050
54 Sqn	Spit	FC	Unnamed pilot	Bf109 destroyed	N France	0845~
71 Sqn	Hurr	FC	P/O W.R.Dunn	Bf109 destroyed	W Lille	0835
603 Sqn	Spit	FC	Sgt W.J.Archibald	Bf109 damaged	N France	0845~
			P/O P.J.Delorme	Bf109 destroyed	N France	0845~
			Sgt G.W.Tabor	Bf109 destroyed	N France	0845~
609 Sqn	Spit	FC	S/L M.Lister-Robinson	Bf109 damaged	St Omer aea	0845~
			P/O V.M.M.Ortmans	Bf109 damaged	N France	0845~
			Sgt J.E.Van Schaick	Bf109 damaged	N Calais	0915~
			Sgt J.E.Van Schaick	Bf109 damaged	N Calais	0915~
610 Sqn	Spit	FC	Sgt E.W.Merriman	Bf109 destroyed	N France	0845~
			Sgt E.W.Merriman	Bf109 destroyed	N France	0845~
616 Sqn	Spit	FC	Sgt D.W.Beedham	Bf109 damaged	N France	0845~
			P/O P.W.E.Heppell	Bf109 prob.dest	N France	0845~
616 Sqn	Spit	FC	F/L H.S.L.Dundas	Bf109 damaged	Merville area	2045~
			P/O P.W.E.Heppell P/O J.E.Johnson	Bf109 prob.dest - shared -	N France	2045~
Hch Wg	Spit	FC	W/C F.S.Stapleton	Bf109 destroyed	Lille	0845~
			W/C F.S.Stapleton	Bf109 destroyed	Lille	0845~
Tang Wg	Spit	FC	W/C D.R.S.Bader	Bf109 destroyed	N France	0845~
Tang Wg	Spit	FC	W/C D.R.S.Bader	Bf109 damaged	N France	2045~

22nd July 1941

72 Sqn	Spit	FC	P/O C.Gosling	Bf109 damaged	nr St Omer	1345~
308 Sqn	Spit	FC	F/L S.Janus	Bf109 destroyed	St Omer	1350
			Sgt J.Kremski	Bf109 destroyed	Near St Inglevert	1350
			S/L M.Pisarek	Bf109 prob.dest	St Omer	1350
			P/O F.Surma	Bf109 destroyed	St Omer	1350

23rd July 1941

54 Sqn	Spit	FC	F/O E.F.J.Charles	Bf109 damaged	St Omer	1330
			P/O V.D.Page	Bf109 destroyed	Eperlecques	1330
			P/O V.D.Page	Bf109 destroyed	Eperlecques	1330
72 Sqn	Spit	FC	Sgt J.Sika	Bf109 destroyed	Mazingarbe	2000~
91 Sqn	Spit	FC	P/O N.D.Warden	He59 damaged	Gravelines	1815~

92 Sqn	Spit	FC	Sgt C.R.Hesketh	Bf109 destroyed	Mazingarbe	2000~
111 Sqn	Spit	FC	P/O G.A.Skelly	Bf109 damaged	Mazingarbe	2000~
145 Sqn	Spit	FC	Sgt R.J.C.Grant	Bf109 destroyed	Ostend	1520~
			S/L P.S.Turner	Bf109 destroyed	Ostend	1520~
145 Sqn	Spit	FC	Sgt F.J.Twitchett	Bf109 damaged	Mazingarbe	2000~
306 Sqn	Spit	FC	Sgt A.Franczak	Bf109 destroyed	Eperlecques	1320
			F/L W.Nowak	Bf109 damaged	Eperleques	1320
			F/L W.Nowak	Bf109 damaged	Eperleques	1320
			F/O J.K.J.Slonski-Ostoja	Bf109 destroyed	Eperlecques	1320
603 Sqn	Spit	FC	Sgt J.Hurst	Bf109 destroyed	Eperlecques	1330~
609 Sqn	Spit	FC	Sgt A.G.Palmer	Bf109 damaged	Mazingarbe	2000~
			F/L P.H.M.Richey	Bf109 destroyed	Foret de Nieppes	2000~
610 Sqn	Spit	FC	P/O J.E.I.Grey	Bf109 prob.dest	Mazingarbe	2000~
			Sgt W.Raine*	Bf109 destroyed	Mazingarbe	2000~

* Shared with Tangmere Wing.

611 Sqn	Spit	FC	Sgt A.C.Leigh	Bf109 prob.dest	Eperlecques	1330~
616 Sqn	Spit	FC	S/L H.F.Burton	Bf109 damaged	Mazingarbe	2000~
			F/L L.H.Casson	Bf109 destroyed	Mazingarbe	2000~
			F/L L.H.Casson	Bf109 damaged	Mazingarbe	2000~
			P/O J.E.Johnson	Bf109 damaged	Mazingarbe	2000~
BH Wg	Spit	FC	W/C A.G.Malan	Bf109 damaged	St Omer-Le Touquet	2000
NW Wg	Spit	FC	W/C J.W.Gillam	Bf109 damaged	15m W Bethune	2000~
Tang Wg	Spit	FC	W/C D.R.S.Bder	Bf109 destroyed	Mazingarbe	2000~

* Shared with 610 Squadron.

Tang Wg	Spit	FC	W/C D.R.S.Bader	Bf109 damaged	Gravelines	1520~

24th July 1941

43 Sqn	Hurr	FC	S/L T.F.Dalton-Morgan P/O D.Bourne	Ju88 destroyed - shared -	12m E May Is	1625
65 Sqn	Spit	FC	Sgt A.H.Johnson	Bf109 destroyed	SE Mardyck	1530~
			Sgt V.Lawson	Bf109 damaged	SE Mardyck	1530~
92 Sqn	Spit	FC	Sgt C.H.Howard	Bf109 prob.dest	Hazebrouck	1530~
			Sgt W.L.H.Johnston	Bf109 prob.dest	Hazebrouck	1530~
			Sgt W.L.H.Johnston	Bf109 prob.dest	Hazebrouck	1530~
			F/L C.B.F.Kingcombe	Bf109 destroyed	Off Le Havre	1530~
			P/O J.Thompson	Bf109 destroyed	Hazebrouck	1530~
257 Sqn	Hurr	FC	F/L T.A.F.Elsdon	Bf109 damaged	SE Mardyck	1530~
306 Sqn	Spit	FC	F/O S.F.Skalski	Bf109 destroyed	SW Gravelines	1525

316 Sqn	Hurr	FC	S/L J.Frey F/O A.K.Gabsewicz	Bf109 destroyed - shared -	20m N Ushant		1426
			F/O A.K.Gabsewicz	Bf109 damaged	20m N Ushant		1426
452 Sqn	Spit	FC	F/O A.H.Humphrey	Bf109 destroyed	15m N Cherbourg		1440
485 Sqn	Spit	FC	F/L E.P.Wells	Bf109 destroyed	Inland Cherbourg		1445
501 Sqn	Spit	FC	S/L A.H.Boyd	Bf109 destroyed	Brest		1500~
			S/L A.H.Boyd	Bf109 destroyed	Brest		1500~
			F/L J.H.Lacey	Bf109 destroyed	5m W Ile de Batz		1500~
			F/L J.H.Lacey	Bf109 destroyed	5m W Ile de Batz		1500~
609 Sqn	Spit	FC	S/L M.Lister-Robinson	Bf109 damaged	Hazebrouck		1530~
			S/L M.Lister-Robinson	Bf109 destroyed	Hazebrouck		1530~
			Sgt T.C.Rigler	Bf109 destroyed	Off Fecamp		1530~
611 Sqn	Spit	FC	P/O W.G.G.D.Smith	Bf109 damaged	Hazebrouck		1530~
			P/O W.G.G.D.Smith	Bf109 prob.dest	Channel		1625
Hch Wg	Spit	FC	W/C F.S.Stapleton	Bf109 destroyed	Dunkirk		1530~

26th July 1941

91 Sqn	Spit	FC	F/L J.E.Demozay	Bf109 destroyed	off Calais	

27th July 1941

242 Sqn	Hurr	FC	F/L R.F.Hamlyn	Bf109 destroyed	Calais	1340
			P/O J.P.McKechnie	Bf109 prob.dest	Calais	1340
			S/L W.W.Straight	Bf109 prob.dest	Calais	1340
			S/L W.W.Straight	Bf109 prob.dest	Calais	1340

27/28th July 1941

29 Sqn	Beau	FC	P/O C.R.Miles	Ju88 destroyed	NE Sheerness	0250
219 Sqn	Beau	FC	F/O A.J.Hodgkinson	Ju88 destroyed	N Horsham	0208
219 Sqn	Beau	FC	W/C C.M.Winter	E/A destroyed	20m SE Selsey	0200

31st July 1941

91 Sqn	Spit	FC	F/O J.J.Le Roux	Ju88 damaged	Griz Nez	1300
91 Sqn	Spit	FC	F/L J.E.Demozay	Bf109 destroyed	Dunkirk	1730
			F/L J.E.Demozay	Bf109 destroyed	Dunkirk	1730
			F/L J.E.Demozay	Bf109 damaged	Dunkirk	1730

31st July/1st August 1941

247 Sqn	Hurr	FC	F/L J.C.Carver	Do17Z destroyed	S Lizard Point	2250
258 Sqn	Hurr	FC	P/O Hutchinson	Do17 damaged	E Lowestoft	2200~

On 24th July, several operations were flown in support of 'Operation Sunrise', the first large-scale heavy bomber attack in daylight. Fighting was heavy and the Luftwaffe lost several fighters. This appears to be one from I./JG 2, possibly that flown by Leutnant Julius Meimberg, who was wounded.

1st August 1941

602 Sqn	Spit	FC	S/L A.C.Deere	Bf109 destroyed	Channel	u/k

2nd August 1941

129 Sqn	Spit	FC	P/O D.O.Cunliffe	Ju88 destroyed	60m ESE Spurn Head	1605

3rd August 1941

71 Sqn	Hurr	FC	P/O G.A.Daymond	Do17 destroyed	Off Orfordness	1318
242 Sqn	Hurr	FC	P/O K.M.Hicks	Bf109 destroyed	Off French coast	1800~
452 Sqn	Spit	FC	P/O W.D.Eccleton	Bf109F destroyed	5m W St Omer	1925
			F/L B.E.Finucane	Bf109F destroyed	m W St Omer	1925
			F/L B.E.Finucane	Bf109F prob.dest	5m W St Omer	1930
602 Sqn	Spit	FC	Sgt K.N.Murray	Bf109F destroyed	St Omer	1930~
			F/L T.D.Williams	Bf109F destroyed	S Marquise	1930~
MSFU	Hurr	FC	Lt W.H.Everett RNVR	FW200 destroyed	350m SW Eire	1531

5th August 1941

91 Sqn	Spit	FC	Sgt F.S.Perkin	Ju88 prob.dest	E Ramsgate	1645
603 Sqn	Spit	FC	Sgt W.Cook	Bf109F prob.dest	St Omer area	1910

6th August 1941

118 Sqn	Spit	FC	F/O D.Fulford	Bf109E destroyed	5m N La Coyne	1610
			F/O P.I.Howard-Williams	Bf109E destroyed	3-4m off La Coyne	1610
263 Sqn	Whir	FC	P/O C.P.Rudland	Bf109 destroyed	Maupertus	1300~
263 Sqn	Whir	FC	F/S R.A.Brackley	Bf109 destroyed	Cherbourg	1600
			S/L A.H.Donaldson	Bf109 damaged	off Cherbourg	1600
			P/O C.P.Rudland	Bf109 destroyed	Nr Querqueville	1600

85

7th August 1941

19 Sqn	Spit FC	Sgt K.W.Charnock	Bf109E destroyed	Mardyck-St Omer	1800~
41 Sqn	Spit FC	Sgt Mitchell	Bf109F prob.dest	Bethune	1800
74 Sqn	Spit FC	Sgt Edwards P/O E.E.L.Winterbeeck	Ju88 damaged - shared -	Off Whitburn	1000~
92 Sqn	Spit FC	F/S D.E.Kingaby	Bf109F prob.dest	St Omer area	1130~
		F/S D.E.Kingaby	Bf109F damaged	St Omer area	1130~
92 Sqn	Spit FC	S/L J.Rankin	Bf109F damaged	Off Gravelines	1830~
602 Sqn	Spit FC	Sgt J.Garden	Bf109E destroyed	10m S Gravelines	1130~
		Sgt H.L.Thorne	Bf109E destroyed	Gravelines area	1130~
603 Sqn	Spit FC	P/O J.A.R.Falconer	Bf109 prob.dest	Bethune area	1800~
609 Sqn	Spit FC	Lt M.Choron	Bf109 damaged	7m NE Calais	0815~
609 Sqn	Spit FC	Sgt P.A.Nash	Bf109 damaged	St Omer	1200~
609 Sqn	Spit FC	F/O J.H.M.Offenberg	Bf109 prob.dest	Channel	0845
609 Sqn	Spit FC	Sgt T.C.Rigler	Bf109 damaged	St Omer area	1200~
611 Sqn	Spit FC	P/O E.J.Lamb	Bf109F prob.dest	Gravelines area	1115~
616 Sqn	Spit FC	Sgt D.W.Beedham	Bf109F damaged	Lille area	1810~
616 Sqn	Spit FC	Sgt J.G.West	Bf109F damaged	Lille area	1810~
BH Wg	Spit FC	W/C M.Lister-Robinson	Bf109F prob.dest	Mardyck-Gravelines	1200
Dux Wg	Spit FC	W/C R.R.S.Tuck	Bf109 destroyed	20m S Mardyck	1800
		W/C R.R.S.Tuck	Bf109 prob.dest	Mardyck-St.Omer	1800
Ken Wg	Spit FC	W/C J.A.Kent	Bf109 destroyed	10m S Gravelines	1115

8th August 1941

121 Sqn	Hurr FC	P/O S.R.Edner	Ju88 prob.dest	15m NE Hull	1450
		Sgt J.J.Mooney	- shared -		
129 Sqn	Spit FC	Sgt H.C.F.Bowman	Bf110 destroyed	65m E Flamboro' Hd	1305
401 Sqn	Hurr FC	F/O E.L.Neal	Ju88 damaged	E Skegness	1750

9th August 1941

71 Sqn	Spit FC	F/O W.R.Dunn	Bf109F destroyed	W Mardyck	1130
91 Sqn	Spit FC	F/L J.E.Demozay	Bf109 destroyed	4m N Calais	1345
92 Sqn	Spit FC	P/O N.F.Duke	Bf109F destroyed	Boulogne area	1830~
		Sgt H.S.Harrison	Bf109F damaged	Boulogne area	1830~
		F/S D.E.Kingaby	Bf109F destroyed	Boulogne area	1830~
		F/S D.E.Kingaby	Bf109F prob.dest	Boulogne area	1830~
		Sgt J.Le Cheminant	Bf109E destroyed	Boulogne area	1830~
		S/L J.Rankin	Bf109F destroyed	Boulogne area	1830~

Flight Lieutenant Cliff Rudland was one of the very few Whirlwind pilots to be successful in air-to-air combat. He claimed two victories, was awarded a DFC and, after a short spell with 19 Squadron, went to Vickers Supermarine's as a test pilot. He returned to operations with 131 Squadron in November 1943 and was promoted to lead 64 Squadron on Mustangs until March 1945. He then became Wing Leader at Andrews Field and survived the war.
(WW2images.com)

			S/L J.Rankin	Bf109F damaged	Boulogne area	1830~
92 Sqn	Spit	FC	S/L J.Rankin	Bf109F damaged	Boulogne area	1830~
111 Sqn	Spit	FC	F/L M.Kellett	Bf109F destroyed	Calais area	1840~
308 Sqn	Spit	FC	F/O W.Rettinger	Bf109F destroyed	St Omer	1140
315 Sqn	Spit	FC	P/O E.Fiedorczuk	Bf109E damaged	St Omer	1130
			P/O J.Gil	Bf109F prob.dest	St Omer	1130
315 Sqn	Spit	FC	F/O J.Gil	Bf109E damaged	5m NW Boulogne	1820
315 Sqn	Spit	FC	Sgt E.Malczewski	Bf109F prob.dest	St Omer	1130
			F/L B.Mickiewicz	Bf109F destroyed	St Omer	1130
315 Sqn	Spit	FC	F/L B.Mickiewicz	Bf109F destroyed	5m NW Boulogne	1820
			F/L W.Szczesniewski	Bf109E damaged	5m NW Boulogne	1820
			S/L S.Pietraszkiewicz	Bf109F prob.dest	5m NW Boulogne	1820
403 Sqn	Spit	FC	P/O K.H.Anthony	Bf109F prob.dest	Gosnay	1130
452 Sqn	Spit	FC	Sgt K.B.Chisholm F/L B.E.Finucane	Bf109F destroyed - shared -	NE France over cloud	1120
			F/L B.E.Finucane	Bf109E destroyed	NE France over cloud	1120
			Sgt K.B.Chisholm P/O D.E.Lewis	Bf109F destroyed - shared -	Mardyck-Bethune	1120
452 Sqn	Spit	FC	P/O R.E.Thorold-Smith F/L B.E.Finucane	Bf109E destroyed - shared -	NE France over cloud	1120
			P/O K.W.Truscott	Bf109E destroyed	Mardyck-Bethune	1120
602 Sqn	Spit	FC	S/L A.C.Deere	Bf109F damaged	near Bethune	1130~
			S/L A.C.Deere	Bf109F damaged	near Bethune	1130~
			S/L A.C.Deere	Bf109F damaged	near Bethune	1130~
			F/L T.D.Williams	Bf109F prob.dest	near Aire	1130~
609 Sqn	Spit	FC	Lt M.Choron	Bf109F prob.dest	NE France	1830~
			P/O A.Nitelet	Bf109F destroyed	NE France	1830~

616 Sqn	Spit	FC	F/O L.H.Casson	Bf109 destroyed	nr St.Omer	1130~
			F/O P.W.E.Heppell	Bf109F destroyed	nr St.Omer	1130~
			F/O J.E.Johnson	Bf109F destroyed	nr St.Omer	1130~
			F/O J.E.Johnson	Bf109F destroyed	nr St.Omer	1130~
			F/L R.Marples	Bf109F prob.dest	Bethune	1130~
			Sgt J.G.West	Bf109F destroyed	nr St.Omer	1130~
			Sgt J.G.West*	Bf109F destroyed	nr St.Omer	1130~

* Shared with Tangmere Wing.

Ntht Wg	Spit	FC	W/C T.H.Rolski	Bf109F prob.dest	St Omer	1140
Tang Wg	Spit	FC	W/C D.R.S.Bader*	Bf109F destroyed	nr St.Omer	1130~

* Shared with 616 Squadron.

SF NW	Spit	FC	G/C F.V.Beamish	Bf109F prob.dest	near Mardyck	1130~
SF NW	Spit	FC	G/C F.V.Beamish	Bf109F prob.dest	near Mardyck	1130~

10th August 1941

3 Sqn	Hurr	FC	Sgt J.T.Shaw	Bf109F destroyed	5m N Gravelines	0935
3 Sqn	Hurr	FC	P/O H.E.Tappin	Bf109F damaged	Off Gravelines	0935
3 Sqn	Hurr	FC	F/L A.E.Berry	Bf109F prob.dest	Off Gravelines	0935
72 Sqn	Spit	FC	P/O E.W.P.Bocock	Bf109 damaged	10m NE Calais	1405~
72 Sqn	Spit	FC	F/O R.B.Newton	Bf109 damaged	St Omer	1400~

12th August 1941

19 Sqn	Spit	FC	P/O D.G.S.R.Cox	Bf109E prob.dest	Coast at Schouwen	1216
41 Sqn	Spit	FC	P/O M.G.Williams	Bf109F destroyed	St Valery	1830
			F/L R.Marples	- shared -		
54 Sqn	Spit	FC	S/L N.Orton	Bf109 destroyed	Near St Omer	1035
			S/L N.Orton	Bf109 destroyed	Near St Omer	1035
65 Sqn	Spit	FC	Sgt R.Baxter	Bf109E prob.dest	Near Antwerp	1545~
			Sgt R.L.Stillwell	Bf109E damaged	7m SW Haamstede	1455~
			S/L J.W.Villa	Bf109E damaged	Near Antwerp	1545~
			Sgt A.H.Johnson	Bf109E destroyed	7m SW Haamstede	1545~
66 Sqn	Spit	FC	Sgt W.J.Corbin	Bf109E damaged	Near Antwerp	1215~
152 Sqn	Spit	FC	S/L J.Darwen	Bf109E damaged	Near Antwerp	1215~
			P/O R.W.C.Miller	Bf109 prob.dest	Near Antwerp	1215~
222 Sqn	Spit	FC	S/L R.C.Love	Bf109 destroyed	4m S Berck-s-Mer	1040
			Sgt R.Ptacek	Bf109 prob.dest	S Berck-s-Mer	1040
			Sgt A.D.Sharples	Bf109 damaged	S Berck-s-Mer	1040
222 Sqn	Spit	FC	F/O R.M.D.Hall	Bf109 prob.dest	St Omer-Griz Nez	1800
234 Sqn	Spit	FC	P/O R.S.Masters	Bf109 damaged	Antwerp area	1215~

On 9th August the Tangmere Wing lost its charismatic leader when Wing Commander Douglas Bader failed to return from operations over St. Omer. Bader was a controversial man, either idolised or loathed. The architect of the 'Big Wing' concept, which was used with no great success during the Battle of Britain, he became one of the original Wing Leaders in 1941. He was credited with at least 20 confirmed kills, the last - a Bf109 destroyed and another probably so - on 9th August, but he was then shot down, baled out and was captured. He ended the war in the high security prison camp at Colditz Castle. Knighted in 1976, he died in 1982.

				S/L H.M.Stephen	Bf109E damaged	Near Antwerp	1215~
485 Sqn	Spit	FC	Sgt J.D.Rae	Bf109F destroyed	Inland Gravelines	1230
603 Sqn	Spit	FC	Sgt K.J.McKelvie	Bf109 damaged	NE France	1800~
Witt Wg	Spit	FC	W/C P.G.Jameson	Bf109E damaged	4m S Haamstede	1545

12/13th August 1941

23 Sqn	Havc	FC	P/O W.A.Bird	E/A prob.dest	Gilze-Rijn	0300~
			P/O W.A.Bird	E/A prob.dest	Gilze-Rijn	0300~
			P/O W.A.Bird	E/A damaged	Gilze-Rijn	0300~
			P/O W.A.Bird	E/A damaged	Gilze-Rijn	0300~
			P/O W.A.Bird	E/A damaged	Gilze-Rijn	0300~
			P/O W.A.Bird	E/A damaged	Gilze-Rijn	0300~

13th August 1941

| 310 Sqn | Hurr | FC | F/O V.Bergman | Ju88 prob.dest | Off Aberdeen | 1535 |

14th August 1941

41 Sqn	Spit	FC	Sgt A.A.Glen	Bf109F destroyed	Pas de Calais	1430
			F/L A.L.Winskill	Bf109F destroyed	Lille-St Omer	1430~
			F/O C.F.Babbage	Bf109F damaged	Near Gravelines	1430~
222 Sqn	Spit	FC	F/O R.M.D.Hall	Bf109 prob.dest	St Omer-Griz Nez	1800
257 Sqn	Hurr	FC	P/O R.A.Jarvis	Ju88 damaged	20m E Happisburgh	2130~
306 Sqn	Spit	FC	S/L J.K.J.Slonski-Ostoja	Bf109 destroyed	W St Omer	1735
			S/L J.K.J.Slonski-Ostoja	Bf109 prob.dest	W St Omer	1735
			Sgt S.Wieprzkowicz	Bf109 destroyed	Calais-Gravelines	1735
308 Sqn	Spit	FC	S/L M.Pisarek	Bf109F destroyed	St Omer area	1730
			P/O W.Rettinger	Bf109 damaged	St Omer area	1730

*Flight Lieutenant W.Szciesniewski of 315 Squadron
claimed a Bf109 probably destroyed on 15th August.
A short while later he was promoted to lead the
squadron, but was lost on the disastrous Circus
operation on 8th November. He was captured.*
(ww2images.com)

		F/O F.F.Szyszka	Bf109E destroyed	St Omer area	1730
		F/L M.Wesolowski	Bf109E destroyed	St Omer area	1730
		F/L M.Wesolowski	Bf109E prob.dest	St Omer area	1730
		F/L M.Wesolowski	Bf109E damaged	St Omer area	1730
		P/O J.Zbierzchowski	Bf109F destroyed	St Omer area	1730
		P/O J.Zbierzchowski	Bf109F damaged	St Omer area	1730
315 Sqn	Spit FC	Sgt A.Chudek	Bf109E destroyed	Ardres	1750
		Sgt A.Chudek	Bf109E damaged	Ardres	1750
		Sgt M.Cwynar	Bf109E destroyed	Ardres	1750
		F/O J.P.Falkowski	Bf109E destroyed	Ardres	1750
		P/O J.Gil	Bf109E destroyed	Ardres	1750
		P/O W.Grudzinski	Bf109E destroyed	Ardres	1750
		P/O W.Grudzinski	Bf109E destroyed	Ardres	1750
		Sgt T.Krieger	Bf109E destroyed	Ardres	1750
		F/L W.Szczesniewski	Bf109E destroyed	Ardres	1750
		F/L W.Szczesniewski	Bf109E prob.dest	Ardres	1750
610 Sqn	Spit FC	F/L R.A.Lee-Knight	Bf109F prob.dest	10-20m E Boulogne	1430~
		Sgt E.W.Merriman	Bf109F damaged	near Gravelines	1430~

16th August 1941

72 Sqn	Spit FC	Sgt C.P.Stone	Bf109 destroyed	St Omer	1840~
		Sgt C.P.Stone	Bf109 damaged	St Omer	1840~
87 Sqn	Hurr FC	F/O C.R.A.Forsyth	Ju88 destroyed	Scilly Isles	1730
92 Sqn	Spit FC	F/O J.Thompson	Bf109F prob.dest	E Dunkirk	0830~
234 Sqn	Spit FC	P/O R.S.Masters	Bf109 destroyed	By evasion Channel	1840~
306 Sqn	Spit FC	Sgt W.Jasinski	Bf109E destroyed	E Hardelot	1244

On 16th August Flight Lieutenant Brendan 'Paddy' Finucane claimed his 9th solo kill in the morning and his 10th and 11th in the evening. He was a controversial figure, an Irish hero at a time when an Irish hero was desperately needed. In time, he would rise firstly to command 602 Squadron and then the Hornchurch Wing, having received a DSO three DFCs. With a score standing at 26 confirmed, plus six 'shared', he was lost to ground fire on 15th July 1942, ditching in the Channel and going down with his Spitfire.

			Sgt J.Jeka	Bf109E destroyed E Hardelot	1244
			P/O Z.Langhamer	Bf109F destroyed E Hardelot	1244
			Sgt H.J.Pietrzak	Bf109E destroyed E Hardelot	1244
			Sgt H.J.Pietrzak	Bf109 damaged E Hardelot	1244
			Sgt O.Pudricki	Bf109E destroyed E Hardelot	1244
			P/O Z.Radomski	Bf109E destroyed E Hardelot	1244
315 Sqn	Spit	FC	S/L S.Pietraszkiewicz	Bf109 destroyed NW St Omer	1840
452 Sqn	Spit	FC	F/L B.E.Finucane	Bf109E destroyed Near Gravelines	0840
452 Sqn	Spit	FC	Sgt K.B.Chisholm	Bf109E destroyed 15m NE Boulogne	1830
			Sgt K.B.Chisholm	Bf109E destroyed 15m NE Boulogne	1830
			F/L B.E.Finucane	Bf109E destroyed 15m NE Boulogne	1830
			F/L B.E.Finucane	Bf109E destroyed 15m NE Boulogne	1830
			Sgt A.R.Stuart	Bf109E destroyed 10-15m NE Boulogne	1830
			Sgt E.B.Tainton	Bf109E destroyed 15m NE Boulogne	1830
			P/O K.W.Truscott	Bf109E destroyed 10-15m NE Boulogne	1830
485 Sqn	Spit	FC	Sgt L.P.Griffith	Bf109E damaged Calais/Marck A/D	0830
			F/L E.P.Wells	Bf109E damaged Calais/Marck A/D	0830
485 Sqn	Spit	FC	Sgt L.J.Frecklington	Bf109E prob.dest Inland Griz Nez	1310
602 Sqn	Spit	FC	Sgt C.A.Booty	Bf109E prob.dest E Dunkirk	0830~
			F/L T.D.Williams	Bf109E damaged Nieuport	0830~
603 Sqn	Spit	FC	Sgt D.F.Ruchwaldy	Bf109F destroyed NW Boulogne	0830~
609 Sqn	Spit	FC	Sgt P.A.Nash	Bf109 damaged Gravelines	1300~
609 Sqn	Spit	FC	F/O B.De Hemptinne	Bf109 destroyed St Omer	1840~
Ken Wg	Spit	FC	W/C J.A.Kent	Bf109E destroyed E Dunkirk	0830~

16/17th August 1941

85 Sqn	Havc	FC	Sgt K.W.Gray	Ju88 damaged	Feltwell	2240~

17th August 1941

3 Sqn	Hurr	FC	Sgt D.J.Scott	Bf109F prob.dest	Le Touquet	1945~
			Sgt D.J.Scott	Bf109F damaged	Le Touquet	1945~
			F/O J.Lonsdale	Bf109F damaged	Le Touquet	1945~
72 Sqn	Spit	FC	S/L D.F.B.Sheen	Bf109 damaged	5m SW Griz Nez	1650~
			Sgt C.P.Stone	Bf109 destroyed	Off Griz Nez	1650~
91 Sqn	Spit	FC	F/O P.P.C.Barthropp	Bf109F damaged	4m NW Calais	1330~
			P/O A.J.Andrews	Bf109F damaged	Off Calais	1330~
91 Sqn	Spit	FC	F/O J.J.Le Roux	Bf109E destroyed	Griz Nez-Boulogne	1635~
			P/O A.J.Andrews	Bf109E prob.dest	Off Griz Nez	1635~
			F/O P.P.C.Barthropp	Bf109E destroyed	Off Griz Nez	1635~
			P/O A.G.Donahue	Bf109E destroyed	Griz Nez-Boulogne	1635~
242 Sqn	Hurr	FC	P/O F.E.Fayolle	Bf109 damaged	Off Gravelines	1300~
242 Sqn	Hurr	FC	P/O H.Quilliam	Bf109E destroyed	Le Touquet	1945~
242 Sqn	Hurr	FC	P/O H.Quilliam	Bf109E destroyed	Le Touquet	1945~
603 Sqn	Spit	FC	F/L F.D.S.Scott-Malden	Bf109E destroyed	5m off Le Touquet	1945~

18th August 1941

41 Sqn	Spit	FC	P/O R.A.Beardsley	Bf109F prob.dest	St Omer-Calais	1510
			P/O R.A.Beardsley	Bf109F damaged	Gravelines	1510
			Sgt W.Brew	Bf109F damaged	Bethune	1510
			Sgt W.Palmer	Bf109F damaged	Lille	1510
			Sgt C.N.Valiquet	Bf109F damaged	Lille	1510
			P/O G.H.Ranger	Bf109F prob.dest	Armentieres	1530
56 Sqn	Hurr	FC	Sgt R.H.Deugo	Bf109F prob.dest	Lille	1515~
65 Sqn	Spit	FC	Sgt S.Stulir	Bf109 destroyed	Lille	1500~
121 Sqn	Hurr	FC	S/L R.P.R.Powell	Bf109 prob.dest	7m S Gravelines	1512
609 Sqn	Spit	FC	P/O D.W.Barnham	Bf109 prob.dest	near Marquise	1950~
			P/O Y.G.A.F.Du Monceau	Bf109 destroyed	7m S Dover	1950~
			F/O V.M.M.Ortmans	Bf109 destroyed	near Marquise	1950~

19th August 1941

71 Sqn	Spit	FC	P/O H.S.Fenlaw	Bf109 damaged	W Bourbourg	1840
			P/O M.W.Fessler	Bf109 prob.dest	Hazebrouck-Gravelines	1840
111 Sqn	Spit	FC	S/L J.S.McLean	Bf109 destroyed	Hazebrouck-Gravelines	1830~
			S/L J.S.McLean	Bf109 damaged	Hazebrouck-Gravelines	1830~

			Sgt M.W.Smyth	Bf109 damaged	Hazebrouck-Gravelines	1830~
222 Sqn	Spit	FC	F/L J.C.Martin	Bf109 prob.dest	Hazebrouck area	1840~
306 Sqn	Spit	FC	S/L S.F.Skalski	Bf109F destroyed	S Gravelines	1055
308 Sqn	Spit	FC	P/O W.Rettinger	Bf109F destroyed	Near Calais	1050
308 Sqn	Spit	FC	P/O A.Pietrasiak	Bf109F destroyed	Dunkirk	1845
315 Sqn	Spit	FC	Sgt S.Blok	Bf109E destroyed	10m SW Dunkirk	1830
			F/O J.P.Falkowski	Bf109 destroyed	10m SW Dunkirk	1830
			F/O T.Nowak	Bf109E destroyed	10m SW Dunkirk	1830
403 Sqn	Spit	FC	P/O N.D.R.Dick	Bf109F destroyed	Gosnay	1050
			P/O N.D.R.Dick	Bf109F destroyed	Gosnay	1050
			S/L B.G.Norris	Bf109F destroyed	N Gosnay	1100
			S/L B.G.Norris	Bf109F damaged	N Gosnay	1100
			Sgt J.B.B.Rainville	Bf109F damaged	N St Omer	1105
			P/O C.P.J.Wood	Bf109E prob.dest	N St Omer	1105
			P/O D.G.E.Ball	Bf109F destroyed	N St Omer	1105
			P/O N.D.R.Dick	Bf109F destroyed	Mid-Channel	1115
452 Sqn	Spit	FC	P/O K.W.Truscott	Bf109F prob.dest	Gravelines-Gosnay	1050
			F/L B.E.Finucane	Bf109F destroyed	Gravelines-Gosnay	1110
			F/L B.E.Finucane	Bf109F prob.dest	Gravelines-Gosnay	1110
485 Sqn	Spit	FC	Sgt J.D.Rae	Bf109E destroyed	Gravelines	1100
			F/L E.P.Wells	Bf109E destroyed	Gravelines	1110
			F/L E.P.Wells	Bf109E damaged	Gravelines	1110
603 Sqn	Spit	FC	Sgt J.Hurst	Bf109 prob.dest	Gosnay area	1100~
			Sgt I.Pager	Bf109 damaged	Gosnay area	1100~
			Sgt D.J.Prytherch	Bf109 prob.dest	Gosnay area	1100~
			Sgt D.F.Ruchwaldy	Bf109 destroyed	NE Dunkirk	1100~
			F/L F.D.S.Scott-Malden	Bf109 destroyed	Gosnay area	1100~
609 Sqn	Spit	FC	P/O B.De Hemptinne	Bf109 damaged	Gravelines-Gosnay	1100~
			F/O V.M.M.Ortmans	Bf109 damaged	Gravelines-Gosnay	1100~
			Sgt E.W.Pollard	Bf109 damaged	Gravelines-Gosnay	1100~
609 Sqn	Spit	FC	P/O Y.G.A.F.Du Monceau	Bf109 damaged	Boulogne-Dover	1845~
611 Sqn	Spit	FC	Sgt A.C.Leigh	Bf109F destroyed	Gravelines-Gosnay	1830~
			P/O W.G.G.D.Smith	Bf109F destroyed	Gravelines-Gosnay	1830~
616 Sqn	Spit	FC	P/O A.Smith	Bf109 destroyed	Gravelines-Gosnay	1830~
NW Wg	Spit	FC	W/C J.W.Gillam	Bf109 destroyed	7m inland Gravelines	1850~

19/20th August 1941

266 Sqn	Spit	FC	F/L D.A.P.McMullen Sgt I.M.Munro	He111 destroyed - shared -	20m E Winterton	2010

20th August 1941

56 Sqn	Hurr	FC	P/O R.A.Ranger	Bf110 destroyed	5m off Holland	1735
66 Sqn	Spit	FC	F/L H.R.Allen P/O P.Olver	Bf109 prob.dest - shared -	10m off Holland	1430
66 Sqn	Spit	FC	S/L A.S.Forbes Sgt F.H.M.Green	Bf109 destroyed - shared -	20m off Holland	1430
66 Sqn	Spit	FC	P/O P.Olver	Bf109 damaged	10m off Holland	1430
152 Sqn	Spit	FC	S/L J.Darwen	Bf110 destroyed	5m off Holland	1430~

21st August 1941

41 Sqn	Spit	FC	Sgt W.Brew S/L L.M.Gaunce	Bf109 prob.dest - shared -	Hesdin	0940-45
41 Sqn	Spit	FC	F/L R.Marples	Bf109F prob.dest	Near Fruges	1400
			Sgt W.Palmer	Bf109 destroyed	Near Fruges	1400
			Sgt W.Palmer	Bf109F prob.dest	Near Fruges	1400
65 Sqn	Spit	FC	Sgt R.H.A.Williams	Bf109F prob.dest	St Omer area	1400~
111 Sqn	Spit	FC	Sgt E.H.Schrader	Bf109E damaged	Target: Choques	0940~
222 Sqn	Spit	FC	P/O J.H.B.Burgess	Bf109F prob.dest	Target: Choques	0940~
			Sgt W.B.Rudd	Bf109E prob.dest	Target: Choques	0940~
306 Sqn	Spit	FC	S/L S.F.Skalski	Bf109 destroyed	S St Omer	1400
315 Sqn	Spit	FC	F/O J.P.Falkowski	Bf109F destroyed	Ardres	1400
403 Sqn	Spit	FC	P/O D.G.E.Ball	Bf109F prob.dest	NW St Omer	0916
			Sgt C.Grigg	Bf109F damaged	S Mardyck	0920
			Sgt C.E.MacDonald	Bf109F damaged	S Mardyck	0920
			S/L B.G.Morris	Bf109F damaged	S Mardyck	0920
603 Sqn	Spit	FC	Sgt W.J.Archibald	Bf109F damaged	Cassel	0940~
			Sgt D.F.Ruchwaldy	Bf109F damaged	Cassel	0940~
609 Sqn	Spit	FC	Lt M.Choron	Bf109 prob.dest	Target: Choques	0940~
			F/O B.De Hemptinne	Bf109 damaged	Target: Choques	0940~
			F/O B.De Hemptinne	Bf109 damaged	Target: Choques	0940~
			Sgt J.E.Van Schaick	Bf109 prob.dest	Target: Choques	0940~
616 Sqn	Spit	FC	F/O J.E.Johnson	Bf109E prob.dest	10m E Le Touquet	

21/22nd August 1941

257 Sqn	Hurr	FC	P/O Johnson	Do17 destroyed	25m E Lowestoft	2110

Wing Commander Michael Lister-Robinson (right), pictured here with Group Captain A.G."Sailor" Malan, claimed his sixteenth and last solo confirmed victory on 27th August while leading the Biggin Hill Wing. Within a few days he was sent on rest. He returned to operations in January 1942 as leader of the Tangmere Wing, but was to be killed in action on 10th April 1942.
(Chris Goss)

22nd August 1941

41 Sqn	Spit	FC	F/L C.F.Gray	Bf109F destroyed	Le Havre A/D	1820
41 Sqn	Spit	FC	F/L C.R.Bush	Bf109E destroyed	Le Havre-Herrault	1820
257 Sqn	Hurr	FC	Sgt J.G.Fogg	He111 destroyed	60m E Winterton	0815
			F/O R.A.Jarvis	- shared -		

22/23rd August 1941

604 Sqn	Beau	FC	W/C J.Cunningham	He111 destroyed	5m NW Wells	2206
604 Sqn	Beau	FC	W/C J.Cunningham	He111 damaged	35m ESE Lowestoft	2206

26th August 1941

452 Sqn	Spit	FC	F/L A.G.Douglas	Bf109E destroyed	Gravelines	1825
			Sgt A.R.Stuart	Bf109E destroyed	Gravelines	1825
603 Sqn	Spit	FC	Sgt D.J.Prytherch	Bf109E damaged	Gravelines	1830~
			Sgt D.F.Ruchwaldy	Bf109F prob.dest	Gravelines-Dunkirk	1830~
			Sgt D.F.Ruchwaldy	Bf109F damaged	Gravelines-Dunkirk	1830~
			F/L F.D.S.Scott-Malden	Bf109E destroyed	E Dunkirk	1830~
615 Sqn	Hurr	FC	Sgt R.M.Hamilton	Ju88 destroyed	40m N Pembroke Dock	1630~
			Lt R.G.O.J.Mouchotte	- shared -		

26/27th August 1941

87 Sqn	Hurr	FC	F/O E.G.Musgrave	Ju88 destroyed	Off Scilly Isles	2130~

27th August 1941

41 Sqn	Spit	FC	S/L L.M.Gaunce	Bf109F damaged	St Omer	0704
			Sgt W.Palmer	Bf109F destroyed	St Omer	0700
			Sgt W.Palmer	Bf109F damaged	Gravelines	0715
71 Sqn	Spit	FC	P/O W.R.Dunn	Bf109 destroyed	Near Ambleteuse	0815
			P/O W.R.Dunn	Bf109 destroyed	Near Ambleteuse	0820
72 Sqn	Spit	FC	Sgt J.Rutherford	Bf109 damaged	St Omer area	0700~
403 Sqn	Spit	FC	P/O C.P.J.Wood.	Bf109E destroyed	Lille	0815
452 Sqn	Spit	FC	F/L B.E.Finucane	Bf109E destroyed	3m NW Gravelines	0720
			F/L B.E.Finucane	Bf109E destroyed	3m NW Gravelines	0720
			P/O R.E.Thorold-Smith	Bf109E destroyed	W Gravelines	0715
			P/O R.E.Thorold-Smith	Bf109E destroyed	8m W Dunkirk	0718
603 Sqn	Spit	FC	F/O R.V.L.Griffiths	Bf109 prob.dest	N Amiens	0800~
			F/O R.V.L.Griffiths	Bf109 damaged	N Amiens	0800~
			S/L M.J.Louden	Bf109 prob.dest	N Amiens	0800~
			F/L W.G.G.D.Smith	Bf109 prob.dest	N Amiens	0800~
609 Sqn	Spit	FC	Lt M.Choron	Bf109F destroyed	St Omer-coast	0700~
			F/O J.H.M.Offenberg	Bf109 prob.dest	St Omer-coast	0700~
BH Wg	Spit	FC	W/C M.Lister-Robinson	Bf109F destroyed	Nr Gravelines	0700
Hch Wg	Spit	FC	W/C F.S.Stapleton	Bf109F destroyed	W St Omer	0815

28th August 1941

41 Sqn	Spit	FC	S/L L.M.Gaunce	Bf109 damaged	Le Havre	1550

29th August 1941

19 Sqn	Spit	FC	Sgt V.Lysicky F/L A.F.Vokes	Bf109 damaged - shared -	Hazebrouck	0720~
19 Sqn	Spit	FC	Sgt S.F.Brooker	Bf110 destroyed	14m off Rotterdam	1015
			Sgt V.Lysicky	Bf110 damaged	14m off Rotterdam	1015
			F/S J.P.Strihavka	Bf110 damaged	14m off Rotterdam	1015
72 Sqn	Spit	FC	P/O E.W.P.Bocock	Bf109 prob.dest	E Hazebrouck	0720~
			P/O E.W.P.Bocock	Bf109 damaged	E Hazebrouck	0720~
			F/L B.K.Kosinski	Bf109 destroyed	E Hazebrouck	0720~
			F/L B.K.Kosinski	Bf109 prob.dest	E Hazebrouck	0720~
			P/O W.J.Rosser	Bf109 destroyed	E Hazebrouck	0720~
			S/L D.F.B.Sheen	Bf109 damaged	6m E Hazebrouck	0720~
91 Sqn	Spit	FC	F/L J.E.Demozay	Bf109 destroyed	Calais-Griz Nez	1415~
			F/L J.E.Demozay	Bf109 damaged	Calais-Griz Nez	1415~

Jean Demozay, a Free French pilot, fought under the nom-de-guerre of Moses Morlaix, first with 1 Squadron and then with 242 and finally with 91 Squadron. A talented and skilful fighter pilot, he was awarded two DFCs and a DSO. In 1942 he was removed from operations, remaining in staff positions until after D-Day, when he formed the 'Groupement Patrie' to operate against German enclaves in by-passed ports. He was killed in a flying accident in December 1944, having attained the rank of Wing Commander. With 18 confirmed victories, he was one of the leading French fighter pilots to fly with the RAF. On 29th August he claimed a Bf109F shot down and a second damaged between Calais and Cap Griz Nez.

			F/O J.J.Le Roux	Bf109E destroyed Calais-Griz Nez		1415~
306 Sqn	Spit	FC	Sgt M.Machowiak	Bf109F destroyed 5m E Dunkirk		0800
308 Sqn	Spit	FC	F/L S.Janus	Bf109 damaged	Near Hazebrouck	0725
			F/L M.Wesolowski	Bf109 damaged	Near Hazebrouck	0725
			Sgt S.Zielinski	Bf109 damaged	Near Hazebrouck	0725
315 Sqn	Spit	FC	Sgt A.Chudek	Bf109E destroyed Lumbres		0720
			Sgt A.Chudek	Bf109E destroyed St Omer		0720
			F/O K.Wolinski	Bf109 damaged	Near Hazebrouck	0720
485 Sqn	Spit	FC	F/L S.C.Norris	Bf109F destroyed Mardyck		0735
			Sgt H.N.Sweetman	Bf109F destroyed 6m NW Mardyck		0736
609 Sqn	Spit	FC	F/O F.X.E.De Spirlet	Bf109 destroyed	Hazebrouck	0720~
			F/O J.H.M.Offenberg	Bf109 prob.dest	Hazebrouck	0720~
			Sgt C.Ortmans	Bf109 damaged	Hazebrouck	0720 -
			Sgt A.G.Palmer	- shared -		

29/30th August 1941

151 Sqn	Deft	FC	F/O A.S.Turnbull	He111 prob.dest	25m N Sheringham	2155

31st August 1941

92 Sqn	Spit	FC	P/O N.F.Duke	Bf109F damaged	Calais-Gravelines	1330~
			P/O P.H.Humphreys	Bf109F damaged	Calais-Gravelines	1330~
			S/L J.Rankin	Bf109F destroyed	Calais-Gravelines	1330~
			P/O B.Bartholomew	Bf109F prob.dest	Calais-Gravelines	1330~
616 Sqn	Spit	FC	Sgt R.D.Bowen	Bf109E destroyed	Calais-Gravelines	1330~
			Sgt R.D.Bowen	Bf109F damaged	Calais-Gravelines	1330~

1/2nd September 1941

406 Sqn	Beau FC	F/O R.C.Fumerton	Ju88 destroyed	Bedlington	2210
604 Sqn	Beau FC	W/C J.Cunningham	Ju88 destroyed	40m E Lowestoft	2355

2nd September 1941

452 Sqn	Spit FC	Sgt A.R.Stuart	Bf109E destroyed	Off Ostend	1200~
452 Sqn	Spit FC	P/O N.S.Willis	Bf109E destroyed	Off Ostend	1200~

4th September 1941

54 Sqn	Spit FC	P/O J.S.Harris	Bf109F prob.dest	10m S Gravelines	1620
71 Sqn	Spit FC	F/L C.G.Peterson	Bf109F destroyed	Near Boulogne	1620
71 Sqn	Spit FC	P/O M.W.Fessler	Bf109 damaged	St Omer-Hardelot	1615
		Sgt G.V.Stone	Bf109 destroyed	Gravelines area	1620~
		P/O G.A.Daymond	Bf109F destroyed	Near Mazingarbe	1625
		P/O R.L.Mannix	Bf109E prob.dest	Mazingarbe-Hardelot	1650
		P/O T.C.Wallace	Bf109E destroyed	Near Mardyck	1620
72 Sqn	Spit FC	P/O D.Clive	Bf109F prob.dest	Mazingarbe-Mardyck	1630~
91 Sqn	Spit FC	F/O J.J.Le Roux	Bf109F destroyed	10m W Berck-sur-Mer	1325~
		F/O J.J.Le Roux	Bf109F destroyed	10m W Berck-sur-Mer	1325~
92 Sqn	Spit FC	P/O E.G.Brettell	Bf109 prob.dest	Mazingarbe-Mardyck	1630~
111 Sqn	Spit FC	F/S O.Hruby	Bf109 destroyed	Mazingarbe-coast	1630~
		Sgt K.Zouhar	Bf109 destroyed	Mazingarbe-coast	1630~
		Sgt K.Zouhar	Bf109 damaged	Mazingarbe-coast	1630~
129 Sqn	Spit FC	Sgt H.C.F.Bowman	Bf109F damaged	10m W Griz Nez	1655
152 Sqn	Spit FC	Sgt E.H.Marsh	Bf109F destroyed	Off The Hague	1245
263 Sqn	Whir FC	F/O D.Stein	Bf109F prob.dest	Cherbourg	1530~
302 Sqn	Spit FC	P/O K.Sporny	Bf109 prob.dest	French coast	1455
		S/L S.Witorzenc	Bf109 destroyed	Off Cherbourg	1500~
308 Sqn	Spit FC	Sgt S.Piatkowski	Bf109 damaged	Near Fruges	1625
		P/O J.Poplawski	Bf109 destroyed	Near Fruges	1625
603 Sqn	Spit FC	Sgt J.Hurst	Bf109F prob.dest	Gravelines area	1620~
		Sgt D.P.Lamb	Bf109 destroyed	5m SSE Dunkirk	1620~
		Sgt D.P.Lamb	Bf109 damaged	10m SW Dunkirk	1620~
		Sgt G.C.M.Neill	Bf109F prob.dest	Gravelines area	1620~
609 Sqn	Spit FC	Sgt A.G.Palmer	Bf109F prob.dest	Mazingarbe-Mardyck	1630~
611 Sqn	Spit FC	Sgt A.C.Leigh	Bf109 destroyed	Gravelines area	1620~
		Sgt T.McN.Ormiston	Bf109 destroyed	Gravelines area	1620~

Acklington, England a detailed photo of Beaufighter crews of 406 Sqn being dropped at dispersal near the waiting HU-Z. (ww2images.com)

616 Sqn	Spit	FC	F/O J.E.Johnson Sgt J.G.West	Bf109 destroyed - shared -	5m off Le Touquet	1630~
Hch Wg	Spit	FC	W/C F.S.Stapleton	Bf109F prob.dest	10m S Gravelines	1620
Hch Wg	Spit	FC	W/C F.S.Stapleton	Bf109E damaged	10m S Gravelines	1620
NW Wg	Spit	FC	W/C J.S.McLean	Bf109 destroyed	NE France	u/k
NW Wg	Spit	FC	W/C J.S.MacLean	Bf109 prob.dest	Mazingarbe-Mardyck	1630~
Tang Wg	Spit	FC	W/C H.de C.A.Woodhouse	Bf109 damaged	Le Touquet	1645~

7/8th September 1941

| 406 Sqn | Beau | FC | F/O R.C.Fumerton | He111 damaged | Near Acklington | 2240 |

8/9th September 1941

| 600 Sqn | Beau | FC | P/O H.V.Ellis | He111 destroyed | NW Scilly Isles | 2132 |

12th September 1941

257 Sqn	Hurr	FC	S/L F.J.Soper	Bf109F damaged	North Sea	1330~
257 Sqn	Hurr	FC	Sgt Wilson	Bf109F damaged	North Sea	1330~
266 Sqn	Spit	FC	P/O H.L.Parry	Bf109 destroyed	Off Holland	1525~

12/13th September 1941

29 Sqn	Beau	FC	F/L J.R.D.Braham	He111 destroyed	10m SE Dover	2120
247 Sqn	Hurr	FC	F/O K.W.Mackenzie	He111 destroyed	Lands End-Scilly Isles	0235
266 Sqn	Spit	FC	F/L D.A.P.McMullen	He111 prob.dest	Off Norfolk coast	2025~

13th September 1941

91 Sqn	Spit	FC	F/L J.E.Demozay	Bf109F destroyed	Calais-Blanc Nez	1620~
91 Sqn	Spit	FC	F/L J.E.Demozay	Bf109F prob.dest	Calais-Blanc Nez	1620~

13/14th September 1941 1941

23 Sqn	Havc	FC	S/L B.R.O'B.Hoare	He111 destroyed	Beauvais	2120~
			S/L B.R.O'B.Hoare	He111 damaged	Beauvais	2120~

15th September 1941

257 Sqn	Hurr	FC	S/L F.J.Soper	Bf109F damaged	Dutch coast	0700~
257 Sqn	Hurr	FC	S/L F.J.Soper	Ju88 destroyed	Happisburgh	1940~
266 Sqn	Spit	FC	Sgt E.S.Dicks-Sherwood	Bf110 damaged	40m off Dutch coast	1535
Witt Wg	Spit	FC	W/C P.G.Jameson	Bf110 destroyed	40m off Dutch coast	1535

15/16th September 1941

23 Sqn	Havc	FC	W/C R.H.A.Leigh	He111 damaged	Evreux	2320~

16th September 1941

91 Sqn	Spit	FC	F/L J.E.Demozay	Bf109F destroyed	5m W Calais	1130
308 Sqn	Spit	FC	P/O K.Krawczynski	Bf109 destroyed	Near Gravelines	1830
			P/O J.Poplawski	Bf109 destroyed	Near Gravelines	1830
			P/O F.Surma	Bf109 destroyed	Near Gravelines	1830
315 Sqn	Spit	FC	Sgt A.Chudek	Bf109F destroyed	N St Omer	1830
			P/O M.Cwynar	Bf109E prob.dest	N St Omer	1830
			F/L Z.Czykowski	Bf109F destroyed	N St Omer	1830
			F/O J.P.Falkowski	Bf109E destroyed	N St Omer	1830
			S/L S.Pietraszkiewicz	Bf109E damaged	N St Omer	1830

16/17th September 1941

85 Sqn	Havc	FC	S/L G.L.Raphael	Ju88 destroyed	Clacton	2220~

17th September 1941

222 Sqn	Spit	FC	P/O J.H.B.Burgess	Bf109 damaged	Marquise	1800~
308 Sqn	Spit	FC	P/O C.Budzalek*	Bf109 destroyed	Mazingarbe	1430~
* by collision						
41 Sqn	Spit	FC	S/L L.M.Gaunce	Bf109F damaged	S Boulogne	1455
54 Sqn	Spit	FC	S/L N.Orton	Bf109 prob.dest	3m E Gravelines	1450~
54 Sqn	Spit	FC	F/L E.F.J.Charles	Bf109F prob.dest	Near Boulogne	1800
			Sgt G.H.Fenton	Bf109F prob.dest	Near Boulogne	1800
			F/O D.Secretan	Bf109E prob.dest	Near Dunkirk	1815
71 Sqn	Spit	FC	F/L C.G.Peterson	Bf109F damaged	Near Mazingarbe	1440

In September 1941 a new German fighter appeared in the skies over northern France. Fast, heavily armed and highly manouvreable, the parity vis-a-vis the Bf109F and the Spitfire Vb was dashed. At first, this aircraft was identified as the old 'Curtiss Hawk 75A', used by the Armee de l'Air in 1940 but, as one pilot said "No Hawk ever had the performance shown by these brutes". Soon it was identified as the Focke Wulf 190A, designed by Kurt Tank, and which was to place the Spitfire Vb pilots at a definite disadvantage for the next eighteen months. The aircraft shown above is one operated by II./JG 2 'Richthofen'.

92 Sqn	Spit	FC	Sgt H.Cox	Bf109F destroyed	Hazebrouck-Calais	1435~
			F/O J.W.Lund	Bf109 prob.dest	Hazebrouck-Calais	1435~
129 Sqn	Spit	FC	P/O J.H.Whalen	Bf109F destroyed	5-10m W Le Touquet	1507
			P/O J.H.Whalen	Bf109F destroyed	5-10m W Le Touquet	1507
306 Sqn	Spit	FC	S/L S.F.Skalski	Bf109F destroyed	Near lens	1433
			S/L S.F.Skalski	Bf109F destroyed	5m SE Dunkirk	1435
402 Sqn	Hurr	FC	Sgt R.J.Emberg	Bf109 prob.dest	NE France	1440~
			F/O F.B.Foster	- shared -		
			P/O S.Graham	Bf109 prob.dest shd	NE France	1440~
			F/O F.W.Kelly	Bf109 prob.dest	NE France	1440~
			Sgt B.P.O'Neill	Bf109 prob.dest shd	NE France	1440~
403 Sqn	Spit	FC	S/L R.A.Lee-Knight	Bf109E destroyed	5-6m off Griz Nez	1600~
			P/O C.P.J.Wood	Bf109E destroyed	Off Griz Nez	1600~
			P/O C.P.J.Wood	Bf109E prob.dest	Off Griz Nez	1600~
485 Sqn	Spit	FC	F/L E.P.Wells	Bf109F prob.dest	E Marquise	1800~
602 Sqn	Spit	FC	Sgt J.B.Niven	Bf109E destroyed	7m NE Boulogne	1800~
602 Sqn	Spit	FC	F/L T.D.Williams	Bf109E destroyed	12m NW Boulogne	1700
609 Sqn	Spit	FC	Lt M.Choron	Bf109 destroyed	NE France	1440~

611 Sqn	Spit	FC	F/L J.C.F.Hayter	Bf109 damaged	5m E Mardyck	1445~
			P/O R.Van Den Honert	Bf109 damaged	near Mardyck	1445~
BH Wg	Spit	FC	W/C J.Rankin	Bf109 damaged	10m off Hardelot	1800~
Hch Wg	Spit	FC	W/C F.S.Stapleton	Bf109F prob.dest	5m S Mardyck	1445~
Tang Wg	Spit	FC	W/C H.De C.A.Woodhouse	Bf109F damaged	Off Le Touquet	1505

18th September 1941

41 Sqn	Spit	FC	Sgt C.J.L.Whiteford	Bf109F destroyed	Ostend	1030~
			Sgt C.J.L.Whiteford	Ju52 destroyed	Offshore Ostend A/D	1110
			P/O G.H.Ranger	- shared -		
			F/L R.Marples	- shared -		
			Sgt G.W.Swanswick	Bf109E prob.dest	Sea off Ostend	1035
			Sgt W.Palmer	Bf109F destroyed	Ostend	1030~
			Sgt W.Palmer	Bf109E prob.dest	Dixmunde-Boulogne	1030
			P/O C.F.Babbage	FW190 destroyed	1m N Ostend	1050
			P/O G.A.F.Buchanon	Hs123 destroyed	Ostend	1030
			F/L C.R.Bush	- shared -		
71 Sqn	Spit	FC	F/L C.G.Peterson	Bf109E destroyed	S Le Touquet	1510
91 Sqn	Spit	FC	Sgt J.Gillies	Bf109E destroyed	Off Nieuport	1400~
402 Sqn	Hurr	FC	Sgt K.B.Handley	Bf109F damaged	Channel	1515~
			Sgt G.McClusky	Bf109F destroyed	Channel	1515~
			F/L R.E.E.Morrow	Bf109F prob.dest	Channel	1515~
			P/O W.H.Pentland	Bf109F damaged	Channel	1515~
			Sgt G.D.Robertson	Bf109F prob.dest	Channel	1515~
452 Sqn	Spit	FC	Sgt K.B.Chisholm	Bf109E destroyed	NE France	1450~
			F/L A.G.Douglas	Bf109E destroyed	Rouen area	1450~
			P/O R.E.Thorold-Smith	Bf109E destroyed	Rouen	1450~
			P/O K.W.Truscott	Bf109F destroyed	NW Rouen	1450~
			P/O K.W.Truscott	Bf109E damaged	N Le Havre	1510~
			Sgt C.N.Wawn	Bf109F destroyed	Rouen area	1450~
			Sgt C.N.Wawn	Bf109 damaged	Rouen area	1450~
485 Sqn	Spit	FC	Sgt A.S.Kronfeld	Bf109E damaged	Yvetot area	1500~
			Sgt H.N.Sweetman	Bf109E prob.dest	Yvetot	1500~
			P/O H.L.Thomas	Bf109E prob.dest	Yvetot area	1500~
			F/L E.P.Wells	Bf109E destroyed	Yvetot area	1500~
602 Sqn	Spit	FC	Sgt S.D.Osborn	Bf109F damaged	Yvetot area	1500~
603 Sqn	Spit	FC	Sgt J.Hurst	Bf109E prob.dest	S Le Touquet	1515~
			F/L F.D.S.Scott-Malden	Bf109E prob.dest	Abbeville	1515~

The first official claim for an FW190 destroyed came on 18th September when Cyril Babbage of 41 Squadron caught the highly experienced Walter Adolph, a Ritterkreuztrager and Kommandeur of II./JG 26, off Ostend. Babbage blew the Focke Wulf into the sea and Adolph was killed.

615 Sqn	Hurr	FC	Lt F.H.De La Bouchere	Bf109 destroyed	Ostend	1030
			Lt F.H.De La Bouchere	Bf109 damaged	Ostend	1030
			Lt F.H.De La Bouchere	Bf109 damaged	Ostend	1030
			P/O J.Slade	Bf109 damaged	Ostend	1030

19th September 1941

71 Sqn	Spit	FC	F/O G.A.Daymond	Bf109F destroyed	Dunkirk	1640
			F/O G.A.Daymond	Bf109F destroyed	Dunkirk-Dover	1655
			P/O J.V.Flynn	Bf109F destroyed	Dunkirk-Dover	1655
72 Sqn	Spit	FC	Sgt J.G.Merrett	Bf109E prob.dest	Off Gravelines	1700~
615 Sqn	Hurr	FC	Sgt P.G.Louis	Bf109F prob.dest	Dover area	1140~

20th September 1941

41 Sqn	Spit	FC	F/O L.L.Bache*	Bf109E destroyed	Doudeville, Nr St Valery	1550
* Shared with Tangmere Wing.						
71 Sqn	Spit	FC	P/O R.O.Scarborough	Bf109 damaged	Hazebrouck-coast	1600
92 Sqn	Spit	FC	F/L J.H.Sanderson	Bf109 prob.dest	Abbeville area	1550~
111 Sqn	Spit	FC	F/L M.Kellett	Bf109 destroyed	Hazebrouck	1550~
129 Sqn	Spit	FC	Sgt V.E.Tucker	Bf109F destroyed	10-20m W St Valery	1620
308 Sqn	Spit	FC	P/O O.Ilinski	Bf109 destroyed	Rouen-Channel	1550-1615
			S/L M.Pisarek	Bf109 destroyed	Rouen-Channel	1550-1615
			P/O F.Surma	Bf109 destroyed	Rouen-Channel	1550-1615
			P/O F.Surma	Bf109 destroyed	Rouen-Channel	1550-1615
452 Sqn	Spit	FC	Sgt K.B.Chisholm	Bf109F destroyed	5m NW Abbeville	1535
			Sgt B.P.Dunstan	Bf109E destroyed	1m NW Berck-s-Mer	1600
			Sgt J.R.H.Elphick	Bf109 damaged	10m W Crotoy	1530

			Sgt J.R.H.Elphick	Bf109 damaged	10m W Crotoy	1530
			F/L B.E.Finucane	Bf109F destroyed	5m NW Abbeville	1535
			F/L B.E.Finucane	Bf109F destroyed	5m NW Abbeville	1535
			F/L B.E.Finucane	Bf109F destroyed	5m NW Abbeville	1535
			F/O K.W.Truscott	Bf109F destroyed	N Abbeville	1540
			F/O K.W.Truscott	Bf109F destroyed	3m off France	1552
			F/O K.W.Truscott	Bf109F damaged	3m off France	1552
603 Sqn	Spit	FC	Sgt J.Hurst	Bf109F prob.dest	French coast	1600~
611 Sqn	Spit	FC	Sgt M.R.B.Ingram	Bf109 damaged	French coast	1600~
Tang Wg	Spit	FC	W/C H.de C.A.Woodhouse	Bf109E destroyed	Doudeville, Nr St Valery*	1550

Shared with 41 Squadron.

20/21st September 1941

219 Sqn	Beau	FC	S/L C.M.Wight-Boycott	He111 destroyed	Near Tangmere	2330~

21st September 1941

41 Sqn	Spit	FC	Sgt C.J.L.Whiteford	Bf109F damaged	Gosnay-Bethune	1520~
			P/O G.H.Ranger	Bf109F damaged	10m NW Gosnay	1515
			F/L C.R.Bush	Bf109F damaged	Near Bethune	1525
71 Sqn	Spit	FC	P/O C.W.Tribken	Bf109F damaged	Lille-Mardyck	1630
			P/O C.W.McColpin	Bf109E destroyed	Lille-coast	1630
111 Sqn	Spit	FC	Sgt K.Zouhar	Bf109 prob.dest	Lille-coast	1630~
129 Sqn	Spit	FC	P/O H.T.Armstrong	Bf109E destroyed	Le Touquet	1510
			P/O D.O.Cunliffe	Bf109E prob.dest	5m S Le Treport	1600
			P/O D.O.Cunliffe	Bf109E damaged	5m S Le Treport	1600
			Sgt A.Drew	Bf109E prob.dest	10m E Le Touquet	1550~
			Sgt V.E.Tucker	Bf109E prob.dest	10m E Le Touquet	1500-15
			P/O J.H.Whalen	Bf109E destroyed	Mid-Channel	1500-45
			P/O J.H.Whalen	Bf109E damaged	Mid-Channel	1500-45
			Sgt J.Wilson	Bf109E prob.dest	10m E Le Touquet	1540
222 Sqn	Spit	FC	Sgt W.B.Maskery	Bf109 prob.dest	Lille-coast	1630~
308 Sqn	Spit	FC	F/L S.Janus	Bf109 destroyed	SW Le Touquet	1512
			S/L M.Pisarek	Bf109 destroyed	SW Le Touquet	1512
			P/O J.Poplawski	Bf109 destroyed	SW Le Touquet	1512
			P/O S.Wandzilak	E/A destroyed	SW Le Touquet	1512
			F/L M.Wesolowski	Bf109 destroyed	SW Le Touquet	1512
			Sgt J.Zielinski	Bf109 prob.dest	SW Le Touquet	1512
			Sgt J.Zielinski	Bf109 damaged	SW Le Touquet	1512

Three Beaufighter crews from 600 Squadron, airborne from Colerne, pose for the camera.

(ww2images.com)

		Sgt S.Zielinski	Bf109 prob.dest	SW Le Touquet	1512
		Sgt S.Zielinski	Bf109 damaged	SW Le Touquet	1512
315 Sqn	Spit FC	Sgt S.Blok	Bf109E destroyed	Fruges	1530
		Sgt S.Blok	Bf109E prob.dest	Fruges	1530
		F/O J.P.Falkowski	FW190 destroyed	Fruges	1530
		S/L S.Pietraszkiewicz	FW190 destroyed	Fruges	1530
		S/L S.Pietraszkiewicz	FW190 destroyed	Fruges	1530
403 Sqn	Spit FC	P/O C.P.J.Wood	Bf109E destroyed	15m NW Lille	1630
452 Sqn	Spit FC	Sgt K.B.Chisholm	Bf109F destroyed	20m E Hardelot	1525
		Sgt K.B.Chisholm	Bf109F damaged	Coast at Hardelot	1530
		F/L B.E.Finucane	Bf109F destroyed	20m E Hardelot	1525
		F/L B.E.Finucane	Bf109F destroyed	20m E Hardelot	1525
		P/O D.E.Lewis	Bf109F damaged	N Desvres	1520
		F/O K.W.Truscott	Bf109E destroyed	N Desvres	1520
		Sgt C.N.Wawn	Bf109F destroyed	N Desvres	1520
485 Sqn	Spit FC	P/O W.V.Crawford-Compton	Bf109F destroyed	5m W Desvres	1525
		P/O G.H.Francis	Bf109F prob.dest	8m NE Hardelot	1515
		F/L E.P.Wells	Bf109F destroyed	Desvres	1530
		F/L E.P.Wells	Bf109F destroyed	5m W Boulogne	1540
602 Sqn	Spit FC	P/O N.C.Macqueen	Bf109F damaged	NE France	1530~
616 Sqn	Spit FC	F/O J.E.Johnson	Bf109F destroyed	5m S Gravelines	1530
		F/O J.E.Johnson	Bf109F destroyed	5m S Gravelines	1530

| | | | P/O W.N.Murray | Bf109F damaged | Gravelines area | 1530~ |
| | | | P/O A.Smith | Bf109F destroyed | Inland Le Touquet | 1530~ |

22nd September 1941

| 91 Sqn | Spit | FC | Sgt F.H.Silk | Bf109 prob.dest | Near Boulogne | 1250~ |

25th September 1941

| 66 Sqn | Spit | FC | Sgt F.H.M.Green | Ju88 damaged | Off Lizard | 1540 |
| | | | P/O Mitchell | - shared - | | |

26th September 1941

91 Sqn	Spit	FC	P/O A.G.Donahue	Klemm destroyed	1-3m NW St Valery-en-Caux	1700
266 Sqn	Spit	FC	Sgt I.M.Munro	Do17 prob.dest	Channel	1910
			Sgt J.C.Thompson	- shared -		

Chapter Four

Enter the Butcher Bird
27th September - 8th November 1941

The new *Luftwaffe* fighter, the Focke Wulf 190, entered unit service in August 1941, but was first met in strength late in September. This remarkable fighter, flown by well-trained, experienced and confident pilots, came as great shock to Fighter Command. It easily out-performed the Spitfire VB and, by the end of the the first week of November, casualties had become so great that *Circus* operations were halted. Even with the clear superiority of the Focke Wulf, the British pilots were still quite prepared to do battle even though, as the great Johnnie Johnson was later to say, "The '190s forced us right back to the French coast". The German pilots were now supremely confident, so much so that two of them, Hans Hahn and Siegfried Schnell, would regularly have wagers on "who would bring down the next Spitfire intact by shooting out its radiator". The RAF were in for a tough time and would face it with quite awesome courage.

27th September 1941

54 Sqn	Spit	FC	Sgt D.Ibbotson	Bf109E damaged	15m NE Le Touquet	1430
			Sgt G.H.Fenton	Bf109 damaged	St Omer-Cassel	1415
			Sgt G.H.Fenton F/L E.F.J.Charles	Bf109F destroyed - shared -	10m S Mardyck	1500~
71 Sqn	Spit	FC	P/O R.O.Scarborough	Bf109F destroyed	Mardyck-Lille	1440
			F/L C.G.Peterson	Bf109F prob.dest	Mardyck-Mazingarbe	1440
			P/O S.A.Mauriello	Bf109F destroyed	Mardyck-Mazingarbe	1435
			P/O S.A.Mauriello	Bf109F prob.dest	Mardyck-Mazingarbe	1435
			P/O J.J.Cowley	Bf109F prob.dest	Mardyck-Mazingarbe	1435
			P/O O.H.Coen	Bf109F damaged	Mazingarbe	1440
72 Sqn	Spit	FC	F/L R.M.D.Hall	Bf109 prob.dest	Mardyck-Mazingarbe	1430~
			Sgt F.Falkiner	Bf109 destroyed	Mardyck-Mazingarbe	1430~
92 Sqn	Spit	FC	S/L R.M.Milne	Bf109 prob.dest	SW St Omer	1430~
			S/L R.M.Milne	Bf109 damaged	near Guines	1430~
			Sgt W.L.H.Johnston	Bf109 prob.dest	Guines area	1430~
			Sgt W.L.H.Johnston	Bf109 damaged	Guines area	1430~
			P/OP.H.Beake	Bf109 damaged	Guines area	1430~
129 Sqn	Spit	FC	Sgt R.A.Hardy	Bf109F destroyed	10m E Boulogne	1440
306 Sqn	Spit	FC	P/O R.Malczewski	Bf109 destroyed	Off Le Touquet	1430
			Sgt S.Krzyzagerski	Bf109 prob.dest	Near Le Crotoy	1423
			Sgt S.Krzyzagerski	Bf109 damaged	Near Le Crotoy	1423
			Sgt S.Krzyzagerski	Bf109 damaged	Near Le Crotoy	1423
			Sgt S.Krzyzagerski	Bf109 destroyed	Le Touquet-Amiens	1430~

		P/O J.Poplawski	Bf109 destroyed	Amiens	1432
		Sgt Z.Rozworski	Bf109E damaged	Off Le Touquet	1420
		Sgt G.Sologub	Bf109E destroyed	Off Le Touquet	1420
		P/O F.Surma	Bf109 prob.dest	Coast-Amiens	1425
		Sgt E.Watolski	Bf109 destroyed	Coast-Amiens	1425
		S/L A.Wczelik	Bf109E damaged	Amiens	1420
315 Sqn	Spit FC	Sgt A.Chudek	FW190 destroyed	Near Abbeville	1430
402 Sqn	Hurr FC	S/L V.B.Corbett	Bf109F destroyed	Near Heuchin	1440
		F/L H.F.Crease	Bf109 damaged	Near Mazingarbe	1435-
		P/O L.S.Ford	Bf109 damaged	Near Mazingarbe	1435
		F/O F.W.Kelly	Bf109 damaged	10m SE Gravelines	1424
		Sgt G.McClusky	Bf109 damaged	10m SE Gravelines	1424
		Sgt G.McClusky	Bf109F destroyed	Near Heuchin	1440
403 Sqn	Spit FC	F/O D.G.E.Ball	Bf109E destroyed	5m SE Cassel	1430
		F/L R.G.Clouston	Bf109E damaged	Cassel	1430
		Sgt E.A.Crist	Bf109E destroyed	Cassel	1430
		F/L R.B.Newton	Bf109E destroyed	Cassel	1430
411 Sqn	Spit FC	F/L K.A.Boomer	Bf109F damaged	Near Mardyck	1520
		P/O R.W.McNair	Bf109F damaged	Near Mardyck	1520
603 Sqn	Spit FC	F/L F.Inness	Bf109E damaged	St Omer-Le Touquet	1430~
		P/O R.G.Marland	Bf109E prob.dest	St Omer-Le Touquet	1430~
		Sgt K.J.McKelvie	Bf109E destroyed	St Omer-Le Touquet	1430~
		Sgt K.J.McKelvie	Bf109F prob.dest	St Omer-Le Touquet	1430~
		Sgt D.J.Prytherch	FW190 destroyed	St Omer-Le Touquet	1430~
609 Sqn	Spit FC	F/O G.E.H.Dieu	Bf109F prob.dest	Mardyck-Mazingarbe	1430~
		P/O Y.G.A.F.Du Monceau	Bf109F destroyed	5-8m N Mardyck	1430~
		F/L J.H.M.Offenberg	Bf109F damaged	5m N St Omer	1430~
611 Sqn	Spit FC	Sgt N.G.Townsend	Bf109E destroyed	St Omer-Le Touquet	1430~
		Sgt K.S.Wright	Bf109F prob.dest	St Omer-Le Touquet	1430~
BH Wg	Spit FC	W/C J.Rankin	Bf109F damaged	Mardyck-Le Touquet	1425
		W/C J.Rankin	Bf109F damaged	Mardyck-Le Touquet	1425-1600
		W/C J.Rankin	Bf109F destroyed	Beach S Le Touquet	1600
Ntht Wg	Spit FC	W/C T.H.Rolski	Bf109 prob.dest	Near le Crotoy	1420
SF Hch	Spit FC	G/C H.Broadhurst	Bf109 destroyed	Near Mardyck	1430~

64 Squadron line-up at Turnhouse, autumn 1941. (WW2images.com)

28/29th September 1941

29 Sqn	Beau	FC	F/L J.R.D.Braham	He111 damaged	10-15m off Belgian coast	2150~

30th September/1st October 1941

406 Sqn	Beau	FC	W/C D.G.Morris	Ju88 destroyed	50m SE Acklington	2209

1st October 1941

72 Sqn	Spit	FC	F/O K.Krosinski	Bf109F destroyed	Channel	1240~
			F/O K.Krosinski	Bf109F prob.dest	Channel	1240~
92 Sqn	Spit	FC	F/S D.E.Kingaby	Bf109F destroyed	Off Griz Nez	1240~
			F/S D.E.Kingaby	Bf109F prob.dest	Off Griz Nez	1240~
485 Sqn	Spit	FC	S/L M.W.B.Knight	Bf109 damaged	Boulogne-5m off Dungeness	1241
602 Sqn	Spit	FC	Sgt J.E.I.Smith	Bf109F damaged	Channel	1240~
			Sgt L.Thorne	Bf109F prob.dest	Channel	1240~
SF Hch	Spit	FC	G/C H.Broadhurst	Bf109E damaged	6m inland Marck	1240~

1/2nd October 1941

25 Sqn	Beau	FC	S/L H.P.Pleasance	Ju88 prob.dest	N Wells	2125
29 Sqn	Beau	FC	F/L J.D.Humphries	Do17 prob.dest	Thames estuary	2330~

2nd October 1941

71 Sqn	Spit	FC	P/O A.F.Roscoe	Bf109E destroyed	Near Abbeville	1305
			P/O R.O.Scarborough P/O N.Anderson	Bf109F destroyed - shared -	Near Abbeville	1345

109

			P/O C.W.McColpin	Bf109E destroyed	Abbeville	1345
			P/O C.W.McColpin	Bf109E destroyed	Abbeville	1345
			S/L S.T.Meares	Bf109F destroyed	Abbeville	1345
72 Sqn	Spit	FC	S/L D.F.B.Sheen	Bf109 destroyed	Abbeville	1345
452 Sqn	Spit	FC	Sgt R.J.Cowan	Bf109F destroyed	Boulogne-Le Touquet	1740
			F/L B.E.Finucane	Bf109F destroyed	Boulogne-Le Touquet	1740
			F/L B.E.Finucane	Bf109F damaged	Boulogne-Le Touquet	1740
485 Sqn	Spit	FC	Sgt J.D.Rae	Bf109F prob.dest	W Boulogne	1730
			F/O P.H.Strang	Bf109E prob.dest	N Calais	1735
			F/L E.P.Wells	Bf109E prob.dest	W Boulogne	1730

2/3rd October 1941

43 Sqn	Hurr	FC	S/L T.F.Dalton-Morgan	Ju88 destroyed	20m off Berwick	2140
406 Sqn	Beau	FC	W/C D.G.Morris	He111 destroyed	Alnwick, N Lesbury	2050
			W/C D.G.Morris	Do17 destroyed	3m E Tynemouth	2120
406 Sqn	Beau	FC	F/L F.W.Hillock	Ju88 damaged	15m E Blythe	2200

3rd October 1941

92 Sqn	Spit	FC	F/S D.E.Kingaby	Bf109F destroyed	10m off Ostend	1500~

5th October 1941

257 Sqn	Hurr	FC	S/L F.J.Soper	Ju88 damaged	30m NE Happisburgh	1308
			Sgt Spencer	- shared -		

9th October 1941

91 Sqn	Spit	FC	F/L J.E.Demozay	Bf109F destroyed	Calais-Offerkerque	1000~
501 Sqn	Spit	FC	Squadron	Ju88 destroyed	Off Cap de la Hague	1420

10/11th October 1941

600 Sqn	Beau	FC	S/L A.D.McN.Boyd	He111 destroyed	10m NW St Ives	0115

12th October 1941

118 Sqn	Spit	FC	F/O P.I.Howard-Williams	Bf109E destroyed	20m N Cap de la Hague	1615
			F/O P.I.Howard-Williams	Bf109E prob.dest	20m N Cap de la Hague	1615
			Sgt J.Lloyd	Bf109E destroyed	20m N Cap de la Hague	1615
			P/O P.Mackenzie	Bf109E destroyed	20m N Cap de la Hague	1615
303 Sqn	Spit	FC	Sgt M.Adamek	Bf109F destroyed	Le Touquet	1240
308 Sqn	Spit	FC	Sgt S.Piatkowski	Bf109F destroyed	Le Touquet	1235
			F/O F.Surma	Bf109F destroyed	Off le Touquet	1235

Squadron Leader F.J.Soper of 257 Squadron shared his last victory claim with Sergeant Spencer on 5th October, when they attacked and claimed damage to a Ju88 off Happisburgh. Soper failed to return from this mission, believed shot down by return fire. (ww2images.com)

452 Sqn	Spit	FC	S/L B.E.Finucane	Bf109F destroyed	SW Le Touquet	1222-40
			F/L K.W.Truscott	Bf109F prob.dest	SW Le Touquet	1222-40
			F/L K.W.Truscott	Bf109 damaged	SW Le Touquet	1222-40

12/13th October 1941

68 Sqn	Beau	FC	P/O M.J.Mansfeld	Ju88 destroyed	Irish Sea	2315~
			P/O M.J.Mansfeld	Ju88 destroyed	Irish Sea	2315~
			P/O M.J.Mansfeld	Ju88 damaged	Irish Sea	2315~

13th October 1941

41 Sqn	Spit	FC	F/S G.W.Swanswick	Bf109 damaged	Arques	1320~
			Sgt C.J.L.Whiteford	Bf109F prob.dest	Arques	1320~
54 Sqn	Spit	FC	Sgt J.W.Guthrie	Bf109E destroyed	Mazingarbe	1430
92 Sqn	Spit	FC	S/L R.M.Milne	Bf109F destroyed	Mazingarbe	1415~
			S/L R.M.Milne	Bf109F destroyed	Mazingarbe	1415~
			S/L R.M.Milne	Bf109E destroyed	Mazingarbe	1415~
			S/L R.M.Milne	Bf109E damaged	Mazingarbe	1415~
118 Sqn	Spit	FC	P/O D.Fulford	Bf109F destroyed	Arques	1320~
129 Sqn	Spit	FC	Sgt R.J.F.Scherk	Bf109F destroyed	6m W Boulogne	1335
			P/O R.J.F.Sherk	Bf109F destroyed	W Boulogne	1335
			P/O J.B.Sillitoe	Bf109F prob.dest	15m E Boulogne	1330
234 Sqn	Spit	FC	Sgt P.H.Fox	Bf109 prob.dest	Arques	1320~
266 Sqn	Spit	FC	F/L C.L.Green	Bf109E damaged	Boulogne-Le Touquet	1330~
			F/L D.A.P.McMullen	Bf109F destroyed	Boulogne-Hardelot	1330~
			F/L D.A.P.McMullen	Bf109E damaged	near Le Touquet	1330~

303 Sqn	Spit	FC	F/L J.E.L.Zumbach	Bf109 destroyed	E Hardelot -mid Channel	1330
			F/L J.E.L.Zumbach	FW190 damaged	E Hardelot -mid Channel	1330
308 Sqn	Spit	FC	S/L M.Pisarek	Bf109 destroyed	Coast-St Omer	1320
			P/O J.Poplawski	Bf109 destroyed	Coast-St Omer	1320
			P/O W.Rettinger	Bf109 destroyed	Coast-St Omer	1320
411 Sqn	Spit	FC	P/O R.W.McNair	Bf109F destroyed	2m off Boulogne	1350
			P/O R.W.McNair	Bf109 damaged	5m off Boulogne	1400
412 Sqn	Spit	FC	Sgt E.N.McDonnell	Bf109E destroyed	10m off France	1400
452 Sqn	Spit	FC	Sgt J.M.Emery	Bf109F destroyed	Gravelines-St Omer	1319
			Sgt J.M.Emery	Bf109F damaged	Gravelines-St Omer	1321
			F/L B.E.Finucane	Bf109F damaged	St Omer-Boulogne	1320
			F/L B.E.Finucane	Bf109F destroyed	St Omer-Boulogne	1320
			F/L B.E.Finucane	Bf109F destroyed	St Omer-Boulogne	1320
			Sgt E.H.Schrader	Bf109F destroyed	Gravelines-St Omer	1320
			F/O R.E.Thorold-Smith	Bf109F destroyed	10m E Hardelot	1320
			F/O R.E.Thorold-Smith	Bf109F damaged	10m E Hardelot	1320
			F/L K.W.Truscott	Bf109F destroyed	NW St Omer	1318
			F/L K.W.Truscott	Bf109F destroyed	NW St Omer	1318
485 Sqn	Spit	FC	P/O W.V.Crawford -Compton	Bf109F destroyed	Cappelle Brouck	1318
			Sgt L.P.Griffith	Bf109 damaged	Cappelle Brouck	1318
602 Sqn	Spit	FC	S/L A.C.Deere	Bf109F damaged	15m NW St Omer	1320~
			Sgt J.B.Niven	Bf109F damaged	St Omer area	1320~
			Sgt D.O'Connor	Bf109F damaged	St Omer area	1320~
			Sgt S.D.Osborn	Bf109F damaged	St Omer area	1320~
			Sgt L.Scorer	Bf109F damaged	St Omer area	1320~
609 Sqn	Spit	FC	P/O J.A.Atkinson	Bf109 damaged	Le Treport area	1415~
			P/O P.A.Nash	Bf109F destroyed	20m W Bethune	1415~
			F/L J.H.M.Offenberg	Bf109 damaged	10m NW Le Treport	1415~
MW Wg	Spit	FC	W/C A.H.Boyd	Bf109F damaged	Arques	1320~
			W/C A.H.Boyd	Bf109F damaged	Arques	1320~

14th October 1941

615 Sqn	Hurr	FC	Capt C.T.M.P.De Scitivaux	He59 destroyed	Off Ostend	1025~
			S/L D.E.Gillam	- shared -		
			F/L P.H.Hugo	- shared -		
			Lt J.A.Maridor	- shared -		

Squadron Leader R.M.Milne of 92 Squadron fought through the Battle of France and the Battle of Britain with 151 Squadron, credited with seven confirmed kills and winning the DFC. Promoted to lead 92 Squadron, he claimed three Messerschmitts destroyed and a fourth damaged on 13th October, winning him a second DFC. On 14th March 1942, now leading the Biggin Hill Wing, he was shot down into the Channel. He was rescued, but unfortunately by the Germans. With 14 confirmed kills, his war was over.

15th October 1941

118 Sqn Spit FC	Sgt D.Claxton	Bf109F destroyed	Le Havre	1300~
	F/O D.Fulford	Bf109F destroyed	Le Havre	1300~
	S/L F.J.Howell F/O P.I.Howard-Williams	Bf109F destroyed - shared -	Le Havre	1300~
	S/L F.J.Howell	Bf109F prob.dest	Le Havre	1300~
	S/L F.J.Howell	Bf109F damaged	Le Havre	1300~
129 Sqn Spit FC	Sgt R.A.Hardy	Bf109F destroyed	Over Le Havre	1140
234 Sqn Spit FC	F/L E.B.Mortimer-Rose	Bf109F damaged	4m N Le Havre	1300~
	F/L E.B.Mortimer-Rose	Bf109F damaged	4m N Le Havre	1300~
	P/O H.B.Shepherd	Bf109F destroyed	Le Havre	1300~
	P/O H.B.Shepherd	Bf109F damaged	Le Havre	1300~
	S/L H.M.Stephen P/O B.Denville	Bf109F destroyed - shared -	Le Havre	1300~
615 Sqn Hurr FC	P/O D.W.Cormack	Bf109E prob.dest	Blankenberghe	0745~
Tang Wg Spit FC	W/C H.de C.A.Woodhouse	Bf109F destroyed	Le Havre	1255
	W/C H.de C.A.Woodhouse	Bf109F damaged	Le Havre	1255

16th October 1941

71 Sqn Spit FC	F/O C.W.McColpin	Hs126 destroyed	Etaples-Hardelot	1115

16/17th October 1941

85 Sqn Havc FC	W/C A.Sanders	Ju88 damaged	25m NE Manston	0019
151 Sqn Hurr FC	P/O R.P.Stevens	Ju88 destroyed	50m E Winterton	u/k

19th October 1941

29 Sqn Beau FC	F/L J.R.D.Braham	Do17Z destroyed	15m off N Foreland	2100~

20th October 1941

87 Sqn	Hurr FC	Sgt A.H.Thom	He111 prob.dest	W Scilly Isles	1740

20/21st October 1941

409 Sqn	Beau FC	S/L R.M.Trousdale	Do17 damaged	Newark	2200
604 Sqn	Beau FC	F/L C.H.Hartley	Do217 damaged	Bath to Ostend	2330~

21st October 1941

65 Sqn	Spit FC	P/O D.C.Mitchell	Bf109F destroyed	St Omer	1200~
		Sgt W.L.Oldhall	Bf109F destroyed	St Omer	1200~
87 Sqn	Hurr FC	Sgt A.H.Thom F/O E.G.Musgrove	Bf110 destroyed - shared -	SE Scilly Isles	0900
111 Sqn	Spit FC	Sgt L.Zadrobilek	Bf109 prob.dest	St Omer	1200~
129 Sqn	Spit FC	Sgt V.E.Tucker	Bf109F destroyed	Boulogne	1145
		Sgt V.E.Tucker	Bf109F destroyed	Boulogne	1145
315 Sqn	Spit FC	Sgt A.Chudek	FW190 destroyed	W St Omer	1200
		P/O Z.Drybanski	Bf109F destroyed	W St Omer	1200
		P/O E.Fiedorczuk	Bf109F prob.dest	W St Omer	1200
		Sgt Z.Gruszczynski	Bf109F prob.dest	W St Omer	1200
		P/O S.Lukaszewicz	Bf109F destroyed	W St Omer	1200
		P/O W.Miksa	Bf109F destroyed	W St Omer	1200
		P/O W.Miksa	Bf109F prob.dest	W St Omer	1200
		P/O W.Miksa	Bf109F damaged	W St Omer	1200
		P/O W.Zajac	Bf109F prob.dest	W St Omer	1200
401 Sqn	Spit FC	F/O C.A.B.Wallace	Bf109F destroyed	Coast S hardelot	1155
		F/O C.A.B.Wallace	Bf109F prob.dest	Coast S hardelot	1155
485 Sqn	Spit FC	Sgt A.S.Kronfeld	Bf109F destroyed	Just inland Boulogne	1155
		Sgt I.J.McNeil	Bf109 damaged	St Omer area	1155
602 Sqn	Spit FC	Sgt H.L.Thorne	Bf109F damaged	St Omer	1200~
609 Sqn	Spit FC	P/O V.M.M.Ortmans	FW190 destroyed	St Omer	u/k
BH Wg	Spit FC	W/C J.Rankin	Bf109F destroyed	Near Le Touquet	1215

21/22nd October 1941

29 Sqn	Beau FC	S/L G.P.Gibson	Ju87 damaged	Dover	1900~
		S/L G.P.Gibson	Ju87 damaged	Dover	1900~

22/23rd October 1941

68 Sqn	Beau FC	F/O W.D.Winward	Ju88 destroyed	Off Nevin	2116
151 Sqn	Hurr FC	F/O R.P.Stevens	Ju88 destroyed	Near Market Drayton	2130
256 Sqn	Deft FC	F/L G.B.S.Coleman	- shared -		

One of the few bomber pilots to make a successful transition to Fighter Command was Guy Gibson, who was - at first unwillingly - moved from 83 Squdron at Scampton, flying Hampdens, firstly to an OTU and then to 29 Squadron, becoming a flight commander on Beaufighters. He was credited with two confirmed kills and a 'damaged' during the spring Blitz, a third destroyed on 6/7th July and, on the night of 21st October, claimed two Ju87 Stukas damaged near Dover. Transferring back to Bomber Command, he was to achieve everlasting fame and a Victoria Cross for his leadership of the Dams raid in 1943. He was killed in action on 19/20th September 1944 while acting as Master Bomber with 627 Squadron.

| 604 Sqn | Beau | FC | F/L J.B.Selway | E/A prob.dest | Channel | 2250 |

24th October 1941

19 Sqn	Spit	FC	F/S J P.Strihavka	Ju88 damaged	35m off Norfolk coast	1327
			Sgt V.Lysicky	- shared -		
303 Sqn	Spit	FC	Sgt M.Belc	Bf109E destroyed	Gravelines-Griz Nez	1510
			P/O B.Drobinski	Bf109E prob.dest	Gravelines-Griz Nez	1510
			F/O B.M.Gladych	FW190 destroyed	Gravelines-Griz Nez	1510
			F/L J.E.L.Zumbach	Bf109E destroyed	Gravelines-Griz Nez	1510
308 Sqn	Spit	FC	P/O J.Jakubowski	Bf109 destroyed	Off Griz Nez	1510
			F/S S.Janus	Bf109 destroyed	Off Griz Nez	1510
			F/S S.Janus	Bf109 destroyed	Off Griz Nez	1510
			Sgt T.Schiele	Bf109 destroyed	Off Griz Nez	1510
			Sgt T.Schiele	Bf109 prob.dest	Off Griz Nez	1510
315 Sqn	Spit	FC	F/L Z.Czykowski	Bf109E prob.dest	Gravelines	1520
			F/L J.P.Falkowski	Bf109E destroyed	Gravelines	1520
			F/O J.Gil	Bf109E prob.dest	Gravelines	1520
			Sgt E.Malczewski	Bf109E destroyed	Gravelines	1520

24/25th October 1941

| 29 Sqn | Beau | FC | F/L J.R.D.Braham | He111 destroyed | Off Gt Yarmouth | 1800 |

25th October 1941

| 71 Sqn | Spit | FC | P/O R.O.Scarborough | Bf109F destroyed | Flushing | 0720 |
| 266 Sqn | Spit | FC | F/L D.A.P.McMullen | Bf109 destroyed | Near Haamstede | 1630~ |

25/26th October 1941

68 Sqn	Beau	FC	W/O W.E.Welch	Ju88 damaged	E Plymouth	2130~
604 Sqn	Beau	FC	P/O F.S.Gonsalves	Ju88 damaged	N Wales	u/k
604 Sqn	Beau	FC	P/O F.S.Gonsalves	Ju88 damaged	N Wales	u/k

Jan Zumbach claimed at least eight confirmed kills with 303 Squadron during the Battle of Britain and would survive the war after leading a Polish Mustang Wing. During his combat career he was awarded two DFCs in addition to numerous Polish decorations. His post-war career was even more colourful, smuggling and flying as a mercenary in the Congo and Biafra. He died in 1986. On 24th October he claimed his eleventh kill, a Bf109E.

26th October 1941

604 Sqn	Beau FC	F/L J.B.Selway	He111 damaged	E Plymouth	2115

27th October 1941

71 Sqn	Spit FC	F/O C.W.McColpin	Bf109E destroyed	5m SE Dunkirk	0725
		F/O C.W.McColpin	Bf109E destroyed	5m SE Dunkirk	0725
91 Sqn	Spit FC	F/O G.C.R.Pannell	Bf109F destroyed	Channel	1410~
152 Sqn	Spit FC	P/O T.R.Thomson	Bf109 damaged	2m N Den Helder	1500~
257 Sqn	Hurr FC	Sgt J.Slaney	Do217 destroyed	Happisburgh	1400~
266 Sqn	Spit FC	Sgt E.S.Dicks-Sherwood F/L C.L.Green	Do217 destroyed - shared -	Off Cromer	1215
401 Sqn	Spit FC	P/O A.E.Harley	Bf109 damaged	7m N Poperinghe	1225
		F/O E.L.Neal	Bf109 prob.dest	6m S Mardyck	1235
		F/O E.L.Neal	Bf109 damaged	6m S Mardyck	1235
		P/O J.A.Small F/O C.A.B.Wallace	Bf109 destroyed - shared -	N Poperinghe	1225~
609 Sqn	Spit FC	Lt M.Choron	FW190 prob.dest	Mardyck area	1230~
609 Sqn	Spit FC	Lt M.Choron	FW190 damaged	Mardyck area	1230~
609 Sqn	Spit FC	S/L G.K.Gilroy	Bf109 destroyed	Near Calais	1600~
		S/L G.K.Gilroy	Bf109 destroyed	Near Calais	1600~
BH Wg	Spit FC	W/C J.Rankin	FW190 destroyed	French coast	1550~
		W/C J.Rankin	Bf109F destroyed	W Folkestone	1550~

28th October 1941

91 Sqn	Spit FC	F/O J.J.Le Roux	Bf109F destroyed	Calais	1545~
91 Sqn	Spit FC	F/O G.C.R.Pannell	Bf109E destroyed	French coast	1140~

28/29th October 1941

307 Sqn	Beau FC	Sgt B.Turzanski	E/A prob.dest	Unknown	u/k
604 Sqn	Beau FC	F/L J.B.Selway	Ju88 destroyed	Near Bridgewater	2105

31st October 1941

65 Sqn	Spit FC	Sgt R.L.Stillwell	Ju88 prob.dest	20-30m S Worthing	1010~

By late 1941 the outlook of Fighter Command was changing radically. The fighter force in the south was not now wholly employed on air defence, Rhubarbs and bomber escort, but was also now being used for direct assault by re-equipping fighters as fighter-bombers. The day of the Hurricane as a pure fighter was over. Here, armourers load bombs beneath a Hurricane's wings. (ww2images.com)

31st October/1st November 1941

151 Sqn	Deft FC	P/O A.I.McRitchie	Ju88 destroyed	25m E Yarmouth	1745
		P/O A.I.McRitchie	Ju88 damaged	25m E Yarmouth	1745

1/2nd November 1941

68 Sqn	Beau FC	P/O M.C.Shipard	He111 destroyed	Anglesey	2205
307 Sqn	Beau FC	Sgt B.Turzanski	Do217 destroyed	N Watchet	2215
		Sgt B.Turzanski	Do217 destroyed	SE Sidmouth	2327
409 Sqn	Beau FC	W/C P.Y.Davoud	Do217 destroyed	100m E Coleby Grange	2225
604 Sqn	Beau FC	F/O E.D.Crew	He111 destroyed	St Albans Head	2200
		F/O E.D.Crew	Ju88 damaged	St Albans Head	2200~
604 Sqn	Beau FC	P/O V.Motion	Do217 damaged	Near Shepton Mallett	2220~

3rd November 1941

91 Sqn	Spit FC	P/O A.J.Andrews	Do17 damaged	15m E North Foreland	1540~
603 Sqn	Spit FC	F/O J.A.R.Falconer	Do17Z damaged	20m E Frinton	1445~
		Sgt D.F.Ruchwaldy	Do17Z damaged	20m E Frinton	1445~

4th November 1941

54 Sqn	Spit FC	Sgt P.McDougall-Black	Bf109F damaged	Off Le Touquet	1335
		S/L F.D.S.Scott-Malden	Bf109F damaged	10m W Le Touquet	1335
403 Sqn	Spit FC	S/L A.G.Douglas	Do217 damaged	12m E Felixstowe	1110

6th November 1941

91 Sqn	Spit FC	P/O G.C.R.Pannell	Do217 damaged	French coast	1745~
303 Sqn	Spit FC	P/O Z.Bienkowski	Bf109E destroyed	Near Nieuport	1420~
		P/O E.Horbaczewski	Bf109E prob.dest	Near Nieuport	1420~
452 Sqn	Spit FC	S/L R.W.Bungey	Bf109F destroyed	6m off Calais	1445
		P/O D.E.Lewis	Bf109F damaged	Off Griz Nez	1445-50

117

The Boulton-Paul defiant, even in late 1941, was still an effective nightfighter. On the night of 31st October P/O A.I.McRitchie of 151 Squadron claimed a Ju88 destroyed and a second damaged east of Yarmouth.

		P/O R.H.C.Sly	Bf109F damaged	5-10m off Griz Nez	1445-50
		F/L R.E.Thorold-Smith	FW190 destroyed	5-10m off Griz Nez	1445-50
		F/L R.E.Thorold-Smith	Bf109F destroyed	5-10m off Griz Nez	1445-50
		F/L K.W.Truscott	Bf109F destroyed	10m off Griz Nez	1445
485 Sqn	Spit FC	P/O W.V.Crawford-Compton	Bf109F prob.dest	Griz Nez-Calais	1445
		Sgt J.D.Rae	Bf109F prob.dest	Griz Nez-Calais	1450

7th November 1941

71 Sqn	Spit FC	P/O T.C.Wallace	Bf109E destroyed	Dunkirk-Gravelines	1330
72 Sqn	Spit FC	P/O W.J.Rosser	FW190 damaged	Berck	1440~
263 Sqn	Whir FC	Sgt C.P.King	Bf109E destroyed	3m W Cap de la Hague	1420
411 Sqn	Spit FC	F/L.K.A.Boomer	Ju88 prob.dest	25m N Sheringham	1800
609 Sqn	Spit FC	P/O P.A.Nash	Bf109F destroyed	3m off Le Treport	1440~
		P/O P.A.Nash	FW190 prob.dest	3m off Le Treport	1440~
		Sgt J.E.Van Schaick	Bf109F destroyed	Berck	1440~

7/8th November 1941

406 Sqn	Beau FC	P/O F.Harding	He111 damaged	Off Hartlepool	2152

8th November 1941

72 Sqn	Spit FC	P/O F.De Naeyer	Bf109E prob.dest	St Pol area	1210~
308 Sqn	Spit FC	P/O J.Poplawski	Bf109F damaged	French coast	1145
		P/O T.Stabrowski	Bf109F damaged	5m N French coast	1145
317 Sqn	Spit FC	Sgt S.Brzeski	Bf109F destroyed	5m E St Omer	1145~
		Sgt S.Brzeski	FW190 damaged	5m E St Omer	1145~

			Sgt T.Koc	Bf109F prob.dest	Ret from Lille	1145~
			Sgt B.Koscik	FW190 destroyed	Merville-Hazeb'k	1145~
412 Sqn	Spit	FC	F/L C.J.Cantrell	Bf109E damaged	10m NW Dunkirk	1210
452 Sqn	Spit	FC	F/L K.W.Truscott	Bf109F destroyed	5m SE Dunkirk	1200
			F/L K.W.Truscott	Bf109F destroyed	Channel N Calais	1200
501 Sqn	Spit	FC	S/L C.F.Currant	Bf109E damaged	Channel	1450~
609 Sqn	Spit	FC	S/L G.K.Gilroy	Bf109 destroyed	St Pol area	1210~
			Sgt C.Ortmans	Bf109 prob.dest	St Pol area	1210~

Chapter Five

Winter 1941-42 - The Daylight Offensive Halted

9th November 1941 - 7th March 1942

Following the high losses incurred on Circus No.101 on 8th November, *Circuses* were suspended, albeit temporarily. The offensive was to be maintained by means of escorted fighter-bomber missions, known as *Fighter Ramrods*. It would not be until early March that the *Circus* missions would be resumed. In the meantime, on 12th February 1942, the Germans put an audacious plan into operation by sailing the battlecruisers *Scharnhorst* and *Gneisenau* from Brest, where they had sheltered for over a year, to Germany via the Dover Straits. The Air Ministry had anticipated this and had a plan, *Operation Fuller*, to employ Bomber and Coastal Commands, plus a shore-based Fleet Air Arm Swordfish unit, to prevent this. In the event, the Germans achieved complete surprise and succeeded in breaking through the Channel defences to reach northern Germany, much to the embarrassment of the British.

9th November 1941

3 Sqn	Hurr FC	F/L J.Lonsdale	Ju88 prob.dest	Margate area	1815
615 Sqn	Hurr FC	Sgt P.G.Louis	Ju88 destroyed	Off Margate	1800

11th November 1941

91 Sqn	Spit FC	F/O J.J.Le Roux	Bf109F destroyed	Off Dover	1355
403 Sqn	Spit FC	F/L R.G.Clouston	Do217 damaged	4m SE Orfordness	1336

12th November 1941

91 Sqn	Spit FC	F/L J.E.Demozay	Bf109F destroyed	N Griz Nez	1350~

15th November 1941

151 Sqn	Deft FC	P/O A.I.McRitchie	Ju88 destroyed	Off Yarmouth	1725

16th November 1941

121 Sqn	Spit FC	P/O H.F.Marting	Ju88 damaged	Off Flambro' Head	1215
145 Sqn	Spit FC	S/L A.D.J.Lovell	Ju88 destroyed	35m NE Hartlepool	1220~

18th November 1941

401 Sqn	Spit FC	P/OD.J.M.Blakeslee	Bf109F damaged	5m W Le Touquet	1120
		P/O I.Gilbert	Bf109F prob.dest	5m W Le Touquet	1120
		Sgt D.R.Morrison	Bf109F prob.dest	Le Touquet-Berck	1115
		F/O E.L.Neal	Bf109F prob.dest	Le Touquet-Berck	1115
		F/O H.A.Sprague	Bf109F prob.dest	8m NW Le Touquet	1115
602 Sqn	Spit FC	S/L A.C.Deere	Bf109E damaged	10m N Le Touquet	1115~
		Sgt J.Garden	Bf109E destroyed	10m N Le Touquet	1115~

On 22nd November, pilots of 401 Squadron (RCAF) fought elements of JG 26 over the Pas de Calais and out over the Channel. Sergeant J.A.O.Levesque claimed an FW190 destroyed between St Omer and Boulogne, but this was to be his sole confirmed victory. On 12th February, during the infamous 'Channel Dash' of the German battlecruisers, he was shot down and captured.

		Sgt J.Garden	Bf109F damaged	10m N Le Touquet	1115~
		P/O J.B.Niven	FW190 damaged	10m NW Le Treport	1115~
		Sgt G.Willis	Bf109E prob.dest	Le Touquet	1115~
		Sgt G.Willis	Bf109E damaged	Le Touquet	1115~
609 Sqn	Spit FC	P/O D.W.Barnham	FW190 destroyed	Griz Nez-Dover	1115~

22nd November 1941

72 Sqn	Spit FC	Sgt E.G.Enright	FW190 damaged	Boulogne-Pas de Calais	1540
		Sgt B.Ingham	Bf109E destroyed	Boulogne-Pas de Calais	1540
		P/O W.J.Rosser S/L C.A.Masterman	- shared - - shared -		
		Sgt B.Ingham	FW190 destroyed	Boulogne-Pas de Calais	1540
		S/L C.A.Masterman P/O W.J.Rosser	- shared - - shared -		
		Sgt C.L.A.Thompson	FW190 damaged	Boulogne-Pas de Calais	1540~
315 Sqn	Spit FC	P/O K.Stembrowicz	Bf109F damaged	Off Le Touquet	1550
401 Sqn	Spit FC	P/O D.J.M.Blakeslee	Bf109E destroyed	10-12m S Calais/Marck	1535-50
		P/O D.J.M.Blakeslee	Bf109E damaged	8m E Dover	1535-50

		Sgt J.A.O.Johnstone	Bf109E damaged	10m SE Griz Nez	1535-50
		Sgt J.A.O.Levesque	FW190 destroyed	St Omer-Boulogne	1530-40
		Sgt D.R.Morrison	FW190 destroyed	Desvres	1535-50
		Sgt D.R.Morrison	FW190 damaged	Channel near Dover	1535-50
		P/O G.W.Northcott	Bf109E damaged	10m S Calais/Marck	1540
		P/O I.C.Ormston	Bf109E destroyed	10m S Calais/Marck	1540

23/24th November 1941

307 Sqn	Beau FC	P/O A.Dziegielewski	Ju88 destroyed	1m W Harrowbeer	2035
604 Sqn	Beau FC	F/L V.Motion	E/A damaged	Bristol Channel	1955

24th November 1941

26 Sqn	Tom AC	S/L Hadfield	Bf109 damaged	Off Ambleteuse	1210~
		S/L Hadfield	FW44 damaged	Off Ambleteuse	1210~

25th November 1941

403 Sqn	Spit FC	F/L R.B.Newton	Do215 damaged	20m E Orfordness	1615

25/26th November 1941

307 Sqn	Beau FC	F/O M.Neyder	Ju88 damaged	Nr.Wellington, S.set	1935

26th November 1941

74 Sqn	Spit FC	P/O A.Williams	Ju88 prob.dest	20m W St Davids Head	1700

27th November 1941

65 Sqn	Spit FC	P/O H.P.Duval	Bf109F destroyed	Off St Valery	1420~
Tang Wg	Spit FC	W/C H.de C.A.Woodhouse	Bf109F destroyed	8m NW Le Havre	1420~

28/29th November 1941

Tang Wg	Spit FC	W/C H.de C.A.Woodhouse	Bf109F destroyed	8m NW Le Havre	1420
307 Sqn	Beau FC	Sgt B.Turzanski	E/A destroyed	4m S Sidmouth	1935

30th November 1941

615 Sqn	Hurr FC	F/L W.Mohr	Ju88 damaged	35m SW Linney Hd	1025

2/3rd December 1941

600 Sqn	Beau FC	S/L A.D.McN.Boyd	He111 destroyed	15m S Plymouth	1930~
600 Sqn	Beau FC	F/O C.G..Imlay	He111 destroyed	Off Portreath	1950~

5th December 1941

607 Sqn	Hurr FC	F/L P.J.T.Stephenson	Bf109E destroyed	Off Le Havre	1445~

6th December 1941

317 Sqn	Spit FC	Sgt S.Brzeski	Ju88 destroyed	Plymouth Sound	1145

7/8th December 1941

23 Sqn	Havc FC	F/O Raymer		Ju88 destroyed	Gilze-Rijn	2145~
		F/O Raymer		Ju88 damaged	Gilze-Rijn	2145~

8th December 1941

303 Sqn	Spit	FC	Sgt M.Adamek	FW190 destroyed	N Le Touquet	1200
315 Sqn	Spit	FC	F/L Z.Czykowski	Bf109F destroyed	N Le Touquet	1202
			S/L S.Janus	Bf109F destroyed	N Le Touquet	1210
401 Sqn	Spit	FC	P/O D.J.M.Blakeslee	Bf109F damaged	10m W Griz Nez	1430
			Sgt W.D.Hagyard	Bf109F destroyed	12m W Griz Nez	1435
			Sgt D.B.Whitney	- shd -	12m W Griz Nez	1435
			Sgt W.D.Hagyard	Bf109F damaged	10m W Griz Nez	1435
			Sgt D.B.Whitney	Bf109F - shd-	10m W Griz Nez	1435
			Sgt D.R.Morrison	Bf109F destroyed	5-8m W Griz Nez	1450
			Sgt D.R.Morrison	Bf109F damaged	5-8m W Griz Nez	1450
603 Sqn	Spit	FC	P/O D.P.Lamb	Bf109 destroyed	2m E Le Touquet	1155~

8/9th December 1941

23 Sqn	Havc FC	P/O Hunt	E/A damaged	Gilze-Rijn	0200~
406 Sqn	Beau FC	W/C D.G.Morris	He111 damaged	Off Acklington	2330

9th December 1941

43 Sqn	Hurr	FC	F/L G.May	Ju88 destroyed	10m E Seaham	1050
43 Sqn	Hurr	FC		Sgt J.Pipa- shd -	10m E Seaham	1050

12/13th December 1941

FIU	Beau FC	W/C D .R.Evans	E/A damaged	Off Lowestoft	u/k

15th December 1941

600 Sqn	Beau FC	F/L C.G.Imlay (shared)	He111 prob.dest	Off Plymouth	1120~
600 Sqn	Beau FC	F/O D.A.B.Ross (shared)	He111 prob.dest	Off Plymouth	1120~

17th December 1941

124 Sqn	SpitFC	S/L R.M.B.Duke-Woolley	Ju88 destroyed	Off North Foreland	1530~

17/18th December 1941

23 Sqn	Havc FC	P/O R.D.Pegram	He111 damaged	Gilze-Rijn	2200~

18th December 1941

234 Sqn	Spit	FC	F/O B.Denville	Bf109F damaged	Brest	1245~
306 Sqn	Spit	FC	Sgt L.Kosmowski	Bf109F destroyed	Brest	1245~
			F/O K.Rutkowski	Bf109F destroyed	Brest	1245~

As the weather worsened, Beaufighters adopted the role of all-weather fighters. This is V8324 RO-B 'Bambi' of 29 Squadron. (ww2images.com)

317 Sqn	Spit	FC	F/L J.Brzezinski	Bf109F destroyed	15m N Pointe Pontusval	1250
			P/O Z.Janicki	Bf109F destroyed	15m N Pointe Pontusval	1245
			F/O T.Kumiega	Bf109F destroyed	15m N Pointe Pontusval	1245
315 Sqn	Hurr	FC	Sgt Finn DFM	Bf109F damaged	Brest	1245~

18/19th December 1941

600 Sqn	Beau	FC	F/O H.V.Ellis	Do217 damaged	Off Falmouth	1930

19th December 1941

Staff	Hurr	FC	W/C P.E.Meagher	Ju88 destroyed	Off St Abbs Head	1230
			W/C P.E.Meagher	Ju88 destroyed	Off St Abbs Head	1230

22nd December 1941

79 Sqn	Hurr	FC	S/L C.D.S.Smith	He115 destroyed	Irish Sea (coll)	1715

23rd December 1941

53 OTU	Spit	TC	F/O D.B.Ogilvie	Do217 destroyed	12m S Mumbles Head	1910

27th December 1941

19 Sqn	Spit	FC	Sgt B.Netopil*	Ju88 damaged	Off Orfordness	1035

* Shared with 71 Squadron.

71 Sqn	Spit	FC	P/O E.M.Potter*	Ju88 damaged	Off Orfordness	1035

* Shared with 19 Squadron.

29/30th December 1941

406 Sqn	Beau	FC	P/O J.R.B.Firth	Ju88 destroyed	Blyth-Newcastle	2110

30th December 1941

130 Sqn	Spit	FC	S/L E.P.P.Gibbs	Bf109F prob.dest	Brest	1415~

152 Sqn	Spit	FC	S/L J.Darwen	Bf109F prob.dest	Brest	1415~
			P/O McLean	Bf109F prob.dest	Brest	1415~
302 Sqn	Spit	FC	P/O R.Budrewicz	Bf109F damaged	Brest	1415~
			P/O C.Glowczynski	Bf109F destroyed	Brest	1415~
			Sgt B.Malinowski	Bf109F prob.dest	Brest	1415~
			F/O A.Rodziewicz	Bf109F damaged	Brest	1415~
			P/O M.Rytka	Bf109F destroyed	Brest	1415~
			P/O K.Sporny	Bf109F destroyed	Brest	1415~
306 Sqn	Spit	FC	P/O Z.Langhamer	Bf109E damaged	N Brest	1415
			F/O K.Rutkowski	Bf109E destroyed	Coast N Brest	1410
			Sgt J.Smigielski	Bf109E destroyed	Coast N Brest	1415
			Sgt G.Solugub	Bf109E prob.dest	Coast N Brest	1410
			P/O S.Szpakowicz	Bf109E prob.dest	Coast N Brest	1413
			S/L A.Wczelik	Bf109E destroyed	Coast N Brest	1413
317 Sqn	Spit	FC	F/S M.M.Maciejowski	Bf109F destroyed	Brest coast	1415~
			F/S M.M.Maciejowski	Bf109F destroyed	Brest coast	1415~

1st January 1942

91 Sqn	Spit	FC	F/L J.E.Demozay	Bf109 destroyed	Off Boulogne	1230
602 Sqn	Spit	FC	F/O E.F.Edsall	He114 destroyed	Off Le Treport	1400
			F/L S.Kempe	- shared -		
			P/O R.L.Lewis	- shared -		
			F/O E.F.Edsall	He114 destroyed	Off Le Treport	1400
			F/L S.Kempe	- shared -		
			P/O R.L.Lewis	- shared -		

5/6th January 1942

3 Sqn	Hurr	FC	Sgt D.J.Scott	Bf110 prob.dest	Near Rotterdam	2100

9th January 1942

71 Sqn	Spit	FC	P/O E.M.Potter	FW190 prob.dest	3m NW Le Treport	1440
			P/O R.S.Sprague	FW190 destroyed	3m NW Le Treport	1440

10/11th January 1942

456 Sqn	Beau	FC	S/L J.S.Hamilton	Do217 destroyed	Near Nuneaton	0155

11th January 1942

71 Sqn	Spit	FC	F/O L.S.Nomis	Ju88 damaged	50m E Lowestoft	0950
317 Sqn	Spit	FC	F/O S.Lukasziewicz	Ju88 destroyed	Off Plymouth	1250
317 Sqn	Spit	FC	F/L P.Ozyra	- shared -		

Tony Lovell joined 41 Squadron pre-war and flew operationally during 1940 and 1941, claiming at least seven solo and four 'shared' confirmed victories. He was then rested, returning to command 145 Squadron in late 1941. On 19th January 1942 he claimed a Ju88 destroyed - probably an aircraft of 3.(F)/122 that was reported missing. His squadron was then posted to the Middle East, where he led 145 Squadron on Malta and 322 Wing in Italy. He won two DSOs, two DFCs and a DFC (US) for his leadership and his combat record of 16 victories and six 'shared'. He was killed in a flying accident at Old Sarum on 17th August 1945.

14th January 1942

607 Sqn	Hurr	FC	Sgt D.A.Blyth	Ju88 prob.dest	Off Calais	1340
607 Sqn	Hurr	FC	P/O W.D.James	- shared -		

14/15th January 1942

29 Sqn	Beau	FC	W/C E.L.Colbeck-Welch	Do217 destroyed	Off North Foreland	1930~
255 Sqn	Beau	FC	P/O J.C.Cox	Do217 destroyed	Off Ostend	2330

17/18th January 1942

85 Sqn	Havc	FC	P/O H.H.Norsworthy Royal Navy	Do217 destroyed - shared -	Off Harwich.	1740

19th January 1942

145 Sqn	Spit	FC	S/L A.D.J.Lovell	Ju88 destroyed	Off Newcastle	1530

22nd January 1942

19 Sqn	Spit	FC	P/O S.F.Brooker	Ju88 damaged	60m E Gt Yarmouth	1735~
			F/L L.V.Chadburn	- shared -		
			S/L P.R.Davies	- shared -		

25/26th January 1942

600 Sqn	Beau	FC	S/L A.D.McN.Boyd	He111 destroyed	80m S Colerne (coll)	1925

30th January 1942

504 Sqn	Spit	FC	Sgt D.A.Barry	Ju88 damaged	Off Ballyquintin Point	1045~
			Sgt I.S.McKenzie	- shared -		

2nd February 1942

19 Sqn	Spit	FC	P/O J.Henderson	Do217 destroyed	Off Cromer	1347
118 Sqn	Spit	FC	F/L P.I.Howard-Williams	Bf109F destroyed	Pointe de Barfleur	1300
			F/L P.I.Howard-Williams	Bf109F damaged	Pointe de Barfleur	1300
			F/L P.I.Howard-Williams	Bf109F damaged	Pointe de Barfleur	1300

Peter Howard-Williams of 118 Squadron was a tough and aggressive fighter pilot. On 2nd February 1942 he needed all his skills to survive against several Bf109 pilots of JG 2, who shot down his wingman and perforated Howard-Williams' own aircraft. He got back, claiming one Messerschmitt shot down and two damaged. (Chris Goss)

4th February 1942

310 Sqn	Spit	FC	F/L F.Burda	Ju88 damaged	45m SW Scillies	1415
			S/L E.A.Foit	- shared -		
			F/S L.Srom	- shared -		
			Sgt F.Vindis	- shared -		

5th February 1942

133 Sqn	Spit	FC	P/O M.E.Jackson*	Do217 destroyed	20m E Spurn Head	1530
			F/L H.A.S.Johnson	- shared -		

* Also shared with 253 Squadron.

			F/L C.W.McColpin	Do217 damaged	15m E Spurn Head	1455
253 Sqn	Hurr	FC	P/O P.Landers*	Do217 destroyed	20m E Spurn Head	1530
			Sgt J.C.Tate	- shared -		

* Also shared with 133 Squadron.

8th February 1942

3 Sqm	Hurr	FC	Sgt J.T.Shaw	Do215 destroyed	8m W Ostend	1810

9th February 1942

603 Sqn	Spit	FC	Sgt D.J.Prytherch	Ju88 damaged	N Aberdeen	1210~
			Sgt G.E.Rapson	- shared -		

10th February 1942

Ken Wg	Spit	FC	W/C R.F.Boyd	Bf109F damaged	Off Beachy Head	1250~

12th February 1942

41 Sqn	Spit	FC	P/O R.F.Cambridge	Bf109F destroyed	Belgian coast	1300~
			F/S R.E.Green	Bf109F destroyed	Belgian coast	1300~
			S/L P.H.Hugo	Bf109F destroyed	Belgian coast	1300~

402 Squadron at Warmwell, January 1942: L-R; Sgts J C Hughes, Mac Macklin, Bob Harmer, J R Scott, B E Innes and I J Eady with Hurricane AE-B in the background. (ww2images.com)

			S/L P.H.Hugo	Bf109F damaged	Belgian coast	1300~
65 Sqn	Spit	FC	S/L H.T.Gilbert	Bf109F destroyed	Dunkirk	1530~
			S/L H.T.Gilbert	Bf109F damaged	Dunkirk	1530~
			P/O C.R.Hewlett	Bf109F damaged	Dunkirk	1530~
72 Sqn	Spit	FC	P/O E.W.P.Bocock	FW190 destroyed	15-20m E Manston	1300~
			P/O E.W.P.Bocock	FW190 damaged	15-20m E Manston	1300~
			P/O E.W.P.Bocock	FW190 damaged	15-20m E Manston	1300~
			F/O F.De Naeyer	FW190 destroyed	Boulogne	1300~
			Sgt J.Garden	FW190 damaged	Boulogne	1300~
			P/O B.Ingham	FW190 destroyed	Boulogne	1300~
			P/O J.Rutherford	FW190 damaged	Boulogne	1300~
111 Sqn	Spit	FC	Sgt P.E.G.Durnford	Bf109F prob.dest	Dunkirk	1530~
			F/S O.Hruby	Bf109F damaged	Dunkirk	1530~
			P/O J.Prihoda	Bf109F destroyed	Dunkirk	1530~
			P/O J.Prihoda	Bf109F damaged	Dunkirk	1530~
124 Sqn	Spit	FC	F/S M.P.Kilburn	FW190 damaged	Off Boulogne	1300~
			F/L J.Kulhanek	Bf109E damaged	Off Boulogne	1300~
			F/L J.Kulhanek	Bf109E damaged	Off Boulogne	1300~
129 Sqn	Spit	FC	F/L H.C.F.Bowman	Bf109F damaged	Belgian coast	1445~
222 Sqn	Spit	FC	Sgt R.Wood	FW190 damaged	Belgian coast	u/k
234 Sqn	Spit	FC	F/L D.A.S.McKay	Bf109 destroyed	5-10m N Dunkirk	1530~

Henry Bowman (left) of 129 Sqn and Geoff Northcott (centre) of 401 each claimed a Bf109 damaged on 12th February. Northcott would survive the war leading 126 Wing, credited with eight confirmed victories, a DSO and two DFCs. Bowman fell to an FW190 of JG 26 on 28th July 1942 after claiming five destroyed. One loss on 12th February was that of Pilot Officer R.Marcinkus of 1 Squadron, whose aircraft is seen being recovered by the Germans. He would be one of the fifty airmen murdered by the Gestapo following the Great Escape from Stalag Luft III in March 1944.

	F/L D.A.S.McKay	Bf109 destroyed	5-10m N Dunkirk	1530~
401 Sqn Spit FC	P/O A.E.Harley	Bf109F destroyed	Calais-Dunkirk	1300
	Sgt D.R.Morrison	- shared -		
	P/O I.C.Ormston	- shared -		
	F/S H.D.MacDonald	Bf109E damaged	5m W Ostend	1310
	P/O G.W.Northcott	Bf109E damaged	Dunkirk-Calais	1300
	P/O I.C.Ormston	Bf109E destroyed	8m off Calais	1300
403 Sqn Hurr FC	F/S G.A.J.Ryckman	Bf109F damaged	Dunkirk-Ostend	1450-1530
	Sgt E.A.Crist	- shared -		
	F/S G.A.J.Ryckman	Bf109F destroyed	Dunkirk-Ostend	1450-1530
485 Sqn Spit FC	P/O D.T.Clouston	Bf109F destroyed	5m W Ostend	1416-
	P/O H.N.Sweetman	- shared -		
	F/L W.V.Crawford- Compton	Bf109F destroyed	5m W Ostend	1410
	F/L W.V.Crawford- Compton	Bf109E destroyed	5m W Ostend	1420
	F/L G.H.Francis	FW190 destroyed	5m W ostend	1430
	P/O R.J.C.Grant	Bf109E destroyed	5m W Ostend	1430
	Sgt J.D.Rae	Bf109F prob.dest	5m W Ostend	1430
607 Sqn Hurr FC	F/S H.L.Gill	Bf109F damaged	Belgian coast	1500~
SF Hch Spit FC	G/C H.Broadhurst	Bf109F prob.dest	Off Gravelines	1330~

13th February 1942

452 Sqn Spit FC	Squadron	He114 destroyed	Off Boulogne	1035
NW Wg Spit FC	G/C F.V.Beamish	- shared -		

15th February 1942

452 Sqn Spit FC	F/S P.Makin	Bf109F damaged	8m W Griz Nez	0945-50

15/16th February 1942

141 Sqn Beau FC	F/L J.G.Benson	Do217 destroyed	SE Blythe	1950

16th February 1942

312 Sqn Spit FC	P/O O.Kucera	Ju88 destroyed	Off Linney Head	0900~

17th February 1942

71 Sqn Spit FC	P/O O.H.Coen	Do217 damaged	10m E. Felixstowe	1605
402 Sqn Hurr FC	F/L R.J.Emberg	Bf109F destroyed	20m SE Start Point	1115

18th February 1942

609 Sqn Spit FC	P/O J.A.Atkinson	Do217 damaged	Off The Humber	1540~
	Sgt A.Evans	- shared -		
	P/O C.Ortmans	- shared -		
	Digby Wing	- shared -		
	P/O J.A.Atkinson	Do217 damaged	Off The Humber	1540~
	Sgt G.Evans	- shared -		
	P/O J.A.Atkinson	- shared -		
	Digby Wing	- shared -		
	F/O Y.G.A.F.Du Monceau	Do217 destroyed	Off The Humber	1545
Dig Wg Spit FC	W/C H.P.Blatchford*	Do217 damaged	E Withernsea	1540~

Shared with 609 Squadron.

	W/C H.P.Blatchford*	Do217 damaged	E Withernsea	1540~

Shared with 609 Squadron.

19th February 1942

151 Sqn Deft FC	Sgt Macpherson	Do217 damaged	Off Cromer	1915~
	S/L I.S.Smith	Do217 destroyed	Off Cromer	1915~
	S/L I.S.Smith	Ju88 damaged	Off Cromer	1915~
	P/O J.A.Wain	Do217 damaged	Off Cromer	1915~

20th February 1942

602 Sqn Spit FC	P/O R.L.Lewis	FW190 destroyed	Dover	1145~
	P/O R.L.Lewis	FW190 damaged	Dover	1145~
	P/O R.L.Lewis	FW190 destroyed	Dover	1155~
	P/O R.L.Lewis	FW190 damaged	Dover	1155~

21st February 1942

308 Sqn Spit FC	Sgt S.Zielinski	Ju88 damaged	Near Isle of Walney	1245

24th February 1942

266 Sqn Spit FC   P/O R.H.L.Dawson   Do217 destroyed   Off Cromer   1815

28th February 1942

401 Sqn Spit FC   Sgt D.R.Morrison   FW190 prob.dest 25m E Ramsgate   1650

28th February/1st March 1942

255 Sqn Beau FC   S/L F.P.J.McGevor   E/A destroyed   NW Cromer   2016

3rd March 1942

485 Sqn Spit FC   W/C D.O.Finlay*   Bf109F destroyed Griz Nez   1600~
11 group E/O visiting.

7th/8th March 1942

600 Sqn Beau FC   S/L A.D.McN.Boyd   He115 destroyed   5m SE S Lizard   0520

263 Squadron, early 1942. (ww2images.com)

Chapter Six

March 1942:

A New Offensive
8th March - 18th August 1942

After exactly four months escorted bomber operations over the occupied territories were resumed. It would not be long before the new Spitfire IX and the Typhoon I would be ready to enter squadron service which, it was hoped, would help to redress the balance of air power. The first of the American units would soon be deployed to England, further outnumbering the German forces. But even so, 1942 would become the blackest period for Fighter Command pilots as the out-classed Spitfire VB units continued to battle the Focke Wulfs and take heavy losses.

8th March 1942

91 Sqn	Spit	FC	F/S W.G.Mart	Bf109F damaged	Gravelines	1825~
121 Sqn	Spit	FC	P/O W.J.Daley Jr	FW190 damaged	10m S Dunkirk	1620
222 Sqn	Spit	FC	F/L L.V.Sanders	Bf109 prob.dest	NE France	1620~
403 Sqn	Spit	FC	P/O N.D.R.Dick	Bf109F damaged	Near St Omer1	1620
			F/S J.B.B.Rainville	Bf109F damaged	1m off Gravelines	1630
			F/L C.P.J.Wood	Bf109F destroyed	1m off Gravelines	1630
609 Sqn	Spit	FC	F/O G.E.F.Dieu	FW190 prob.dest	Off Gravelines	1620~
			F/O Y.G.A.F.Du Monceau	FW190 destroyed	10m N Griz Nez	1620~
			F/O Y.G.A.F.Du Monceau	FW190 prob.dest	10m N Griz Nez	1620~
			S/L G.K.Gilroy	FW190 damaged	Off Gravelines	1620~
			P/O J.E.J.Morai	FW190 damaged	Off Gravelines	1620~

8/9th March 1942

3 Sqn	Hurr	FC	P/O B.H.Hay	Do217 damaged	Gilze-Rijn	0200
23 Sqn	Bost	FC	Sgt J.E.Millard	E/A damaged	Poix	0030~
23 Sqn	Bost	FC	P/O Z.Van Riel	Do217 damaged	Poix	0110~
409 Sqn	Beau	FC	S/L R.M.Trousdale	He111 destroyed	North Coates	2125

9th March 1942

118 Sqn	Spit	FC	P/O I.W.Jones	Bf109F damaged	NE France	1540~
452 Sqn	Spit	FC	S/L K.W.Truscott	Bf109F destroyed	5m W Lilliers	1540
			S/L K.W.Truscott	Bf109F damaged	5m W Lilliers	1550
			F/L C.N.Wawn	Bf109F destroyed	5m W Lilliers	1540
			F/L C.N.Wawn	Bf109E prob.dest	Coast near Hardelot	1550
485 Sqn	Spit	FC	P/O M.R.D.Hume	FW190 prob.dest	Le Touquet	1535

501 Sqn	Spit	FC	S/L C.F.Currant	Bf109E damaged	NE France	1540~
			P/O R.A.Newbery	Bf109F destroyed	15m off Bethune -Hardelot	1540~
602 Sqn	Spit	FC	Sgt S.D.Osborn	FW190 damaged	Hardelot area	1530~
			F/S L.Scorer	FW190 destroyed	Hardelot area	1530~
			F/S L.Scorer	FW190 damaged	Hardelot area	1530~
Ken Wg	Spit	FC	G/C F.V.Beamish	FW190 destroyed	Off Hardelot	1530~

9/10th March 1942

85 Sqn	Mosq	FC	F/O P.W.Arbon	E/A destroyed	Off Manston	2015

13th March 1942

72 Sqn	Spit	FC	P/O J.Rutherford	FW190 destroyed	St Omer area	1530~
			P/O J.Rutherford	FW190 prob.dest	St Omer area	1530~
118 Sqn	Spit	FC	Cmdt A.Jubelin (shared) Sgt V.K.Moody	Ju88 prob.dest - shared -	Casquettes	1730~
131 Sqn	Spit	FC	F/L R.H.Harries (shared) Sgt A.P.F.Vilboux	Ju88 destroyed - shared -	SW Valley	1400~
303 Sqn	Spit	FC	F/O B.Drobinski	Bf109F destroyed	8m NW Hazebrouck	1510
			S/L W.Kolaczkowski	Bf109F destroyed	8m NW Hazebrouck	1510
			F/O M.Lipinski	Bf109F destroyed	8m NW Hazebrouck	1510
316 Sqn	Spit	FC	P/O M.Wyszkowski	Bf109F destroyed	5m N St Omer	1510
401 Sqn	Spit	FC	S/L A.G.Douglas	FW190 prob.dest	15m W St Omer	1530
			P/O H.J.L.Merritt	FW190 damaged	8m NW St Omer	1515
			F/S J.Witham	FW190 prob.dest	15m W St Omer	1535
452 Sqn	Spit	FC	P/O R.H.C.Sly	FW190 destroyed	5m S Gravelines	1500
501 Sqn	Spit	FC	P/O R.C.Lynch*	Ju88 prob.dest - shared -	Casquettes	1730~

* Shared with Ibsley Wing.

602 Sqn	Spit	FC	F/L E.W.P.Bocock	FW190 destroyed	3m SE Ambleteuse	1530~
			P/O J.R.Dennehey	FW190 damaged	Griz Nez-St Omer	1530~
			S/L B.E.Finucane	FW190 destroyed	E Griz Nez	1530~
			S/L B.E.Finucane P/O H.Johnston	FW190 destroyed - shared -	Griz Nez-St Omer	1530~
			P/O H.Johnston	FW190 damaged	Griz Nez-St Omer	1530~
			P/O J.B.Niven	FW190 prob.dest	Griz Nez-St Omer	1530~
Ibs Wg	Spit	FC	W/C I.R.Gleed*	Ju88 prob.dest	Casquettes	1730~

* Shared with 501 Squadron.

13th March 1942

41 Sqn	Spit	FC	P/O J.J.Allen	Bf109E destroyed	Fecamp	1100~
			P/O R.F.Cambridge	Bf109E destroyed	Fecamp	1100~

Left: 313 Squadron pilots at Fairlop. (l to r) Sergeant F.Kotiba, Pilot Officer V.Jicha, Sergeant J.Hlouzek and Warrant Officer F.Vavrinek (Z.Hurt). Right: Squadron Leader C.F. 'Bunny' 'Currant of 501 Squadron claimed a Bf109 damaged on 9th March, but was himself wounded in the fight. He would end the war with a DSO, two DFCs, a score of at least ten destroyed and the rank of Wing Commander.

			F/L F.A.Coker	Bf109E destroyed Fecamp		1100~
			P/O A.A.Glen	Bf109E destroyed Fecamp		1100~
			P/O A.A.Glen	Bf109E destroyed Fecamp		1100~
			S/L P.H.Hugo	Bf109E destroyed Fecamp		1100~
			P/O B.Van Der Stock	Bf109E destroyed Fecamp		1100~
72 Sqn	Spit	FC	P/O J.Rutherford	FW190 destroyed	NE France	1530~
			P/O J.Rutherford	FW190 prob.dest	NE France	1530~
118 Sqn	Spit	FC	Sgt Moody	Ju88 prob.dest	Casquettes	1530~
			Cmdr A.Jubelin	- shared -		
129 Sqn	Spit	FC	P/O H.T.Armstrong	Bf109F destroyed 5m off Etretat		1100~
			P/O R.E.Bush	FW190 destroyed 5m off Etretat		1100~
			Sgt A.J.Edwards	- shared -		
303 Sqn	Spit	FC	S/L W.Kolaczkowski	Bf109F destroyed 8m NW Hazebrouck		1510
			F/O B.Drobinski	Bf109F destroyed 8m NW Hazebrouck		1510
			F/O M.Lipinski	Bf109F destroyed 8m NW Hazebrouck		1510
316 Sqn	Spit	FC	P/O M.Wyszkowski	Bf109F destroyed 5m N St Omer		1510
401 Sqn	Spit	FC	S/L A.G.Douglas	FW190 prob.dest 15m W St Omer		1530
			F/S J.Witham	FW190 prob.dest 15m W St Omer		1535
			P/O H.J.L.Merritt	FW190 damaged 8m NW St Omer		1515
452 Sqn	Spit	FC	P/O R.H.C.Sly	FW190 destroyed 5m S Gravelines		1500
501 Sqn	Spit	FC	P/O R.C.Lynch*	Ju88 prob.dest	Casquettes	1530~
602 Sqn	Spit	FC	S/L B.E.Finucane	FW190 destroyed NE France		1530~

* *Shared with Ibsley Wing.*

			F/L E.W.P.Bocock	FW190 destroyed	NE France	1530~
			F/L E.W.P.Bocock	FW190 destroyed	NE France	1530~
			S/L B.E.Finucane	FW190 destroyed	NE France	1530~
			P/O H.Johnston	- shared -		
			P/O J.B.Niven	FW190 prob.dest	NE France	1530~
			P/O J.R.Dennehey	FW190 damaged	NE France	1530~
			P/O H.Johnston	FW190 damaged	NE France	1530~
Ibs Wg	Spit	FC	W/C I.R.Gleed*	Ju88 prob.dest	Casquettes	1530~

Shared with 501 Squadron.

14th March 1942

41 Sqn	Spit	FC	S/L P.H.Hugo	Bf109E destroyed	Fecamp	1115~
			F/L F.A.Coker	Bf109E destroyed	Fecamp	1115~
			P/O A.A.Glen	Bf109E destroyed	Fecamp	1115~
			P/O A.A.Glen	Bf109E destroyed	Fecamp	1115~
			P/O J.J.Allen	Bf109E destroyed	Fecamp	1115~
			P/O R.F.Cambridge	Bf109E destroyed	Fecamp	1115~
			P/O B.Van Der Stock	Bf109E destroyed	Fecamp	1115~
129 Sqn	Spit	FC	P/O H.T.Armstrong	Bf109F destroyed	5m off Etretat	1050-1100
			P/O R.E.Bush	FW190 destroyed	5m off Etretat	1050-1100
			Sgt A.J.Edwards	- shared -		
452 Sqn	Spit	FC	P/O F.A.Coker	Bf109E destroyed	Le Havre	1700
			Sgt J.McA.Morrison	Bf109F prob.dest	50m N Le Havre	1700
			S/L K.W.Truscott	FW190 destroyed	½-1m off Le Havre	1700
602 Sqn	Spit	FC	P/O J.R.Dennehey	Ju88 prob.dest	Off Le Havre	1700~
			Sgt P.F.Green	- shared -		

21st March 1942

312 Sqn	Spit	FC	Sgt J.Dobrovolny	Ju88 destroyed	8m E Saltee Island	1510
			F/L B.Dvorak	Ju88 destroyed	8m E Saltee Island	1510

23rd March 1942

118 Sqn	Spit	FC	Sgt S.A.Jones	Ju88 damaged	Portland	2100~
			Sgt V.K.Moody	Ju88 damaged	Portland	2100~
121 Sqn	Spit	FC	P/O J.J.Mooney	FW190 destroyed	NE Calais	1605
Ibs Wg	Spit	FC	W/C I.R.Gleed	Ju88 destroyed	Portland	2100~

24th March 1942

121 Sqn	Spit	FC	P/O R.F.Tilley	FW190 prob.dest	Commines-1m off Griz Nez	1545
129 Sqn	Spit	FC	P/O H.T.Armstrong	FW190 destroyed	Abbeville	1550~

135

Two pilots who braved great dangers to fight with the British were Mike Donnet (Left) who stole a light aircraft and flew it from Belgium in July 1941, (3 kills) and Alexander Gabszewicz, who escaped from Poland in 1939, fought with the French in 1940 and then escaped to England. Donnet claimed three confirmed kills with 64 Squadron and ended the war leading the Bentwaters Mustang Wing (ww2images. com). Gabszewicz, credited with eight victories, ended the war as Station Commander of Coltishall. Both pilots claimed FW190s damaged on 27th March.

403 Sqn	Spit	FC	F/S L.J.Somers	FW190 destroyed	N Commines, nr Lille	1535
411 Sqn	Spit	FC	Unknown pilot	FW190 damaged	Near Ballieul	1545~
			Unknown pilot	FW190 damaged	Near Ballieul	1545~
412 Sqn	Spit	FC	W/O L.W.Powell	FW190 damaged	Abbeville	1540
602 Sqn	Spit	FC	F/L J.H.Lacey	FW190 damaged	Gravelines-Dover	1550~

25th March 1942

32 Sqn	Hurr	FC	F/S R.S.Davidson	Ju88 damaged	Off Harwich	1115~
129 Sqn	Spit	FC	P/O R.E.Bush	FW190 destroyed	Boulogne area	1610~
			P/O R.J.F.Sherk	FW190 destroyed	Boulogne area	1610~
303 Sqn	Spit	FC	F/O M.Kolubinski	FW190 damaged	Near Desvres	1535

26th March 1942

41 Sqn	Spit	FC	S/L P.H.Hugo	Bf109E destroyed	Le Havre	1610~
			S/L P.H.Hugo	Bf109E damaged	Le Havre	1610~
457 Sqn	Spit	FC	S/L P.M.Brothers	Bf109E destroyed	5m off Le Havre	1605
485 Sqn	Spit	FC	F/L W.V.Crawford -Compton	Bf109E destroyed	1m W Le Havre	1609

			F/L W.V.Crawford -Compton	Bf109E destroyed	2m S Fecamp	1610
			P/O E.D.Mackie	- shared -		
			Sgt I.J.P.Maskill	Bf109E destroyed	Off Le Havre	1610
602 Sqn	Spit	FC	P/O A.M.Charlesworth	Bf109F damaged	Le Havre	1610~
			S/L B.E.Finucane	FW190 destroyed	Le Havre	1610~
SF Ken	Spit	FC	G/C F.V.Beamish	Bf109E destroyed	Le Havre	1610~
			G/C F.V.Beamish	FW190 destroyed	Le Havre	1610~

26/27th March 1942

3 Sqn	Hurr	FC	Sgt D.J.Scott	E/A destroyed	Eindhoven	0010~
3 Sqn	Hurr	FC	Sgt J.T.Shaw	Do217 destroyed	Gilze-Rijn	2350~

27th March 1942

64 Sqn	Spit	FC	P/O M.G.L.M.Donnet	FW190 damaged	Ostend	1545~
			P/O M.G.L.M.Donnet	FW190 damaged	Ostend	1545~
124 Sqn	Spit	FC	F/L T.Balmforth	FW190 damaged	Ostend	1545~
313 Sqn	Spit	FC	Sgt F.J.Dohnal	Bf109E damaged	5m off Ostend	1545
			F/O F.W.Vancl	Bf109E damaged	5m off Ostend	1545
			F/L Z.Czykowski	FW190 damaged	10m N Ostend	1535
316 Sqn	Spit	FC	Sgt M.Dolcinski	FW190 damaged	10m off Ostend	1535
			S/L A.K.Gabszewicz	FW190 damaged	10m off Ostend	1535
			F/O M.Piotrowski	FW190 damaged	10m off Ostend	1535
			F/O T.Szumowski	FW190 damaged	10m off Ostend	1535
411 Sqn	Spit	FC	P/O D.W.P.Donnelly	FW190 damaged	Ostend	1535
			P/O F.E.Green	Bf109 destroyed	Ostend	1535
			P/O J.H.Long	Bf109 prob.dest	Ostend	1535
72 Sqn	Spit	FC	F/S F.E.Jones	FW190 damaged	Ostend	1545~

28th March 1942

64 Sqn	Spit	FC	Sgt W.Walker	FW190 prob.dest	Channel area	1730~
			Sgt J.K.Stewart	FW190 damaged	Channel area	1730~
			P/O C.Thomas	FW190 destroyed	Channel area	1730~
			P/O F.A.H.L.A.Conard	FW190 prob.dest	Channel area	1730~
313 Sqn	Spit	FC	P/O V.Jicha	FW190 destroyed	N Calais	1720-30
			S/L K.Mrazek	Bf109E destroyed	N Calais	1720-30
313 Sqn	Spit	FC	Sgt J.Reznicek	FW190 prob.dest	5m off Folkestone	1730
313 Sqn	Spit	FC	P/O F.W.Vancl	FW190 prob.dest	Off Calias	1720
457 Sqn	Spit	FC	P/O K.E.James*	Bf109 destroyed	5m SE Calais	1745

* Shared with 602 Squadron.

Above: The guns of a Hurricane being tested at the butts (WW2images. com). Right: Flying Officer J.D.Rae of 485 Squadron claimed his second confirmed victory on 28th March. He became a prisoner on 22nd August 1943 with a score of at least eleven.

	F/L H.L.North	FW190 damaged	Griz Nez-Calais	1745
	P/O G.G.Russell	FW190 prob.dest	Griz Nez-Calais	1745
	F/L R.H.C.Sly	FW190 destroyed	Griz Nez-Calais	1745
	Sgt W.Wright	FW190 damaged	Griz Nez-Calais	1745
485 Sqn Spit FC	F/L W.V.Crawford-Compton	FW190 destroyed	Marquise	1735
	F/L R.J.C.Grant	FW190 destroyed	5m inland Calais	1745
	F/L R.J.C.Grant	FW190 prob.dest	5m inland Calais	1745
	F/S J.R.Liken	FW190 damaged	5m inland Griz Nez-Calais	1735
	P/O G.J.Palmer	FW190 prob.dest	Marquise	1735
	Sgt J.D.Rae	FW190 destroyed	5m inland Griz Nez-Calais	1745
	Sgt J.D.Rae	FW190 damaged	20m inland Griz Nez-Calais	1800
602 Sqn Spit FC	Sgt S.A.Catarall	FW190 prob.dest	Channel-Calais area	1745~
	Sgt S.A.Catarall	FW190 damaged	Channel-Calais area	1745~
	S/L B.E.Finucane	FW190 destroyed	Channel-Calais area	1745~
	S/L B.E.Finucane*	Bf109 destroyed	5m SE Calais	1745

* Shared with 457 Squadron.

	F/S J.Garden	FW190 destroyed	5m NE Marquise	1745~
	P/O D.G.Maxwell	FW190 destroyed	Channel-Calais area	1745~
	F/S F.W.Schofield	FW190 damaged	Channel-Calais area	1745~
Hch Wg Spit FC	W/C R.P.R.Powell	FW190 prob.dest	St Omer-Calais	1740~
Ken Wg Spit FC	W/C R.F.Boyd	FW190 prob.dest	near Griz Nez	1745~

29th March 1942

401 Sqn	Spit	FC	P/O I.C.Ormston	FW190 prob.dest	10m off Dover	1615

1/2nd April 1942

1 Sqn	Hurr	FC	F/L K.Kuttelwascher	Ju88 destroyed	Melun	0100~
			F/L K.Kuttelwascher	Ju88 damaged	Melun	0100~

1/2nd April 1942

602 Sqn	Spit	FC	Sgt S.D.Osborn	Bf109F damaged	Channel	1445~
			P/O C.K.Tait	FW190 damaged	Channel	1445~

2/3rd April 1942

23 Sqn	Havc	FC	P/O Z.Van Riel	E/A damaged	St Andre	0200~
23 Sqn	Havc	FC	S/L B.R.O'B.Hoare	Do217 damaged	Near Evreux	0015~
			S/L B.R.O'B.Hoare	Do217 damaged	Near Evreux	0015~
604 Sqn	Beau	FC	S/L S.H.Skinner	E/A damaged	Near Channel Islands	2335
604 Sqn	Beau	FC	F/L E.D.Crew	He111 destroyed	Off Portland	2130

3/4th April 1942

23 Sqn	Bost	FC	F/L J.Brown	He111 destroyed	Bombing Evreux	2350~
23 Sqn	Bost	FC	Sgt E.Williams	E/A damaged	Beauvais	2320~

4th April 1942

72 Sqn	Spit	FC	P/O R.C.Kitchen	FW190 damaged	Abbeville	1020~
			P/O R.C.Kitchen	Bf109 damaged	Abbeville	1020~
			W/O J.G.L.Robillard	FW190 destroyed	Abbeville	1020~
129 Sqn	Spit	FC	F/O H.T.Armstrong	FW190 damaged	Ramsgate-Gravelines	1245
303 Sqn	Spit	FC	F/L Z.Kustrzynski	FW190 destroyed	St Omer area	0941
			F/L Z.Kustrzynski	FW190 destroyed	St Omer area	0941
303 Sqn	Spit	FC	F/O E.Horbaczewski	FW190 destroyed	St Omer-Calais	1030
			F/S M.Popek	FW190 destroyed	St Omer-Calais	1030
316 Sqn	Spit	FC	Sgt T.Szymanski	FW190 prob.dest	St Omer area	1030
			Sgt T.Szymanski	FW190 prob.dest	St Omer area	1030
317 Sqn	Spit	FC	S/L H.Scczesny	FW190 destroyed	St Omer area	1030
			S/L H.Scczesny	FW190 destroyed	St Omer area	1030
457 Sqn	Spit	FC	F/L H.L.North	FW190 damaged	St Omer	1030
485 Sqn	Spit	FC	Sgt G.E.Brown	FW190 damaged	St Omer-Calais	1030
			F/L W.V.Crawford Compton	FW190 damaged	St Omer	1030
			P/O I.J.McNeil	FW190 prob.dest	St Omer	1030

On 4th April, the RAF flew Circus No.119 against St.Omer. FW190s and Bf109s of Jagdgeschwader 26 rose in force to oppose them and there was savage fighting between the target and the Channel. Flight Lieutenant Z.Kustrzynski of 303 Squadron claimed two FW190s but was jumped and forced to crash-land. His aircraft was one of fourteen Spitfires lost this day.

602 Sqn Spit FC	P/O J.R.Dennehey	FW190 damaged	Aire	1030~
	P/O J.R.Dennehey	FW190 damaged	Sangatte	1030~
	Sgt P.F.Green	Bf109F damaged	Aire	1030~
	F/S L.Scorer	FW190 damaged	Aire	1030~
	F/S L.Scorer	Bf109F damaged	Aire	1030~
604 Sqn Beau FC	S/L E.D.Crew	He111 damaged	S Swanage	1800
604 Sqn Beau FC	W/C J.Cunningham	He111 damaged	Brockworth	1850
BH Wg Spit FC	W/C J.Rankin	FW190 damaged	4m off Dunkirk	1040
Ntht Wg Spit FC	W/C T.H.Rolski	FW190 prob.dest	St Omer area	1030
	W/C T.H.Rolski	FW190 prob.dest	St Omer area	1030

5/6th April 1942

23 Sqn Bost FC	W/C W.J.Crisham	Do217 damaged	Evreux	u/k
FIU Beau FC	F/O D.L.Ryalls	Do217 destroyed	Thames estuary	2100~

6th April 1942

91 Sqn Spit FC	F/O G.C.R.Pannell	Bf109F destroyed	Dungeness	0830~

6/7th April 1942

29 Sqn Beau FC	W/C E.L.Colbeck-Welch	Do217 prob.dest	Off North Foreland	2215~

On 10th April, Frantisek Fajtl of 313 Squadron claimed a Bf109 damaged. He would end the war on the Eastern Front, leading a Czech unit of the Red Air Force.

7/8th April 1942

409 Sqn	Beau FC	S/L R.M.Trousdale	Do217 destroyed	N Cromer	0004

10th April 1942

41 Sqn	Spit FC	F/L W.Palmer	FW190 prob.dest	4m off Boulogne	1745~
		F/L W.Palmer	FW190 damaged	4m off Boulogne	1745~
		F/L B.Van Der Stock	FW190 damaged	Le Touquet area	1745~
		F/L B.Van Der Stock	FW190 damaged	Le Touquet area	1745~
		F/L B.Van Der Stock	FW190 damaged	Le Touquet area	1745~
313 Sqn	Spit FC	F/L F.Fajtl	Bf109E damaged	15m S Gravelines	1735
		F/S V.Foglar	Bf109E destroyed	15m S Gravelines	1735
		F/L V.Hajek	FW190 prob.dest	15m S Gravelines	1735
316 Sqn	Spit FC	P/O A.Cholajda	FW190 prob.dest	NE Hardelot	1740
		F/O J.Dec	FW190 prob.dest	NE Hardelot	1740
		S/L A.K.Gabsewicz	FW190 destroyed	NE Hardelot	1740
		Sgt T.Gora	FW190 damaged	NE Hardelot	1740
		F/L S.F.Skalski	FW190 destroyed	NE Hardelot	1740
		F/O T.Szumowski	FW190 destroyed	NE Hardelot	1740
		P/O J.Szymankiewicz	FW190 prob.dest	NE Hardelot	1740
		P/O J.Szymankiewicz	FW190 damaged	NE Hardelot	1740
		P/O M.Wyszkowski	FW190 destroyed	NE Hardelot	1740
		P/O M.Wyszkowski	FW190 damaged	NE Hardelot	1740
317 Sqn	Spit FC	Sgt A.Kolczynski	FW190 prob.dest	S Boulogne	1740
		Sgt E.Olzewski	Bf109E destroyed	S Boulogne	1740

340 Sqn	Spit FC	Capt B.Duperier	FW190 damaged	Le Touquet	1745~
602 Sqn	Spit FC	S/L B.E.Finucane	FW190 damaged	Dunkirk-Mardyck	1745~

11/12th April 1942

3 Sqn	Hurr FC	Sgt J.T.Shaw	E/A damaged	Schipol	2355~

12th April 1942

64 Sqn	Spit FC	S/L W.G.G.D.Smith	Bf109E prob.dest	Hazebrouck	1335
65 Sqn	Spit FC	S/L H.T.Gilbert	FW190 prob.dest	St Omer	1445~
121 Sqn	Spit FC	F/L T.W.Allen	FW190 prob.dest	N Hazebrouck	1335
		F/L T.W.Allen	FW190 damaged	N Hazebrouck	1335
		S/L H.C.Kennard	FW190 damaged	Aire	1330
		P/O J.B.Mahon	FW190 damaged	Aire	1325
		P/O L.A.Skinner	FW190 destroyed	Aire-Hazebrouck	1330
		P/O L.A.Skinner	FW190 damaged	Aire-Hazebrouck	1330
129 Sqn	Spit FC	F/L H.C.F.Bowman	FW190 destroyed	St Omer	1340
303 Sqn	Spit FC	P/O S.Socha	Bf109F prob.dest	S St Omer	1445
313 Sqn	Spit FC	Sgt P.Brazda	Bf109E destroyed	N Hazebrouck-Cassel	1335
		F/L F.Fajtl	- shared -		1335
		S/L K.Mrazek	FW190 damaged	N Hazebrouck-Cassel	1335
316 Sqn	Spit FC	Sgt T.Szymanski	FW190 destroyed	S Gravelines	1340
602 Sqn	Spit FC	F/O J.B.Niven	FW190 damaged	10m S Calais	1440~
Ken Wg	Spit FC	W/C R.F.Boyd	FW190 damaged	nr Gravelines	1445~
		W/C R.F.Boyd	FW190 damaged	nr Gravelines	1445~
Tang Wg	Spit FC	W/C P.H.Hugo	FW190 damaged	NE France	u/k

12/13th April 1942

3 Sqn	Hurr FC	P/O B.H.Hay	He111 damaged	Willemstadt	0100~

13th April 1942

602 Sqn	Spit FC	Lt R.De La Poype	Bf109F damaged	Gravelines	1515~
		F/O J.B.Niven	FW190 destroyed	Griz Nez-Boulogne	1515~
		F/S G.Willis	FW190 damaged	Gravelines	1515~

14th April 1942

124 Sqn	Spit FC	P/O M.P.Kilburn	FW190 damaged	Griz Nez	1850~
303 Sqn	Spit FC	Sgt M.Adamek	Bf109F destroyed	10m N R Orne	1248
		F/O M.Lipinski	Bf109F prob.dest	27m N R Orne	1248
306 Sqn	Spit FC	F/O A.Flisnik	Bf109E destroyed	6-8m off St Aubin	1245
		P/O J.Zulikowski	Bf109F destroyed	6-8m off St Aubin	1245

Far right: Squadron Leader Brendan Finucane of 602 Squadron claimed an FW190 damaged on 10th April. He would be credited with 26 kills before his death on 15th July. Right: Squadron Leader H.T.Gilbert made his last claim on 12th April. He was killed in a flying accident on 2nd May. (ww2images.com)

457 Sqn	Spit	FC	P/O D.H.MacLean	FW190 destroyed	Desvres-St Inglevert	1840
71 Sqn	Spit	FC	F/L N.Anderson	FW190 damaged	Guines	1850
			P/O M.G.H.McPharlin	FW190 damaged	Guines	1850

15th April 1942

72 Sqn	Spit	FC	S/L C.B.F.Kingcombe	FW190 damaged	Boulogne	1615~
			Sgt F.Malan	FW190 damaged	Boulogne	1615~
			F/O B.O.Parker	FW190 prob.dest	Boulogne	1615~
			F/O B.O.Parker	FW190 damaged	Boulogne	1615~
121 Sqn	Spit	FC	F/L T.W.Allen	FW190 destroyed	Hazebrouck-St Omer	1910
			P/O S.R.Edner	FW190 destroyed	Near St Omer	1915
			P/O L.A.Skinner	FW190 destroyed	Off Calais harbour	1915
403 Sqn	Spit	FC	F/S E.B.Argue	FW190 prob.dest	Near Griz Nez	1900
411 Sqn	Spit	FC	P/O H.W.McLeod	FW190 damaged	Le Touquet	1615~
			P/O H.W.McLeod	Bf109F damaged	Le Touquet	1615~
			S/L R.B.Newton	FW190 prob.dest	Le Touquet	1615~
602 Sqn	Spit	FC	P/O A.M.Charlesworth	FW190 prob.dest	Ambleteuse	1615~
609 Sqn	Spit	FC	S/L G.K.Gilroy	FW190 destroyed	Le Touquet	1615~
616 Sqn	Spit	FC	F/L J.E.Johnson	FW190 damaged	Le Touquet	1615~

15/16th April 1942

141 Sqn	Beau	FC	F/L I.H.Cosby	E/A damaged	Off Tyne	0040~

16th April 1942

71 Sqn	Spit	FC	P/O O.H.Coen	FW190 damaged	Hucqueliers	1359
118 Sqn	Spit	FC	Cdt A.Jubelin	Bf109 damaged	St Albans Head	1830~
303 Sqn	Spit	FC	F/O E.Horbaczewski	Bf109E destroyed	5-6m SW Le Havre	1138
306 Sqn	Spit	FC	P/O G.Solugub	Bf109E destroyed	2-3m off Cabourg	1145

			P/O G.Solugub	Bf109E destroyed	2-3m off Cabourg	1145
308 Sqn	Spit	FC	F/O B.Kudrewicz	Bf109F destroyed	10m NW Le Havre	1130
317 Sqn	Spit	FC	F/O S.Lukaszewicz	FW190 prob.dest	Marquise	1820
401 Sqn	Spit	FC	P/O D.J.M.Blakeslee	FW190 damaged	Le Touquet-Sangatte	1430~
			F/O E.L.Neal	FW190 damaged	Le Touquet-Sangatte	1430~
			P/O I.C.Ormston	FW190 damaged	Le Touquet-Sangatte	1430~
			P/O J.Witham	FW190 damaged	Le Touquet-Sangatte	1430~
457 Sqn	Spit	FC	F/L H.L.North	FW190 prob.dest	Dunkirk	0730
485 Sqn	Spit	FC	F/L W.V.Crawford -Compton	FW190 destroyed	Abbeville	1430~
			F/L J.R.C.Killian	FW190 destroyed	Abbeville	1430~
			S/L E.P.Wells	FW190 destroyed	Abbeville	1430~
Tang Wg	Spit	FC	W/C P.H.Hugo	Bf109F damaged	Le Havre	1130~

16/17th April 1942

1 Sqn	Hurr	FC	F/L K.Kuttelwascher	Do217 destroyed	St Andre	0230~

17th April 1942

71 Sqn	Spit	FC	P/O J.J.Lynch	Ju88 destroyed	8m E Felixstowe	0715
			P/O L.S.Nomis	-.shared -		
118 Sqn	Spit	FC	Sgt F.T.Brown	Bf109F damaged	Cherbourg	0935~
234 Sqn	Spit	FC	P/O B.Wydrowski	Bf109E damaged	Cherbourg	0935~
302 Sqn	Spit	FC	P/O M.Rytka	Bf109 destroyed	15m N Cherbourg	1555~
			P/O E.Wardzinski	Bf109 damaged	15m N Cherbourg	1555~
306 Sqn	Spit	FC	Sgt Z.Horn	Bf109F destroyed	10m N Cherbourg	1555
501 Sqn	Spit	FC	S/L C.F.Currant	Bf109F prob.dest	Cherbourg	0935~
Ibs Wg	Spit	FC	W/C I.R.Gleed	Bf109 destroyed	Cherbourg	0935~

17/18th April 1942

23 Sqn	Bost	FC	Sgt J.E.Millard	E/A destroyed	Montdidier	0015~

22nd April 1942

234 Sqn	Spit	FC	Sgt R.R.Barnfather	Bf109 destroyed	off Cherbourg	u/k

23/24th April 1942

307 Sqn	Beau	FC	Sgt W.Illaszewicz	Ju88 prob.dest	5m S Sidmouth	2254
604 Sqn	Beau	FC	P/O J.D.A.Tharp	Do217 destroyed	W Seaton	2328

24th April 1942

72 Sqn	Spit	FC	F/O F.De Naeyer	FW190 damaged	Calais	1500~
			Sgt R.J.H.Robertson	FW190 prob.dest	SE Calais	1500~

144

121 Sqn	Spit	FC	P/O W.J.Daley	Ju52/3M dest.	5m W Knocke A/D	1450
			P/O L.A.Skinner	- shared -		
175 Sqn	Hurr	FC	F/L A.H.Humphrey	Bf109 prob.dest	S Portland	0735~
			P/O Mackay	- shared -		
313 Sqn	Spit	FC	P/O V.Jicha	FW190 damaged	10-35m NW Ostend	1450
457 Sqn	Spit	FC	P/O P.H.Watson	FW190 damaged	Compeigne	1745
485 Sqn	Spit	FC	F/L W.V.Crawford Compton	FW190 destroyed	Near Hesdin	1745
			F/L J.R.C.Killian	FW190 damaged	W Hesdin	1745
			P/O G.J.Palmer	FW190 destroyed	Near Hesdin	1745
			S/L E.P.Wells	FW190 destroyed	Near Hesdin	1745

25th April 1942

43 Sqn	Hurr	FC	S/L D.A.R.G.L.Du Vivier	Ju88 destroyed	Acklington	1330~
71 Sqn	Spit	FC	S/L C.G.Peterson	FW190 damaged	Dunkirk	1027
72 Sqn	Spit	FC	F/O F.De Naeyer	FW190 prob.dest	Huquelieres	1630~
111 Sqn	Spit	FC	F/L R.C.Brown	FW190 damaged	Dunkirk	1025~
118 Sqn	Spit	FC	Sgt F.T.Brown	Bf109 prob.dest	Channel	1640~
124 Sqn	Spit	FC	P/O F.H.J.Ashton	Bf109F destroyed	NE France	1630~
313 Sqn	Spit	FC	F/L S.B.Fejfar	FW190 damaged	5m off Berck	1635-45
316 Sqn	Spit	FC	P/O A.Cholajda	FW190 damaged	SE Dunkirk	1035
			F/O J.Dec	FW190 destroyed	S Dunkirk	1035
			P/O L.Przygocki	- shared -		
			S/L A.K.Gabszewicz	FW190 destroyed	Near Hazebrouck	1030
			F/O J.Radomski	FW190 damaged	5m S Dunkirk	1035
			P/O M.Wyszkowski	FW190 destroyed	S Dunkirk	1035
316 Sqn	Spit	FC	F/L S.F.Skalski	Bf109F damaged	SW Le Havre	1430
317 Sqn	Spit	FC	F/S S.Brzeski	FW190 destroyed	2m N Dunkirk	1035
			F/O T.Koc	FW190 destroyed	4m off Dunkirk	1030
			F/O Z.Slomski	- shared -		
412 Sqn	Spit	FC	F/L F.E.Green	FW190 damaged	Le Treport-Abbeville	1630
485 Sqn	Spit	FC	S/L E.P.Wells	FW190 damaged	Nieuport	1630
602 Sqn	Spit	FC	F/L J.H.Lacey	FW190 damaged	Hesdin-Fruges	1630~
609 Sqn	Spit	FC	P/O T.C.Rigler	Bf109 destroyed	Le Crotoy-Le Treport	1640~
Dig Wg	Spit	FC	W/C H.P.Blatchford	FW190 destroyed	5m NW le Treport	1650
Ibs Wg	Spit	FC	W/C I.R.Gleed	Bf109F damaged	Cherbourg	0945~

25/26th April 1942

23 Sqn	Bost	FC	P/O T.Offord	Bf110 damaged	Caen	2330
219 Sqn	Beau	FC	S/L J.G.Topham	Do217 destroyed	40m S Worthing	2345

255 Sqn	Beau FC	F/O H.G.S.Wyrill	Ju88 destroyed	Llandrydod	2350
307 Sqn	Beau FC	Sgt W.Illaszewicz	Ju88 damaged	S Sidmouth	2343-58
307 Sqn	Beau FC	F/L M.Neyder	Ju88 destroyed	Start Point	2236
418 Sqn	Bost FC	Sgt G.W.C.Harding	E/A damaged	Evreux	0135

26th April 1942

41 Sqn	Spit FC	P/O A.A.Glen	FW190 prob.dest	Marquise	2100~
111 Sqn	Spit FC	P/O G.Stenborg	FW190 destroyed	Cassel-St Omer	1045~
133 Sqn	Spit FC	F/L C.W.McColpin	FW190 destroyed	Boulogne	1800~
302 Sqn	Spit FC	S/L J.Kowalski	FW190 prob.dest	Dunkirk-St Omer	1800~
306 Sqn	Spit FC	S/L T.Czerwinski	FW190 destroyed	3m E Calais	1800~
		P/O J.Zulikowski	FW190 damaged	3m E Calais	1800~
317 Sqn	Spit FC	F/O T.Kumiega	FW190 damaged	Gravelines	1050
		F/O Z.Slomski	FW190 damaged	Gravelines	1050
457 Sqn	Spit FC	Sgt A.H.Blake	FW190 damaged	5m S Calais	1800
		P/O D.H.MacLean	FW190 damaged	Calais-St Omer	1800
		F/L R.H.C.Sly	FW190 damaged	5m S Calais	1800
485 Sqn	Spit FC	P/O E.D.Mackie	FW190 prob.dest	Boulogne-St Omer	1800
602 Sqn	Spit FC	S/L B.E.Finucane	FW190 destroyed	St Omer	1100~
		F/S H.L.Thorne	FW190 destroyed	St Omer	1100~
		F/S H.L.Thorne	FW190 damaged	St Omer	1100~

26/27th April 1942

1 Sqn	Hurr FC	S/L J.A.F.MacLachlan	Do217 destroyed	Evreux/St Andre	0035~
		S/L J.A.F.MacLachlan	Do217 damaged	Evreux/St Andre	0035~
1 Sqn	Hurr FC	F/L K.Kuttelwascher	He111 destroyed	Boos	0300~
		F/L K.Kuttelwascher	Ju88 damaged	Boos	0300~
23 Sqn	Havc FC	Sgt Paterson	E/A damaged	Dinard	0415~
87 Sqn	Hurr FC	P/O F.A.Grantham	Do217 damaged	Bath	0120~
125 Sqn	Beau FC	P/O R.White	He111 prob.dest	Bath	0210~
125 Sqn	Beau FC	W/C D.V.Ivins	Do217 damaged	Bath	0200~
307 Sqn	Beau FC	F/O M.Neyder	Ju88 damaged	15-20m S Bridport	2334
307 Sqn	Beau FC	F/O M.Pietrzyk	Ju88 prob.dest	10m S Exmouth	2334
604 Sqn	Beau FC	F/L E.D.Crew	He111 damaged	Portland	0115~
604 Sqn	Beau FC	Sgt T.S.Atkinson	Do217 damaged	Bath	0230~

27th April 1942

65 Sqn	Spit FC	P/O T.A.Burke	FW190 destroyed	Holque	1220~
		P/O T.A.Burke	FW190 destroyed	Holque	1220~

Left: Gray Stenborg, a New Zealander, claimed his first victory on 26th April with 111 Squadron. He later served with 185 Squadron on Malta before returning to 91, but was killed in action on 24th September 1943 with a score of at least fourteen. Right: Polish pilots from 306 Squadron. (ww2images.com)

			F/L A.C.Bartley	FW190 damaged	Holque	1220~
71 Sqn	Spit	FC	P/O R.S.Sprague	FW190 damaged	near St Omer	1215
			P/O A.F.Roscoe	FW190 prob.dest	St Omer	1215
			P/O E.M.Potter	FW190 damaged	St Omer	1215
			S/L C.G.Peterson	FW190 destroyed	St Omer	1215-25
			S/L C.G.Peterson	FW190 destroyed	St Omer	1215-25
			S/L C.G.Peterson	FW190 damaged	St Omer	1215-25
			F/O O.H.Coen (shared) P/O M.G.H.McPharlin	FW190 destroyed (shared)	St Omer-Coast	1215-25
			F/O O.H.Coen (shared) P/O M.G.H.McPharlin	FW190 destroyed (shared) -	St Omer-Coast	1215-25
			F/O O.H.Coen (shared) P/O M.G.H.McPharlin	FW190 destroyed (shared) -	St Omer-Coast	1215-25
72 Sqn	Spit	FC	P/O S.W.Daniel	FW190 prob.dest	Lille	1545~
			F/L H.T.Armstrong	FW190 damaged	Lille	1545~
111 Sqn	Spit	FC	P/O G.Stenborg	FW190 destroyed	Holque	1220~
			S/L P.R.W.Wickham	Bf109E damaged	Holque	1220~
122 Sqn	Spit	FC	P/O W.B.Poulton	Bf109E damaged	Near Clairmarais	1220~
133 Sqn	Spit	FC	P/O W.H.Baker Jr	FW190 prob.dest	5m W Ostend	1430~
			P/O R.L.Pewitt	FW190 prob.dest	Ostend	1430~
303 Sqn	Spit	FC	P/O A.Glowacki	FW190 prob.dest	5m from Lille	1537
			F/L J.E.L.Zumbach	FW190 prob.dest	5m from Lille	1537

313 Sqn	Spit	FC	P/O J.Prihoda	FW190 destroyed	10m NW St Omer	1215-25
316 Sqn	Spit	FC	S/L A.K.Gabszewicz	FW190 destroyed	NE Lille	1545
317 Sqn	Spit	FC	F/O P.Sadowski	FW190 prob.dest	Lille	1545~
457 Sqn	Spit	FC	F/L H.L.North	FW190 damaged	Lille	1540
			F/L R.H.C.Sly	FW190 prob.dest	St Omer-Calais/Marck	1550
			F/L R.H.C.Sly	FW190 damaged	St Omer-Calais/Marck	1550
485 Sqn	Spit	FC	F/S A.R.Robson	FW190 prob.dest	5m SE Gravelines	1600
610 Sqn	Spit	FC	P/O L.E.Hoken	Ju88 destroyed	Off Lowestoft	0617
SF Hch	Spit	FC	G/C H.Broadhurst	FW190 damaged	St Omer	1220
			G/C H.Broadhurst	Bf109 damaged	St Omer	1220
Tang Wg	Spit	FC	W/C P.H.Hugo	FW190 prob.dest	Dunkirk	1430~
			W/C P.H.Hugo	FW190 damaged	Dunkirk	1430~

28th April 1942

72 Sqn	Spit	FC	F/L E.N.Woods Sgt R.J.H.Robertson	FW190 damaged - shared -	Calais-Gravelines	1120~
121 Sqn	Spit	FC	P/O S.R.Edner	FW190 prob.dest	15m S Dunkirk	1120
222 Sqn	Spit	FC	P/O R.Beaumont	FW190 prob.dest	Dunkirk	1120~
310 Sqn	Spit	FC	F/L E.A.Foit F/S F.Vindis	Ju88 destroyed - shared -	15m NW Trevose Hd	2100
317 Sqn	Spit	FC	F/L M.Duryasz	FW190 destroyed	10m N St Omer	1125
			F/O T.Koc	FW190 destroyed	10m N St Omer	1125
			Sgt A.Kolczynski	FW190 destroyed	10m N St Omer	1125
			F/O J.Mencel	FW190 damaged	10m N St Omer	1125
			F/O J.Walawski	FW190 damaged	10m N St Omer	1125
401 Sqn	Spit	FC	P/O D.J.M.Blakeslee	FW190 prob.dest	S Dunkirk	1150-1200
			P/O D.J.M.Blakeslee	FW190 prob.dest	S Dunkirk	1150-1200
602 Sqn	Spit	FC	P/O J.R.Dennehey	FW190 damaged	Calais-Gravelines	1120~
			S/L B.E.Finucane	FW190 damaged	Calais-Gravelines	1120~
NW Wg	Spit	FC	W/C F.D.S.Scott-Malden	FW190 prob.dest	N St Omer	1130

28/29th April 1942

68 Sqn	Beau	FC	S/L V.Vesely	Ju88 damaged	Norfolk coast	0400~
68 Sqn	Beau	FC	Sgt Jenkinson	He111 prob.dest	Off Harwich	0420~
68 Sqn	Beau	FC	W/O L.Bobek	Do217 destroyed	Off Yarmouth	0445~
133 Sqn	Spit	FC	P/O E.Doorly.	Do217 damaged	Nr Church Fenton	0410
253 Sqn	Hurr	FC	Sgt W.I.H.Maguire	Do217 damaged	Near York	0350~
253 Sqn	Hurr	FC	W/O Y.Mahe	Ju88 destroyed	Near York	0330
253 Sqn	Hurr	FC	F/O H.D.Seal	He111 prob.dest	S York	0310

Right: Prosser Hanks, one of the 1939 'originals' of 1 Squadron in France, commanded the Coltishall Wing from February 1942. On 29/30th April, he claimed a Do217 probably destroyed, shared a second 'probable' with AA Command and claimed strikes on a third. He was to survive the war with a score of at least thirteen victories, the rank of Group Captain and with a DSO, a DFC and an AFC.

406 Sqn	Beau	FC	P/O A.G.Lawrence	Ju88 destroyed	70-80m E Whitby	0409
406 Sqn	Beau	FC	F/O D.C.Furse	Do217 destroyed	E Bridlington	0400~

29th April 1942

129 Sqn	Spit	FC	Sgt A.Drew	Bf109F damaged	Isle of Wight	1400~
266 Sqn	Typh	FC	F/L A.C.Johnston	Ju88 damaged	Near Norwich	0040~
316 Sqn	Spit	FC	Sgt W.Kiedrzynski	FW190 damaged	SE Hardelot	1605
			Sgt K.Sumara	FW190 destroyed	SE Hardelot	1605
317 Sqn	Spit	FC	F/O T.Koc	FW190 destroyed	Coast near Boulogne	1600
			F/O T.Koc	FW190 prob.dest	Coast near Boulogne	1600
457 Sqn	Spit	FC	S/L P.M.Brothers	FW190 prob.dest	Griz Nez	1550-1610
			P/O D.H.MacLean	FW190 damaged	Calais-Griz Nez	1615
485 Sqn	Spit	FC	F/S A.R.Robson	FW190 damaged	Le Touquet-Boulogne	1615

29/30th April 1942

Dux Wg	Typh	FC	W/C P.P.Hanks	Do217 prob.dest	Coltishall	2340~
			W/C P.P.Hanks*	Do217 prob.dest	Coltishall	2340~

* Shared with AA Command.

			W/C P.P.Hanks	Do217 damaged	Near Norwich	2340~
68 Sqn	Beau	FC	S/L G.L.Howden	He111 damaged	Near Norwich	0115~

30th April 1942

64 Sqn	Spit	FC	F/L L.O.J.Prevot	Bf109E damaged	Flushing	1520~
71 Sqn	Spit	FC	S/L C.G.Peterson	FW190 damaged	W Le Crotoy	1925
			P/O S.A.Mauriello	Bf109E damaged	10m W Berck	1930
111 Sqn	Spit	FC	Sgt P.E.G.Durnford	FW190 destroyed	Calais area	1030~

Pilots of 133 Squadon, Spring 1942. (ww2images.com)

			P/O G.Stenborg	FW190 destroyed	W Ardres	1930~
			P/O G.Stenborg	FW190 destroyed	Abbeville	1930~
122 Sqn	Spit	FC	P/O G.A.Y.F.F.X.Muller	Bf109F prob.dest	Zeebrugge	1520~
124 Sqn	Spit	FC	P/O M.P.Kilburn	Bf109F prob.dest	Le Havre	1140~
222 Sqn	Spit	FC	P/O R.H.Fletcher	FW190 prob.dest	Abbeville	1930~
313 Sqn	Spit	FC	Sgt J.Hlouzek	FW190 damaged	40m W Flushing	1520
313 Sqn	Spit	FC	Sgt J.Hlouzek	Bf109E destroyed	5m NW Abbeville	1925-35
401 Sqn	Spit	FC	S/L A.G.Douglas	Bf109E damaged	10m NNW Le Havre	1145
501 Sqn	Spit	FC	F/S V.Bauman	Bf109F destroyed	Mid-Channel	1730~
602 Sqn	Spit	FC	F/L E.W.P.Bocock	FW190 destroyed	7-10m NW Le Havre	1140~
			P/O J.R.Dennehey	FW190 damaged	Le Havre	1140~
			S/L B.E.Finucane	FW190 prob.dest	Le Havre	1140~
			F/S H.L.Thorne	FW190 prob.dest	Le Havre	1140~
			F/S G.Willis	FW190 prob.dest	Le Havre	1140~
BH Wg	Spit	FC	W/C J.Rankin	Bf109F damaged	NW Le Havre	1140

30th April/1st May 1942

1 Sqn	Hurr	FC	F/L K.Kuttelwascher	He111 destroyed	Rennes	0130~
			F/L K.Kuttelwascher	Ju88 destroyed	Dinard	0200~
3 Sqn	Hurr	FC	F/L J.T.Shaw	Ju88 destroyed	1m E Chievres AD	0445
29 Sqn	Beau	FC	S/L D.Parker	He111 destroyed	Off Orfordness	0200~
68 Sqn	Beau	FC	W/C J.W.M.Aitken	Do217 destroyed	Off East Anglia	0500~
68 Sqn	Beau	FC	P/O M.J.Mansfeld	He111 destroyed	Off East Anglia	0200~

		P/O M.J.Mansfeld	He111 destroyed	Off East Anglia	0200~
		P/O M.J.Mansfeld S/L V.Vesely	Do217 destroyed - shared -	North Sea	0330~
141 Sqn	Beau FC	W/C F.W.Heycock	Do217 damaged	Off Blythe	0310
253 Sqn	Hurr FC	S/L D.S.Yapp*	He111 destroyed	NE Highbaldstow	0230~
with Havoc 1459 Flt (F/L C.V.Winn)					
406 Sqn	Beau FC	F/O D.C.Furse	Ju88 damaged	N Tyne	0307
		F/O D.C.Furse	Ju88 damaged	NE Tyne	0314
		F/O D.C.Furse	Do217 damaged	40m E Teesmouth	0356
406 Sqn	Beau FC	Sgt A.J.Harper	Do217 damaged	100m NE Scorton	0330
406 Sqn	Beau FC	Sgt G.Stephen	Ju88 destroyed	Off Tyne	0230

1st May 1942

41 Sqn	Spit FC	Sgt G.F.Beurling	FW190 destroyed	Channel	1415~
401 Sqn	Spit FC	F/S G.B.Murray	FW190 damaged	N Le Havre	1605
		P/O I.C. Ormston	FW190 damaged	35m SW Shoreham	1630
411 Sqn	Spit FC	P/O H.W.McLeod	FW190 damaged	E Griz Nez	1620
457 Sqn	Spit FC	Sgt G.L.C.Gifford	FW190 damaged	Calais-Griz Nez	1925
		P/O D.H. MacLean	FW190 prob.dest	Calais-Griz Nez	1930
485 Sqn	Spit FC	F/S A.R.Robson	FW190 damaged	10m E Boulogne	1930
602 Sqn	Spit FC	F/L E.W.P.Bocock	FW190 prob.dest	Boulogne	1935~
		F/L E.W.P.Bocock	FW190 damaged	35-40m SE Beachy Head	1935~
		Sgt W.W.J.Loud	FW190 prob.dest	Guines	1935~
		Sgt W.W.J.Loud	FW190 damaged	Guines	1935~
		F/S H.L.Thorne	FW190 prob.dest	Marquise	1935~
		F/S H.L.Thorne	FW190 damaged	Marquise	1935~
616 Sqn	Spit FC	F/O C.B.Brown	FW190 prob.dest	Channel	1620~

3rd May 1942

41 Sqn	Spit FC	Sgt G.F.Beurling	FW190 destroyed	2-3m off Griz Nez	1145~
		F/S R.E.Green	FW190 damaged	Guines	1145~
41 Sqn	Spit FC	Sgt J.S.Wilson	FW190 damaged	Abbeville	1710~
308 Sqn	Spit FC	F/S W.Majchryzyk	Ju88 damaged	Cap De La Hague -Alderney	2130
		F/O T.Stebrowski	- shared -		
315 Sqn	Spit FC	F/O K.Stembrowicz*	Ju88 damaged	Near Heysham, Lancs	0720
Shared with 452 Squadron.					
316 Sqn	Spit FC	P/O C.Jaworowski	FW190 destroyed	SE Guines	1610
		Sgt W.Kiedrzynski	FW190 damaged	SE Calais	1610

			F/L S.F.Skalski	FW190 prob.dest	SW Calais	1605
340 Sqn	Spit	FC	Lt F.L.De Tedesco	FW190 destroyed	10m E Boulogne	1140
			Capt B.Duperier	FW190 destroyed	Calais-Guines	1145
			Lt F.Chauvin F/L F.E.Fayolle	FW190 destroyed - shared -	Calais-Guines	1143
452 Sqn	Spit	FC	P/O W.J.Lamerton*	Ju88 damaged	Near Heysham, Lancs	0720

* Shared with 315 Squadron.

3/4th May 1942

1 Sqn	Hurr	FC	S/L J.A.F.MacLachlan	He111 destroyed	Dinard	0400~
			S/L J.A.F.MacLachlan	Ju88 destroyed	Dinard	0400~
307 Sqn	Beau	FC	F/L M.Neyder	Ju88 destroyed	20m S Seaton	0255
307 Sqn	Beau	FC	Sgt W.Illaszewicz	Ju88 destroyed	Topsham, Exeter	0142
			Sgt W.Illaszewicz	Ju88 destroyed	Colyton	0225
307 Sqn	Beau	FC	F/O S.Andrzejewski	Ju88 destroyed	8m E Torbay	0146
604 Sqn	Beau	FC	S/L S.H.Skinner	Do217 prob.dest	Portland	0218
604 Sqn	Beau	FC	F/L E.D.Crew	Do217 destroyed	Portland	0140

4th May 1942

72 Sqn	Spit	FC	P/O R.C.Kitchen	Bf109F destroyed	N Le Havre	1020~
			P/O D.O.Waters P/O O.L.Hardy	Do217 prob.dest - shared -	N Le Havre	1020~
			F/L H.T.Armstrong	Bf109F destroyed	N Le Havre	1020~
			F/L H.T.Armstrong	- shared -		
				Bf109F destroyed	N Le Havre	1020~
124 Sqn	Spit	FC	F/S B.J.Hull	Bf109 destroyed	Le Havre	1040~
129 Sqn	Spit	FC	Sgt E.E.O.Irish	FW190 damaged	Off Le Havre	1545~
154 Sqn	Spit	FC	F/L G.T.Hugill	Bf109E damaged	Dutch coast	1240~
222 Sqn	Spit	FC	P/O R.Beaumont* Sgt F.Ogden Sgt N.K.T.Stanton	Bf109F damaged - shared - - shared -	Le Havre	1040~

* Also shared with Station Flight Biggin Hill

340 Sqn	Spit	FC	Lt F.Chauvin	FW190 damaged	25m NW Le Havre	1600
457 Sqn	Spit	FC	Sgt G.L.C.Gifford	FW190 damaged	Griz Nez-Boulogne	1945
485 Sqn	Spit	FC	F/S A.R.Robson	FW190 prob.dest	Ambleteuse	1945
			F/L M.M.Shand	FW190 prob.dest	Ambleteuse	1945
BH Wg	Spit	FC	W/C J.Rankin	Bf109F destroyed	Le Havre	1040~
			W/C J.Rankin	Bf109F damaged	Le Havre	1040~
NW Wg	Spit	FC	W/C F.D.S.Scott-Malden	Bf109F damaged	Le Havre	1040~

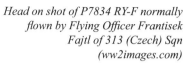

Head on shot of P7834 RY-F normally flown by Flying Officer Frantisek Fajtl of 313 (Czech) Sqn (ww2images.com)

			W/C F.D.S.Scott-Malden*	Bf109F damaged	Le Havre	1040~

* Shared with 222 Squadron.

SF BH	Spit	FC	G/C P.R.Barwell	Do217 prob.dest	Le Havre	1040~
72 Squadron				- shared -		

4/5th May 1942

1 Sqn	Hurr	FC	F/L K.Kuttelwascher	He111 destroyed	St Andre	0130~
			F/L K.Kuttelwascher	He111 destroyed	St Andre	0130~
			F/L K.Kuttelwascher	He111 destroyed	St Andre	0130~
23 Sqn	Havc	FC	P/O E Williams	E/A damaged	Rennes	0130~
604 Sqn	Beau	FC	F/L E.D.Crew	Do217 destroyed	Isle of Wight	0430~
604 Sqn	Beau	FC	P/O R.J.Foster	Do217 damaged	Channel	2240

5th May 1942

122 Sqn	Spit	FC	P/O E.J.Bland	FW190 prob.dest	Abbeville	1530~
			P/O J.L.Crisp	FW190 prob.dest	Abbeville	1530~
			F/L H.J.L.Hallowes	FW190 destroyed	Abbeville	1530~
			F/L H.J.L.Hallowes	FW190 damaged	Abbeville	1530~
			P/O W.T.E.Rolls	FW190 destroyed	Abbeville	1530~
129 Sqn	Spit	FC	Sgt B.Bjornstad	FW190 destroyed	Desvres	1440
			Sgt E.T.Hiskens	FW190 damaged	SE Boulogne	1445
			S/L R.H.Thomas	FW190 prob.dest	Desvres-Boulogne	1440
313 Sqn	Spit	FC	F/L S.B.Fejfar	FW190 prob.dest	Lille	1535
			F/L S.B.Fejfar	FW190 destroyed	Lille	1535
			P/O O.Kucera	FW190 damaged	Lille	1535
316 Sqn	Spit	FC	S/L A.K.Gabszewicz	FW190 prob.dest	10m E Hardelot	1440
			Sgt W. Kiedrzynski	FW190 destroyed	10m E Hardelot	1440
BH Wg	Spit	FC	W/C J.Rankin	FW190 damaged	5m SE Dunkirk	1545
Ibs Wg	Spit	FC	W/C I.R.Gleed	FW190 prob.dest	Hardelot	1440

On the night of 7th May, Luftwaffe bombers attacked Chatham. This aircraft, an He111H-6 of 7./KG 100, was caught near Ashford by a Beaufighter of 29 Squadron, flown by Pilot Officer Carr. All the crew baled out, but two were killed when their parachutes failed.

6th May 1942

72 Sqn	Spit	FC	Sgt R.J.H.Robertson	Bf109F destroyed	Caen	1845~
316 Sqn	Spit	FC	S/L A.K.Gabszewicz	FW190 prob.dest	Sea Calais-Griz Nez	1845
			F/O J.Radomski	- shared -		
			F/O W.Walendowski	- shared -		

6/7th May 1942

3 Sqn	Hurr	FC	Sgt D.J.Scott	E/A destroyed	Gilze-Rijn	0230~
418 Sqn	Bost	FC	P/O A.Lukas	- shared -		

7th May 1942

118 Sqn	Spit	FC	P/O J.Veen	Ju88 destroyed	Off Portland	2105

7/8th May 1942

29 Sqn	Beau	FC	P/O R.M.Carr	He111 destroyed	Patcham, nr Ashford	0245
219 Sqn	Beau	FC	S/L J.G..Topham	He111 destroyed	3m N Brighton	0255

8th May 1942

340 Sqn	Spit	FC	S/Lt M.Boudier	Bf109E damaged	Off Littlehampton	1235-55
			S/Lt A.Dubec	Bf109E destroyed	Off Littlehampton	1235-55

8/9th May 1942

3 Sqn	Hurr	FC	P/O B.H.Hay	He111 destroyed	Off Dutch Coast	0315~
			P/O B.H.Hay	Do217 destroyed	Schipol	0315~
3 Sqn	Hurr	FC	Sgt D.J.Scott	E/A prob.dest	Soesterburg	0300~

9th May 1942

64 Sqn	Spit	FC	S/L W.G.G.D.Smith	FW190 damaged	Near Bruges	1750~
71 Sqn	Spit	FC	P/O A.F.Roscoe	E/A prob.dest	En route Hazebrouck	1320~
72 Sqn	Spit	FC	F/O B.O.Parker	FW190 destroyed	Off Ostend	1740~

Harry Broadhurst (centre front row) sits with Spitfire pilots of the Hornchurch Wing.
(ww2images.com)

122 Sqn	Spit	FC	F/L H.J.L.Hallowes	FW190 damaged	Hazebrouck	1330~
129 Sqn	Spit	FC	Sgt S.G..Jenssen	FW190 damaged	Gravelines	1345~
175 Sqn	Hurr	FC	F/L A.H.Humphrey	Bf109F destroyed	S Lulworth	0700~
			F/L A.H.Humphrey	Bf109F destroyed	S Lulworth	0700~
313 Sqn	Spit	FC	P/O J.Prihoda	FW190 damaged	5m NE Dunkirk	1740-50
350 Sqn	Spit	FC	F/L Y.G.A.F.Du Monceau	FW190 damaged	Calais	1345
457 Sqn	Spit	FC	Sgt G.L.C.Gifford	FW190 damaged	Hazebrouck	1330

11th May 1942

340 Sqn	Spit	FC	F/L F.E.Fayolle	Ju88 destroyed	30m S Selsey Bill	1745
602 Sqn	Spit	FC	F/L E.W.P.Bocock	FW190 damaged	Mid-Channel	2045~

14th May 1942

610 Sqn	Spit	FC	S/L G.S.K.Haywood	Ju88 prob.dest	Off Southwold	1850~
			Sgt F.Mares	- shared -		

15th May 1942

137 Sqn	Whir	FC	F/S G.V.Brennan (shared)	Ju88 damaged	Off Yarmouth	0900~
			F/S A.G..Brunet	- shared -		
610 Sqn	Spit	FC	F/L R.N.Courtney (shared)	Do217 damaged	12m N Sheringham	u/k
610 Sqn	Spit	FC	S/L G.S.K.Haywood	Do217 damaged	Off Sherringham	1600~
			Sgt F.Mares	- shared -		
610 Sqn	Spit	FC	S/L G.S.K.Haywood	Do217 destroyed	Off Yarmouth	1800
			P/O L.E.Hoken	- shared -		
			Sgt F.Mares	- shared -		
			P/O L.A.Smith	- shared -		

155

16th May 1942

412 Sqn	Spit	FC	P/O R.A.Ellis		Do217	destroyed	30-35m E Southwold	1650
			P/O J.D.Stephenson		- shared -		
412 Sqn	Spit	FC	P/O M D(?)Boyd		Do217 damaged	E Southwold	u/k
610 Sqn	Spit	FC	S/L G.S.K.Haywood		Ju88 prob.dest	Off Lowestoft	1915~
			Sgt F.Mares		- shared	
Colt Wg	Spit	FC	W/C P.P.Hanks		- shared -	

17th May 1942

64 Sqn	Spit	FC	Sgt P.S.Hannan	FW190 damaged	Audricq	1140~
			S/L W.G.G.D.Smith	FW190 destroyed	Audricq	1140~
			Sgt J.K.Stewart	FW190 destroyed	Audricq	1140~
			F/L C.Thomas	FW190 prob.dest	Audricq	1140~
72 Sqn	Spit	FC	P/O S.W.Daniel	Bf109E damaged	Le Treport	1030~
72 Sqn	Spit	FC	F/L E.N.Woods	FW190 damaged	Channel	1445~
			P/O J.R.Ratten	FW190 damaged	15m W Griz Nez	1445~
121 Sqn	Spit	FC	P/O W.J.Daley Jr	FW190 destroyed	St Omer	1600~
			F/O S.R.Edner	FW190 destroyed	St Omer	1600~
			P/O J.B.Mahon	FW190 damaged	St Omer	1600~
			P/O J.J.Mooney	FW190 damaged	St Omer	1600~
122 Sqn	Spit	FC	P/O J.G.Durkin	FW190 damaged	Audricq	1140~
			F/L L.P.Griffith	FW190 prob.dest	Audricq	1140~
			F/L H.J.L.Hallowes	FW190 prob.dest	Audricq	1140~
			F/L H.J.L.Hallowes	FW190 damaged	Audricq	1140~
			F/L H.J.L.Hallowes	FW190 damaged	Audricq	1140~
			P/O W.H.Prest	FW190 damaged	Audricq	1140~
			S/L L.O.J.Prevot	FW190 destroyed	Audricq	1140~
			P/O W.T.E.Rolls	FW190 destroyed	Audricq	1140~
			P/O W.T.E.Rolls	FW190 prob.dest	Audricq	1140~
133 Sqn	Spit	FC	F/L C.W.McColpin	Bf109F destroyed	NW Le Treport	1030
			F/L C.W.McColpin	Bf109F prob.dest	NW Le Treport	1030
			P/O M.S.Morris	Bf109F prob.dest	NW Le Treport	1030
402 Sqn	Spit	FC	F/S B.E.Innes	FW190 damaged	Channel	1140~
602 Sqn	Spit	FC	S/L B.E.Finucane	FW190 destroyed	Guines	1140~
			P/O C.K.Tait	FW190 destroyed	Guines	1140~
BH Wg	Spit	FC	W/C J.Rankin	Bf109F destroyed	5m off Le Treport	1015
BH Wg	Spit	FC	W/C J.Rankin	FW190 damaged	4m off Boulogne	1445~
Hch Wg	Spit	FC	W/C R.P.R.Powell	FW190 destroyed	Audricq	1140~

Left: Carroll W. 'Red' McColpin flew with 71 and 133 'Eagle' Squadrons before transferring to the USAAF. He claimed a Bf109 destroyed on 17th May, his last - of eight - confirmed victories with the RAF. Right: on 17th May Jamie Rankin, leading the Biggin Hill Spitfires, claimed his seventeenth solo confirmed kill. (Chris Goss)

18th May 1942

412 Sqn Spit FC	P/O G.G.Davidson	Ju88 damaged	15-20m E Felixstowe	0605
	P/O R.A.Ellis	- shared -		
456 Sqn Beau FC	F/O D.B.Wills	Ju88 destroyed	St George's Channel	1700

19th May 1942

71 Sqn Spit FC	S/L C.G.Peterson	FW190 prob.dest	Calais	2035
133 Sqn Spit FC	F/S C.W.Harp	FW190 destroyed	10m NW Fecamp	1520
	F/S C.W.Harp	FW190 destroyed	10m NW Fecamp	1520
	P/O M.S.Morris	Bf109F destroyed	10m NW Fecamp	1515
	P/O M.S.Morris	Bf109F damaged	10m NW Fecamp	1515
	P/O G.B.Sperrey*	Bf109F damaged	N Le Havre	1520

* Shared with Biggin Hill Wing.

331 Sqn Spit FC	Lt H.Leifseth	FW190 damaged	Calais	2050
	2/Lt T.Weisteen	FW190 damaged	E Calais	2050
350 Sqn Spit FC	F/L Y.G.A.F.Du Monceau	Bf109 prob.dest	Calais	2050
	Sgt J.Ester	Bf109E prob.dest	Calais	2040
BH Wg Spit FC	W/C J.Rankin*	Bf109F damaged	N Le Havre	1520

* Shared with 133 Squadron.

NW Wg Spit FC	W/C F.D.S.Scott-Malden	FW190 prob.dest	St Omer	2030

19/20th May 1942

3 Sqn Hurr FC	Sgt D.J.Scott	E/A destroyed	Leeuwarden	0350~

21st May 1942

610 Sqn	Spit	FC	Sgt J.H.Tanner (shared)	Ju88 damaged	Off Cromer	0645~
			P/O P.B.Wright	- shared -		

22nd May 1942

411 Sqn	Spit	FC	P/O P.R.Eakins	Ju88 damaged	Off Skegness	2010
			S/L R.B.Newton	- shared -		

23rd May 1942

65 Sqn	Spit	FC	P/O V.Lawson	FW190 damaged	Calais area	1145~
111 Sqn	Spit	FC	Sgt H.D.Christian	FW190 damaged	Near St Omer	1140~
350 Sqn	Spit	FC	F/L A.L.T.J.Boussa	FW190 damaged	E Calais/Marck	1145
			P/O R.J.L.Laumans	FW190 damaged	St Omer-Boulogne	1155-1215
			P/O A.M.Plisnier	FW190 destroyed	St Omer-Calais	1145
			P/O A.M.Plisnier	FW190 damaged	St Omer-Calais	1145
604 Sqn	Beau	FC	W/C J.Cunningham	He111 destroyed	Near Shaftesbury	1703

24th May 1942

124 Sqn	Spit	FC	P/O F.H.J.Ashton	FW190 damaged	Off Griz Nez	1910~
			Sgt P.E.G.Durnford	FW190 destroyed	N Sangatte	1910~
			P/O M.P.Kilburn	Bf109 destroyed	Sangatte	1910~
			P/O M.P.Kilburn	FW190 damaged	Sangatte	1910~
			S/L D.A.P.McMullen	FW190 destroyed	Off Griz Nez	1910~
			S/L D.A.P.McMullen	FW190 destroyed	Off Griz Nez	1910~
133 Sqn	Spit	FC	P/O M.E.Jackson	Bf109F damaged	Off Dungeness-France	1700
167 Sqn	Spit	FC	Sgt J.R.Taggart*	Ju88 prob.dest	Hartlepool	0720

* Shared with 332 Squadron.

332 Sqn	Spit	FC	2/Lt P.Mollestad*	Ju88 prob.dest	Hartlepool	0720
			2/Lt T.Strand	- shared -		

* Shared with 167 Squadron.

401 Sqn	Spit	FC	SgtI R.MacLennan	FW190 damaged	Off Griz Nez	1920
			F/S D.R.Morrison	FW190 damaged	8m NW Sangatte	1910
			F/S D.R.Morrison	FW190 damaged	8-10m NW Griz Nez	1920
BH Wg	Spit	FC	W/C J.Rankin	Bf109F damaged	Off Griz Nez	1910
Ken Wg	Spit	FC	W/C E.P.Wells	Bf109F damaged	Off Griz Nez	1910
SF BH	Spit	FC	G/C P.R.Barwell	Bf109F damaged	Off Griz Nez	1910

24/25th May 1942

604 Sqn	Beau	FC	S/L S.H.Skinner	He111 destroyed	Off Studland	0100

Left: famous for his phenomenal eyesight, Edward Wells of New Zealand became known as 'Hawkeye'. Initially with 41 Squadron in 1939, he tranferred to 485 (RNZAF) Squadron in 1941 and rose to command the unit. On 5th May he became Kenley Wing Leader, claiming a Bf109 damaged on 24th. He ended the war with a DSO, two DFCs and a score of twelve confirmed kills. Right: Mike Kilburn, known as 'Slim', claimed his second confirmed kill - an FW190 - on 24th May as well as another damaged. He also survived the war, leading a Tempest unit. His final score was six confirmed and one 'shared'.

25th May 1942

411 Sqn	Spit	FC	P/O D.W.P.Connolly*	Do217 damaged	6m E Leicester-Wash	2100~

* Shared with 616 Squadron.

616 Sqn	Spit	FC	F/O C.B.Brown*	Do217 damaged	6m E Leicester-Wash	2100~
			F/L J.E.Johnson	- shared -		
			Sgt J.H.Smithson	- shared -		
			Sgt N.G.Welch	- shared -		

* Also shared with 616 Squadron.

MSFU	Hurr	FC	F/O J.B.Kendal	Ju88 destroyed	Russian convoy	0900
MSFU	Hurr	FC	P/O A.J.Hay	He111 destroyed	Russian convoy	1900
			P/O A.J.Hay	He111 damaged	Russian convoy	1900

26th May 1942

234 Sqn	Spit	FC	S/L F.E.W.Birchfield	Ju88 prob.dest	SW Portreath	1155~

27th May 1942

41 Sqn	Spit	FC	P/O J.J.Allen (shared)	Bf109F destroyed	Isle of Wight	1505
			F/L D.W.Wainright	- shared -		
72 Sqn	Spit	FC	S/L C.B.F.Kingcombe	Bf109F damaged	St Valery-en-Caux	1140~
			F/L H.T.Armstrong	Bf109F destroyed	Nr St Valery	1140~
121 Sqn	Spit	FC	F/O W.J.Daley Jr	Bf109F destroyed	2m W Walcheren	1645
			F/O J.B.Mahon	Bf109F damaged	N Walcheren	1645

		Sgt F.R.Vance	Bf109F damaged	N Walcheren		1645
222 Sqn	Spit FC	P/O D.H.Evans	Bf109F damaged	N Walcheren		1645
BH Wg	Spit FC	W/C J.Rankin*	Bf109F prob.dest	Near Fecamp		1140

* Shared with Station Flight Biggin Hill.

NW Wg	Spit FC	W/C F.D.S.Scott-Malden	Bf109F damaged	10-15m N Blankenberghe		1648
SF BH	Spit FC	G/C P.R.Barwell*	Bf109F prob.dest	Near Fecamp		1140

* Shared with Station Flight Biggin Hill.

27/28th May 1942

416 Sqn	Spit FC	F/S J.Moul	He111 damaged	40m ENE Peterhead	2317

28th May 1942

416 Sqn	Spit FC	P/O E R.Burrows	He111 damaged	5m E Peterhead	1900

28/29th May 1942

68 Sqn	Beau FC	W/O L.Bobek	Ju88 damaged	Off Hornsea	0115~
151 Sqn	Mosq FC	F/L D.A.Pennington	He111 damaged	Off Hornsea	0550~
151 Sqn	Mosq FC	P/O J.A.Wain	Do217 damaged	Off Cromer	0045~

29th May 1942

111 Sqn	Spit FC	Sgt Y.Henricksen	FW190 damaged	Dunkirk	0820~
		Sgt A.Williams	FW190 damaged	Dunkirk	0820~
124 Sqn	Spit FC	Sgt P.E.G.Durnford	FW190 destroyed	SE Dunkirk	0820~
		F/S B.J.Hull	FW190 destroyed	Off Dunkirk	0820~
133 Sqn	Spit FC	S/L E.H.Thomas	FW190 damaged	5m S Dunkirk	0820
401 Sqn	Spit FC	S/L A.G.Douglas	FW190 destroyed	1m E Dunkirk	0820

29/30th May 1942

25 Sqn	Beau FC	F/O A.J.Picknett	Do217 destroyed	E Hull	0115~
68 Sqn	Beau FC	F/L W.D.Winward	D0217E destroyed	Happisburgh	0525~
68 Sqn	Beau FC	W/C J.M.W.Aitken	Do217E destroyed	Norfolk coast	0245~
		W/C J.M.W.Aitken	Ju88 damaged	Norfolk coast	0245~
68 Sqn	Beau FC	S/L G.L.Howden	Ju88 destroyed	Off Spurn Head	u/k
68 Sqn	Beau FC	P/O A.E.Marshall	He111 destroyed	Off Cromer	0100~
		P/O A.E.Marshall	He111 damaged	Off Cromer	0100~
151 Sqn	Mosq.FC	P/O J.A.Wain	Do217E prob.dest	N Sea	u/k
157 Sqn	Mosq.FC	S/L G.Ashfield	Do217E destroyed	Dover Straits	0540~

30th May 1942

401 Sqn	Spit FC	F/O D.J.M.Blakeslee	FW190 damaged	8m W Hesdin	1440
BH Wg	Spit FC	W/C J.Rankin	Bf109F damaged	Near St Pol	1445

Max Aitken, son of Lord Beaverbrook, Minister of Aircraft Production, flew with 601 Squadron during the Battle of France and the early part of the Battle of Britain. He later led 68 Squadron and, after several staff appointments, he led the Banff Strike Wing Mosquitos. On 29/30th May he claimed a Do217 destroyed and a Ju88 damaged. He ended the war with a DSO, a DFC and a score of fourteen confirmed kills. He is pictured at his investiture with the DFC in 1940

30/31st May 1942

1 Sqn	Hurr	FC	W/O G.Scott	Ju88 damaged	St Trond	u/k
3 Sqn	Hurr	FC	F/S D.J.Scott	Ju88 prob.dest	Soesterburg	0230~
			F/S D.J.Scott	Ju88 damaged	Soesterburg	0230~
3 Sqn	Hurr	FC	P/O B.H.Hay	Ju88 prob.dest	S Venlo	u/k
3 Sqn	Hurr	FC	F/S C.H.Smith	E/A damaged	Gilze-Rijn	u/k

31st May 1942

72 Sqn	Spit	FC	P/O J.R.Ratten	FW190 destroyed	W St Valery-en-Caux	1935~
			Sgt R.J.H.Robertson	FW190 destroyed	St Valery-en-Caux	1935~
			Sgt R.J.H.Robertson	FW190 damaged	Dieppe	1935~
124 Sqn	Spit	FC	F/S B.J.Hull	Bf109F destroyed	Dieppe	1935~
133 Sqn	Spit	FC	P/O E.D.Taylor	FW190 damaged	Nr St Valery-en-Caux	1945-2000
164 Sqn	Spit	FC	P/O S.Blok	Ju88 damaged	E Orkneys	2000~
			P/O W.J.Cleverly	- shared -		
303 Sqn	Spit	FC	F/O M.Lipinski	FW190 damaged	Coast near Dieppe	1950
331 Sqn	Spit	FC	Lt S.Sem	Bf109F destroyed	Near Flushing	1610
			F/S F.A.S.Fearnley	- shared		
			2/Lt M.Y.Gran	Bf109F damaged	Off Walcheren	1625
			Lt R.A.Berg	- shared -		
602 Sqn	Spit	FC	P/O C.K.Tait	FW190 damaged	Abbeville	1940~

31st May/1st June 1942

3 Sqn	Hurr	FC	F/S C.H.Smith	Do217 destroyed	Gilze-Rijn	0245~
			F/S C.H.Smith	Do217 damaged	Gilze-Rijn	0245~
29 Sqn	Beau	FC	S/L D.Parker	Do217 prob.dest	Off Calais	0050~
219 Sqn	Beau	FC	F/OJ C.I.Hooper	Ju88 destroyed	Dungeness	0023

1st June 1942

Sqn			Pilot	Claim	Location	Time
71 Sqn	Spit	FC	P/O R.S.Sprague	FW190 damaged	Near Bruges	1345
			F/L G.A.Daymond	FW190 destroyed	Off Ostend	1345
			S/L C.G.Peterson	FW190 destroyed	Near Bruges	1340
			S/L C.G.Peterson	FW190 damaged	Near Bruges	1340
			P/O E.M.Porter	FW190 damaged	Near Bruges	1345
175 Sqn	Hurr	FC	Sgt W.J.A.McLachlan	Bf109F damaged	Off Weymouth	1120
			F/S R.A.Peters	- shared -		
350 Sqn	Spit	FC	F/L Y.G.A.F.Du Monceau	FW190 destroyed	Off Nieuport	1505
403 Sqn	Spit	FC	P/O L.J.Somers	FW190 damaged	N Ostend	1845~

1/2nd June 1942

Sqn			Pilot	Claim	Location	Time
1 Sqn	Hurr	FC	Sgt G.S.M.Pearson	Ju88 destroyed	St Trond	0340~
1 Sqn	Hurr	FC	F/S G.C.English	Do217 destroyed	Eindhoven	0315~
3 Sqn	Hurr	FC	Sgt P.M.Gawith	E/A damaged	Twente	0330~
85 Sqn	Havc	FC	P/O B.A.Burbridge	Ju88 damaged	Ipswich	0330~

2nd June 1942

Sqn			Pilot	Claim	Location	Time
64 Sqn	Spit	FC	Sgt H.V.Warnock	FW190 damaged	Le Crotoy area	0715~
			Sgt P.S.Hannan	FW190 damaged	Le Crotoy area	0715~
			F/L D.E.Kingaby	FW190 damaged	Le Crotoy	0715~
81 Sqn	Spit	FC	F/L L.G.Bedford	FW190 destroyed	Off Le Touquet	1100~
			F/L J.E.Walker	FW190 destroyed	10m off Le Touquet	1100~
122 Sqn	Spit	FC	Sgt R.A.G.Nadon	FW190 destroyed	Le Crotoy	0715~
			P/O W.T.E.Rolls	- shared -		
			S/L L.O.J.Prevot	FW190 damaged	Le Crotoy area	0715~
			S/L L.O.J.Prevot	FW190 prob.dest	Le Crotoy area	0715~
			P/O W.T.E.Rolls	FW190 damaged	Le Crotoy	0715~
122 Sqn	Spit	FC	S/L L.O.J.Prevot	FW190 damaged	Off Le Touquet	1100~
331 Sqn	Spit	FC	Sgt H.G.E.Grundt-Spang	FW190 prob.dest	5m W Le Touquet	1105
Hch Wg	Spit	FC	W/C R.P.R.Powell	FW190 prob.dest	W Le Touquet	0725~

2/3rd June 1942

Sqn			Pilot	Claim	Location	Time
1 Sqn	Hurr	FC	F/L K.Kuttelwascher	Do217 destroyed	5m off Dunkirk	0415~
3 Sqn	Hurr	FC	Sgt R.Inwood	Do217 destroyed	Eindhoven	0400~
3 Sqn	Hurr	FC	F/S D.J.Scott	Do217 damaged	Canterbury	0320~
29 Sqn	Beau	FC	F/L R.F.Robinson	Ju88 destroyed	E Foreness	0145
85 Sqn	Havc	FC	P/O B.A.Burbridge	Do217 prob.dest	Canterbury	0250
85 Sqn	Havc	FC	S/L H.R.Maud	Do217 destroyed	Off North Foreland	0235~

Two Hurricane night intruder pilots of 1 Squadron; the one-armed James MacLachlan and, far right, Karel Kuttelwascher. MacLachlan was credited with sixteen kills, but was lost on 29th June. Kuttelwascher was credited with eighteen and died post-war. Both made several claims on the night of 3rd June 1942

175 Sqn	Hurr	FC	F/L A H.Humphrey	FW190 damaged	Channel	0330~

3rd June 1942

242 Sqn	Spit	FC	F/S J.M.Portz	Ju88 prob.dest	E Fife Ness	1600~
316 Sqn	Spit	FC	Sgt T.Gora	FW190 destroyed	10m W Le Havre	1635
316 Sqn	Spit	FC	P/O M.Wyszkowski	FW190 prob.dest	3m W Le Havre	1635
401 Sqn	Spit	FC	F/S S.C.Cosburn F/L E.L.Neal	Caudron dest. - shared -	7-8m NE Le Treport	1220-
Ex Wg	Spit	FC	W/C A.Vasatko	Do215 prob.dest	10m NE Cherbourg	1500

3/4th June 1942

1 Sqn	Hurr	FC	F/L K.Kuttelwascher	Do217 destroyed	E St Andre	0345~
			F/L K.Kuttelwascher	Do217 damaged	St Andre	0345~
			F/L K.Kuttelwascher	He111 destroyed	St Andre	0345~
1 Sqn	Hurr	FC	S/L J.A.F.MacLachlan	Do217 destroyed	St Andre	0330~
			S/L J.A.F.MacLachlan	Do217 destroyed	St Andre	0330~
			S/L J.A.F.MacLachlan	Do217 damaged	St Andre	0330~
			S/L J.A.F.MacLachlan	Do217 damaged	St Andre	0330~
219 Sqn	Beau	FC	S/L A.Alexandrowicz	He111 destroyed	Off Isle of Wight	0135~
			S/L A.Alexandrowicz	Ju88 destroyed	Off Isle of Wight	0135~

4th June 1942

91 Sqn	Spit	FC	P/O Brady	He111 damaged	Off Hastings	0615~
118 Sqn	Spit	FC	S/L J.C.Carver	FW190 damaged	Off Cap Levy	1300~
			F/L R.A.Newbery	FW190 damaged	Off Cap Levy	1300~
			F/L R.A.Newbery	FW190 prob.dest	Off Cap Levy	1300~
340 Sqn	Spit	FC	Lt J.H.Schloesing	Ju88 damaged	Beachy Head-Berck	0830
501 Sqn	Spit	FC	Sgt J.K.Jerabek	FW190 destroyed	Cap Levy	1300~
			P/O R.C.Lynch F/L P.J.Stanbury	FW190 damaged - shared -	Cap Levy	1300~
610 Sqn	Spit	FC	F/L R.N.Courtney P/O P.R.Pabiot	Ju88 damaged - shared -	Dutch coast	1530~

163

4/5th June 1942

25 Sqn	Beau FC	F/L J.F.Inkster	E/A damaged	Off Whitby	0230~
141 Sqn	Beau FC	F/O J.G.Benson	Do217 damaged	25-30m E Tyne	0230~
141 Sqn	Beau FC	W/O R.C.Hamar	Do217 damaged	Seaham	0200~

5th June 1942

72 Sqn	Spit FC	F/L H.T.Armstrong	Bf109 destroyed	Abbeville	1545~
		P/O F.F.Colloredo -Mansfeld	Bf109F prob.dest	Somme estuary	1545~
		P/O O.L.Hardy	FW190 damaged	Abbeville	1545~
		Sgt E.S.Hughes	Bf109 destroyed	Abbeville	1545~
		Sgt B.J.Oliver	Bf109F damaged	Abbeville	1545~
		F/L E.N.Woods	Bf109 destroyed	Abbeville	1545~
131 Sqn	Spit FC	F/L R.H.Harries	FW190 prob.dest	N Le Havre	1530~
		F/L R.H.Harries	FW190 damaged	N Le Havre	1530~
		P/O K.A.H.Mason	FW190 prob.dest	N Le Havre	1530~
		P/O K.A.H.Mason	FW190 damaged	N Le Havre	1530~
		S/L M.G.F.Pedley	FW190 destroyed	N Le Havre	1530~
133 Sqn	Spit FC	S/L E.H.Thomas	Bf109F prob.dest	S Abbeville	1545
303 Sqn	Spit FC	F/L V.Bergman	FW190 damaged	W Ile de Batz	1510
		S/L F.Dolezal	FW190 damaged	W Ile de Batz	1510
		F/L E.A.Foit	FW190 damaged	W Ile de Batz	1510
		F/O B.M.Gladych	FW190 destroyed	10m NW Le Havre	1532
		F/S M.Petr	FW190 damaged	W Ile de Batz	1510
		P/O K.Samofal	FW190 prob.dest	N Le Havre	1535
		Sgt J.Stasik	FW190 destroyed	10m NW Le Havre	1532
		P/O M.Szelestowski	FW190 destroyed	10m NW Le Havre	1532
		F/S F.Trejtnar	FW190 damaged	W Ile de Batz	1510
316 Sqn	Spit FC	F/O W.S.Krol	FW190 destroyed	N Le Havre	1535
401 Sqn	Spit FC	F/S S.C.Cosburn	FW190 damaged	Abbeville	1540
		P/O J.K.Ferguson	FW190 damaged	Near Abbeville	1535
		F/S D R.Morrison	FW190 damaged	Abbeville	1545
		F/S D.R.Morrison*	FW190 destroyed	Abbeville	1534

* Shared with Biggin Hill.

BH Wg	Spit FC	W/C J.Rankin*	W190 destroyed - shared -	Abbeville	1534

* Shared with 401 Squadron.

		W/C J.Rankin	FW190 prob.dest	Abbeville area	1540

Graham Robertson of 402 Squadron, here showing his first 'victory swastika' in 1941, went on to claim four solo kills and finally commanded 411 Squadron. On 8th June he claimed strikes on an FW190 near St Omer.

6/7th June 1942

3 Sqn	Hurr	FC	Sgt P.M.Gawith	E/A destroyed	Eindhoven	0140~
29 Sqn	Beau	FC	S/L J.R.D.Braham	Do217 destroyed	15m E Sandwich	0300~
29 Sqn	Beau	FC	W/C E.L.Colbeck-Welch	Do217 prob.dest	Canterbury	0145~
600 Sqn	Beau	FC	P/O A.B.Harvey	He111 destroyed	Off St Eval	2315

8th June 1942

121 Sqn	Spit	FC	P/O J.B.Mahon	FW190 destroyed	St Omer area	1330
			P/O J.B.Mahon	FW190 destroyed	St Omer area	1330
			F/L J.J.Mooney	FW190 destroyed	St Omer area	1330
			F/L J.J.Mooney	FW190 destroyed	St Omer area	1330
			P/O J.G.Durkin	FW190 damaged	Mardyck	1340~
402 Sqn	Spit	FC	F/L N.H.Bretz	FW190 damaged	St Omer	1345
			P/O W.Q.Dewar	FW190 damaged	St Omer	1345
			S/L R.E.E.Morrow	FW190 damaged	St Omer	1345
			P/O G.D.Robertson	FW190 damaged	St Omer	1345
602 Sqn	Spit	FC	F/L E.W.P.Bocock	FW190 damaged	2-3m SE St Omer	1345~
			S/L B.E.Finucane	FW190 prob.dest	St Omer	1345~
			Sgt W.N.J.Loud	FW190 damaged	7m N St Omer	1345~
			F/L J.B.Niven	FW190 prob.dest	SE St Omer	1345~
611 Sqn	Spit	FC	P/O M.Graham	FW190 damaged	St Omer	1345~
			S/L D.H.Watkins	FW190 damaged	N St Omer	1345~

8/9th June 1942

219 Sqn Beau FC	S/L J.G.Topham	Ju88 destroyed	N Bembridge	0100~

9th June 1942

131 Sqn Spit FC	P/O K.A.H.Mason	Bf109 destroyed	Off Selsey Bill	2135~

10th June 1942

41 Sqn Spit FC	P/O T.R.Poynton	FW190 destroyed	Off St Catherines Pt	0715
310 Sqn Spit FC	Sgt K.Janata	FW190 prob.dest	Channel N Lannion	1411
	F/S M.Petr	FW190 destroyed	Channel N Lannion	1411
	F/S L.Strom	FW190 destroyed	Channel N Lannion	1411
	F/S F.Trejtnar	FW190 destroyed	Channel N Lannion	1411
	F/S F.Trejtnar	FW190 damaged	Channel N Lannion	1411
313 Sqn Spit FC	F/L K.Kasel	FW190 damaged	Channel N Lannion	1411
	Sgt V.Prerest	FW190 damaged	Channel N Lannion	1411

10/11th June 1942

175 Sqn Hurr FC	F/S R.A.Peters	Ju88 destroyed	S Portland	2255~
	F/S R.A.Peters	Ju88 prob.dest	S Portland	2255~
219 Sqn Beau FC	S/L A.Alexandrowicz	Do217 destroyed	St Catherines Point	0100~

11th June 1942

340 Sqn Spit FC	Sgt M.Bouguen	FW190 damaged	N Cherbourg	1430~
	Lt R.G.O.J.Mouchotte	FW190 damaged	N Cherbourg	1430~
411 Sqn Spit FC	F/S J.R.Mowbray	Ju88 destroyed	42m E Spurn Head	0712
	F/S S.A.Taylor	- shared -		

13/14th June 1942

600 Sqn Beau FC	Sgt J.Boyd	He111 prob.dest	Bude Bay	2321

14th June 1942

MSFU Hurr FC	P/O A.V.Sanders	FW200 damaged	Inward from Gibralter	1341

15/16th June 1942

FIU Beau FC	W/C D.R.Evans	Do217 destroyed	Off Littlehampton	0100~

16th June 1942

310 Sqn Spit FC	Sgt K.Janata (shared)	Ju88 damaged	20m E Berry Head	2133
	F/S F.Mlejnecky	- shared -		
	F/S L.Srom (shared)	Ju88 damaged	20m E Berry Head	2133

16/17th June 1942

604 Sqn Beau FC	P/O B.R.Keele	He111 damaged	N Swanage	0100~

Far Right: Flight Lieutenant H.C.F.Bowman of 129 Squadron claimed his fourth victory on 20th June. He was killed on 28th July in combat with JG 2 after being seen to destroy another FW190. Right: Squadron Leader N.H.Bretz who, as a Flight Commander with 402 Squadron, claimed an FW190 damaged

17th June 1942

91 Sqn	Spit	FC	F/L F.H.Silk	Ju88 damaged	Channel	2150~
			Sgt M.K.Eldrid	- shared -		
118 Sqn	Spit	FC	F/L R.A.Newbery	FW190 damaged	Off Barfleur	1100~
			F/O R.Claude	- shared -		

19th June 1942

222 Sqn	Spit	FC	F/L J.R.C.Kilian	FW190 destroyed	Knocke	1120~
			Sgt F.Ogden*	FW190 destroyed	15m N Ostend	1120

* *Shared with North Weald Wing.*

			P/O R.Seed	FW190 damaged	Belgian coast	1120~
331 Sqn	Spit	FC	Lt K.Birksted	FW190 destroyed	Flushing	1115
			Lt K.Birksted	FW190 damaged	Flushing	1115
			Sgt F.Cleve	FW190 destroyed	Flushing	1115
			Lt A.C.Gerup	FW190 destroyed	NW Flushing	1115
			Sgt S.Heglund	FW190 damaged	NW Flushing	1115
			Capt H.O.Mehre	FW190 damaged	4-5m off Knocke	1105-25
			Sgt H.Soggnes	FW190 damaged	Knocke	1115
NW Wg	Spit	FC	W/C F.D.S.Scott-Malden*	FW190 destroyed	15m N Ostend	1120

* *Shared with 222 Squadron.*

20th June 1942

118 Sqn	Spit	FC	Sgt T.J.De Courcey	FW190 damaged	French coast	1550~
129 Sqn	Spit	FC	F/L H.C.F.Bowman	FW190 destroyed	35m S Beachy Head	1545
			F/S E.T.Hiskens	FW190 damaged	35m S Beachy Head	1550
			P/O J.B.Shillitoe	FW190 destroyed	35m S Beachy Head	1555
			F/L F.W.Vancl	FW190 destroyed	N Le Havre	1545~
137 Sqn	Whir	FC	F/S Ashton	Do217 damaged	Off Yarmouth	2200~
			W/O Mercer	- shared -		
501 Sqn	Spit	FC	P/O J.A.G.Jackson	FW190 prob.dest	St Omer	1550~
611 Sqn	Spit	FC	P/O T.Felc (shared)	FW190 prob.dest	Le Havre	1535~

			P/O M.Graham	FW190 destroyed	Le Havre	1535~
			Sgt B.M.L.Taylor	- shared -		
72 Sqn	Spit	FC	P/O R.J.H.Robertson	FW190 damaged	Hardelot-St Omer	1550~
Ken Wg	Spit	FC	W/C E.P.Wells	FW190 destroyed	20m N Le Havre	1535

21st June 1942

| 234 Sqn | Spit | FC | F/L E.D.Glaser | Bf110 destroyed | S Dodman Point | 2120 |
| | | | P/O W.F.Webster | - shared - | | |

21/22nd June 1942

1 Sqn	Hurr	FC	F/L K.Kuttelwascher	Ju88 destroyed	St Andre	0300~
			F/L K.Kuttelwascher	Ju88 damaged	St Andre	0300~
1 Sqn	Hurr	FC	F/S G.S.M.Pearson	E/A damaged	Evreux	0315~
3 Sqn	Hurr	FC	Sgt P.M.Gawith	He111 destroyed	Soesterburg	0330~
			Sgt P.M.Gawith	Do217 prob.dest	Zuider Zee	0330~
3 Sqn	Hurr	FC	Sgt J.R.Collins	E/A damaged	Eindhoven	0245
29 Sqn	Beau	FC	S/L Scott	He177 destroyed	Off Somme	0130
604 Sqn	Beau	FC	P/O R.J.Foster	He111 destroyed	Off Ventnor	0100

22nd June 1942

64 Sqn	Spit	FC	F/S G.A.Mason	FW190 damaged	Off Dunkirk	1210
			S/L W.G.G.D.Smith	FW190 prob.dest	Off Dunkirk	1210
610 Sqn	Spit	FC	P/O L.E.Hoken	Ju88 destroyed	E Yarmouth	2310~

23rd June 1942

19 Sqn	Spit	FC	P/O J.Henderson	FW190 prob.dest	Off Start Point	1935~
			S/L P.B.G.Davies	FW190 damaged	7m E Berry Head	1935~
310 Sqn	Spit	FC	F/L E.A.Foit	FW190 destroyed	E Ile de Batz	1910-15
313 Sqn	Spit	FC	S/L K.Mrazek	FW190 damaged	NE Ile de Batz	1905-10
			P/O J.Prihoda	FW190 destroyed	NE Ile de Batz	1905-10
Ex Wg	Spit	FC	W/C A.Vasatko*	FW190 destroyed	8m E Start Point	1935

* Collided and MIA.

23/24th June 1942

3 Sqn	Hurr	FC	P/O B.H.Hay	Ju88 destroyed	Ijmuiden	0230~
			P/O B.H.Hay	Ju88 destroyed	Ijmuiden	0230~
68 Sqn	Beau	FC	P/O W.J.Gough	Do217 destroyed	East coast	0014

24/25th June 1942

| 25 Sqn | Beau | FC | P/O A.M.Hill | Do217 destroyed | Off Humber | 0100~ |
| 68 Sqn | Beau | FC | P/O P.H.Cleaver | Do217 destroyed | Wash | 0030~ |

On 23rd June Wing Commander Alois Vasatko,leading the Exeter Wing, collided with an FW190 and was killed. Following this action Oberleutnant Armin Faber (above inset) of JG 2 landed his FW190 at Pembrey after shooting down two Spitfires and becoming lost.

151 Sqn	Mosq FC	S/L D.F.W.Darling	Do217 damaged	Hammonds Knoll	0100~
151 Sqn	Mosq FC	W/C I.S.Smith	Do217 destroyed	Off Gt Yarmouth	0030~
		W/C I.S.Smith	Do217 destroyed	Off Gt Yarmouth	0030~
		W/C I.S.Smith	He111 prob.dest	Off Gt Yarmouth	0030~
151 Sqn	Mosq FC	P/O J.A.Wain	He111 destroyed	Off Norfolk coast	0030~

25th June 1942

303 Sqn	Spit FC	F/O B.M.Gladych	Ju88 destroyed	35m E Grimsby	0550
		F/O O.Sobiecki	- shared -		

26th June 1942

602 Sqn	Spit FC	F/L E.W.P.Bocock	FW190 damaged	30m N Cap d'Antifer	1745~
		S/L P.M.Brothers	FW190 damaged	N Etretat	1745~
		S/L P.M.Brothers	FW190 damaged	N Etretat	1745~
		F/S J.S.Fifield	FW190 prob.dest	N Etretat	1745~
		Sgt B.A.Schaefer	FW190 damaged	N Etretat	1745~
		Sgt A.Strudwick	FW190 destroyed	N Etretat	1745~

26/27th June 1942

29 Sqn	Beau FC	P/O G.Pepper	He111 destroyed	40m nE Foreness	0300~
151 Sqn	Mosq FC	F/L D.G.Moody	Do217 destroyed	Off Norfolk coast	0235~
151 Sqn	Deft FC	F/L C.Robertson	Do217 damaged	Off Norfolk coast	0245~
		F/L C.Robertson	Do217 damaged	Off Norfolk coast	0245~
610 Sqn	Spit FC	S/L G.S.K.Haywood	Ju88 destroyed	Off Happisburgh	0245~

27th June 1942

125 Sqn	Beau FC	S/L F.D.Hughes	Ju88 destroyed	Off Hook Head	0933
133 Sqn	Spit FC	F/L D.J.M.Blakeslee	Ju88 damaged	Dungeness-Boulogne	0715

27/28th June 1942

87 Sqn	Hurr FC	P/O R.J.McNair	E/A damaged	Dinant	0235
247 Sqn	Hurr FC	F/L Gray	Do217 destroyed	Lannion	0315~
307 Sqn	Beau FC	F/O K.Rach	Do217 destroyed	30m ESE Exeter	0129
307 Sqn	Beau FC	F/O G.K.Ranoszek	Do217 damaged	Nr Weston-S-Mare	0330~
307 Sqn	Beau FC	Sgt E.Wojczynski	Do217 damaged	20m S Seaton	0210

28/29th June 1942

1 Sqn	Hurr FC	F/L K.Kuttelwascher	Do217 destroyed	Trevieres, W Bayeux	0330~
264 Sqn	Mosq FC	F/O A.J.Hodgkinson	Do217 damaged	Off Portland	0215~
307 Sqn	Beau FC	F/S B.Turzanski	Do217 destroyed	Off Exmouth	0230~

29th June 1942

64 Sqn	Spit FC	Sgt J.K.Stewart	FW190 damaged	Hazebrouck	1645~
124 Sqn	Spit FC	P/O M.P.Kilburn	FW190 damaged	Calais	2145~
133 Sqn	Spit FC	F/L D.J.M.Blakeslee	Ju88 damaged	Dungeness-Boulogne	0715
222 Sqn	Spit FC	P/O D.H.Evans	FW190 damaged	Gravelines	1700~
		Sgt L.F.Foster	- shared -		
		2/Lt K.G.Kuhlmann	- shared -		
		P/O R.Wood	- shared -		
		Sgt F.Ogden*	FW190 destroyed	5m N Gravelines	1700

Shared with North Weald Wing.

		Sgt F.Ogden	FW190 damaged	Gravelines	1700~
331 Sqn	Spit FC	2/Lt M.Y.Gran	FW190 damaged	St Omer	u/k
		Capt H.O.Mehre	FW190 damaged	St Omer	u/k
350 Sqn	Spit FC	P/O H.A.Picard	FW190 destroyed	Off Sangatte	1640
		P/O H.A.Picard	FW190 destroyed	Off Sangatte	1650
NW Wg	Spit FC	W/C F.D.S.Scott-Malden*	FW190 destroyed	5m N Gravelines	1700

Shared with 222 Squadron.

1/2nd July 1942

1 Sqn	Hurr FC	Sgt J RCampbell	Do217 damaged	Rennes	0400~
1 Sqn	Hurr FC	F/L K.Kuttelwascher	Do217 destroyed	5m N Dinard	0400~
		F/L K.Kuttelwascher	Do217 destroyed	5m N Dinard	0400~
		F/L K.Kuttelwascher	Do217 damaged	N Dinard	0400~
1 Sqn	Hurr FC	Sgt G.S.M.Pearson	Do217 damaged	Rennes	0345~
23 Sqn	Bost FC	Sgt R.E.Wakeford	E/A damaged	Evreux	0350~
125 Sqn	Deft FC	W/C E.G.Barwell	Do17 damaged	nr Cardiff	u/k
307 Sqn	Beau FC	P/O S.Podgorski	Do217 damaged	5m NE Exeter	0233

The only two claims on 27th June were made by Don Blakeslee of 133 Squadron for a Ju88 damaged, and by Desmond Hughes of 125 Squadron, who shot down a Ju88 of Wekusta 51 off the Irish coast. Blakeslee would claim three victories with the RAF and another eleven with the USAAF. (ww2images.com). Hughes, initially a Defiant pilot with 264 Squadron, would claim a total of eighteen solo kills and would win a DSO and three DFCs.

3rd July 1942

303 Sqn	Spit	FC	F/O T.Kolecki	Ju88 destroyed	E Lincoln	2025
			F/S M.Popek	- shared -		
			Sgt A.Rokitnicki	- shared -		
			F/S K.Wunsche	- shared -		
			F/O T.Kolecki	Ju88 destroyed	E Lincoln	2025
			F/S M.Popek	- shared -		
			Sgt A.Rokitnicki	- shared -		
			F/S K.Wunsche	- shared -		

5/6th July 1942

600 Sqn	Beau	FC	F/S C.Spry	He111 prob.dest	S Scilly Isles	0405

6th July 1942

137 Sqn	Whir	FC	F/L L.H.Bartlett	Ju88 damaged	Off Yarmouth	1025~
313 Sqn	Spit	FC	P/O O.Kucera*	Ju88 damaged	S Lyme Regis	2130
			Sgt K.Valasek	- shared -		

* Also shared with 421 Squadron.

421 Sqn	Spit	FC	F/L G.D.Robertson	Bf109F damaged	Near Start Point	1125
421 Sqn	Spit	FC	F/L G.D.Robertson*	Ju88 damaged	S Lyme Regis	2130

* Shared with 313 Squadron.

6/7th July 1942

23 Sqn	Mosq	FC	W/C B.R.O'B.Hoare	Do217 destroyed	Near Chartres	0140~
219 Sqn	Beau	FC	S/L J.G.Topham	Do217 destroyed	S Amble	0140~
219 Sqn	Beau	FC	F/L J.E.Willson	Do217 damaged	Off Seaham	0330~

7/8th July 1942

406 Sqn	Beau	FC	P/O R.H.Harrison	Do217 prob.dest	Middlesborough	0130
			P/O R.H.Harrison	Do217 destroyed	30m SE Hartlepool	0200

406 Sqn	Beau FC	P/O A.G.Lawrence	He111 destroyed	Off Hartlepool	0130
406 Sqn	Beau FC	W/C D.G.Morris	Do217 destroyed	70m E Tyne	0205
406 Sqn	Beau FC	W/C G.G.Stockdale	Do217 destroyed	130m E Scarborough	0225
600 Sqn	Beau FC	P/O A.B.Harvey	He111 prob.dest	S Lizard	0342

8th July 1942

121 Sqn	Spit FC	P/O G.O.Halsey Sgt A.C.Stanhope	Ju88 damaged - shared -	Off Griz Nez	0740
1449 Flt	Hurr FC	P/O B.S.Thompson	Ju88 damaged	SE Scilly Isles	2150~

8/9th July 1942

23 Sqn	Mosq FC	S/L K.H.Salusbury-Hughes	Do217 destroyed	Near Etampes	0245~
		S/L K.H.Salusbury-Hughes	He111 destroyed	Near Evreux	0245~

9th July 1942

610 Sqn	Spit FC	W/O W.M.Jackson Sgt J.G.Leach	Ju88 damaged - shared -	E Spurn Head	0618

11/12th July 1942

600 Sqn	Beau FC	P/O W.G.H.King	Do217 destroyed	Off Lands End	0040

12th July 1942

310 Sqn	Spit FC	Sgt K.Pernicka (shared) F/S L.Srom	Ju88 destroyed - shared -	55m off Bolt Head	2127

12/13th July 1942

157 Sqn	Mosq FC	P/O W.Taylor	Do217 damaged	Off Orfordness	u/k

13th July 1942

72 Sqn	Spit FC	Sgt A.R.Menzies	FW190 damaged	Abbeville	1455~
616 Sqn	Spit FC	F/L F.A.O.Gaze	FW190 prob.dest	Abbeville	1455~

15th July 1942

66 Sqn	Spit FC	S/L R.D.Yule P/O K.M.Barclay P/O B.F.G.Darbey F/L E.P.F.L.T.Magruder Lt V.R.E.Nissen	FW190 destroyed - shared - - shared - - shared - - shared -	20m N Pte de Barfleur	0945
		S/L R.D.Yule P/O K.M.Barclay P/O B.F.G.Darbey F/L E.P.F.L.T.Magruder Lt V.R.E.Nissen	FW190 damaged - shared - - shared - - shared - - shared -	20m N Pte de Barfleur	0945
317 Sqn	Spit FC	F/O S.Lukaszewicz	FW190 damaged	Off Boulogne	1420
		F/O J.Mencel F/O T.Szymankiewicz	FW190 destroyed - shared -	Off Boulogne	1420

172

On 13th July, Flight Lieutenant Tony Gaze of 616 Squadron, on a sweep near Abbeville, sighted a lone FW190 climbing towards his squadron. He peeled off and attacked, claiming a 'probable'. In fact, this aircraft, from 4./JG 26, went into the ground at high speed, killing Oberfeldwebel Helmut Ufer.

		P/O J.Zbrozek	FW190 prob.dest	Off Boulogne	1420
402 Sqn	Spit	FC	P/O J.C.Bayly	FW190 destroyed	Le Touquet-Dover	1515
			F/S J.C.Hughes	- shared -		
			F/S N.A.Keene	- shared -		
			F/L D.G.Malloy	- shared -		
			S/L R.E.E.Morrow	- shared -		
			F/L N.B.Trask	- shared -		

15/16th July 1942

3 Sqn	Hurr	FC	Sgt R.Inwood	E/A damaged	Eindhoven	0245~
29 Sqn	Beau	FC	P/O G.Pepper	Ju88 prob.dest	5m E Thamesmouth	0010~

16th July 1942

421 Sqn	Spit	FC	Sgt R.Clasper	Ju88 damaged	30m W Milford Haven	2110
			P/O C.B.Handley	- shared -		
1449 Flt	Hurr	FC	Sgt D.H.Rogers	Ju88 damaged	40m SW Scilly Isles	1910~
			P/O B.S.Thompson	- shared -		

17th July 1942

71 Sqn	Spit	FC	P/O J.J.Lynch	Ju88 destroyed	8m E Orfordness	0715
			P/O L.S.Nomis	- shared -		
412 Sqn	Spit	FC	F/S F.H.Richards	Ju88 destroyed	SE St Catherines Pt	0630
			F/S H.V.Thompson	Ju88 destroyed	SE St Catherines Pt	0630

18th July 1942

340 Sqn	Spit	FC	S/Lt M.Albert	FW190 damaged	5m S Worthing	0625
416 Sqn	Spit	FC	F/L P.L.I.Archer	Do217 destroyed	15m E Orfordness	1430
616 Sqn	Spit	FC	F/L F.A.O.Gaze	FW190 destroyed	Off Le Touquet	0900~
			F/L F.A.O.Gaze	FW190 damaged	Off Le Touquet	0900~

19th July 1942

71 Sqn	Spit	FC	P/O J.F.Helgason	FW190 destroyed	Dunkirk-Nieuport	1340

		P/O J.J.Lynch		- shared -		
121 Sqn	Spit	FC	F/L S.R.Edner	FW190 damaged	Off Dunkirk-Nieuport	1315
222 Sqn	Spit	FC	Sgt F.Ogden	FW190 damaged	Channel	1600
411 Sqn	Spit	FC	F/L R.W.McNair	Do217 damaged	15m E Skegness	1615

21/22nd July 1942

151 Sqn	Mosq	FC P/O G.Fisher		Do217 destroyed	50m E Humber	0100

22/23rd July 1942

68 Sqn	Beau	FC	S/L G.L.Howden	Do217 damaged	Off Spurn Head	0500~
247 Sqn	Hurr	FC	S/Lt C.E.Helies	Ju88 destroyed	E Start Point	2330~

23/24th July 1942

68 Sqn	Beau	FC	Sgt J.C.Truscott	Do217 destroyed	E Mablethorpe	2308
68 Sqn	Beau	FC	S/L V.Vesely	He177 destroyed	North Sea	0130~
68 Sqn	Beau	FC	W/C J.W.M.Aitken	Ju88 destroyed	E Spurn Head	2330~
			W/C J.W.M.Aitken	Do217 destroyed	E Spurn Head	2330~
68 Sqn	Beau	FC	W/O L.Bobek	Do217 destroyed	Off Lowestoft	2324
406 Sqn	Beau	FC	P/O A.G.Lawrence	Ju88 destroyed	Hartlepool	u/k
409 Sqn	Beau	FC	W/O H.Brooks	Do217 prob.dest	Off Lincs coast	2355~
409 Sqn	Beau	FC	F/L E.L.McMillan	Do217 damaged	Lincs Coast	0145
			F/L E.L.McMillan*	Do217 destroyed	Holbeach	0008

* Shared with 486 Squadron.

486 Sqn	Typh	FC	F/L H.N.Sweetman*	Do217 destroyed	Holbeach	0008

* Shared with 409 Squadron.

24th July 1942

308 Sqn	Spit	FC	P/O A.T.Habela	Ju88 damaged	60m Off Withernsea	1830
			F/O J.K.Zuromaski	- shared -		

25th July 1942

91 Sqn	Spit	FC	F/L R.L.Spurdle	Bf109F destroyed	Calais	0840~
137 Sqn	Hurr	FC	P/O J.E.McLure	Ju88 destroyed	E Yarmouth	1950~
			W/O R.L.Smith	- shared -		
234 Sqn	Spit	FC	F/L E.D.Glaser	Ju88 destroyed	Off Hartland Point	2135
			Sgt W.T.Hinds	- shared -		

25/26th July 1942

3 Sqn	Hurr	FC	Sgt R.Inwood	Ju88 damaged	Haamstede	0215~
3 Sqn	Hurr	FC	F/S D.J.Scott	Ju88 destroyed	Noordwijk	0330~
23 Sqn	Mosq	FC	F/O F B.McCullach	He111 destroyed	Bretigny	0130~
219 Sqn	Beau	FC	S/L J.G.Topham	Do217 destroyed	E Blythe	0230~

Right: Paddy Finucane's luck ran out on 15th July when he was forced to ditch in the Channel. The Spitfire sank immediately, taking the pilot down. Far Right: Harvey Sweetman, a New Zealander with 486 Squadron shared a night victory with a 409 Squadron Beaufighter crew on 23/24th July. He would later become an accomplished flying-bomb killer during 1944 and would survive the war, his last operational post being CO of 3 Squadron.

S/L J.G.Topham		Do217 destroyed	E Blythe	0230~

26th July 1942

72 Sqn	Spit FC	F/L H.T.Armstrong	FW190 destroyed	W Calais	1345~
		P/O D.G.S.R.Cox	FW190 damaged	W Calais	1345~
		P/O R.C.Kitchen	FW190 destroyed	W Calais	1345~
		S/L R.W.Oxspring DFC	FW190 prob.dest	W Calais	1345~
91 Sqn	Spit FC	F/O E.F.Clarkson	FW190 damaged	Off Dungeness	1340~
		F/L R.L.Spurdle	FW190 destroyed	5-10m S Dungeness	1340
		F/L R.L.Spurdle	FW190 damaged	5-10m S Dungeness	1340~
131 Sqn	Spit FC	S/L M.G.F.Pedley	FW190 damaged	N Calais	1345
222 Sqn	Spit FC	Sgt D.G.Mercer	FW190 damaged	Off Gravelines	1710~
		Sgt D.C.Mercer	FW190 damaged	Off Gravelines	1700~
302 Sqn	Spit FC	S/L J.Kowalski	FW190 destroyed	8-12m N Calais	1345
		Sgt H.Mikusek	FW190 damaged	Desvres	1345
		F/O A.Rodziewicz	FW190 destroyed	3-5m N Mardyck	1345
		P/O M.Wedzik	FW190 damaged	10m N Calais	1345
317 Sqn	Spit FC	P/O S.Brzeski	FW190 prob.dest	5m N Calais	1340-45
		Sgt W.Grobelny	FW190 damaged	2m N Calais	1340-45
401 Sqn	Spit FC	P/O D.R.Morrison	FW190 damaged	Griz Nez	1345
		F/L J.Witham	FW190 damaged	Griz Nez	1345
412 Sqn	Spit FC	P/O G.G.Davidson	FW190 prob.dest	NE Abbeville/Drucat	1340~
		F/L F.E.Green	FW190 destroyed	NE Abbeville/Drucat	1330
		F/L F.E.Green	FW190 damaged	NE Abbeville/Drucat	1340
		P/O K.I.Robb	FW190 damaged	NE Abbeville/Drucat	1340~
		P/O K.I.Robb	FW190 damaged	NE Abbeville/Drucat	1340~
Ntht Wg	Spit FC	W/C S.Janus	FW190 damaged	NE Calais	1345

175

27th July 1942

421 Sqn Spit	FC	Sgt C.D.Myers	Ju88 destroyed	15-20m W St Govans Light	1855
		Sgt J.A.Omand	- shared -		

27/28th July 1942

3 Sqn	Hurr FC	Sgt R.Inwood	Ju88 destroyed	Noordwijk	0400~
		Sgt R.Inwood	He111 prob.dest	Noordwijk	0400~
3 Sqn	Hurr FC	F/L D.J.Scott	Do217 damaged	Schouwen Island	0400~
3 Sqn	Hurr FC	F/S V.Smith	Ju88 damaged	Schipol	0415~
29 Sqn	Beau FC	P/O S.Handley	He111 prob.dest	N Dunkirk	0400~
29 Sqn	Beau FC	S/L S.P.Richards	He111 destroyed	NE Foreness	0100~
68 Sqn	Beau FC	P/O W.E.Welch	Do217 destroyed	Off Norfolk coast	0115~
		P/O W.E.Welch	Do217 damaged	Off Norfolk coast	0115~
68 Sqn	Beau FC	W/O L.Bobek	Do217 destroyed	Off Norfolk coast	0100~
68 Sqn	Beau FC	W/O L.Bobek	Do217 prob.dest	Off Norfolk coast	0100~
125 Sqn	Beau FC	F/L A.H.Drummond	He111 damaged	NW Aberporth	0250~
125 Sqn	Beau FC	P/O G.E.Jameson	He111 destroyed	NW The Smalls	0208
125 Sqn	Beau FC	P/O D.R.McLachlin	He111 destroyed	Cenmoes	0200~
		P/O D.R.McLachlin	He111 destroyed	15 S Cenmoes Pt	0330~
151 Sqn	Mosq	FC P/O E.A.Fielding	Do217 destroyed	E Cromer	0130~
151 Sqn	Mosq	FC S/L D.A.Pennington	Do217 destroyed	Off Norfolk coast	0055
157 Sqn	Mosq	FC S/L G.Ashfield	He111 destroyed	East Anglia	u/k
157 Sqn	Mosq	FC F/L A.S.Worthington	Do217 damaged	Off Southwold	0140
253 Sqn	Hurr FC	F/L J.L.W.Ellacombe*	Do217 prob.dest	Near Highbaldstow	0115~

* Shared with 1459 Flight.

255 Sqn	Beau FC	F/S P.S.Kendall	He111 damaged	Near Birmingham	0200~
287 Sqn	Deft FC	F/O Russell	Ju88 prob.dest	Near Tring	0240
409 Sqn	Beau FC	W/O H.Brooks	Do217 damaged	Wash area	2315
600 Sqn	Beau FC	F/L J.Arnsby	He111 damaged	Off Scilly Isles	0015
600 Sqn	Beau FC	S/L P.B.Elwell	He111 destroyed	50m SSE Predannack	0145~
		S/L P.B.Elwell	He111 damaged	50m SSE Predannack	0145~
1459 Flt	Havc FC	S/L C.V.Winn*	Do217 prob.dest	Near Highbaldstow	0115~

* Shared with 253 Squadron.

28th July 1942

91 Sqn	Spit FC	F/L R.L.Spurdle	FW190 damaged	Dungeness	2020~
129 Sqn	Spit FC	F/L H.C.F.Bowman	FW190 destroyed	S Selsey	2110
130 Sqn	Spit FC	F/S R.P.M.Leblond	Ju88 destroyed	S Lizard	1030

Desmond Scott of 3 Squadron (left) and Bob Spurdle of 91 were both New Zealanders and successful 'lone wolf' pilots. Scott operated as a night intruder pilot, ending the war as a highly decorated Group Captain (DSO, DFC, OBE) and five confirmed kills, while Spurdle ended as a Squadron Leader DFC* with at least ten confirmed, including two Japanese fighters in the Far East in 1943.

29th July 1942

137 Sqn	Hurr FC	F/S J.R.Rebbetoy	Ju88 destroyed	Happisburgh	2050
		Sgt L.O'Neill	- shared -		
412 Sqn	Spit FC	F/L F.E.Green	FW190 destroyed	10m S Brighton	1955

29/30th July 1942

25 Sqn	Beau FC	F/O A J.Picknett	Do217 damaged	S Humber	0300~
29 Sqn	Beau FC	P/O E.P.Heybroek	He111 damaged	SE Foreness	0300~
68 Sqn	Beau FC	F/O E.V.Raybould	Do217 destroyed	Near Clay	0200
125 Sqn	Beau FC	P/O W.V.Hall	He111 damaged	W The Smalls	0200~
151 Sqn	Mos FC	F/O A.I.McRitchie	Do217 destroyed	The Wash	0106
		F/O A.I.McRitchie	Do217E damaged	The Wash	0100~
253 Sqn	Hurr FC	Lt D.M.Beguin*	Do217 damaged	Off Mablethorpe	0200~

* Shared with 1459 Flight.

409 Sqn	Beau FC	W/C P.Y.Davoud	He111 prob.dest	8m NE Skegness	0127
		W/C P.Y.Davoud	Do217 damaged	Grantham	0151
456 Sqn	Beau FC	W/C E.C.Wolfe	He111 destroyed	3m SE Pwlheli	0137
604 Sqn	Beau FC	F/L W.Hoy	He111 destroyed	NW Scillies	1213
1459 Flt	Havc FC	Unknown crew*	Do217 damaged	Off Mablethorpe	0200~

* Shared with 253 Squadron.

30th July 1942

64 Sqn	Spit FC	F/L D.E.Kingaby	FW190 destroyed	5m W Boulogne	1230~
64 Sqn	Spit FC	S/L W.G.G.D.Smith	FW190 destroyed	St Omer	1915~
		S/L W.G.G.D.Smith Lt A.Austeen	FW190 destroyed - shared -	St Omer	1915~
		P/O J.K.Stewart	FW190 destroyed	St Omer	1915~
		F/O M.G.L.M.Donnet	FW190 destroyed	St Omer	1915~
121 Sqn	Spit FC	F/L W.J.Daley	FW190 damaged	Le Touquet	1225~
122 Sqn	Spit FC	F/L L.P.Griffith	FW190 damaged	St Omer	1915~
		S/L L.O.J.Prevot	FW190 destroyed	St Omer	1915~

177

154 Sqn	Spit FC	S/L D.C.Carlson	FW190 destroyed	5m N St Omer	1915~
		Sgt F.J.Flote	- shared -		
332 Sqn	Spit FC	Sgt M.Eriksen	FW190 destroyed	S Le Touquet	1225
		Sgt J.Loftsgaard	FW190 damaged	15-20m off Le Touquet	1235
340 Sqn	Spit FC	Sgt A.R.Moynet	FW190 prob.dest	10m NW St Omer	1915
350 Sqn	Spit FC	F/L Y.G.A.F.Du Monceau	Bf109F prob.dest	Mid-Channel	1925-30
		F/L Y.G.A.F. Du Monceau	Bf109F damaged	Mid-Channel	1925-30
		Sgt J.Ester	Bf109 destroyed	Dover Straits	1930
		P/O H.E.Marchal	- shared -		
616 Sqn	Spit FC	P/O R.G.Large	FW190 damaged	St Omer	1915~
Hch Wg	Spit FC	W/C D.O.Finlay	FW190 prob.dest	St Omer	1915~

30/31st July 1942

3 Sqn	Hurr FC	F/L D.J.Scott	Do217/Bf110 dam	Off Schouwen Island	u/k
23 Sqn	Mosq FC	W/C B.R.O'B.Hoare	E/A destroyed	Orleans	0245~
68 Sqn	Beau FC	F/O P.F.Allen	Ju88 destroyed	Off Yarmouth	0330~
		F/O P.F.Allen	Do217 prob.dest	Off Yarmouth	0330~
68 Sqn	Beau FC	P/O D.L.Ward	Do217 destroyed	Off Norfolk coast	0130~
85 Sqn	Havc FC	W/C G.L.Raphael	Ju88 damaged	Near Cambridge	0250~
157 Sqn	Mosq FC	F/L A.S.Worthington	Do217 damaged	SE Harwich	0100~
255 Sqn	Beau FC	F/O H.G.S.Wyrill	He111 damaged	Gloucester	u/k
264 Sqn	Mosq FC	S/L C.A.Cooke	Ju88 destroyed	Malvern Wells	0205
604 Sqn	Beau FC	P/O B.R.Keele	He111 destroyed	Preston, S Warmwell	0104
		P/O B.R.Keele	He111 destroyed	12m S Swanage	0030

31st July 1942

121 Sqn	Spit FC	P/O F.R.Boyles	Bf109F prob.dest	Off Berck	1500
		F/L S.R.Edner	Bf109F destroyed	Off Berck	1500
		F/L S.R.Edner	Bf109F destroyed	Off Berck	1500
		Sgt W.P.Kelly	Bf109F destroyed	Le Crotoy	1455
		S/L H.C.Kennard	Bf109F destroyed	Somme estuary	1520
		F/L J.B.Mahon	FW190 destroyed	Off Berck	1500
		F/L J.B.Mahon	FW190 destroyed	Off Berck	1500
133 Sqn	Spit FC	P/O W.H.Baker Jr	FW190 destroyed	Inland Le Crotoy	1450
		P/O E.D.Taylor	FW190 destroyed	8m off Le Crotoy	1455
		P/O E.D.Taylor	Bf109F damaged	8m off Le Crotoy	1455
222 Sqn	Spit FC	Sgt D.G.Mercer	Bf109F destroyed	Off Berck-sur-Mer	1500~
		F/L R.Barrett	FW190 damaged	Off Berck	1500~
		Sgt D.C.Mercer	Bf109F destroyed	Off Berck	1500~

The ill-fated Turbinlite Havoc with its nose-mounted searchlight and paired with a Hurricane for the 'kill' was not a great success. Right, Squadron leader L.O.J.Prevot of 122 Squadron claimed his third success on 30th July, but was then shot down. He evaded and returned, later commanding 65 and 197 Squadrons and rising to Wing Commander DFC.

331 Sqn	Spit	FC	2/Lt S.Heglund	FW190 damaged	Off Berck	1515
			Sgt N.K.Jorstad	FW190 damaged	Off Berck	1515
332 Sqn	Spit	FC	Sgt S.K.Liby	Bf109F destroyed	Mid Channel N Berck	1500
			Maj W.Mohr	FW190 damaged	Mid Channel N Berck	1455
			Sgt T.A.Waerner	FW190 destroyed	Mid Channel N Berck	1500

31st July/1st August 1942

68 Sqn	Beau	FC	W/O L.Bobek	Do217 destroyed	E Spurn Head	0330

1st August 1942

71 Sqn	Spit	FC	P/O J.A.Gray	FW190 destroyed	10-15m off Flushing	1505
			P/O R.S.Sprague	FW190 damaged	10-15m off Flushing	1505
412 Sqn	Spit	FC	P/O G.G.Davidson	FW190 destroyed	10-15m S Brighton	1000
			P/O G.G.Davidson	FW190 damaged	10-15m S Brighton	1010
412 Sqn	Spit	FC	P/O R.A.Ellis	FW190 damaged	8m SW Selsey Bill	2047
			P/O R.A.Ellis	FW190 damaged	8m SW Selsey Bill	2050

1/2nd August 1942

141 Sqn	Beau	FC	W/C F.W.Heycock	Ju88 prob.dest	S Selsey Bill	2300~

2nd August 1942

409 Sqn	Beau	FC	S/L W.A.Emmett	Do217 damaged	Spalding	1657
416 Sqn	Spit	FC	F/S T.C.Gates	Do217 destroyed	15-20m NE Martlesham Heath	1520
			P/O J.S.McKendy	Do217 destroyed	- shared -	
610 Sqn	Spit	FC	W/O W.M.Jackson	Do217 damaged	Off Winterton	1735
			P/O F.Musgrove	Do217 damaged	Off Winterton	1735

179

2/3rd August 1942

29 Sqn	Beau FC	S/L D.Parker	Do217 destroyed	N Ostend	0400~
85 Sqn	Havc FC	W/C G.L.Raphael	Ju88 destroyed	Off Dengle Flats	0300~
85 Sqn	Havc FC	S/L V.R.Snell	Ju88 damaged	Off Clacton	0400~
157 Sqn	Mosq FC	P/O E.Cave-Brown	Ju88 damaged	Off Southwold	0400~

3rd August 1942

68 Sqn	Beau FC	S/L G.L.Howden	Do217 damaged	Off Norfolk coast	1310~
91 Sqn	Spit FC	F/O E.F.Clarkson	Bf109 damaged	S Dungeness2	200~
		F/L R.L.Spurdle	Bf109 damaged	S Dover	2200~
406 Sqn	Beau FC	P/O R.H.Harrison	Do217 damaged	30m E Flamboro' Hd	1255
409 Sqn	Beau FC	S/L B.G.Miller	Do217 damaged	Off Yorkshire coast	1357
485 Sqn	Spit FC	P/O L.S.Black	Do217 destroyed	Near Wellingborough	1812

3/4th August 1942

68 Sqn	Beau FC	F/O P.F.Allen DFC	Do217 damaged	Off Norfolk coast	0430~

4th August 1942

64 Sqn	Spit FC	F/O M.G.L.M.Donnet	FW190 damaged	N Berck-sur-Mer	2100~
Hawkers Hurr —		Unknown pilot	Do217 damaged	S Cranwell	1730

4/5th August 1942

125 Sqn	Beau FC	P/O R.Bastow	He111 destroyed	Off Milford Haven	0330~
125 Sqn	Beau FC	P/O G.E.Jameson	He111 destroyed	Near Lundy Island	0209
307 Sqn	Beau FC	F/O G.K.Ranoszek	Ju88 destroyed	Off Start Point	0130
		F/O G.K.Ranoszek	Ju88 destroyed	6m S Kingsbridge	0147
307 Sqn	Beau FC	F/O S.Szablowski	Ju88 destroyed	50m S Bolt Head	0258
604 Sqn	Beau FC	F/S D.Fraser	Ju88 prob.dest	SW Portland	2330~
604 Sqn	Beau FC	P/O S.A.Spencer	E/A destroyed	S Swanage	0035

6/7th August 1942

68 Sqn	Beau FC	F/S J.Adam	Do217 prob.dest	SW Norwich	0100

7/8th August 1942

68 Sqn	Beau FC	F/O P.H.Cleaver	Do217 destroyed	Coningsby	0115

8th August 1942

91 Sqn	Spit FC	P/O R.M.Batten	Ju88 damaged	Dungeness	2150~
		P/O L.E.Mairs	- shared -		

8/9th August 1942

29 Sqn	Beau FC	P/O G.Pepper	He111 destroyed	10-12m S Dungeness	2240

Wing Commander Douglas 'Zulu' Morris, born in Wales but educated in South Africa, took his first operational command leading 406 Squadron, from its formation in May 1941 until August 1943. He ended the war as an Air Commodore, DSO, DFC CBE. His score is uncertain - at least four destroyed, possibly six. On 7/8th July 1942 he claimed a Do217, one of two Dorniers lost by Kampfgeschwader 2 this night. He is pictured here in late 1941. (ww2images.com)

9th August 1942

266 Sqn	Typh FC	P/O N.J.Lucas (shared)	Ju88 destroyed	50m off Cromer	2030~
		P/O I.M.Munro	- shared -		

9/10th August 1942

25 Sqn	Beau FC	S/L H.P.Pleasance	Do217 destroyed	2m E Hornsea	2330~
29 Sqn	Beau FC	S/L J.R.D.Braham	Do217 destroyed	40m NE NE Foreness	0010~
219 Sqn	Beau FC	S/L W.R.L.Beaumont	Do217 destroyed	Unknown	2315~

10/11th August 1942

23 Sqn	Mosq FC	S/L K.H.Salusbury-Hughes	Do217 destroyed	Beauvais	0215~

11th August 1942

610 Sqn	Spit FC	W/O W.M.Jackson	Ju88 damaged	Off Norfolk coast	1845
		Sgt E.S.Roberts	- shared -		

11/12th August 1942

25 Sqn	Beau FC	F/S H.L.Middlemast	Ju88 damaged	SE Hornsea	0230~
68 Sqn	Beau FC	F/O P.F.Allen	He111 destroyed	E Mablethorpe	0100~
141 Sqn	Beau FC	P/O F.H.Street	He111 damaged	W Beach Head	2300~
253 Sqn	Hurr FC	F/S L.McCarthy*	E/A damaged	Goole	0100~
* Shared with 1459 Flight.					
409 Sqn	Beau FC	F/S A,E.Thomas	Do217 damaged	Lincoln	0130
1459 Flt	Havc FC	S/L Winn*	E/A damaged	Goole	0100
* Shared with 253 Squadron.					

12/13th August 1942

85 Sqn	Havc FC	Sgt A.W.Sullivan*	Ju88 destroyed	Colchester	0235
* Shared with AA Command.					

13th August 1942

266 Sqn	Typh FC	F/L A.C.Johnston	Me210 destroyed	E Cromer	1936

14th August 1942

131 Sqn	Spit FC	F/L R.H.Harries	FW190 damaged	S Selsey	0600
141 Sqn	Beau FC	F/L S.S.Duff	Ju88 destroyed	E St Albans Head	1945
315 Sqn	Spit FC	Sgt J.Malec	Ju88 damaged	NW Barrow	1205

15/16th August 1942

406 Sqn	Beau FC	F/L D.C.Furse	E/A damaged	20m E Newcastle	2259

16/17th August 1942

68 Sqn	Beau FC	F/L W.D.Winward	Do217 damaged	E Coltishall	u/k

17th August 1942

64 Sqn	Spit FC	F/L M.G.L.M.Donnet	FW190 damaged	Yvetot	1800~
		F/L D.E.Kingaby	FW190 damaged	10-12m S Dieppe	1800~
		P/O J.K.Stewart	FW190 prob.dest	Yvetot	1800~
401 Sqn	Spit FC	Sgt L.J.Armstrong	FW190 prob.dest	Somme Estuary	1800
		F/S E.L.Gimbel	FW190 prob.dest	10m W Rouen	1750
		S/L K.L.B.Hodson	FW190 damaged	10m W Rouen	1750
		P/O G.B.Murray	FW190 destroyed	Coast, Somme Estuary	1800
		F/L J.Witham	- Shared -		
		F/L R.D.Reesor	FW190 prob.dest	Somme Estuary	1800
		P/O H.A.Westhaver	FW190 prob.dest	Somme Estuary	1800
		F/S E.L.Gimbel	- Shared -		
402 Sqn	Spit FC	Sgt H.P.Fuller	FW190 damaged	10m SW Rouen	1800

17/18th August 1942

141 Sqn	Beau FC	P/O F.H.Street	Do217 destroyed	50m S Ford	2350~
418 Sqn	Bost FC	S/L G.L.Caldwell	Ju88 destroyed	Criel	0105

18th August 1942

129 Sqn	Spit FC	P/O E.S.Hall	He115 prob.dest	10-15m off Cherbourg	1010
		Whole Squadron	He59 destroyed	10-15m off Cherbourg	1010
133 Sqn	Spit FC	F/L D.J.M.Blakeslee	FW190 destroyed	Sangatte	1345
137 Sqn	Whir FC	P/O J.F.Luing	Ju88 damaged	30m E Yarmouth	2100
		Sgt L.O'Neill	- Shared -		
602 Sqn	Spit FC	S/L P.M.Brothers	FW190 damaged	Griz Nez	1400~

452 Squadron in 1942. Standing 4th from left is Bill Crawford-Compton, kneeling 2nd from left is Johnny Checketts and standing, with cap, is 'Hawkeye' Wells, the Wing Leader.

Chapter Seven

Dieppe, Jabos and the

Baedekker Raids

19th August - 31st December 1942

It was apparent to the Allies that, at some time in the future, an invasion of France must surely be attempted. There were two overriding criteria to be met before this could be attempted. Firstly, the Allied fighter forces must establish sufficient air superiority over the beachhead to protect the warships, transports, landingcraft and troops. Second, there must be a deep water anchorage for succeeding troops and equipment to be landed in support. At first sight, this seemed to require an established port. Plans were laid for a 'dress rehearsal', the harbour selected was Dieppe, the code name was *Operation Jubilee* and the date was set as 19th August 1942. The result was, for the mainly Canadian troops, a disaster.

Landed at dawn under a massive air umbrella, the ground forces found themselves pinned down by withering gunfire. The port of Dieppe was never in any danger of capture and the operation ended in retreat shortly after noon, when troops began to be taken off the blood-soaked beaches. It was clear that the capture of a defended port was out of the question and that other means needed to be devised. For the RAF, over 100 fighters were lost, but the fighter pilots fought determinedly and maintained sufficient air cover to provide protection for their charges and the *Luftwaffe* did surprisingly little damage to the seaborne forces. The Dieppe adventure, as a raid, was an utter failure. However the results of that raid were to lead directly to the overwhelming success of the D-Day landings in June 1944. Without Dieppe the Allied invasion of the continent would almost certainly have ended in a bloody tragedy.

In the early summer of 1942, Luftwaffe bombers returned in what was to become known as the *Baedekker* raids, attacking towns and cities by night and employing fighter-bombers on 'hit and run' raids against coastal targets. Against these latter, the newly formed Typhoon units were to prove very successful.

19th August 1942

19 Sqn	Spit	FC	P/O J.Henderson	FW190 damaged	SW outskirts Dieppe	0930
			F/L H.F.Bradley	FW190 damaged	Mid-Channel	1005
19 Sqn	Spit	FC	Sgt I.M.Moody	FW190 damaged	Mid-Channel	1640
41 Sqn	Spit	FC	Sgt A.Imbert	FW190 damaged	Dieppe	1015~
			F/L M.L.Stepp	FW190 damaged	Dieppe	1015~
64 Sqn	Spit	FC	F/S W.J.Batchelor	Do217 destroyed	Dieppe	1240~
			P/O J.Doherty	Do217 destroyed	Dieppe	1240~
			F/L D.E.Kingaby	Do217 destroyed	Dieppe	1240~
			S/L W.G.G.D.Smith	Do217 destroyed	Dieppe	1240~
			F/L C.Thomas	Bf109 damaged	Dieppe	1240~
64 Sqn	Spit	FC	F/S G.A.Mason	FW190 damaged	Dieppe	1520~
			S/L W.G.G.D.Smith	Do217 destroyed	Dieppe	1520~
			F/L C.Thomas	FW190 destroyed	Dieppe	1520~

			P/O H.F.Withy	Do217 damaged	Dieppe	1520~
65 Sqn	Spit	FC	Sgt R.Biggs	Do217 destroyed	Dieppe	1100~
			Sgt R.Brown	- shared -		
			Sgt T.D.Tinsey	Do217 destroyed	Dieppe	1100~
65 Sqn	Spit	FC	S/L D.A.P.McMullen	Do217 damaged	Dieppe	1245~
71 Sqn	Spit	FC	P/O H.H.Strickland	FW190 damaged	10m W Dieppe	0530
71 Sqn	Spit	FC	S/L C.G.Peterson	Ju88 damaged	Off Dieppe	1125
71 Sqn	Spit	FC	F/O S.M.M.Anderson	Ju88 damaged	5m off Dieppe	1350
			F/L O.H.Coen DFC	Ju88 prob.dest	Off Dieppe	1400
			F/O M.G.H.McPharlin	Ju88 prob.dest	Off Dieppe	1400
			S/L C.G.Peterson	Ju88 destroyed	Off Dieppe	1415
81 Sqn	Spit	FC	P/O P.J.Anson	FW190 prob.dest	Dieppe	0830~
			F/L L.G.Bedford	FW190 prob.dest	Dieppe	0830~
111 Sqn	Spit	FC	Sgt B.A.C.Spranger	Do217 damaged	Dieppe	1015~
			F/L F.W.Vancl	- shared -		
111 Sqn	Spit	FC	F/L H.R.Baraldi	Do217 damaged	Dieppe	1245~
			P/O B.E.Gale	FW190 damaged	Dieppe	1245~
			Sgt Y.Henricksen	Do217 damaged	Dieppe	1245~
			S/L P.R.W.Wickham	FW190 damaged	Dieppe	1245~
			S/L P.R.W.Wickham	FW190 damaged	Dieppe	1245~
118 Sqn	Spit	FC	Sgt T.J.De Courcey*	Do217 destroyed	Dieppe	1525~

* Shared with Tangmere Wing.

			F/L J.B.Shepherd	Do217 destroyed	Dieppe	1525~
			F/O I.G.Stewart	- shared -		
			F/S S.Watson	- shared -		
121 Sqn	Spit	FC	Sgt L.M.Blanding	FW190 prob.dest	6m off Dieppe	0925
			F/L S.R.Edner	FW190 destroyed	6m W Dieppe	0930
			P/O G.O.Halsey	FW190 prob.dest	2m off Dieppe	0930
			P/O F.D.Smith	FW190 damaged	Off Dieppe	0930
122 Sqn	Spit	FC	P/O L.C.Collignon	Do217 destroyed	Dieppe	1015~
			F/L L.P.Griffith	Do217 destroyed	Dieppe	1015~
			S/L J.R.C.Kilian	Do217 destroyed	Dieppe	1015~
			Sgt W.W.Peet	- shared -		
			Sgt G.Williams	- shared -		
122 Sqn	Spit	FC	F/L L.P.Griffith	Do217 prob.dest	Dieppe	1240~
124 Sqn	Spit	FC	F/S P.E.G.Durnford	FW190 damaged	Dieppe	1130~
			F/S P.E.G.Durnford	Ju88 destroyed	Dieppe	1130~
			F/L W.Gregson	FW190 destroyed	Dieppe	1130~
			F/L W.Gregson	FW190 damaged	Dieppe	1130~

185

 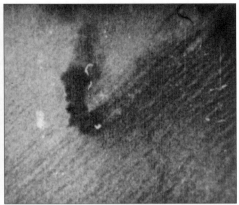

Operation Jubilee: (Left): A Do217 of KG 2 under attack. (Right): The bomber goes into the sea in flames. The "air umbrella" provided by Fighter Command proved costly, but afforded adequate protection to the Royal Navy. This was a vital experiment, one that was ultimately to lead to success in 1944 when the Allies invaded in force. (ww2images.com)

		P/O M.P.Kilburn	FW190 prob.dest	Dieppe	1130~
124 Sqn	Spit FC	F/L W.Gregson	FW190 damaged	Dieppe	1415~
		F/S B.J.Hull	FW190 destroyed	Dieppe	1415~
		F/S B.J.Hull	FW190 damaged	Dieppe	1415~
		F/S B.J.Hull	Ju88 damaged	Dieppe	1415~
		Sgt A.G.Russell	FW190 damaged	Dieppe	1415~
129 Sqn	Spit FC	Sgt R.L.Reeves	FW190 prob.dest	SE Brighton	0540
		P/O J.B.Shillitoe	FW190 damaged	SE Dieppe	0620
129 Sqn	Spit FC	S/L R.H.Thomas	Do217 damaged	SW Dieppe	1535
		F/L B.Ingham	Do217 destroyed	Channel W Dieppe	1535
130 Sqn	Spit FC	F/L W.J.Rosser	FW190 damaged	Dieppe	0930~
130 Sqn	Spit FC	Sgt A.S.Braybrook	Ju88 damaged	Dieppe	1400~
		P/O R.P.M.Leblond	FW190 prob.dest	Dieppe	1400~
		Sgt O.C.S.Snell	FW190 damaged	Dieppe	1400~
131 Sqn	Spit FC	F/L R.H.Harries	FW190 destroyed	Dieppe	0930~
131 Sqn	Spit FC	S/L H.R.Allen	Do217 damaged	5-10m S Selsey Bill	1525
		F/L R.H.Harries F/O N.S.Wilson P/O A.F.Eckert Sgt A.W.Bower	Do217 destroyed - shared - - shared - - shared -	Dieppe	1525~
		P/O I.K.Crawford F/L J.C.S.Doll F/O H.S.Jackson P/O E.A.J.Williams	Do217 destroyed - shared - - shared - - shared -	Dieppe	1525~
		S/L M.G.F.Pedley	Do217 damaged	Dieppe	1525~

131 Sqn	Spit	FC	P/O H.G.Copeland	Do217 prob.dest	Dieppe area	1840~
			Sgt J.L.Davidson	- shared -		
			Sgt J.Thorogood	- shared -		
			P/O H.G.Copeland	Ju88 prob.dest	Dieppe area	1840~
			F/O H.S.Jackson	- shared -		
			P/O H.G.Copeland	Do217 damaged	Dieppe area	1840~
133 Sqn	Spit	FC	F/S R.L.Alexander	FW190 prob.dest	Dieppe	0800
			P/O W.H.Baker Jr	FW190 destroyed	Dieppe harbour/town	0800
			F/L D.J.M.Blakeslee	FW190 destroyed	N Dieppe harbour	0800
133 Sqn	Spit	FC	P/O R.N.Beaty	FW190 damaged	5m N Dieppe	1050
			P/O R.N.Beaty	Do217 damaged	5m N Dieppe	1050
			F/L D.J.M.Blakeslee	FW190 damaged	N Dieppe	1050
			F/L D.J.M.Blakeslee	Do217 destroyed	N Dieppe	1050
			F/L E.G.Brettell	FW190 destroyed	2m E Dieppe	1050
			P/O D.S.Gentile	FW190 destroyed	E Dieppe	1050
			P/O D.S.Gentile	Ju88 destroyed	E Dieppe	1050
			P/O G.G.Wright	FW190 damaged	5m N Dieppe	1050
			P/O D.D.Gudmundsen	Do217 damaged	7m NE Dieppe	1100
			F/O E.Doorly	Do217 damaged	7m NE Dieppe	1100
			P/O W.H.Baker Jr	FW190 damaged	Dieppe harbour-town	1100
			F/L E.G.Brettell	Do217 damaged	Dieppe	1100
133 Sqn	Spit	FC	F/L D.J.M.Blakeslee	FW190 damaged	N Dieppe	1310
			F/O J.C.Nelson	Do217 damaged	S Dieppe	1310
			F/S R.L.Alexander	Do217 destroyed	Dieppe area	1315
137 Sqn	Whir	FC	F/L J.E.Van Schaick	Ju88 damaged	E Happisburgh	1000~
			Sgt A.K.Brown	- shared -~		
137 Sqn	Whir	FC	P/O J.M.Bryan	Do217 destroyed	E Cromer	1030~
			Sgt Roberts	- shared -		
141 Sqn	Beau	FC	Sgt R.O.Cleo	Ju88 destroyed	Channel	1800~
154 Sqn	Spit	FC	W/O J.G.Buiron	Do217 destroyed	Dieppe	1015~
			S/L D.C.Carlson	- shared -		
			P/O H.W.Chambers	- shared -		
			P/O M.Davies	- shared -		
			P/O I.T.Garrett	- shared -		
			F/L G.A.Harrison	- shared -		
			F/O A.S.Turnbull	- shared -		
			Sgt J.S.Whaley	- shared -		
165 Sqn	Spit	FC	F/L E.W.Campbell -Colquhoun	Do217 destroyed	Dieppe	1100~
			P/O A.Pederson	- shared -		

	S/L H.J.L.Hallowes	Do217 destroyed	Dieppe	1100~
	S/L H.J.L.Hallowes	Do217 damaged	Dieppe	1100~
	P/O H.C.Richardson	Ju88 damaged	Dieppe	1100~
	P/O B.Warren	Do217 destroyed	Dieppe	1100~
	P/O D.Warren	- shared -		
174 Sqn Hurr FC	S/L F.E.Fayolle	FW190 dest.*	Dieppe	0530~

By collision. Fayolle KIA

175 Sqn Hurr FC	F/L J.E.Meredith	He111 destroyed	Dieppe	1045~
	P/O R.A.Peters	FW190 prob.dest	Dieppe	1045~
	P/O R.A.Peters	FW190 damaged	Dieppe	1045~
239 Sqn Must AC	F/L E.K.Barnes	FW190 dest.*	Dieppe	0830~

Shared with an unidentified Spitfire.

266 Sqn Typh FC	F/L R.H.L.Dawson	Do217 destroyed	E Le Treport	1430~
	F/L A.C.Johnson	FW190 prob.dest	N Le Treport	1430~
	P/O I.M.Munro	Do217 prob.dest	Near Le Treport	1430~
277 Sqn Deft FC	P/O R.F.F.Harris	Bf109F damaged	Dieppe	1500
303 Sqn Spit FC	F/S W.Giermer	FW190 prob.dest	E Dieppe	1025
	Sgt J.Karczmarz	FW190 prob.dest	E Dieppe	1030
	P/O T.Kolecki	Ju88 destroyed	1-2m N Dieppe	1030
	F/L J.Marciniak	FW190 prob.dest	2m N Dieppe	1030
	P/O S.Socha	FW190 destroyed	3m NW Dieppe	1030
	P/O S.Socha	Ju88 destroyed	3m NW Dieppe	1030
	S/L J.E.L.Zumbach	FW190 destroyed	NE Dieppe	1030
	S/L J.E.L.Zumbach	FW190 prob.dest	NE Dieppe	1030
	P/O A.Glowacki	FW190 prob.dest	N Dieppe	1035
303 Sqn Spit FC	P/O E.Horbaczewski	FW190 destroyed	N Dieppe	1340
	F/S M.Popek	FW190 dest.*	Off Dieppe	1340

Shared with an unidentified Spitfire.

	Sgt J.Stasik	FW190 destroyed	N Dieppe	1340
303 Sqn Spit FC	F/S W.Giermer	He111 destroyed	N Dieppe	1630
	S/L J.E.L.Zumbach	- shared -		
317 Squadron		- shared -		
	P/O A.Glowacki	He111 destroyed	N Dieppe	1630
	Sgt A.Rokitnicki	- shared -		
	Sgt A.Rutecki	- shared -		
310 Sqn Spit FC	F/L V.Chocholin	Do217 damaged	Dieppe	1105
	S/L F.Dolezal	Do217 prob.dest	Dieppe	1105
	S/L F.Dolezal	FW190 damaged	Dieppe	1110
	P/O J.Doucha	Do217 damaged	Dieppe	1115

Spitfire Vbs at Redhill for Operation Jubilee. Note the prominent white stripes. (Z Hurt)

	F/L E.A.Foit	Do217 damaged	Dieppe	1100
	W/O A.Fornusek	Do217 damaged	Dieppe	1110
	P/O J.Hartman	Do217 damaged	Dieppe	1105
	F/L J.Kimlicka	Do217 damaged	Dieppe	1105
	Sgt K.Pernicka	Do217 prob.dest	Dieppe	1125
	Sgt V.Popelka	Do217 prob.dest	Dieppe	1105
	Sgt V.Popelka	Do217 damaged	Dieppe	1110
	Sgt A.Skach	FW190 damaged	Dieppe	1100-10
	Sgt J.Stivar	Do217 damaged	Dieppe	1110
312 Sqn Spit FC	F/S T.Motycka	FW190 prob.dest	Dieppe coast	1130
	Sgt V.Ruprecht	FW190 prob.dest	Dieppe coast	1130
	P/O V.Smolik	FW190 damaged	Dieppe	1130
312 Sqn Spit FC	Sgt J.Liskutin	Do217 destroyed*	mid-Channel	1520
* Shared with an unidentified Spitfire.				
	F/S J.Pipa	Do217 damaged	Convoy mid-Channel	1520
	F/O J.Keprt	Do217 destroyed	Convoy mid-Channel	1525
317 Sqn Spit FC	P/O M.M.Maciejowski	FW190 destroyed	Dieppe	1020-35
	P/O M.M.Maciejowski	Ju88 destroyed	Dieppe	1020-35
	Sgt W.Pawlowski	FW190 damaged	Dieppe	1020-35
	F/L K.Rutkowski	Do217 destroyed	Dieppe	1020-35
317 Sqn Spit FC 303 Squadron	Sgt K.Sztramko	He111 destroyed - shared -	N Dieppe	1630
	P/O S.Brzeski	He111 destroyed	Near Dieppe	1620-35
	Sgt A.Kolczynski P/O M.M.Maciejowski	Do217 destroyed - shared -	Near Dieppe	1620-35
	F/O S.Lukaszewicz	FW190 destroyed	Near Dieppe	1620-35
	F/L K.Rutkowski	He111 destroyed	Near Dieppe	1620-35
331 Sqn Spit FC	Lt R.A.Berg Sgt H.G.E.Grundt-Spang	FW190 damaged - shared -	W Dieppe	0710

Everyone was invited: the entire fighter force in the south was involved in the Dieppe operation. Left, Lieutenant Rolf Arne Berg of 331 Squadron flew four sorties, claiming an FW190 destroyed and two damaged, one shared with Helmer Grundt-Spang. Right: Spitfire VBs of 303 Squadron.

	Capt K.Birksted	FW190 prob.dest	NE Dieppe		0710
	Sgt F.A.S.Fearnley	- shared -			
	Capt K.Birksted	FW190 prob.dest	Dieppe		0710
	Lt S.Sem	FW190 prob.dest	Dieppe		0710
	Sgt G.Owren	- shared -			
	Maj H.O.Mehre	FW190 destroyed	E Dieppe		0705-20
	Maj H.O.Mehre	FW190 damaged	E Dieppe		0705-20
331 Sqn Spit FC	F/S F.A.S.Fearnley	Do217 prob.dest	N Dieppe		1215
	2/Lt H.Sognnes	Do217 destroyed	N Dieppe		1205-20
	Capt A.C.Hagerup	- shared -			
	Lt S.Sem	Do217 damaged	Dieppe-Somme		1215
332 Squadron		- shared -			
	Lt T.Weisteen	Do217 damaged	N Dieppe		1210-20
331 Sqn Spit FC	Lt R.A.Berg	FW190 destroyed	8m W Dieppe		1505-15
	Lt R.A.Berg	FW190 damaged	8m W Dieppe		1505-15
	Sgt H.G.E.Grundt-Spang	FW190 destroyed	Dieppe		1515-20
	Sgt H.G.E.Grundt-Spang	FW190 damaged	Dieppe		1515-20
	Lt M.Ree	Do217 damaged	20m off Dieppe		1520
	Lt S.Heglund	FW190 prob.dest	N Dieppe		1515~
331 Sqn Spit FC	Sgt E.Fossum	Do217 damaged	Dieppe		1935
	Lt S.Sem	- shared -			
332 Sqn Spit FC	Sgt M.Eriksen	FW190 destroyed	Dieppe		0655-0710
	Sgt M.Eriksen	FW190 damaged	Dieppe		0655-0710
	Capt R.From	FW190 destroyed	Dieppe		0645-0725
	Capt R.From	FW190 damaged	Dieppe		0645-0725
	Sgt J.Loftsgaard	FW190 destroyed	Dieppe		0645-0710

Major Finn Thorsager first saw action in April 1940, flying Gladiators for the Royal Norwegian Air Force. He escaped to England and served with 331 and 332 Squadrons, rising to command the latter. Although his score was not high, he was an inspirational leader and won a DFC. On 19th August he claimed three FW190s damaged.

	Lt J.Ryg	FW190 damaged	Dieppe	0700-25
	Capt F.Thorsager	FW190 damaged	E Dieppe	0645-0710
	Capt F.Thorsager	FW190 damaged	E Dieppe	0645-0710
332 Sqn Spit FC	Lt O.Kristiansen	Do217 damaged*	Dieppe	1200
* Shared with an unidentified Spitfire.				
331 Squadron	Lt W.Christie	Do217 destroyed - shared -	Dieppe-Somme	1215
	Sgt O.Djonne	Do217 destroyed	Dieppe	1200-15
	Sgt M.Eriksen	Do217 destroyed	W Dieppe	1210
	Sgt J.Loftsgaard	Do217 destroyed	Dieppe	1215
	Lt J.Ryg	Do217 destroyed	Dieppe	1200-10
332 Sqn Spit FC	2/Lt E.Lindseth	FW190 damaged	N Dieppe	1500
	Capt F.Thorsager	FW190 damaged	Dieppe	1510
340 Sqn Spit FC	2/Lt M.Boudier	FW190 damaged	10m N Dieppe	0540
340 Sqn Spit FC	S/Lt O.Massart Capt F.H.De La Bouchere	Do217 destroyed - shared -	Off Dieppe	1000-15
	Adj J.Guignard	Do217 damaged	4m N Dieppe	1015
	S/Lt P.F.Kennard	Do217 destroyed	5m N Dieppe	1000
	Cdt B.Duperier Capt F.H.De La Bouchere	Do217 damaged - shared -	Off Dieppe	1000
	Capt F.H.De La Bouchere	Do217 destroyed	Off Dieppe	1000
	Sgt M.Bouguen	Do217 damaged	3m N Dieppe	1000
340 Sqn Spit FC	Capt F.H.De La Bouchere Cdt B.Duperier Capt A.Gilbert S/Lt P.F.Kennard S/Lt A.R.Moynet Lt J.H.Schloesing	Do217 destroyed - shared - - shared - - shared - - shared - - shared -	Off Dieppe	1245-1300
340 Sqn Spit FC	Capt R.Bechoff	Do217 damaged	20m S Beachy Head	1910
350 Sqn Spit FC	Sgt L.V.Flohimont	FW190 damaged	Dieppe	0800

		F/L Y.G.A.F.Du Monceau	FW190 destroyed	Dieppe	0810
		P/O H.A.Picard P/O E.J.Plas	FW190 destroyed - shared -	SW Dieppe	0810-20
350 Sqn	Spit FC	Sgt R.A.Alexandre	FW190 prob.dest	Dieppe harbour	1030
		Sgt R.A.Alexandre	FW190 damaged	Dieppe harbour	1030
		F/L A.L.T.J.Boussa	FW190 destroyed	Dieppe	1035-45
		F/L A.L.T.J.Boussa	FW190 damaged	Dieppe	1035-45
		Sgt F.E.Boute	FW190 damaged	2m off E Dieppe	1035
		F/L Y.G.A.F.Du Monceau	FW190 damaged	Dieppe	1040-50
		P/O G.M.H.Seydel	FW190 damaged	2m off E Dieppe	1035
		P/O F.A.Venesoen	FW190 destroyed	Dieppe harbour	1040-45
350 Sqn	Spit FC	Sgt J.L.Vanlerberghe P/O H.J.L.Smets P/O A.M.Plisnier Sgt F.E.Boute	Ju88 destroyed - shared - - shared - - shared -	3m off Dieppe	1240
350 Sqn	Spit FC	Sgt L.V.Flohimont	FW190 damaged	Convoy mid-Channel	1520
		Sgt R.A.Alexandre	FW190 damaged	Mid Channel-Dieppe	1600
		Sgt R.A.Alexandre	FW190 damaged	Mid Channel-Dieppe	1600
		P/O A.M.Plisnier	FW190 destroyed	20m NE Dieppe	1600
		P/O G.M.H.Seydel	FW190 damaged	Off Dieppe	1600
		P/O F.A.Venesoen	FW190 damaged	Convoy-Dieppe	1600
		P/O E.J.Plas	FW190 damaged	25m N Dieppe	1550-1600
		Sgt J.L.Vanlerberghe	Do217 damaged	25m NW Dieppe	1600~
401 Sqn	Spit FC	S/L K.L.B.Hodson	FW190 damaged	Off Dieppe	1035
		F/S S.Coburn	Do217 damaged	Dieppe	1038
		F/S S.Coburn	Do217 damaged	Dieppe	1038
		S/L K.L.B.Hodson	Do217 damaged	Dieppe	1038
		F/S R.M.Zobell	Do217 damaged	Dieppe	1038
		P/O D.R.Morrison	FW190 destroyed	Dieppe	1040
401 Sqn	Spit FC	P/O G.B.Murray	FW190 prob.dest	Dieppe	1400
		P/O G.B.Murray	FW190 damaged	Dieppe	1400
		P/O H.A.Westhaver	FW190 damaged	Dieppe	1400
		F/L J.Whitham	FW190 prob.dest	Dieppe	1400
		F/L J.Witham	FW190 damaged	Dieppe	1400
402 Sqn	Spit FC	F/L E.A.Bland	FW190 damaged	Near Dieppe	1310
		S/L N.H.Bretz	FW190 damaged	Near Dieppe	1310
		P/O G.N.Keith	FW190 damaged	Near Dieppe	1310
403 Sqn	Spit FC	P/O H.J.Murphy	Bf109F prob.dest	S Dieppe	0730

Eagles of the Luftwaffe (l-r) Oberleutnant Erich Leie, Major Walter Oesau, Oberleutnant Rudolf Pflanz, and Oberfeldwebel Gunther Seeger of JG 2 in front of a Bf109. Both Leie and Seeger claimed Spitfires on 19th August. Pflanz had fallen to Spitfires in late July. (ww2images.com).

403 Sqn Spit FC	Sgt M.K.Fletcher F/L G.U.Hill	FW190 destroyed - shared -	S Dieppe		0745
403 Sqn Spit FC	F/L P.T.O'Leary	FW190 damaged	1m N Dieppe		1220
	F/L G.U.Hill	FW190 prob.dest	1m N Dieppe		1225
	F/L G.U.Hill	FW190 damaged	1m N Dieppe		1225
403 Sqn Spit FC	Sgt M.K.Fletcher	FW190 damaged	10m NE Dieppe		1710
	S/L L.S.Ford	FW190 destroyed	15m NW Dieppe		1710
	P/O H.J.Murphy	FW190 destroyed	25m NW Dieppe		1710
411 Sqn Spit FC	F/L R.W.McNair	FW190 prob.dest	2-3m N Dieppe		0830
	S/L R.B.Newton Unknown fighter	FW190 destroyed - shared -	2-3m N Dieppe		0830
411 Sqn Spit FC	F/S D.R.Matheson S/L R.B.Newton	Do217 damaged - shared -	25m-2m off Dieppe		1845
414 Sqn Must AC	F/O H.H.Hills	FW190 destroyed	5m S Dieppe		1055
416 Sqn Spit FC	P/O R.A.Buckham	Ju88 damaged	3-5m off Dieppe		1400
	S/L L.V.Chadburn	Ju88 prob.dest	3-5m off Dieppe		1400
	S/L L.V.Chadburn	Ju88 damaged	3-5m off Dieppe		1400
	P/O J.S.McKendy	Bf110 damaged	3-5m off Dieppe		1400
	P/O J.S.McKendy	FW190 damaged	3-5m off Dieppe		1400
	F/S R.D.Phillip	FW190 destroyed	3-5m off Dieppe		1400
	F/L H.Russel	FW190 destroyed	3-5m off Dieppe		1400
	F/L F.H.Boulton	Ju88 damaged	3-5m off Dieppe		1405

193

		F/S H.McDonald	Ju88 damaged	3-5m off Dieppe	1405
		P/O J.A.Rae	Ju88 damaged	3-5m off Dieppe	1405
		P/O R.A.Buckham	FW190 destroyed	3-5m off Dieppe	1400-05
		P/O R.G.Large	FW190 damaged	Dieppe	1430~
485 Sqn	Spit FC	P/O L.S.Black	FW190 damaged	N Dieppe 4m out	0830
		P/O C.Chrystall	FW190 destroyed	Off Dieppe	0840
485 Sqn	Spit FC	F/L R.W.Baker	Do217 damaged	10m NW Dieppe	1830
501 Sqn	Spit FC	P/O G.A.Mawer	Do217 destroyed	Dieppe	1525~
		F/L P.J.Stanbury	FW190 damaged	Dieppe	1525~
602 Sqn	Spit FC	S/L P.M.Brothers	FW190 damaged	Dieppe	0700~
		P/O R.W.F.Sampson	FW190 damaged	Dieppe	0700~
602 Sqn	Spit FC	F/L E.W.P.Bocock	Do217 destroyed	Dieppe	1130~
		F/L E.W.P.Bocock	FW190 damaged	Dieppe	1130~
		Sgt W.W.J.Loud Sgt W.E.Caldecott	Do217 destroyed - shared -	off Dieppe	1130~
		Sgt W.E.Caldecott	Do217 prob.dest	Dieppe	1130~
		Sgt P.Hauser	Do217 destroyed	Dieppe	1130~
		Sgt W.Lethbridge	Do217 damaged	Dieppe	1130~
		Sgt J.Marryshow	FW190 damaged	Dieppe	1130~
		F/L J.B.Niven	Do217 damaged	Dieppe	1130~
		F/L J.B.Niven	FW190 damaged	6-10m N Dieppe	1130~
		F/O E.D.M.Rippon	Do217 damaged	Dieppe	1130~
		F/O E.D.M.Rippon	Ju88 damaged	Dieppe	1130~
		P/O R.W.F.Sampson	Do217 damaged	N Dieppe	1130~
		P/O R.W.F.Sampson	Do217 damaged	N Dieppe	1130~
602 Sqn	Spit FC	P/O R.W.F.Sampson	FW190 destroyed	Dieppe	1415~
610 Sqn	Spit FC	S/L J.E.Johnson F/S S.C.Creagh P/O L.A.Smith	Bf109 destroyed - shared - - shared -	Dieppe	0830~
		F/L D.E.Crowley-Milling	FW190 damaged	Dieppe	0830~
		F/L D.E.Crowley-Milling	Bf109 destroyed	Dieppe	0830~
		P/O L.E.Hoken	FW190 damaged	Dieppe	0830~
		S/L J.E.Johnson	FW190 destroyed	Dieppe	0830~
		S/L J.E.Johnson P/O L.A.Smith	FW190 destroyed - shared -	Dieppe	0830~
		P/O L.A.Smith	FW190 damaged	Dieppe	0830~
611 Sqn	Spit FC	F/L W.V.Crawford -Compton	FW190 damaged	2m W Dieppe	0540~

The Mustang Is of Army Co-operation Command were employed for low-level tactical reconnaissance during the Dieppe raid and sustained several casualties. Here, Winston Churchill visits 613 Squadron at Twinwood Farm to inspect the Mustangs. (ww2images.com)

			F/L J.Manak	FW190 damaged	Dieppe	0540~
			S/L D.H.Watkins	FW190 destroyed	6m N Dieppe	0540~
616 Sqn	Spit	FC	Sgt M.H.F.Cooper	FW190 damaged	Dieppe	1130~
			S/L J.S.Fifield	FW190 damaged	Dieppe	1130~
			F/L F.A.O.Gaze	Do217 destroyed	Dieppe	1130~
			F/O G.B.MacLachlan	FW190 damaged	Dieppe	1130~
			P/O J.H.Smithson	FW190 damaged	Dieppe	1130~
616 Sqn	Spit	FC	P/O J.H.Smithson	FW190 damaged	Dieppe	1430~
Ntht Wg	Spit	FC	S/L T.Nowierski	Do217 damaged	Near Dieppe	1030
			S/L T.Nowierski	Do217 damaged	Near Dieppe	1030
Port Wg	Spit	FC	W/C M.V.Blake	FW190 destroyed	Dieppe	0930~
SF Hch	Spit	FC	G/C H.Broadhurst	FW190 destroyed	Dieppe	0720~
SF Hch	Spit	FC	G/C H.Broadhurst	FW190 damaged	Dieppe	1015~
			G/C H.Broadhurst	FW190 damaged	Dieppe	1015~
			G/C H.Broadhurst	FW190 damaged	Dieppe	1015
Tang Wg	Spit	FC	W/C E.P.P.Gibbs*	Do217 destroyed	Dieppe	1525~
WM Wg	Spit	FC	W/C P.G.Jameson	FW190 destroyed	Dieppe	0830~
Witt Wg	Typh	FC	W/C D.E.Gillam	FW190 damaged	Dieppe	1430~

* Shared with 118 Squadron.

20th August 1942

91 Sqn	Spit	FC	P/O J.R.Heap	Do24 destroyed	10-15m W Dieppe	1300~
137 Sqn	Whir	FC	Sgt J.M.Barclay	Ju88 damaged	N Yarmouth	0845~
317 Sqn	Spit	FC	F/O F.Martini	FW190 destroyed	15m W Le Havre	1730-35
411 Sqn	Spit	FC	F/L R.W.McNair	FW190 damaged	Near Cayeux	1810
610 Sqn	Spit	FC	S/L J.E.Johnson	FW190 prob.dest	Cayeux	1810~

Both Harry Broadhurst, the Horchurch Station Commander (left) and Johnnie Johnson, newly promoted CO of 610 Squadron (right), made claims over Dieppe. (ww2images.com - Broadhurst)

20/21st August 1942

| 29 Sqn | Beau FC | F/O G.Pepper | He177 destroyed | 35m SE Beachy Head | 2330~ |

21st August 1942

65 Sqn	Spit FC	Sgt J.A.Long	FW190 damaged	4m off Ramsgate	1010
		Sgt T.D.Tinsey	FW190 prob.dest	4m off Ramsgate	1010
		Sgt T.D.Tinsey	FW190 damaged	15m off Dunkirk	1010

22/23rd August 1942

| 68 Sqn | Beau FC | P/O W.J.Gough | Do217 prob.dest | E North Coates | 2345~ |
| 157 Sqn | Mosq FC | W/C R.G.Slade | Do217 destroyed | 20m from Castle Camps | 2259 |

23rd August 1942

| 152 Sqn | Spit FC | F/S M.McPherson F/L W.M.Sizer | Ju88 destroyed - shared - | Irish Sea | 0832 |
| 504 Sqn | Spit FC | Sgt W.E.Francis Sgt J.D.J.Hawkins | Ju88 destroyed - shared - | Off Gormanston | 0832 |

23/24th August 1942

25 Sqn	Beau FC	S/L W.J.Alington	Do217 destroyed	East Walton	2325
25 Sqn	Beau FC	W/C H.P.Pleasance	Do217 destroyed	20m Mablethorpe	2345~
25 Sqn	Beau FC	F/O J.Singleton	E/A damaged	S Bourne	0015~
255 Sqn	Beau FC	F/O H.G.S.Wyrill	Do217 damaged	S Peretborough	2350~

Left: a senior pilot's meeting. 'Sailor' Malan second left and Bill Crawford-Compton far right. Right: Joe Singleton of 25 Squadron made his first combat claim on 23/24th August. This was for a Do217 damaged. He would raise his score to seven destroyed, winning a DSO and DFC.

	F/O H.G.S.Wyrill	Do217 damaged	S Peretborough	2350~
409 Sqn Beau FC	P/O W.D.Gibson	Do217 prob.dest	Off Skegness	2325

24th August 1942

129 Sqn Spit FC	Sgt J.R.Spiers	FW190 destroyed	Off St Catherines Pt	1930
	F/L E.A.Bland	FW190 destroyed	Bolbec	1610
	S/L N.H.Bretz	FW190 destroyed	Bolbec	1610
	Sgt W.A.Hayes	FW190 damaged	Bolbec	1610
	P/O N.A.Keene	FW190 prob.dest	Bolbec	1610
	F/L I.G.Keltie	FW190 damaged	10-15m N Fecamp	1620
	P/O K.L.Magee	FW190 damaged	Bolbec	1610
	F/L D.G.Malloy	FW190 damaged	Bolbec	1610
611 Sqn Spit FC	F/L W.V.Crawford -Compton	FW190 destroyed	W Fauville	1730~

24/25th August 1942

29 Sqn Beau FC	S/L J.R.D.Braham	Ju88 prob.dest	30m SE Beachy Head	2220~
418 Sqn Bost FC	P/O S.H.D.Venables	Do217 damaged	N Aubigny	2320

25th August 1942

141 Sqn Beau FC	P/O H.D.Venables	Ju88 prob.dest	S Isle of Wight	0825~

27th August 1942

71 Sqn Spit FC	S/L G.A.Daymond	FW190 destroyed	S Gravelines	1120
	Sgt A.J.Seaman	FW190 damaged	15m S Gravelines	1120
154 Sqn Spit FC	P/O A.F.Aikman	FW190 damaged	Channel	1410~

197

After the storm: pilots of from 501, 66 and 118 Squadrons gather for a photo after the Dieppe raid.

			F/L A.F.Eckford	FW190 damaged	5m S Dover	1410~
350 Sqn	Spit	FC	F/L Y.G.A.F.Du Monceau	FW190 destroyed	N Le Crotoy	1235
			F/O E.J.Plas	FW190 prob.dest	Le Crotoy	1230
			F/O E.J.Plas	FW190 damaged	Le Crotoy	1240
412 Sqn	Spit	FC	W/O H.V.Thompson	FW190 damaged	25-30m SE Selsey Bill	1945-50
Deb Wg	Spit	FC	W/C R.M.B.Duke -Woolley	FW190 destroyed	8m S Gravelines	1242
Ken Wg	Spit	FC	W/C C.B.F.Kingcombe	FW190 damaged	Off Boulogne	1230~

28th August 1942

310 Sqn	Spit	FC	S/L F.Dolezal*	Bf109E destroyed	S Exmouth	0940~

* Shared with Exeter Wing.

401 Sqn	Spit	FC	F/S J.Chaplin	FW190 damaged	Amiens	1330-40
			F/S L.F.Foster	FW190 damaged	Amiens-Abbeville	1330-40
			P/O T.K.Ibbotson	FW190 prob.dest	Near Amiens	1330-40
			P/O D.R.Morrison	FW190 prob.dest	E Amiens	1330-40
			P/O G.B.Murray	FW190 prob.dest	Near Meaulte	1330-40
			F/S A.L.Sinclair	FW190 damaged	Amiens	1330-40
611 Sqn	Spit	FC	F/L W.V.Crawford -Compton	FW190 destroyed	Near Amiens	1340~
			F/L W.V.Crawford -Compton	FW190 destroyed	Near Albert	1340~
			F/L W.V.Crawford -Compton Section claim	FW190 prob.dest - shared -	Near Albert	1340~
Ex Wg	Spit	FC	W/C K.Mrazek*	Bf109E destroyed	S Exmouth	0940~

* Shared with 310 Squadron.

28/29th August 1942

3 Sqn	Hurr FC	F/S J.R.Collins	E/A damaged	St Trond	0115~
23 Sqn	Mosq FC	Sgt G RWright	E/A damaged	Gilze-Rijn	0200~
29 Sqn	Beau FC	S/L J.R.D.Braham	Ju88 destroyed	30m SE Beachy Head	2230~
		S/L J.R.D.Braham	Ju88 damaged	25m S Beachy Head	0510~
32 Sqn	Hurr FC	P/O R.S.Davidson	Ju88 destroyed	Unknown	u/k
219 Sqn	Beau FC	F/L A.W.Horne	He111 destroyed	Off Blyth	2350~
406 Sqn	Beau FC	F/L J.R.B.Firth	E/A destroyed	22m E Whitby	2304

29th August 1942

124 Sqn	Spit FC	Sgt A.Herreman	FW190 destroyed	Off Griz Nez	1045~
		P/O M.P.Kilburn	FW190 destroyed	Le Touquet	1045~
125 Sqn	Beau FC	F/O J.A'B.P.Boyd	Ju88 destroyed	45m SW Angle	1830~
331 Sqn	Spit FC	Sgt K.Bache Lt S.Sem	FW190 damaged - shared -	Off Calais	1100
		Sgt F.Cleve	FW190 prob.dest	Off Griz Nez	1100
		Maj H.O.Mehre	FW190 damaged	Off Griz Nez	1100
		2/Lt H.Sognnes	FW190 damaged	10m S Dover	1100
401 Sqn	Spit FC	P/O G.B.Murray	FW190 damaged	20m S Ostend	1135
Deb Wg	Spit FC	W/C R.M.B.Duke -Woolley	FW190 prob.dest	3m NW Griz Nez	1045

2nd September 1942

401 Sqn	Spit FC	P/O D.R.Morrison	FW190 destroyed	Off Shoreham	1000
		F/S R.D.Reesor	FW190 destroyed	Off Shoreham	1000

2/3rd September 1942

25 Sqn	Beau FC	F/O J.Singleton	He111 destroyed	20m E Ely	2330~

3rd September 1942

131 Sqn	Spit FC	P/O I.K.Crawford	FW190 damaged	S Selsey	1035~
		P/O A.F.Eckart	FW190 destroyed	S Selsey	1035~

4th September 1942

133 Sqn	Spit FC	P/O R.N.Beaty	Ju86 damaged	Off Ramsgate	1500~

4/5th September 1942

23 Sqn	Mosq FC	F/O L.W.H.Welch	FW190 prob.dest	Melun	0500~
307 Sqn	Beau FC	Sgt J.Pacholczyk	Ju88 damaged	Lyme Bay	2211

5th September 1942

64 Sqn	Spit	FC	F/L M.G.L.M.Donnet	FW190 damaged	Rouen	1040~
			F/L C.Thomas	FW190 destroyed	Rouen	1030-40~
121 Sqn	Spit	FC	P/O N.D.Young	Ju88 destroyed	Unknown	u/k
340 Sqn	Spit	FC	S/L M.Boudier	FW190 destroyed	5m N Le Treport	1030
			S/L M.Boudier	FW190 destroyed	15m N Le Treport	1040
401 Sqn	Spit	FC	P/O D.R.Morrison	FW190 prob.dest	Dieppe	1030
610 Sqn	Spit	FC	F/S S.C.Creagh Sgt R.H.W.Gregory	Me210 destroyed - shared -	E Southend	1510~
611 Sqn	Spit	FC	F/L J.Manak	FW190 damaged	Rouen	1040~
			P/O R.T.Williams	FW190 damaged	Rouen	1040~

6th September 1942

1 Sqn	Typh	FC	P/O D.P.Perrin	Me210 destroyed	2m SW Redcar	1143
			P/O T.G.B.Bridges	Me210 destroyed	Robin Hood's Bay	1150
401 Sqn	Spit	FC	F/S E.L.Gimbel	FW190 damaged	Somme Estuary	1810
402 Sqn	Spit	FC	F/L F.H.Boulton	FW190 damaged	Near Meaulte	1750
			S/L N.H.Bretz	FW190 damaged	Near Meaulte	1800
			F/L D.G.Malloy	FW190 prob.dest	Near Meaulte	1755
611 Sqn	Spit	FC	F/L W.V.Crawford -Compton	FW190 damaged	Cayeux-Berck	1800~
			F/L W.V.Crawford -Compton	FW190 damaged	Cayeux-Berck	1800~
			P/O MGraham	FW190 damaged	Abbeville	1800~
			F/L F.W.Vancl	FW190 prob.dest	Abbeville	1800~

6/7th September 1942

25 Sqn	Beau	FC	F/L J.L.Shaw	He111 damaged	E Spurn Head	0005~
410 Sqn	Beau	FC	P/O R.R.Ferguson	Ju88 damaged	24m NE Whitby	2335

7th September 1942

91 Sqn	Spit	FC	P/O J.A.Maridor	Ju88 prob.dest	Off Ostend	1920~
133 Sqn	Spit	FC	P/O W.H.Baker Jr	FW190 damaged	Off Rotterdam	1030
302 Sqn	Spit	FC	P/O E.Ebenrytter	FW190 damaged	Near Dover	1020
			S/L S.H.Lapka	FW190 damaged	4-5m off Dover	1020
			P/O C.Sniec	FW190 destroyed	4-5m off Dover	1020
308 Sqn	Spit	FC	F/L T.Koc	FW190 damaged	Near English coast	u/k
310 Sqn	Spit	FC	W/O A.Fornusek	Do217 damaged	5m WSW Guernsey	1730
402 Sqn	Spit	FC	Sgt G.D.A.T.Cameron	FW190 damaged	10m W Rotterdam	1025

85 Squadron: Two pilots, Flying Officer Gonzales, left, and Flight Lieutenant McLannahan sit with recognition charts. (ww2images.com)

7/8th September 1942

85 Sqn	Mosq FC	Sgt K.R.McCormick		He111 destroyed	E Foulness	2234
157 Sqn	Mosq FC	P/O G.Deakin		Do217 damaged		u/k

8th September 1942

26 Sqn	Must AC	P/O R.C.Cooper		E/A damaged	S Hastings	0620~
		F/O C.D.North-Lewis		- shared -		
315 Sqn	Spit FC	S/L M.Wiorkiewicz		FW190 damaged	10-15m N Le Havre	1335

8/9th September 1942

141 Sqn	Beau FC	W/O R.C.Hamer	He111 destroyed	12m SSE St Albans Hd	0210
151 Sqn	Mosq FC	F/O A.I.McRitchie	Do217 destroyed	Near Duxford	2338
151 Sqn	Mosq FC	F/L H.G.Bodien	Do217 damaged	Near Framlington	0030~

10/11th September 1942

23 Sqn	Mosq FC	W/C B.R.O'B.Hoare	E/A destroyed	S Enschede	2345~

11th September 1942

91 Sqn	Spit FC	F/L A.G.Donahue	Ju88 damaged	Off Belgian coast	0630

12th September 1942

HA Flt	Spit FC	P/OPrince E.Galitzine	Ju86P damaged	Near Southampton	1005-45

14th September 1942

56 Sqn	Typh	FC P/O W.E.Coombes	Ju88 destroyed	40m E Cromer	1730~
		F/L M.R.Ingle-Finch	- shared -		

15/16th September 1942

25 Sqn	Beau FC	S/L W.J.Alington*	Do217 destroyed	7m N Sheringham	0010~

Upgraded from 'damaged'

68 Sqn	Beau FC	W/O L.Bobek	Do217 damaged	NE Cromer	0120~

16th September 1942

133 Sqn	Spit FC	P/O C.H.Miley	FW190 damaged	15m E Deal	0640
402 Sqn	Spit FC	P/O G.N.Keith	FW190 damaged	10m SE Le Treport	1210
		Sgt E.J.Ross	FW190 damaged	10m SE Le Treport	1210
602 Sqn	Spit FC	Sgt G.F.Emes	He111 damaged	E Fair Isle	1830~
		F/S J.F.Kistruck	- shared -		
611 Sqn	Spit FC	F/L W.V.Crawford -Compton	FW190 damaged	Eu-Le Treport	1210~
		P/O M.Graham	FW190 damaged	Le Treport	1210~

17th September 1942

412 Sqn	Spit FC	P/O W.B.Needham	FW190 damaged	10m N Le Havre	1540
		P/O L.W.Powell	FW190 destroyed	10m N Le Havre	1540

17/18th September 1942

25 Sqn	Beau FC	F/O J.Singleton	Do217 damaged	Near Hunstanton	2230~
151 Sqn	Mosq FC	F/L H.G.Bodien	Do217 destroyed	Near Kings Lynn	2155
157 Sqn	Mosq FC	Sgt L.R.Watts	Do217 damaged	20m NW Haamstede	2240~

18th September 1942

MSFU	Hurr FC	F/O A.H.Burr	He111 destroyed	Russian Convoy	1155

19/20th September 1942

25 Sqn	Beau FC	P/O J.L.V.Norris	Do217 prob.dest	10m E Seaham	0020~
25 Sqn	Beau FC	Sgt J.H.Staples	Do217 prob.dest	E Whitby	2200~
68 Sqn	Beau FC	W/O L.Bobek	Do217 damaged	70m E Happisburgh	2120~
219 Sqn	Beau FC	S/L J.G.Topham	Do217 destroyed	SE Cambois Bay	2204

20th September 1942

91 Sqn	Spit FC	F/L A.J.Andrews DFC	Ju88 damaged	Near Flushing	0640~
125 Sqn	Beau FC	F/L J.R.A.Bailey	Ju88 damaged	S Waterford	1015~

23rd September 1942

19 Sqn	Spit FC	Sgt D.J.Love P/O A.A.Simpson	Ju88 damaged - shared -	35m SE Falmouth	0945
91 Sqn	Spit FC	F/L J.E.Demozay	FW190 destroyed	10m NW Griz Nez	1125~

23/24th September 1942

25 Sqn	Beau FC	P/O R.Peake	Do217 destroyed	E Flamborough Head	0100~

24/25th September 1942

307 Sqn	Beau FC	S/L G.K.Ranoszek	E/A destroyed	SW Eddystone LH	2340

25/26th September 1942

406 Sqn	Beau FC	Sgt E.S.P.Fox	Ju88 prob.dest	SW Lizard	0145
406 Sqn	Beau FC	S/L D.C.Furse	Do217 destroyed	St Just	0215

26th September 1942

91 Sqn	Spit FC	P/O F.N.Gillitt	Ju88 prob.dest	Off Dover	1200~

27th September 1942

257 Sqn	Typh FC	P/O M.J.Coombe	Ju88 damaged	40m S Start Point	1300~
		P/O C.W.C.Henman	Ju88 damaged	40m S Start Point	1300~

28th September 1942

257 Sqn	Typh FC	F/S A.J.Addington	Ju88 destroyed	24m SW Bridport	0710~

30th September 1942

91 Sqn	Spit FC	F/L A.J.Andrews DFC	Ju88 destroyed	Griz Nez	1135~
91 Sqn	Spit FC	F/L J.J.Le Roux	FW190 damaged	Over Hawkinge	1820
		F/L J.J.Le Roux	FW190 damaged	Over Hawkinge	1820
157 Sqn	Mosq	FC W/C R.F.H.Clerke	Ju88 destroyed	30m off Holland	1150~

2nd October 1942

124 Sqn	Spit FC	F/O P.E.G.Durnford	FW190 prob.dest	N St Omer	1545~
306 Sqn	Spit FC	P/O W.Walendowski	FW190 destroyed	Aux-le-Chateau	1545
331 Sqn	Spit FC	Capt R.A.Berg	FW190 prob.dest	Gravelines	1430
401 Sqn	Spit FC	P/O S.C.Cosburn	FW190 damaged	Somme Estuary	1540
		F/L D.R.Morrison	Bf109F prob.dest	Somme Estuary	1540
611 Sqn	Spit FC	S/L H.T.Armstrong	FW190 prob.dest	Off French coast	1430~
		F/L W.V.Crawford -Compton	Bf109F prob.dest	E Foret de Crecy	1430~
616 Sqn	Spit FC	F/O R.G.Large	FW190 destroyed	St Omer	1545~
Deb Wg	Spit FC	W/C R.M.B.Duke -Woolley	FW190 destroyed*	6m SE Calais	1435

Shared with 4 FG

203

The new fighter for the RAF was to be the Hawker Typhoon. Employed in the home defence role, it proved to be an excellent fighter. Faster than the Spitfires and with the far superior armament of four 20mm cannon, it appeared to be a worthy successor to the Spitfire VBs. However, the weight and wing loading made it a poor dogfighter and its shape caused much confusion with the FW190 and led to recognition stripes being painted as shown. This example is from 56 Squadron.

9th October 1942

306 Sqn	Spit FC	F/L J.Gil	FW190 destroyed	Audricque-Cassel	1000
		F/L J.Gil	Bf109F damaged	Audricque-Cassel	1000
		F/O S.Kedzierski	FW190 destroyed	Audricque-Cassel	1000
		P/O H.J.Pietrzak	FW190 destroyed	Audricque-Cassel	1000
		F/L J.Zulikowski	FW190 prob.dest	Audricque-Cassel	1000
401 Sqn	Spit FC	F/L G.B.Murray F/S E.L.Gimbel	FW190 destroyed - shared -	Lille	0940
		F/L G.B.Murray	FW190 damaged	Lille	0940
BH Wg	Spit FC	W/C E.H.Thomas	FW190 destroyed	N Gravelines	1010
		W/C E.H.Thomas	FW190 damaged	W Gravelines	1010

10th October 1942

132 Sqn	Spit FC	Sgt R.A.Carr F/L D.Fopp	Do217 prob.dest - shared -	E Felixstowe	0845~

11th October 1942

64 Sqn	Spit FC	S/L F.A.O.Gaze	FW190 damaged	Near Cassel	1435~
122 Sqn	Spit FC	Sgt G.S.Hulse	FW190 damaged	10m ENE St Omer	1435~
		P/O D.G.Mercer	FW190 damaged	Near Cassel	1435~
332 Sqn	Spit FC	Sgt E.Samuelsen	FW190 damaged	Cassel	1433

12th October 1942

91 Sqn	Spit FC	Sgt K.Hawkins	FW190 destroyed	Off Dover	1025

13th October 1942

| 125 Sqn | Beau FC | S/L G.A.Denby | He111 prob.dest | 110m NNE Sumburgh | 0730~ |

14th October 1942

| 91 Sqn | Spit FC | F/L A.J.Andrews DFC | FW190 damaged | Le Touquet | 0740~ |

16/17th October 1942

| 29 Sqn | Beau FC | F/L I.G.Esplin | Ju88 destroyed | Off Cap d'Antifer | 0700~ |
| 219 Sqn | Beau FC | P/O D.W.B.Farrer | Do217 destroyed | Off Whitburn | 2150~ |

17th October 1942

| 486 Sqn | Typh FC | Sgt A.N.Sames
P/O G.G.Thomas | FW190 destroyed
- shared - | 5-9m S Hastings | 1325-30 |

18th October 1942

| 91 Sqn | Spit FC | F/L A.J.Andrews DFC
Sgt D.H.Davy | Ju88 destroyed
- shared - | Off Dunkirk | 0745~ |

19th October 1942

29 Sqn	Beau FC	S/L J.R.D.Braham	Do217 damaged	30m ENE Foulness	1200~
68 Sqn	Beau FC	S/L V.Vesely	Do217 damaged	S Crtiomer Knoll	1040~
68 Sqn	Beau FC	F/L W.D.Winward	Ju88 destroyed	Off Cromer Knoll	1145~
85 Sqn	Mosq FC	F/L E.N.Bunting	Ju88 damaged	45m NNW Foreness	1050
85 Sqn	Mosq FC	Sgt D.I.Clunes	Do217 damaged	35m E Clacton	1100
157 Sqn	Mosq FC	F/S N.Munro	Do217 damaged	E Clacton	0945~
		F/S N.Munro	Ju88 destroyed	Southwold	0945~
157 Sqn	Mosq FC	S/L G.Ashfield	Ju88 damaged	SE Harwich	1300~

21st October 1942

| 125 Sqn | Beau FC | F/O J.O.Mathews | Ju88 damaged | 120m NW Sumburgh | 1330~ |

24/25th October 1942

| 68 Sqn | Beau FC | F/O E.V.Raybould | Do217 damaged | N Burnham Market | 2200~ |
| 409 Sqn | Beau FC | P/O J.T.MacDonald | Do217 prob.dest | 8m E Mablethorpe | 2137 |

25th October 1942

| 141 Sqn | Beau FC | P/O G.L.Selman | Ju88 damaged | Beachy Head | 1740 |

26th October 1942

29 Sqn	Beau FC	S/L J.R.D.Braham	Ju88 destroyed	10-20m S Beachy Hd	1215~
91 Sqn	Spit FC	F/L A.J.Andrews	FW190 damaged	Off Dungeness	1640~
		F/O J.A.Maridor	FW190 damaged	nr Griz Nez	1640~
157 Sqn	Mosq FC	F/O E.Cave-Brown	Ju88 destroyed	S Beachy Head	1200~

27th October 1942

125 Sqn	Beau FC	F/O G.E.Jameson	Ju88 damaged	10m N Lerwick	1800~
340 Sqn	Spit FC	S/Lt M.Boudier	FW190 damaged	12m NW Griz Nez	1715
611 Sqn	Spit FC	F/L W.V.Crawford -Compton	FW190 damaged	5m NE Griz Nez	1715

28th October 1942

85 Sqn	Mosq	FC Sgt A.W.Sullivan	Do217 prob.dest	Thames estuary	1600~

31st October 1942

91 Sqn	Spit FC	F/O J.P.Coudray	FW190 damaged	Near Dover	1715~
		S/L J.E.Demozay	FW190 destroyed	10m S Dover	1700~
		S/L J.E.Demozay	FW190 destroyed	10m S Dover	1700~
		S/L J.E.Demozay	FW190 damaged	10m S Dover	1700~
		F/L J.J.Le Roux	FW190 destroyed	15m E Dover	1720~
		F/L J.J.Le Roux	FW190 destroyed	15m E Dover	1720~
		P/O J.A.Maridor	FW190 destroyed	Dover Straits	1720~
		P/O J.A.Maridor	FW190 damaged	Dover Straits	1720~
		Sgt J.A.Round	FW190 damaged	15m E Dover	1720~
122 Sqn	Spit FC	P/O D.G.Mercer	FW190 destroyed	Near Deal	1715~
453 Sqn	Spit FC	P/O A.G.B.Blumer	Ju88 damaged	Off North Foreland	1645~
		Sgt N.F.Swift	Ju88 damaged	Deal	1615-1715

31st October/1st November 1942

29 Sqn	Beau FC	S/L J.R.D.Braham	Do217 destroyed	7m off East Foreland	2000~
29 Sqn	Beau FC	F/O G.Pepper	Do217 destroyed	18m e Foreness	1850~
		F/O G.Pepper	Do217 destroyed	W Canterbury	0100~

1st November 1942

322 Sqn	Spit FC	2/Lt T.A.Waerner	FW190 damaged	N St Omer	1400
MSFU	Hurr FC	P/O N.Taylor	FW200 destroyed	43.00N 15.24W	u/k

2nd November 1942

340 Sqn	Spit FC	Adj J.G.Buiron	FW190 damaged	Berck-Le Touquet	1510
		Cdt B.Duperier	FW190 destroyed	5m SE Berck	1510
		Cdt B.Duperier	FW190 destroyed	S Le Touquet A/D	1510
		Adj R.G.Gouby	FW190 destroyed	Somme mouth	1510
		S/Lt A.R.Moynet Capt J.H.Schloesing	FW190 prob.dest - shared -	Somme mouth	1510
611 Sqn	Spit FC	S/L H.T.Armstrong	FW190 destroyed	Somme estuary	1510~
		S/L H.T.Armstrong	Bf109 prob.dest	Somme estuary	1510~

206

		P/O L.De Tedesco	FW190 destroyed	Le Touquet	1510~
		P/O P.E.Helmore	FW190 damaged	Le Touquet	1510~
		P/O P.M.Sims	FW190 damaged	Le Touquet	1510~

3rd November 1942

257 Sqn	Typh FC	F/O G.F.Ball	FW190 destroyed	35m W Guernsey	1315~
		P/O P.G.Scotchmer	FW190 destroyed	35m W Guernsey	1315~

4th November 1942

56 Sqn	Typh FC	P/O K.L.Storey	Ju88 damaged	E Yarmouth	1710~
125 Sqn	Beau FC	S/L F.D.Hughes	Ju88 destroyed	130m E Stonehaven	0925~
		F/O J.H.Turnbull	- shared -		

7th November 1942

340 Sqn	Spit FC	S/Lt A R Moynet	FW190 destroyed	30m S Beachy Head	1615
		S/Lt A R Moynet	FW190 destroyed	30m S Beachy Head	1615
400 Sqn	Must AC	P/O F.E.W.Hanton	Bf109 prob.dest	3m off Cabourg	1100~

8th November 1942

165 Sqn	Spit FC	S/L H.J.L.Hallowes	FW190 damaged	Calais	1250~
401 Sqn	Spit FC	P/O D.R.Manley	FW190 destroyed	Near Audricq	1215~
		F/L D.R.Morrison	- shared -		
611 Sqn	Spit FC	F/L W.V.Crawford -Compton	FW190 damaged	Gravelines	1250~

9th November 1942

331 Sqn	Spit FC	F/S H.G.E.Grundt-Spang	FW190 prob.dest	Griz Nez	1630~
611 Sqn	Spit FC	S/L H.T.Armstrong	FW190 prob.dest	Calais	1630~
		F/L W.V.Crawford -Compton	FW190 destroyed	Calais-Griz Nez	1630~
611 Sqn	Spit FC	P/O G.R.Lindsay	FW190 damaged	Calais	1630~

10th November 1942

91 Sqn	Spit FC	F/S I W.Downer	FW190 destroyed	Off Calais	1100~
125 Sqn	Beau FC	F/L J.R.A.Bailey	Ju88 destroyed	118m E Inverberie	0900~
401 Sqn	Spit FC	P/O E.L.Gimbel	FW190 destroyed	3m W Fecamp	1505
		S/L K.L.B.Hodson	- shared -		

16th November 1942

350 Sqn	Spit FC	F/O A.M.Plisnier	Ju52 destroyed	St Aubin A/D	1620
		F/O F.A.Venesoen	- shared -		

Whirlwind pilots had little opportunity for combat as they were employed mainly on anti-shipping and ground attack duties. Warrant Officer Don McPhail of 263 Squadron was shot down and killed by Flak on 7th December whilst attacking shipping off Jersey.

19th November 1942

350 Sqn Spit FC	Sgt L.J.Harmel	Bf110 dest.	5m W Ghent	1220
	F/O A.M.Plisnier	- shared -		

26th November 1942

268 Sqn Must AC	F/O R.A.Bethell	Bf109F dest.	nr Elburg	1500~
	F/O R.A.Bethell	Ju52/3M dest.	Nr Oldebroeck	1500~
485 Sqn Spit FC	S/L R.J.C.Grant	He115 destroyed	3m W Zierikzee	1210

29th November 1942

331 Sqn Spit FC	Maj K.Birksted	FW190 damaged	Nieuport-Flushing	1200
	Capt R.A.Berg	FW190 damaged	Nieuport-Flushing	1200
	2/Lt S.Heglund	- shared -		
	2/Lt N.K.Jorstad	- shared -		
	Sgt G.Owren	FW190 damaged	Nieuport-Flushing	1200
340 Sqn Spit FC	S/Lt P.F.Kennard	FW190 damaged	Near St Pol	1440

1st December 1942

340 Sqn Spit FC	S/L M.Bouguen	FW190 destroyed	Lumbres	1530
	Adj R.G.Gouby	FW190 destroyed	Lumbres	1540
	Lt O.Massart	FW190 damaged	Lumbres	1530
	S/Lt A.R.Moynet	FW190 destroyed	Lumbres	1530
	S/Lt A.R.Moynet	FW190 damaged	Lumbres	1530
	Lt E.Reilhac	FW190 damaged	Lumbres	1530
MW Wg Spit FC	W/C T.F.Dalton-Morgan	Bf109F damaged	Cap de la Hague	1700~

3rd December 1942

19 Sqn Spit FC	P/O D.W.Connor	FW190 damaged	80m W Pte du Raz	1005

4th December 1942

402 Sqn Spit FC	P/O N.A.Keene	FW190 destroyed	Samer	1450

64 Squadron was one of the first units to receive the Spitfire IXB. Flying Officer Patterson posed in front of "Brazil". (ww2images.com)

			F/O H.A.Simpson	FW190 damaged	5m E Griz Nez	1445
			F/O H.A.Simpson	FW190 damaged	5m E Griz Nez	1445
611 Sqn	Spit	FC	F/L F.W.Vancl	FW190 damaged	Off Calais	1450~
Ken Wg	Spit	FC	W/C J.C.Fee	FW190 prob.dest	5m NE Boulogne	1445-1500

5th December 1942

609 Sqn	Typh	FC	F/S A.Haddon	FW190 prob.dest	Off Dover	1445~

6th December 1942

122 Sqn	Spit	FC	P/O D.G.Mercer	FW190 destroyed	NW Calais	1245~
131 Sqn	Spit	FC	Sgt A.W.Bower	FW190 damaged	Off Calais	1245~
			P/O H.De Bordas	FW190 destroyed	Off Calais	1245~
			S/L R.H.Harries	FW190 destroyed	Off Calais	1245~

8th December 1942

23 Sqn	Mosq	FC	F/L L.W.H.Welch	Bucker trainer destroyed	Bricy	1200
			F/L L.W.H.Welch	Bucker trainer damaged	Bricy	1200
			F/L L.W.H.Welch	Ju87 destroyed	Bricy	1200
			F/L L.W.H.Welch	FW200 damaged	Bricy	1200

10/11th December 1942

3 Sqn	Hurr	FC	P/O H.K.Dalton	E/A damaged	Gilze-Rijn	2137
3 Sqn	Hurr	FC	P/O V.Smith	E/A damaged	Soesterburg	2315~
68 Sqn	Beau	FC	F/L M.J.Mansfeld	Do217 destroyed	50m off Cromer	2025~

11th December 1942

164 Sqn	Spit	FC	W/O W.Cook Sgt W.Nowoczyn	Ju88 damaged - shared -	NE Aberdeen	1400~
401 Sqn	Spit	FC	P/O S.C.Cosburn	FW190 destroyed	4m S Hastings	1205
			F/O T.K.Ibbotson	FW190 damaged	4m S Hastings	1205

Frank Murphy of 486 Squadron and Andre Plisnier (far right) of 350 were both successful in December. Plisniere claimed two FW190s damaged on 12th December and Murphy, flying the big Typhoon against 'hit and run' raiders, claimed a Bf109 destroyed on 17th December and another on 24th, his first two victories. Both men survived the war.

12th December 1942

124 Sqn Spit FC	S/L T.Balmforth	FW190 destroyed	Fecamp	1330~
	P/O B.J.Hull	FW190 destroyed	Fecamp	1330~
	F/L M.P.Kilburn	FW190 destroyed	N Fecamp	1330~
	F/L M.P.Kilburn Sgt J.Saphir	FW190 destroyed - shared -	N Fecamp	1330~
167 Sqn Spit FC	F/O A.R.Hall	FW190 destroyed	Off Ijmuiden	1300~
	F/O A.R.Hall	FW190 destroyed	Off Ijmuiden	1300~
340 Sqn Spit FC	S/L M.Boudier	FW190 destroyed	Near Les Andelys	1335
	Lt O.Massart	FW190 damaged	N St Valery	1350
	Lt O.Massart	FW190 prob.dest	SE Beachy Head	1400
	S/Lt M.Renaud	FW190 damaged	SW Grandvilliers	1330
350 Sqn Spit FC	F/O L.C.Collignon	FW190 damaged	Near St Omer	1130
	F/L Y.G.A.F.Du Monceau	FW190 damaged	Near St Omer	1125
	F/O A.M.Plisnier	FW190 damaged	St Omer	1120
	F/O A.M.Plisnier	FW190 damaged	St Omer	1130
401 Sqn Spit FC	P/O S.C.Cosburn	FW190 damaged	10m S Hastings	1410

13th December 1942

91 Sqn Spit FC	P/O J.G.Johnson	FW190 damaged	12m N Griz Nez	1500~

14th December 1942

263 Sqn Whir FC	F/O J.P.Coyne	FW190 damaged	N Cherbourg	1550~

15th December 1942

137 Sqn Whir FC	P/O R.L.Smith	FW190 damaged	SE Ramsgate	1550~
609 Sqn Typh FC	F/O J.R.Baldwin	FW190 damaged	Off Goodwin Sands	1610~
	F/S A.Haddon	FW190 destroyed	E Ramsgate	1600
	F/S A.Haddon	FW190 damaged	E Ramsgate	1600

Squadron Leader Geoffrey Warnes, one of the Gladiator 'originals' of 263 Squadron's ill-fated Norwegian adventure in 1940, climbs aboard Whirlwind HE-S 'Bellows'. (ww2images.com)

16th December 1942

29 Sqn	Beau	FC	S/L G.H.Goodman	Do217 damaged	45m SE Beachy Head	1500~
141 Sqn	Beau	FC	F/O Cook	Do217 destroyed	Bognor Regis	1445
609 Sqn	Typh	FC	F/S J.M.De Selys Longchamps	FW190 damaged	N Boulogne	1510~
			Sgt S.Turek	FW190 destroyed	N Boulogne	1510~

17th December 1942

486 Sqn	Typh	FC	F/S F.Murphy	Bf109F destroyed	6m S St Catherines Pt	1620
			Sgt K.G.Taylor-Cannon	Bf109F destroyed	6m S St Catherines Pt	1620

18th December 1942

486 Sqn	Typh	FC	F/O G.G.Thomas	Do217E destroyed	6m S Brighton & Hove	1150

19th December 1942

137 Sqn	Whir	FC	F/O J.M.Bryan P/O J R Rebbetoy	FW190 prob.dest - shared -	Off Deal	1415~
486 Sqn	Typh	FC	Sgt A.N.Sames	FW190 destroyed	50m S Bognor Regis	1510
			F/L H.N.Sweetman	FW190 damaged	50m S Bognor Regis	1510
609 Sqn	Typh	FC	F/S A.Haddon	FW190 prob.dest	Off Deal	1412
			F/O R.A.Lallemant	FW190 destroyed	Deal-Griz Nez	1412

20th December 1942

412 Sqn	Spit	FC	F/O W.B.Needham	FW190 damaged	Dieppe-Le Treport	1330-45
609 Sqn	Typh	FC	Sgt S.Turek	FW190 destroyed	Off Dungeness	0900~

Spitfire NN-E EP464 of 310 Squadron, photographed in late 1942. This aircraft was one of two shot down by FW190s of 8./JG 2 on 29th January 1943. Warrant Officer J.Petr went down off Morlaix and was killed. (ww2images.com)

		Sgt S.Turek	FW190 prob.dest	Off Dungeness	0900~

22nd December 1942

234 Sqn	Spit FC	F/L J.Henderson	FW190 damaged	Off Ushant	1635
486 Sqn	Typh FC	F/S C.N.Gall F/O A.E.Umbers	Do217 destroyed - shared -	15m S St Catherines Pt	1020
609 Sqn	Typh FC	F/O J.C.Wells	Ju88 damaged	Cayeux	1540~

24th December 1942

486 Sqn	Typh FC	F/S F.Murphy	Bf109F destroyed	30m S St Catherines Pt	1335
		F/O G.G.Thomas	Bf109F destroyed	40m S St Catherines Pt	1335

31st December 1942

306 Sqn	Spit FC	F/O K.Gorniak	FW190 prob.dest	SE Berck	1440
		F/O Z.Langhamer	FW190 destroyed	SE Berck	1440
		F/O Z.Langhamer	FW190 damaged	SE Berck	1440
		P/O H.J.Pietrzak	FW190 destroyed	NE Le Crotoy	1440
		W/O J.Smigielski	FW190 damaged	Berck	1440
		P/O W.Szajda	FW190 prob.dest	Berck	1440

Chapter Eight

The Allied Build-Up
1st January - 30th June 1943

With a few squadrons now operating the Spitfire IX and more re-equipping or preparing to do so, the general mood of Fighter Command was one of optimism. The USAAF 8th Army Air Force heavy bomber units had begun to deploy in England and had already commenced raids in France with RAF escort. In late January attacks against Germany would begin, commencing the daylight strategic offensive. How the Germans would react to this could only be imagined.

The most sweeping change was to come in June, with the official formation of 2nd Tactical Air Force. This would place almost all fighter-bomber units and a high proportion of fighter squadrons directly under centralised 2nd TAF control, these units to be transferred to the continent following a successful invasion to work in close co-operation with the ground forces in precisiely the same way that the *Luftwaffe* had operated during the Blitzkrieg of 1940. The term 'Fighter Command' was to to be abolished and replaced with the unwieldy 'Air Defence of Great Britain' (ADGB). There were to be difficulties in the change of command, however, and the actual operational debut of 2nd TAF as an entity would not occur until November. Therefore, until that time, the units will still be referred to as 'FC'.

4/5th January 1943

29 Sqn	Beau FC	P/O R RDensham	Do217 damaged	15m N Ostend	2100~

9th January 1943

340 Sqn	Spit FC	S/Lt M.Lorand	FW190 damaged	Foret de Crecy	1330
		Lt E.Reilhac	FW190 destroyed	Foret de Crecy	1330
		Lt E.Reilhac	FW190 damaged	Foret de Crecy	1330
611 Sqn	Spit FC	Sgt R.L.Due	FW190 damaged	Abbeville	1345~
		Sgt H.E.Walmsley	FW190 prob.dest	Abbeville	1345~

10th January 1943

266 Sqn	Typh FC	P/O S.J.Blackwell	FW190 damaged	Off Torquay	1435~
		F/O J.Small	FW190 destroyed	500 yards off Teignmouth	1435~

13th January 1943

340 Sqn	Spit FC	S/L F.Hardy	FW190 destroyed	S Abbeville	1345
		Lt E.Reilhac	FW190 destroyed	Foret de Crecy	1345
		S/Lt M.Renaud	FW190 damaged	Abbeville area	1345
402 Sqn	Spit FC	P/O O.R.Brown	FW190 destroyed	N Abbeville	1345~
		F/O J.M.Checketts	FW190 damaged	N Abbeville	1345~
611 Sqn	Spit FC	F/L F.F.Colloredo -Mansfeld	FW190 destroyed	S Abbeville	1345

213

One-way tickets: (left) The wreckage of Ju88 3E+BB of Stab./KG 6 scattered across the Town End Recreation Ground at Caterham, Surrey. (right) Do217 U5+MR of 7./KG 2 met a similar fate at Westerham, Kent. Both shot down by Wing Commander Mike Wight-Boycott of 29 Squadron (opposite page), who destroyed a third bomber and claimed two more damaged during two sorties this night.

15th January 1943

340 Sqn Spit FC S/Lt R.G.Gouby	FW190 destroyed 20m W Cayeux	1600
S/Lt R.G.Gouby	FW190 damaged 20m W Cayeux	1600

15/16th January 1943

25 Sqn Mosq FC F/L J.Singleton	Do217 destroyed Off Humber	2100~
151 Sqn Mosq FC Sgt E.A.Knight	Do217 destroyed 8m SW Lincoln	2050

16th January 1943

609 Sqn Typh FC F/O G.Evans	FW190 damaged 3m S Dover	1630

17th January 1943

332 Sqn Spit FC Sgt R.Hassel	FW190 damaged Walcheren	1245
Lt P.Mollestad	FW190 destroyed Noord Beveland	1245
Lt T.Strand	- shared -	
401 Sqn Spit FC F/S F.B.Evans	FW190 damaged Bolbec-Goderville	1530
P/O E.L.Gimbel	FW190 destroyed Goderville	1525
F/O H.C.Godefroy	FW190 damaged 10m S Fecamp	1525
F/O H.C.Godefroy	FW190 damaged 10m S Fecamp	1525
F/L F.E.Grant	FW190 damaged 10m S Fecamp	1525
F/L G.B.Murray	FW190 damaged 10m S Fecamp	1525
402 Sqn Spit FC P/O M.Johnston	FW190 damaged Bolbec area	1525
S/L D.G.Malloy	FW190 destroyed Bolbec area	1525
P/O D.J.McCrimmon	FW190 damaged 5m N Fecamp	1530
W/O J.D.Mitchner	FW190 damaged Bolbec area	1525
P/O E.J.Ross	FW190 damaged Bolbec area	1525
P/O E.J.Ross	FW190 damaged Bolbec area	1525

Right: The wreck of another KG 6 Ju88. 3E+GK of 2 Staffel fell at Bethersden, shot down by Squadron Leader I.G.Esplin. also of 29 Squadron.

412 Sqn	Spit	FC	F/L R.A.Ellis	FW190 destroyed	Near Fontaine -le-Dun	1527-30
			S/L F.W.Kelly	FW190 destroyed	Near Fontaine -le-Dun	1527-30
486 Sqn	Typh	FC	Sgt K.G.Taylor-Cannon	Bf109F destroyed	40m SE St Catherines Pt	1505
611 Sqn	Spit	FC	P/O G.R.Lindsay	FW190 damaged	Abbeville	1150~

17/18th January 1943

29 Sqn	Beau	FC	W/C C.M.Wight-Boycott	Ju88 destroyed	Brenzett	2025
			W/C C.M.Wight-Boycott	Do217 damaged	Off Dungeness	2025~
29 Sqn	Beau	FC	W/C C.M.Wight-Boycott	Do217 destroyed	Westerham	0430
			W/C C.M.Wight-Boycott	Do217 damaged	S England	0500~
			W/C C.M.Wight-Boycott	Ju88 destroyed	Caterham	0530
29 Sqn	Beau	FC	F/S T.C.Wood	Ju88 destroyed	SE London	2100~
29 Sqn	Beau	FC	F/O A.C.Musgrove	Ju88 damaged	Off Beachy Head	2130~
29 Sqn	Beau	FC	F/O R.M.Carr	Do217 damaged	Off Dungeness	2020~
29 Sqn	Beau	FC	S/L I.G.Esplin	Ju88 destroyed	Bethersdem	0550
85 Sqn	Mosq	FC	W/C G.L.Raphael	Ju88 destroyed	SE England	2045~

18th January 1943

19 Sqn	Spit	FC	F/L P.H.Bell	FW190 damaged	N Ushant	1455

18/19th January 1943

609 Sqn	Typh	FC	S/L R.P.Beamont	Ju88 damaged	Dover	2015~

20th January 1943

64 Sqn	Spit	FC	S/L W.V.Crawford -Compton	FW190 destroyed	3m NE Calais	1700~
			2/Lt E.Lindseth	FW190 damaged	NW Calais	1700~
			F/L H.R.G.Poulton	FW190 damaged	NW Calais	1700~
91 Sqn	Spit	FC	S/L R.H.Harries	Bf109F destroyed	S Pevensey Bay	1300~
			S/L R.H.Harries	Bf109F damaged	S Pevensey Bay	1300~
			S/L R.H.Harries	FW190 damaged	S Pevensey Bay	1300~
122 Sqn	Spit	FC	F/L C.Haw	Bf109F damaged	S Guines	1315~
			S/L D.E.Kingaby	Bf109F destroyed	S Guines	1315~
332 Sqn	Spit	FC	Sgt N.Fuglesang	FW190 damaged	Griz Nez-10m inland	1320
			Sgt E.Westly	FW190 damaged	Mid Channel-Griz Nez	1320
340 Sqn	Spit	FC	S/Lt R.G.Gouby	FW190 destroyed	10m SE Beachy Hd	1245-1300
			S/Lt R.G.Gouby	FW190 destroyed	20m S Dungeness	1245-1300
			S/Lt R.G.Gouby	FW190 prob.dest	20m S Dungeness	1245-1300
			Lt F.P.M.Roos	Bf109F damaged	S Hastings	1245-1300
401 Sqn	Spit	FC	F/O H.C.Godefroy	FW190 destroyed	S Friston	1250
			P/O H.D.MacDonald	FW190 damaged	S Friston	1250
			P/O H.D.MacDonald	FW190 damaged	S Friston	1250
609 Sqn	Typh	FC	F/O R.A.Lallemant	FW190 destroyed	Off Dungeness	0915
609 Sqn	Typh	FC	F/O J.R.Baldwin	Bf109F destroyed	E Manston	1245
			F/O J.R.Baldwin	Bf109F destroyed	E Manston	1245
			F/O J.R.Baldwin	Bf109F destroyed	E Manston	1245
			F/L J.A.Atkinson	FW190 destroyed	15m SE Dover	1300~
609 Sqn	Typh	FC	F/O P.E.Raw	FW190 damaged	S Dover	1440~
			F/O R Van Lierde	FW190 destroyed	12m S Dover	1440~
611 Sqn	Spit	FC	S/L H.T.Armstrong	Bf109F destroyed	1m S Pevensey Bay	1315~
			S/L H.T.Armstrong	Bf109F destroyed	1m S Pevensey Bay	1315~
BH Wg	Spit	FC	W/C R.M.Milne	FW190 destroyed	S Dungeness	1300
			W/C R.M.Milne	Bf109F destroyed	S Pevensey Bay	1300

20/21st January 1943

29 Sqn	Beau	FC	F/S T.C.Wood	Ju88 damaged	5m W Ashford	2100~
141 Sqn	Beau	FC	W/C J.R.D.Braham	Do217 destroyed	10m SW Dungeness	0100~
FIU	Beau	FC	F/L W.K.Davison	Do217 destroyed	40m S Dungeness	2359

21st January 1943

122 Sqn	Spit	FC	S/L D.E.Kain	FW190 destroyed	Calais	1530~

*On 20th January Dickie
Milne, the Biggin Hill Wing
leader (left) claimed a Bf109
and a FW190 destroyed
between Dungeness and
Pevensey Bay, while Johnny
Baldwin (right) fought an
entire Staffel of Bf109s from
JG 26, destroyed three and
was then shot down himself.
(Milne - ww2images.com)*

			S/L D.E.Kingaby	FW190 destroyed	10m S Calais	1530~
			S/L D.E.Kingaby	FW190 damaged	Gravelines	1530~
306 Sqn	Spit	FC	S/L K.Rutkowski	FW190 prob.dest	E Abbeville	1525
			F/O S.Szpakowicz	FW190 prob.dest	E Abbeville	1520
			F/O S.Szpakowicz	FW190 damaged	N Abbeville	1525
			Sgt H.Szwaba	FW190 prob.dest	E Abbeville	1525
316 Sqn	Spit	FC	F/S P.Gallus	FW190 prob.dest	N Abbeville	1530
			P/O J.Szymankiewicz	FW190 prob.dest	N Berck	1530
609 Sqn	Typh	FC	F/O P.J.Nankivell	FW190 destroyed	E Deal	0850

21/22nd January 1943

264 Sqn	Mosq		FC S/L M.H.Maxwell	Do217 damaged	Deelen	2250~

22nd January 1943

331 Sqn	Spit	FC	F/L H.G.E.Grundt-Spang	Bf109F destroyed	Off Westhoofd	1540
			F/L H.G.E.Grundt-Spang	Bf109F destroyed	Off Westhoofd	1540
350 Sqn	Spit	FC	P/O R.A.Alexandre	FW190 destroyed	Near Mardyck	1515
			F/L A.M.Plisnier	FW190 prob.dest	St Omer-Mardyck	1515

22/23rd January 1943

410 Sqn	Mosq FC		F/S B.M.Haight	Do217 destroyed	4m E Hartlepool	2050

23rd January 1943

66 Sqn	Spit	FC	F/L G.Elcombe	FW190 damaged	15m N Sept Isles	1415
167 Sqn	Spit	FC	Sgt G.J.Cassidy	Do217 prob.dest	40m NE Happisburgh	1250~
			P/O L.C.M.Van Eendenburg	- shared -		

26th January 1943

64 Sqn	Spit	FC	Sgt F.R.Burnard	FW190 damaged	St Omer	1345~
			P/O G.A.Mason	FW190 destroyed	St Omer	1345~
165 Sqn	Spit	FC	F/L B.Warren	FW190 destroyed	Off Hardelot	1400~
167 Sqn	Spit	FC	P/O C.T.K.Cody	Ju88 destroyed	Off Yarmouth	1500
			Sgt W.P.Nash	- shared -		
266 Sqn	Typh	FC	F/O C.R.M.Bell	FW190 destroyed	4m E Start Point	1610~
Tang Wg	Spit	FC	W/C P.M.Brothers	FW190 destroyed	4m W Hardelot	1400

29th January 1943

118 Sqn	Spit	FC	Sgt J.Hollingsworth	FW190 damaged	Ijmuiden	1528
			Sgt L.M.Lack	FW190 destroyed	Ijmuiden	1528
			S/L E.W.Wootten	FW190 damaged	Ijmuiden	1526
310 Sqn	Spit	FC	F/L V.Chocholin	FW190 prob.dest	15m N Off Morlaix	1430
			F/L V.Chocholin	FW190 damaged	15m N Off Morlaix	1430
			S/L E.A.Foit	FW190 destroyed	15m N Morlaix	1430
			F/L H.Hrbacek	FW190 damaged	15m N Morlaix	1430
			F/S V.Popelka	FW190 destroyed	N Morlaix	1430

2nd February 1943

308 Sqn	Spit	FC	F/L T.Koc	FW190 prob.dest	Courtrai-Calais	1100-15
			S/L W.Zak	FW190 prob.dest	Courtrai-Mid Channel	1050-1115
315 Sqn	Spit	FC	F/O S.Blok	FW190 destroyed	3-4m E Calais	1525
			P/O M.Cwynar	FW190 destroyed	3-4m E Calais	1525
331 Sqn	Spit	FC	Sgt E.Berg-Olsen	FW190 prob.dest	E Dieppe	1610
			2/Lt B.Bjornstad	FW190 damaged	E Dieppe	1610
			Lt M.Y.Gran	FW190 prob.dest	E Dieppe	1610
			Lt S.Heglund	FW190 damaged	E Dieppe	1610
332 Sqn	Spit	FC	2/Lt M.Eriksen	FW190 prob.dest	Dieppe-Caveux	1615-20
416 Sqn	Spit	FC	S/L F.H.Boulton	FW190 prob.dest	St Omer	1515
			F/L R.A.Buckham	FW190 destroyed	St Omer	1515
NW Wg	Spit	FC	W/C P.G.Jameson	FW190 damaged	S Somme	1615
SF Ntht	Spit	FC	G/C M.Mumler	FW190 prob.dest	Courtrai-Calais	1100-15

3rd February 1943

219 Sqn	Beau	FC	F/L J.E.Willson	Do217 destroyed	Muston, near Filey	2035

Warmwell: a superbly detailed photo of a Whirlwind at dispersal with Typhoons in the background.
(ww2images.com)

4th February 1943

331 Sqn Spit FC	Capt R.A.Berg	FW190 destroyed	Ypres area	1225-35
	2/Lt N.K.Jorstad	FW190 prob.dest	Ypres area	1225-35
332 Sqn Spit FC	F/S E.Westly	FW190 damaged	W Ypres	1220

4/5th February 1943

609 Sqn Typh FC	F/O P.J.Nankivell	FW190 destroyed	S Eastbourne	0945~
611 Sqn Spit FC	F/L F.F.Colloredo -Mansfeld	FW190 damaged	7m W Boulogne	1210~
	F/O J.A.C.Aitken	- shared -		

8th February 1943

| 486 Sqn Typh FC | F/L H.N.Sweetman | FW190 damaged | 20m SW Shoreham | 1410-15 |
| | Sgt L.Walker | FW190 damaged | 20m SW Shoreham | 1410-15 |

9th February 1943

| 91 Sqn Spit FC | F/O R.M.Batten | Do217 destroyed | Mid Channel | 1115~ |
| 609 Sqn Typh FC | F/L J.A.Atkinson | Do217 damaged | Manston | 0845~ |

10th February 1943

165 Sqn Spit FC	F/L E.W.C.Colquhoun	FW190 prob.dest	St Aubin	1115~
	Sgt A.J.Osborne	FW190 damaged	St Aubin	1115~
	F/O B.Warren	FW190 damaged	St Aubin	1115~
609 Sqn Typh FC	F/L J.C.Wells	Bf109 destroyed	Off St Margarets Bay	u/k
611 Sqn Spit FC	F/O J.C.Minto	FW190 damaged	Near Desvres	1115~

13th February 1943

64 Sqn	Spit FC	Sgt W.Bilstand	FW190 damaged	Boulogne	1020~
167 Sqn	Spit FC	P/O C.T.K.Cody	FW190 damaged*	Ijmuiden	1630~

* Probably not confirmed

340 Sqn	Spit FC	Capt J.A.M.Fournier	FW190 damaged	5m N Le Touquet	1020
		F/S P.R.Hubidos	FW190 damaged	SE Boulogne	1020
		Lt O.Massart	FW190 destroyed	SE Boulogne	1030
		F/L E.Reilhac	FW190 damaged	5-6m E Hardelot	1010
485 Sqn	Spit FC	F/O D.G.E.Brown	FW190 damaged	Le Touquet area	1215
		S/L R.J.C.Grant	FW190 destroyed	Hardelot	1225
		F/O M.R.D.Hume	FW190 destroyed	Off Hardelot	1220
610 Sqn	Spit FC	S/L J.E.Johnson	FW190 prob.dest	Le Touquet	1215~

13/14th February 1943

605 Sqn	Mosq FC	S/L R.E.X.Mack	Do217 damaged	Evreux	0010~

14th February 1943

609 Sqn	Typh FC	F/O J.M.De Selys -Longchamp	FW190 destroyed	Mid-Channel-N Calais	1150~
		F/O R.A.Lallemant	FW190 destroyed	Dover-Griz Nez	1150~
		F/O R.A.Lallemant	FW190 destroyed	Dover-Griz Nez	1150~
		F/O R.A.Lallemant	FW190 prob.dest	Dover-Griz Nez	1150~
		F/O R.H.Payne	FW190 destroyed	Mid-Channel-N Calais	1150~
		F/O A.Polek	FW190 destroyed	Off Calais	1150~
		F/O A.Polek	FW190 prob.dest	Off Calais	1150~

15th February 1943

64 Sqn	Spit FC	S/L W.V.Crawford -Compton	FW190 destroyed	10m off Dunkirk	1550~
		F/L M.G.L.M.Donnet	FW190 destroyed	Dunkirk	1545~
		F/O J.V.Draper	FW190 damaged	Dunkirk	1550~
122 Sqn	Spit FC	Sgt W.W.Peet	FW190 prob.dest	Dunkirk	1550~
266 Sqn	Typh FC	Sgt G.M.R.Eastwood	FW190 damaged	S Start Point	1700~
306 Sqn	Spit FC	S/L K.Rutkowski	FW190 destroyed	10m N Calais	1420
		W/O J.Smigielski	FW190 destroyed	5-10m N Calais	1420
		W/O S.Piatkowski	FW190 prob.dest	10m SE Deal	1400
		F/O J.K.Zuromski	FW190 damaged	10m SE Deal	1400
331 Sqn	Spit FC	2/Lt H.G.E.Grundt-Spang	FW190 destroyed	Mid Channel	1550
		Capt L.Lundsten	FW190 destroyed	Mid Channel	1550
		F/S K.Bache	FW190 damaged	Mid Channel	1550

Slightly 'bent' 409 Squadron Beaufighter at Acklington after a landing accident. Note the AI transmitter 'arrow' behind the propeller and the receiving aerials on the wing. (ww2images.com)

			2/Lt H.Sognnes	FW190 damaged	Mid Channel	1550
332 Sqn	Spit	FC	2/Lt M.Eriksen	FW190 destroyed	Off Dunkirk	1540
			2/Lt M.Eriksen	FW190 destroyed	Off Dunkirk	1550
			2/Lt J.B.Gilhuus	FW190 destroyed	Off Dunkirk	1540
403 Sqn	Spit	FC	S/L L.S.Ford	FW190 damaged	Off Goodwin Sands	1402
			S/L C.M.Magwood	FW190 damaged	Off Goodwin Sands	1401
NW Wg	Spit	FC	W/C P.G.Jameson	FW190 destroyed	Off Dunkirk	1540

15/16th February 1943

307 Sqn	Mosq	FC	F/O R.Zwolinski	Ju88 prob.dest	S Seaton	2342
605 Sqn	Mosq	FC	P/O Ponsford	Do217 destroyed	Melun	2130~

16th February 1943

402 Sqn	Spit	FC	F/O N.A.Keene	FW190 damaged	Le Touquet area	1720
486 Sqn	Typh	FC	F/S F.Murphy	Ju88 destroyed	30m SE St Catherines Pt	1850
611 Sqn	Spit	FC	F/L F.F.Colloredo-Mansfeld	FW190 prob.dest	Guines	1300~
			S/L A.C.Deere	FW190 destroyed	Guines	1300~
			F/S T.Harris	FW190 damaged	Guines	1300~

16/17th February 1943

125 Sqn	Beau	FC	P/O H.B.Newton	Do17 destroyed	Off South Wales	2225
			P/O H.B.Newton	Do217 damaged	Off South Wales	2225~
			P/O H.B.Newton	E/A destroyed	Off South Wales	2225~
			P/O H.B.Newton	Do217 prob.dest	Off South Wales	2225~

125 Sqn	Beau FC	W/C R.F.H.Clerke	Do217 destroyed	Exmoor	2230
125 Sqn	Beau FC	F/L G.E.Jameson	Do217 destroyed	SW England	2300~
125 Sqn	Beau FC	P/O J.O.Mathews	Ju88 damaged	Fairwood Common	2245
605 Sqn	Mosq FC	F/O R.R.Smart	Do217 prob.dest	Evreux	2355~
605 Sqn	Mosq FC	Sgt J.Brochocki	E/A destroyed	Evreux	2100~

19th February 1943

130 Sqn	Spit FC	F/L K.Matheson	FW190 damaged	5m SE Dodman Point	1700
		S/L W.H.A.Wright	FW190 damaged	5m SE Dodman Point	1700

26th February 1943

122 Sqn	Spit FC	Sgt N.Lawson	FW190 damaged	St Omer	1550~
266 Sqn	Typh FC	S/L C.L.Green	FW190 destroyed	50m S Exmouth	1235~
		S/L C.L.Green F/O R.K.Thompson	FW190 destroyed - shared -	50m S Exmouth	1235~
331 Sqn	Spit FC	2/Lt B.Bjornstad	FW190 destroyed	St Omer area	1550
		Capt L.Lundsten	FW190 prob.dest	St Omer area	1550
		2/Lt H.Sognnes	FW190 destroyed	St Omer area	1550
		2/Lt H.Sognnes	FW190 damaged	St Omer area	1550
402 Sqn	Spit FC	F/L I.G.Keltie	FW190 damaged	Le Touquet area	1615
609 Sqn	Typh FC	F/L J.A.Atkinson	FW190 destroyed	Off Boulogne	0900~
		F/O E.R.A.Roberts	FW190 damaged	Off Boulogne	0900~

26/27th February 1943

29 Sqn	Beau FC	W/C C.M.Miller	Do217 destroyed	Foreness	2245~
		W/C C.M.Miller	Do217 destroyed	Foreness	2245~

27th February 1943

313 Sqn	Spit FC	S/L J.Himr	FW190 damaged	Ushant area	1520
402 Sqn	Spit FC	F/O L.M.Cameron	FW190 destroyed	N Dunkirk	1425
403 Sqn	Spit FC	S/L L.S.Ford	FW190 destroyed	NW Dunkirk	1425
		S/L L.S.Ford	FW190 damaged	NW Dunkirk	1425
		P/O E.L.Gimbel	FW190 destroyed	15m NNW Dunkirk	1425

27/28th February 1943

418 Sqn	Bost FC	F/L R.J.Bennell	E/A damaged	Near Melun A/D	2130

28th February 1943

130 Sqn	Spit FC	P/O J.Andrieux	FW190 destroyed	W Barfleur	1635~

1st March 1943

486 Sqn	Typh	FC F/S W.B.Tyerman	FW190 destroyed	4m S Bognor	1220~

Left: Alan Deere, Battle of Britain veteran, claimed his fifteenth solo kill on 16th February while leading 611 Squadron. He survived the war as a Wing Commander DSO, DFC* with seventeen 'confirmed'. Right Harry Newton, a New Zealander like Al Deere, had a successful fight off the Welsh coast on 16/17th, claiming two destroyed, a 'probable' and a 'damaged'. He also survived the war.

(ww2images.com)

3rd March 1943

609 Sqn	Typh	FC	F/O J.R.Baldwin	FW190 destroyed	2-3m off Griz Nez	1000~
			F/O J.R.Baldwin	FW190 damaged	2-3m off Griz Nez	1000~
609 Sqn	Typh	FC	F/O J.M.De Selys -Longchamp	FW190 prob.dest	Griz Nez	u/k
			Sgt T.D.L.Leslie	FW190 damaged	Griz Nez	u/k

3/4th March 1943

29 Sqn	Beau	FC	P/O T.C.Wood	Ju88 destroyed	Near Maidstone	0425
29 Sqn	Beau	FC	F/L R.M.Carr	Do217 damaged	E Foreness	2200~
418 Sqn	Mosq	FC	F/L R.J.Bennell	Do217 destroyed	Deelen	2245

4th March 1943

91 Sqn	Spit	FC	S/L R.H.Harries	FW190 destroyed	Calais	1200~
			F/O R.S.Nash	- shared -		1200~

6th March 1943

313 Sqn	Spit	FC	F/S J.Slepica	FW190 damaged	NW Brest	1415

7th March 1943

331 Sqn Spit FC	2/Lt K.Bache	Bf109F destroyed	10m off France	1343
	Maj K.Birksted	Bf109F destroyed	8m NE North Foreland	1343

7/8th March 1943

29 Sqn Beau FC	S/L G.H.Goodman	Do217 destroyed	Linchmere	0124
604 Sqn Beau FC	F/L W.Hoy	He177 destroyed	S Beachy Head	0130~
604 Sqn Beau FC	W/C V.C.Wood	Do217 destroyed	30m S Ford	0130~

8th March 1943

64 Sqn Spit FC	S/L W.V.Crawford -Compton	FW190 destroyed	Cleres	1410~
	S/L W.V.Crawford -Compton	FW190 destroyed	Cleres	1410~
122 Sqn Spit FC	S/L D.E.Kingaby	FW190 destroyed	Cleves-Pont d'Ailly	1410~
331 Sqn Spit FC	Lt H.Sognnes	Bf109F damaged	Off Griz Nez	1745
403 Sqn Spit FC	P/O C.G.Cumming	FW190 damaged	5m N Pointe de la Percee	1500
	F/L C.M.Magwood	- shared -		
	F/L H.C.Godefroy	FW190 destroyed	W Bayeux	1500
	F/O H.D.MacDonald	FW190 destroyed	Off Pointe de la Percee	1500

9th March 1943

331 Sqn Spit FC	F/S R.H.Olsen	Bf109F damaged	Le Touquer-St Omer	1630
340 Sqn Spit FC	S/Lt R.G.Gouby	FW190 destroyed	15m S Dover	1540
	2/Lt P.F.Kennard	FW190 destroyed	E Calais	1545-55
	2/Lt P.F.Kennard	FW190 destroyed	E Calais	1545-55
	2/Lt P.F.Kennard	FW190 damaged	E Calais	1545-55

9/10th March 1943

406 Sqn Beau FC	F/O A.G.Lawrence	Do217 destroyed	20m S Portland Bill	2105

10th March 1943

331 Sqn Spit FC	2/Lt B.Bjornstad	FW190 damaged	Knocke-Ostend	1615
332 Sqn Spit FC	2/Lt M.Eriksen	FW190 damaged	Knocke	1620
	2/Lt B.Raeder*	FW190 prob.dest	Off Knocke	1620

* Shared with North Weald Wing.

	F/S K.Ronhof	FW190 damaged	Knocke area	1620
	Lt T.Strand	FW190 prob.dest	Knocke area	1620
	Maj F.Thorsager	Bf109F damaged	Near Knocke	1615
	2/Lt E.Westly	Bf109F damaged	Knocke	1620

In March 1943, Johnnie Johnson was promoted to lead the Canadian Kenley Wing. (l to r) Harry MacDonald , Bob 'Trapper' Bowen, Hugh Godefroy, Wally Conrad and Johnson. MacDonal and Godefroy each claimed an FW190 destroyed on 8th March.

BH Wg	Spit	FC	W/C R.M.Milne	FW190 prob.dest	SW Bethune	1750~
NW Wg	Spit	FC	W/C P.G.Jameson*	FW190 prob.dest	Off Knocke	1620

* Shared with 32 Squadron.

11th March 1943

118 Sqn	Spit	FC	F/L R.A.Newbery	FW190 damaged	Ijmuiden	1755
			P/O C.Tallalla	FW190 destroyed	Ijmuiden	1755
610 Sqn	Spit	FC	F/L P.I.Howard-Williams	FW190 destroyed	30m S Beachy Head	1900~

11/12th March 1943

68 Sqn	Beau	FC	F/O J.Vopalecky	Ju88 destroyed	35m NE Cromer	u/k
219 Sqn	Beau	FC	Sgt A.Hollingsworth	Do217 destroyed	Off Yorkshire coast	u/k
219 Sqn	Beau	FC	F/O A.Wallace	Do217 prob.dest	15m E Hartlepool	u/k
219 Sqn	Beau	FC	F/L J.E.Willson	Do217 destroyed	4m E Cullercoats	2325
			F/L J.E.Willson	Do217 destroyed	Great Stainton	2325~
			F/L J.E.Willson	Do217 prob.dest	4m NW West Hartlepool	2325~
605 Sqn	Mosq	FC	W/C G.L.Denholm	E/A prob.dest	Gilze-Rijn	0030~

12th March 1943

64 Sqn	Spit	FC	F/O J.V.Draper	FW190 damaged	Near Hardelot	1630
			F/L E.F.J.Charles	FW190 damaged	10m inland Dunkirk	1630
122 Sqn	Spit	FC	P/O M.Edwards	FW190 damaged	Bradwell Bay	0820~

225

On 13th March, Hauptmann Heinrich Setz, Kommandeur of I./JG 27, was shot down and killed by a Spitfire pilot, believed to have been Michal Najbicz of 315 Squadron. Setz had been credited with 132 kills in Russia and six in the west. He was a holder of the Ritterkreuz mit Eichenlaub (Oak Leaves).

316 Sqn	Spit	FC	F/O C.Jaworowski	Bf109G destroyed S Foret de Bretanne	1255
			P/O W.Kiedrzynski	FW190 destroyed 40m N Etretat	1315
331 Sqn	Spit	FC	2/Lt B.Bjornstad	FW190 destroyed Off Bradwell	0750
			Sgt F.Eitzen	FW190 destroyed Mid Channel	0750
			2/Lt R.Engelsen Lt E.Fossum	FW190 destroyed Off Bradwell - shared -	0750
			Capt L.Lundsten	FW190 destroyed North Foreland-Calais	0750
			Capt L.Lundsten	FW190 destroyed North Foreland-Calais	0750
			F/S R.H.Olsen	FW190 damaged Off Bradwell	0750
			2/Lt B.Bjornstad F/S R.H.Olsen	FW190 damaged Off Bradwell - shared -	0750
			Lt H.Sognnes	FW190 destroyed Off Bradwell	0750
			Lt H.Sognnes	FW190 damaged Off Bradwell	0750
			Lt H.Sognnes	FW190 damaged Off Bradwell	0750
332 Sqn	Spit	FC	2/Lt M.Eriksen	FW190 destroyed 10m W Rouen	1245-1300
			Capt J.Ryg	Bf109G prob.dest St Valery-Fecamp	1255
			Lt T.Strand	FW190 damaged Off St Valery	1300
340 Sqn	Spit	FC	F/L O.Massart	FW190 prob.dest 5m S Rouen	1250-55
609 Sqn	Typh	FC	Sgt T.D.L.Leslie	FW190 damaged Off Dunkirk	1010~
			F/S L.W.F.Stark	FW190 destroyed Off Dunkirk	1010~

12/13th March 1943

219 Sqn	Beau	FC	F/L J.C.I.Hooper	Do217 destroyed Off Tyne	2240~
605 Sqn	Mosq	FC	S/L I.M.T.deK.De Bocock	Do217 destroyed Eindhoven	2350~

13th March 1943

1 Sqn	Typh	FC	F/L L.S.B.Scott	FW190 destroyed SW Beachy Head	1740~
			Sgt R.W.Hornall	FW190 destroyed SW Beachy Head	1740~

In the spring of 1943 the Allison-powered North American Mustang I and II became a more frequent visitor to the skies of northern France. Although fast and manoeuvrable, the Mustangs often fell victim to FW190s. (ww2images.com)

122 Sqn	Spit	FC	Sgt N.Lawson	FW190 destroyed	Lumbres	1530~
			F/L W.H.Prest	FW190 destroyed	Lumbres	1530~
			P/O O.Smik	Bf109G damaged	Lumbres	1530~
266 Sqn	Typh	FC	F/O J.H.Deall	FW190 destroyed	20m S Start Point	1225~
			F/O J.H.Deall (shared)	FW190 destroyed	20m S Start Point	1225~
			Sgt D.S.Eadie (shared)	FW190 destroyed	20m S Start Point	1225
315 Sqn	Spit	FC	F/O M.Najbicz	Bf109G destroyed	S Poix	1510-15
316 Sqn	Spit	FC	F/O L.Zakrewski	FW190 destroyed	Grandvilliers	1510
331 Sqn	Spit	FC	Sgt T.Larssen	Bf109 damaged	Somme Estuary	1520
			Lt H.Sognnes	FW190 damaged	Mid Channel-Berck	1520
402 Sqn	Spit	FC	F/O L.M.Cameron	FW190 damaged	S Cayeux	1520
403 Sqn	Spit	FC	S/L L.S.Ford	FW190 destroyed	10-20m SW Amiens	1515

13/14th March 1943

29 Sqn	Beau	FC	S/L I.G.Esplin	Ju88 prob.dest	S Beachy Head	0130~

14th March 1943

340 Sqn	Spit	FC	S/Lt R.G.Gouby	FW190 destroyed	SW Boulogne	1755
			S/Lt R.G.Gouby	FW190 damaged	SW Boulogne	1755
			S/Lt P.F.Kennard	FW190 destroyed	S St Omer	1800
486 Sqn	Typh	FC	F/S R.H.Fitzgibbon	FW190 destroyed	35-40m S Beachy Hd	1115

611 Sqn	Spit	FC	F/L F.F.Colloredo -Mansfeld	FW190 damaged	Boulogne-Le Touquet	1800~
BH Wg	Spit	FC	W/C R.M.Milne	FW190 destroyed	Berck-Montreuil	1810~

14/15th March 1943

219 Sqn	Beau	FC	S/L J.S.Morton	Do217 destroyed	12m NE Hartlepool	2330~
219 Sqn	Beau	FC	F/O A.E.Sloman	Do217 destroyed	E Teesmouth	0000~

15th March 1943

SF Egl	Spit	FC	W/C R.F.Boyd	Ju88 damaged	Off Malin Head	1125~

15/16th March 1943

68 Sqn	Beau	FC	F/L M.J.Mansfeld	Ju88 destroyed	50m E Spurn Head	2200~
219 Sqn	Beau	FC	F/L J.E.Willson	Do217 destroyed	Spurn Head	2140
			F/L J.E.Willson	E/A destroyed	Near Cleethorpes	2130~
18th March 1943						
118 Sqn	Spit	FC	Sgt R.J.Flight	FW190 prob.dest	North Sea	1630~
			F/L R.A.Newbery	FW190 destroyed	North Sea	1630~
Dig Wg	Spit	FC	W/C H.P.Blatchford	FW190 destroyed	Dutch coast off Voorne	1630~
			W/C H.P.Blatchford	FW190 prob.dest	Dutch coast off Voorne	1630~

18/19th March 1943

29 Sqn	Beau	FC	F/L J.G.Strauss	Ju88 destroyed	35m off Foreness	2300~
68 Sqn	Beau	FC	F/O P.F.Allen	Do217 destroyed	Off Winterton	2330~
			F/O P.F.Allen	Do217 destroyed	Off Winterton	2330~
157 Sqn	Mosq	FC	F/O G.Deakin	Ju88 destroyed	Norwich	2245~
410 Sqn	Mosq	FC	F/O D.Williams*	Do217 destroyed	Kings Lynn	2310

Shared with AA Command.

22nd March 1943

264 Sqn	Mosq	FC	W/O D.McKenzie	Ju88 destroyed	W Bordeaux	1030~
			F/L W.F.Gibb	Ju88 destroyed	W Bordeaux	1030~
			F/O R.M.Muir	- shared -		

24th March 1943

91 Sqn	Spit	FC	S/L R.H.Harries	FW190 destroyed	S Hythe	1020~
			S/L R.H.Harries	FW190 damaged	S Hythe	1020~
			P/O A. O'Shaughnessy	- shared -		
234 Sqn	Spit	FC	Sgt R.Lane	Ju88 destroyed	5m W Sumburgh	1754
			Sgt Wilson	- shared -		

24/25th March 1943

219 Sqn Beau FC	F/O J R Robinson	Do217 prob.dest	20m E Tynemouth	0100~
409 Sqn Beau FC	S/L G.H.Elms	Ju88 destroyed	Earlstone	0030

25th March 1943

64 Sqn Spit FC	2/Lt T.Johnsen	FW190 prob.dest	Somme	1600~
609 Sqn Typh FC	Sgt C.E.West	FW190 damaged	Off North Foreland	1815~

26th March 1943

609 Sqn Typh FC	F/O R.Van Lierde	Ju52 destroyed	Ath, Belgium	1230~

27th March 1943

604 Sqn Beau FC	F/L T.Wood (shared AA)	Ju88 destroyed	S Worthing	1417

28th March 1943

421 Sqn Spit FC	P/O R.T.Heeney	FW190 damaged	30-35m S Beachy Hd	1235
602 Sqn Spit FC	P/O A.Strudwick	FW190 prob.dest	Off Ile de Batz	1600~

28/29th March 1943

68 Sqn Beau FC	F/O J.Vopalecky*	Do217 destroyed	Southwold	2200~
* Shared with 157 Squadron.				
68 Sqn Beau FC	P/O L.Bobek	Ju88 destroyed	60m E Lowestoft	2230~
157 Sqn Mosq FC	F/O J.R.Beckett*	Do217 destroyed	Southwold	2200~
* Shared with 68 Squadron.				

29th March 1943

91 Sqn Spit FC	F/O G.W.Bond	FW190 damaged	Somme estuary	1125~
610 Sqn Spit FC	P/O F.A.Venesoen	FW190 destroyed	Off Brighton	1115

30th March 1943

264 Sqn Mosq FC	S/L M.H.Maxwell	He111 prob.dest	8m N Redon	1430~

1st April 1943

331 Sqn Spit FC	Lt H.Sognnes	FW190 destroyed	Caen-20m N coast	1640

3rd April 1943

234 Sqn Spit FC	P/O W.G.Gadsden	Ju88 damaged	25m E Sumburgh	1825~
	F/L E.D.Glaser	- shared -		
403 Sqn Spit FC	S/L L.S.Ford	FW190 destroyed	Near Fruges	1503
	F/O H.D.MacDonald	FW190 destroyed	Near Fruges	1503
	F/L C.M.Magwood	FW190 destroyed	Near Fruges	1503
416 Sqn Spit FC	S/L F.H.Boulton	FW190 destroyed	Near le Touquet	1500
	F/L R.A.Buckham	FW190 destroyed	Near le Touquet	1500
	P/O N.A.Keene	- shared -		

		F/O J.A.Rae	FW190 damaged	Near le Touquet	1500
Ken Wg	Spit	FC	W/C J.E.Johnson	FW190 destroyed	E Montreuil	1505-10
Ntht Wg	Spit	FC	W/C W.Kolaczkowski	FW190 damaged	10m NNW Dieppe	1630

3/4th April 1943

29 Sqn	Beau	FC	S/L A.R.Wright	Ju88 destroyed	14m W Schouwen	2130~
			S/L A.R.Wright	Ju88 damaged	14m W Schouwen	2130~

4th April 1943

118 Sqn	Spit	FC	V.C.Simmonds	FW190 damaged	20-50m off Hook of Holland	1945~
			F/S C.Anderton	FW190 destroyed	Off Dutch Coast	1945~
			Sgt J.Hollingsworth	FW190 destroyed	Off Dutch Coast	1945~
			Sgt J.Hollingsworth	FW190 damaged	Off Dutch Coast	1945~
			Unknown pilot	FW190 damaged	Off Dutch Coast	1945~
			S/L E.W.Wootten	FW190 damaged	20-60m off Hook of Holland	1945~
			S/L E.W.Wootten	FW190 damaged	20-60m off Hook of Holland	1945~
167 Sqn	Spit	FC	Sgt W.P.Nash	FW190 damaged	Off Dutch coast	1945~
312 Sqn	Spit	FC	F/S S.Tocauer	FW190 prob.dest	E St Brieuc	1654
315 Sqn	Spit	FC	P/O T.Andersz	FW190 destroyed	N Rouen	1430
			F/S M.Matus	FW190 damaged	15m NNW Rouen	1435
			S/L T.Sawicz	FW190 damaged	15m NNW Rouen	1435
316 Sqn	Spit	FC	S/L H.Szczesny	FW190 destroyed	Near Rouen	1430~
			S/L H.Szczesny*	FW190 destroyed	Near Rouen	1430~
* by collision						
331 Sqn	Spit	FC	2/Lt B.Bjornstad	FW190 destroyed	Rouen-Channel	1440
			Sgt G.K.Koren	FW190 damaged	Rouen-Channel	1440
			F/S R.H.Olsen	FW190 prob.dest	Rouen-Channel	1440
			F/S R.H.Olsen	FW190 damaged	Rouen-Channel	1440
332 Sqn	Spit	FC	Lt M.Eriksen	Bf109 destroyed	10m off Dieppe	1450-55
			Lt M.Eriksen	Bf109 damaged	10m off Dieppe	1450-55
			Sgt K.Herford	Bf109 prob.dest	10m off Dieppe	1450-55
			2/Lt E.Westly	Bf109 damaged	10m off Dieppe	1450-55
			2/Lt E.Westly	Bf109 damaged	10m off Dieppe	1450-55
403 Sqn	Spit	FC	S/L L.S.Ford	FW190 destroyed	20m N Rouen	1435
			P/O E.L.Gimbel*	FW190 destroyed	Near Pavilly	1435
*by collision						
			F/L C.M.Magwood	FW190 destroyed	Bellencombre	1435

Three great Canadian aces were all successful on 3rd April. Bob Buckham of 416 Squadron (left) shared the destruction of an FW190, his CO Foss Boulton got another and Charlie Magwood of 403 Squadron claimed a third. All would survive the war. Boulton was captured on 13th May and was repatriated due to his injuries. Buckham died in 1947 in a flying accident.

			F/O H.D.MacDonald	FW190 destroyed	Near St Valery	1445
			F/L C.M.Magwood	FW190 destroyed	10m NW St Valery	1447
			Sgt L.J.Deschamps	FW190 destroyed	Bellencombre	1435-47
504 Sqn	Spit	FC	S/L J.R.C.Kilian	FW190 damaged	Mid-Channel	1005~
			F/L C.C.McCarthy-Jones	FW190 prob.dest	Mid-Channel	1005~
Colt Wg	Spit	FC	W/C H.P.Blatchford	FW190 damaged	North Sea	1045~
			W/C H.P.Blatchford	FW190 damaged	North Sea	1945~
2Pol Wg	Spit	FC	W/C A.K.Gabszewicz	FW190 destroyed	60m off Dutch coast	1945

5th April 1943

129 Sqn	Spit	FC	P/O R.L.Reeves	FW190 damaged	Landunvez, N Brest	1800
			S/L H.A.C.Gonay	FW190 damaged	Landunvez, N Brest	1750
332 Sqn	Spit	FC	Sgt K.Herfjord	FW190 destroyed	30m N Haamstede	1600
			Lt B.Raeder	FW190 destroyed	30m N Haamstede	1600
			2/Lt E.Westly	FW190 prob.dest	30m N Haamstede	1600
416 Sqn	Spit	FC	S/L F.H.Boulton	FW190 damaged	20m W Ghent	1518
			F/O J.A.Rae	FW190 damaged	20m W Ghent	1520
616 Sqn	Spit	FC	Sgt M.H.F.Cooper	FW190 damaged	Landunvez	1745
Ibs Wg	Spit	FC	W/C T.F.Dalton-Morgan	FW190 destroyed	Landunvez	1745
			W/C T.F.Dalton-Morgan	FW190 prob.dest	Landunvez	1745
Ken Wg	Spit	FC	W/C J.E.Johnson	FW190 damaged	Knocke-Ostend	1535
			W/C J.E.Johnson	FW190 damaged	Knocke-Ostend	1535
			W/C J.E.Johnson	FW190 damaged	Knocke-Ostend	1535

6th April 1943

350 Sqn	Spit	FC	S/L A.L.T.J.Boussa	Do217 destroyed	70m E Acklington	1057

Left, Jack Rae of 416 Squadron, who survived the war and became a singer! On 5th April he claimed an FW190 damaged. Right: a nice study of Flight Lieutenant (later Wing Commander) Walter Dring standing on Typhoon R8884 HF-L at Gatwick. (ww2images.com)

7th April 1943

257 Sqn	Typh FC	F/O P.F.Steib	Bf109 destroyed	30m S Isle of Wight	0745~
609 Sqn	Typh FC	Sgt T.D.L.Leslie	Do217 prob.dest	Off Cap Griz Nez	1400~

8th April 1943

65 Sqn	Spit FC	Sgt I.Evans	FW190 damaged	N Brest	1100~
453 Sqn	Spit FC	F/L D.G.Andrews	FW190 damaged	NE Abbeville	1840
		S/L J.R.Ratten	FW190 damaged	NE Abbeville	1840
Perr Wg	Spit FC	W/C P.G.St.G.O'Brian	FW190 damaged	N Brest	1100~

9th April 1943

1 Sqn	Typh FC	Sgt R.W.Hornall	FW190 destroyed	Dover Straits	1950~
486 Sqn	Typh FC	S/L D.J.Scott F/L H.N.Sweetman F/L A.E.Umbers F/O I.D.Waddy	FW190 prob.dest - shared - - shared - - shared -	Etretat	1935
		S/L D.J.Scott F/L H.N.Sweetman F/L A.E.Umbers F/O I.D.Waddy	FW190 prob.dest - shared - - shared - - shared -	Etretat	1935
609 Sqn	Typh FC	Lt E.Haabjoern	FW190 destroyed	Dover Straits	1925~
611 Sqn	Spit FC	P/O H.E.Walmsley	FW190 damaged	Dungeness -Ambleteuse	1845~
611 Sqn	Spit FC	S/L B.Berthold	FW190 destroyed	Dover Straits	1930~
		F/O G.R.Lindsay	FW190 destroyed	Dover Straits	1930~
611 Sqn	Spit FC	F/S A.Haynes	FW190 damaged	Dover Straits	2030~

11th April 1943

602 Sqn Spit FC P/O W.W.J.Loud FW190 prob.dest 2m N Guisseny 1620~

11/12th April 1943

418 Sqn Bost FC S/L P.Burton-Gyles E/A destroyed Beauvais 0120

13th April 1943

331 Sqn	Spit	FC	Maj H.O.Mehre	FW190 damaged	SW Caen	1640
			Sgt T.Woxen	FW190 damaged	Caen	1640
332 Sqn	Spit	FC	Capt W.Christie	FW190 damaged	Caen-20m N Coast	1640
			2/Lt O.Djonne	FW190 destroyed	Caen-20m N Coast	1640

14th April 1943

400 Sqn Must AC F/O D.M.Grant Do217 destroyed Melun/Villaroche A/D 2230

14th April 1943

65 Sqn	Spit	FC	F/L R.Barrett	FW190 destroyed	Cambret	1700~
			P/O J.A.Long	JuW34 destroyed	Cambret	1700~
257 Sqn	Typh	FC	F/O C.W.C.Henman	Bf109F destroyed	S Portland	1905~
			P/O S.J.Khin	Bf109F prob.dest	S Portland	1905~
411 Sqn	Spit	FC	P/O C.S.Pope	FW190 destroyed	30-40m NE Cherbourg	1805
			F/O A.M.Barber F/L G.C.Semple	FW190 destroyed - shared -	30-40m NE Cherbourg	1805
486 Sqn	Typh	FC	F/S R.H.Fitzgibbon S/L D.J.Scott	Bf109 destroyed - shared -	20m NW St Aubin	1010

14/15th April 1943

85 Sqn	Mosq	FC	S/L W.P.Green	Do217 destroyed	Thames estuary	0007
85 Sqn	Mosq	FC	F/L G.L.Howitt	Do217 destroyed	Clacton	0041
157 Sqn	Mosq	FC	F/L J.G.Benson	Do217 destroyed	Near Colchester	0045
418 Sqn	Mosq	FC	W/C J.H.Little	E/A destroyed	Beauvais	0246
605 Sqn	Mosq	FC	S/L C.D.Tomalin DFC	E/A damaged	Soesterburg	0200~

15/16th April 1943

605 Sqn	Mosq	FC	F/O R.R.Smart	Ju87 destroyed	Avord	0150~
605 Sqn	Mosq	FC	F/O R.R.Smart	Ju87 destroyed	Avord	0150~

16th April 1943

197 Sqn	Typh	FC	F/L J.R.Hyde	Bf109 prob.dest	Off Fecamp	1800~
			F/O J.Turton	FW190 prob.dest	Off Fecamp	1800~
331 Sqn	Spit	FC	Sgt F.Eitzen	FW190 destroyed	5m W Flushing	1430
			2/Lt H.G.E.Grundt-Spang	FW190 destroyed	5m W Flushing	1430

			Capt L.Lundsten	FW190 destroyed	Flushing	1430
332 Sqn	Spit	FC	2/Lt J.B.Gilhuus	FW190 prob.dest	Flushing area	1430
			Maj F.Thorsager	FW190 destroyed	Flushing area	1430
412 Sqn	Spit	FC	S/L F.W.Kelly	FW190 prob.dest	15m N Ushant	2005-10
486 Sqn	Typh	FC	Squadron claim	Bf109 destroyed	5m N Le Havre	0825
616 Sqn	Spit	FC	Sgt T.D.Dean	FW190 prob.dest	Brest	1540
Ntht Wg	Spit	FC	W/C W.Kolaczkowski	FW190 damaged	25m NW St Valery -en-Caux	0900

17th April 1943

41 Sqn	Spit	FC	F/O R.H.W.Hogarth	Ju88 destroyed	Ostend	2045~
266 Sqn	Typh	FC	F/O J.H.Deall	FW190 damaged	N Brest	2000~
			S/L C.L.Green	FW190 damaged	N Brest	2000~
403 Sqn	Spit	FC	F/L H.C.Godefroy	FW190 destroyed	Le Treport area	1503-20
			P/O P.K.Gray	FW190 destroyed	Le Treport area	1503-20
16 Sqn	Spit	FC	S/L F.H.Boulton	Bf109 destroyed	15-20m N Dieppe	1850
			Squadron claim	FW190 destroyed	15-20m N Dieppe	1850

Opposite page: Pilot Officer Max Cotton of 263 Squadron returned to Warmwell on 28th April with this flak damage to the starboard wing of P6981 following a convoy attack (ww2images.com)

Right: on 24/25th April John Lintott of 85 Squadron claimed his first - of four - victories. He was killed in action on 9/10th July 1943..

18th April 1943

611 Sqn	Spit	FC	F/L E.F.J.Charles	FW190 destroyed	Bay d'Authie	1710~

20th April 1943

315 Sqn	Spit	FC	F/O R.Dubielecki	FW190 destroyed	10-15m N Fecamp	1935
			Sgt T.Jankowski	FW190 damaged	10-15m N Fecamp	1935
			S/L J.Poplawski	FW190 damaged	10-15m N Fecamp	1935
332 Sqn	Spit	FC	Lt M.Eriksen	Ju88 destroyed	10m off Clacton	1150
416 Sqn	Spit	FC	S/L F.H.Boulton	FW190 destroyed	Dieppe coast	1925
			P/O R.D.Phillip	FW190 damaged	Dieppe coast	1925

21st April 1943

485 Sqn	Spit	FC	S/L H.E.Meagher	Bf109 destroyed	3m W Cayeux	1235
610 Sqn	Spit	FC	S/L W.A.Laurie	FW190 damaged	Cayeux	1230~
			F/O F.A.Venesoen	FW190 damaged	Cap St Mathieu	1230~
			F/O F.A.Venesoen	FW190 damaged	Cap St Mathieu	1230~

23/24th April 1943

85 Sqn	Mosq FC	S/L E.D.Crew	Do217 damaged	North Foreland	0359

24/25th April 1943

85 Sqn	Mosq FC	F/O J.P.M.Lintott	Ju88 destroyed	Bromley	0030

27th April 1943

41 Sqn	Spit	FC	F/O C.R.Birbeck	FW190 destroyed	W Somme estuary	1705

28/29th April 1943

256 Sqn	Beau FC	F/O J.A.Green	Do217 destroyed	35m S Worthing	2230~

29th April 1943

268 Sqn	Must AC	F/L Bird	Ju88 destroyed	Sea	u/k
		F/O Browne	- shared -		
486 Sqn	Typh FC	P/O F.Murphy	Bf109 destroyed	30m S Isle of Wight	1910-15
		F/O A.H.Smith	Bf109 destroyed	30m S Isle of Wight	1910-15

2nd May 1943

167 Sqn	Spit FC	F/L A.R.Hall	FW190 damaged	Off Dutch coast	1935~
		S/L A.C.Stewart	FW190 damaged	Off Dutch coast	1935~
302 Sqn	Spit FC	F/O S.Brzeski	FW190 destroyed	20m W The Hague	1935
331 Sqn	Spit FC	Lt N.K.Jorstad	FW190 destroyed	Walcheren	1930-35
		Lt N.K.Jorstad	FW190 damaged	Walcheren	1930-35
		Lt N.K.Jorstad	FW190 destroyed	Walcheren	1930-35
		Lt H.Sognnes	FW190 destroyed	Walcheren	1930-35
332 Sqn	Spit FC	2/Lt M.Eriksen	FW190 destroyed	Walcheren	1930-35
		2/Lt O.Djonne	FW190 destroyed	Walcheren	1930-35
		2/Lt O.Djonne	FW190 destroyed	Walcheren	1930-35
		2/Lt J.B.Gilhuus	FW190 damaged	Walcheren	1930-35
Colt Wg	Spit FC	W/C H.P.Blatchford	FW190 prob.dest	Off Dutch coast	1935~

3rd May 1943

118 Sqn	Spit FC	Sgt R.J.Flight	FW190 destroyed	Ijmuiden	1750
		Sgt R.J.Flight	FW190 destroyed	Ijmuiden	1750
		Sgt R.J.Flight	FW190 damaged	Ijmuiden	1750
167 Sqn	Spit FC	F/O C.T.K.Cody	FW190 destroyed	Ijmuiden	1800~
		F/O F.J.Reahill	FW190 prob.dest	Ijmuiden	1800~
		S/L A.C.Stewart	FW190 damaged	Ijmuiden	1800~
		F/O J.Van Arkel	FW190 damaged	Ijmuiden	1800~
416 Sqn	Spit FC	S/L F.H.Boulton	FW190 destroyed	Samer	1821
		F/L R.A.Buckham	FW190 destroyed	Samer	1821
134 Wg	Spit FC	W/C F.Dolezal	FW190 damaged	9-10m W Ile de Batz	1513

4th May 1943

315 Sqn	Spit FC	F/O R.Dubielecki	FW190 damaged	N Sas Van Gent	1850
316 Sqn	Spit FC	F/O M.M.Maciejowski	FW190 prob.dest	10m S Flushing	1850
		F/O M.M.Maciejowski	FW190 damaged	10m S Flushing	1850
331 Sqn	Spit FC	Sgt F.H.Berg-Olsen	Bf109 destroyed	Somme mouth	1950-55
		2/Lt H.G.E.Grundt-Spang	Bf109 destroyed	Somme mouth	1950-55
		Lt N.K.Jorstad	Bf109 damaged	Somme mouth	1950-55

Marius Eriksen of 332 Squadron claimed his last victory - an FW190 - in combat with JG 1 on 2nd May 1943. He was then himself shot down and captured. With nine kills he was then the top-scoring Norwegian fighter pilot.

		Sgt T.Larssen	Bf109 destroyed	Somme mouth	1950-55
		Capt L.Lundsten	Bf109 damaged	Somme mouth	1950-55
		Lt H.Sognnes	Bf109 damaged	Somme mouth	1950-55
611 Sqn	Spit FC	S/L E.F.J.Charles	FW190 damaged	20m W Antwerp	1840~
BH Wg	Spit FC	W/C A.C.Deere	FW190 destroyed	15m W Antwerp	1840~

4/5th May 1943

605 Sqn	Mosq FC	F/O B.Williams	Do217 destroyed	Eindhoven	0430~

7th May 1943

332 Sqn	Spit FC	2/Lt H.R.Isachsen	Bf109 damaged	SE St Omer	1855
		2/Lt E.Westly	Bf109 damaged	SE St Omer	1855
611 Sqn	Spit FC	S/L E.F.J.Charles	Bf109 damaged	3m N Le Touquet	1620~

7/8th May 1943

418 Sqn	Mosq FC	P/O H.O.Craft	Ju88 destroyed	Near Bretigny	0058

8th May 1943

122 Sqn	Spit FC	Sgt R.J.Williams	Ju88 destroyed	Near Laindon	0715
		F/O L .W.Burt	Ju88 damaged	Pitsea	0715~
331 Sqn	Spit FC	2/Lt K.Bache	Ju88 destroyed	6m SW North Weald	0750
		Capt L.Lundsten	- shared -		

11th May 1943

613 Sqn	Must AC	F/O W.Bodington	FW190 damaged	North Sea	0900
		F/O The Hon H.Sackville	FW190 damaged	North Sea	0900
		F/O R.Smith	FW190 damaged	North Sea	0900
		F/O J.R.C.Townsend	FW190 destroyed	10m off Holland	0900
Ken Wg	Spit FC	W/C J.E.Johnson	FW190 destroyed	Gravelines coast area	1310

12/13th May 1943

418 Sqn	Mosq FC	F/L M.W.Beveridge	Ju88 damaged	Orleans/Bricy A/D	0052
		F/L M.W.Beveridge	Ju87 damaged	Orleans/Bricy A/D	0052
		F/L M.W.Beveridge	E/A damaged	Orleans/Bricy A/D	0052

13th May 1943

122 Sqn	Spit FC	S/L W.V.Crawford -Compton	FW190 damaged	E Doullons	1630~
		P/O J.Hlado	FW190 damaged	Le Touquet	1630~
315 Sqn	Spit FC	F/O S.Blok	FW190 damaged	Abbeville	1620
316 Sqn	Spit FC	P/O T.Gora	FW190 prob.dest	Amiens-Doullens	1630-35
		S/L S.Bienkowski	FW190 damaged	Bernaville	1635-40
331 Sqn	Spit FC	Lt G.G.W.Gran	FW190 destroyed	St Omer-Cassel	1220
		Lt H.Sognnes	FW190 destroyed	St Omer-Cassel	1220
331 Sqn	Spit FC	Lt H.Sognnes	FW190 prob.dest	Berck-Albert	1620-40
		Lt H.Sognnes	FW190 damaged	Berck-Albert	1620-40
332 Sqn	Spit FC	2/Lt H.R.Isachsen	FW190 damaged	Berck-Albert	1625
		Lt E.Westly	FW190 destroyed	Berck-Albert	1630
		Lt E.Westly	FW190 damaged	Berck-Albert	1630
403 Sqn	Spit FC	S/L C.M.Magwood	FW190 destroyed	St Omer-Gravelines	1205
		S/L C.M.Magwood	FW190 damaged	St Omer-Gravelines	1218
403 Sqn	Spit FC	P/O W.T.Lane	FW190 damaged	Near Meaulte	1628
		P/O H.J.Dowding	Bf109 destroyed	5m S Le Touquet	1630
		F/L H.D.MacDonald	Bf109 damaged	Meaulte	1632
		Sgt R.D.Bowen*	FW190 destroyed	Mid Channel	1648

* Shared with Kenley Wing.

		F/L H.C.Godefroy	Bf109 damaged	Meaulte	1630
		P/O H.J.Dowding	FW190 destroyed	Mid Channel	1648
416 Sqn	Spit FC	F/L R.H.Walker	FW190 destroyed	Dunkirk area	1200
		F/O J.A.Rae	FW190 destroyed	15m S Mardyck	1220
		S/L F.H.Boulton	FW190 destroyed	Hazebrouck -Gravelines	1205-15
		S/L F.H.Boulton	FW190 damaged	Hazebrouck -Gravelines	1205-15
Ken Wg	Spit FC	W/C J.E.Johnson	FW190 destroyed	Berck-Le Touquet	1630
		W/C J.E.Johnson*	FW190 destroyed	Mid Channel	1648

* Shared with 403 Squadron.

Ntht Wg	Spit FC	W/C W.Kolaczkowski	Bf109 prob.dest	Near Meaulte	1630

Left: Warmwell, Squadron Leader E.C.R.Baker after being hit by flak over Abbeville and nursing his 182 Squadron Typhoon home to a crash landing near Ford on May 13th. Right: 'Spike' Umbers of 486 Squadron was eventually to lose his life to Flak while leading the Tempest-equipped squadron in 1945.

13/14th May 1943

157 Sqn Mosq FC P/O L.R.Watts	Do217 destroyed	Off Orfordness	0245~
605 Sqn Mosq FC F/O A.G.Woods	He111 damaged	Laon	0100~

14th May 1943

122 Sqn Spit FC P/O G.le Gal*	FW190 destroyed	W Flushing	1330~
* Shared with Hornchurch Wing.			
P/O G.le Gal	FW190 damaged	W Flushing	1330~
268 Sqn Must AC F/S F.J.Barnes	FW190 destroyed	Ijmuiden	1340~
315 Sqn Spit FC F/O M.Najbicz	FW190 damaged	Near Amiens	1225
315 Sqn Spit FC F/O M.Najbicz	FW190 damaged	Near Amiens	1225
F/O T.Zurakowski	FW190 damaged	Near Amiens	1225
316 Sqn Spit FC F/O C.Jaworowski	FW190 damaged	5m N Courtrai	1230
P/O T.Karnkowski	FW190 prob.dest	2-3m N Courtrai	1247
341 Sqn Spit FC Capt L.C.Martel	FW190 destroyed	Dixmunde-Roulers	1237
403 Sqn Spit FC F/L H.C.Godefroy	FW190 destroyed	S Ostend	1240
F/L H.D.MacDonald	FW190 destroyed	Off Ostend	1250
416 Sqn Spit FC F/L R.A.Buckham	FW190 destroyed	Near Ypres	1225
611 Sqn Spit FC F/L E.F.J.Charles	FW190 destroyed	nr Courtrai	1340~

	Sgt E.Clark*	Bf109 destroyed Nieuport	1340~

By collision.

Hch Wg Spit FC	W/C J.R.Ratten*	FW190 destroyed W Flushing	1330~

Shared with 122 Squadron.

Ken Wg Spit FC	W/C J.E.Johnson	FW190 destroyed Near Nieuport	1245

14/15th May 1943

157 Sqn Mosq FC	F/L H.E.Tappin	FW190 destroyed Evreux	0120~
609 Sqn Typh FC	F/O R.Van Lierde	He111 destroyed NW Blankenburghe	0010~

15th May 1943

19 Sqn Spit FC	F/L P.Wigley	Bf109 damaged 10m NW Poix	1702
	F/L P.Wigley	Bf109 damaged Poix-Le Treport	1705
124 Sqn Spit FC	F/O D.E.Willis	FW190 destroyed 55m W Start Point	1330~
195 Sqn Typh FC	Sgt R.A.Hough	Bf109 destroyed N Southwold	2200~
315 Sqn Spit FC	F/O S.Blok	FW190 destroyed 5m SW Trouville	1705
	F/O R.Dubielecki	FW190 damaged 5m SW Trouville	1705
317 Sqn Spit FC	P/O W.Kirchner	FW190 prob.dest 10m off Orfordness	2210
	Sgt T.Tamowicz	FW190 damaged 10m off Orfordness	2210
331 Sqn Spit FC	Maj H.O.Mehre	FW190 destroyed N Amiens	1710
	Capt T.Weisteen	FW190 damaged N Amiens	1710
332 Sqn Spit FC	Capt J.Ryg	FW190 destroyed N Amiens	1710
341 Sqn Spit FC	Cdt R.G.O.J.Mouchotte	FW190 destroyed 10m S Caen	1711
403 Sqn Spit FC	F/L H.D.MacDonald	Bf109 damaged NW Poix	1710
	F/L H.D.MacDonald	Bf109 destroyed NW Poix	1710
421 Sqn Spit FC	F/O J.D.F.McFarlane	Bf109 damaged NW Poix	1702
611 Sqn Spit FC	S/L E.F.J.Charles	FW190 destroyed 10m SE Caen	1710~
	S/L E.F.J.Charles	FW190 destroyed 10m SE Caen	1710~

15/16th May 1943

604 Sqn Beau FC	F/O B.R.Keele	Do217 destroyed 30m E Tynemouth	0215

16th May 1943

65 Sqn Spit FC	F/L J.R.Heap	FW190 destroyed 12m N Tregastel	1740~
263 Sqn Whir FC	F/O J.P.Coyne	FW190 damaged Coquettes	0910~
	F/O A.Lee-White	FW190 damaged Coquettes	0910~
412 Sqn Spit FC	F/O L.W.Powell	FW190 destroyed 10-15m NW Sept Iles	1740
416 Sqn Spit FC	F/L R.A.Buckham	FW190 damaged Triqueville-Le Havre	1735
611 Sqn Spit FC	P/O H.E.Walmsley	FW190 damaged Morlaix	1740~

Two great fighter leaders of the Biggin Hill squadrons were (left) Rene Mouchotte, commanding 341 'Alsace' Squadron, and Jack Charles, CO of 611. Both claimed Focke Wulfs destroyed on 16th May 1943 and vied for the honour of destroying the 1,000 enemy aircraft claimed by Biggin Hill units. Mouchotte was killed in action by Unteroffizier Schöhl of 8./JG 26 on 27th August, but Jack Charles survived the war as a Wing Commander with a DSO, two DFCs and a confirmed total of at least fifteen victories.

16/17th May 1943

85 Sqn	Mosq FC	S/L W.P.Green	FW190 destroyed	Dover Straits	0130~
85 Sqn	Mosq FC	F/O J.D.R.Shaw	FW190 destroyed	Near Gravesend	0200~
85 Sqn	Mosq FC	F/O B.J.Thwaites	FW190 destroyed	Dover Straits	0100~
		F/O B.J.Thwaites	FW190 destroyed	Dover Straits	0100~
85 Sqn	Mosq FC	F/L G.L.Howitt	FW190 destroyed	Dover Straits	2345~

17th May 1943

315 Sqn	Spit FC	F/L W.Zajac	FW190 damaged	10m SW Amiens	1530~
316 Sqn	Spit FC	S/L J.Zurakowski	Bf109 damaged	Abbeville-Amiens	1520
		F/O A.F.Prochnicki	FW190 prob.dest	Near Abbeville	1525-30
331 Sqn	Spit FC	2/Lt K.Bache	FW190 destroyed	10m N Guernsey	1300
		Lt M.Y.Gran	FW190 destroyed	10m N Guernsey	1300
		Lt M.Y.Gran	FW190 damaged	10m N Guernsey	1300
341 Sqn	Spit FC	Cdt R.G.O.J.Mouchotte	Bf109 destroyed	10m N Caen	1048
		Capt M.Boudier	FW190 destroyed	Caen	1050
		Lt M.Bouguen	FW190 destroyed	3m N Houlgate	1105
611 Sqn	Spit FC	S/L E.F.J.Charles	FW190 destroyed	Cabourg	1100~
		F/L J.M.Checketts	FW190 damaged	N Caen AD	1100~
		F/L F.F.Colloredo -Mansfeld	FW190 prob.dest	Caen AD	1100~
		Sgt G.A.Jones	Bf109 damaged	5-10m SE Cabourg	1100~
		Sgt V.A.Lancaster	Bf109 destroyed	10m NE Caen	1100~

17/18th May 1943

151 Sqn Mosq FC F/S H.K.Kemp	Ju88 destroyed	Near Minehead	0330

18th May 1943

332 Sqn Spit FC Capt W.Christie	FW190 destroyed	Hesdin	1510
2/Lt E.Westly	FW190 damaged	Hesdin	1510

18/19th May 1943

85 Sqn Mosq FC F/L J.P.M.Lintott	FW190 destroyed	Off Whitstable	0100~

19th May 1943

611 Sqn Spit FC F/L J.M.Checketts	FW190 damaged	Nr Hazebrouck	2130~
Sgt G.AJones	FW190 damaged	15m E St Omer	2130~
F/O G.R.Lindsay	FW190 destroyed	St Omer	2130~
F/O J.C.Minto	FW190 damaged	Nr Hazebrouck	2130~

20/21st May 1943

29 Sqn Mosq FC F/O D.A.Crone	He111 destroyed	Dijon	0300~
418 Sqn Mosq FC S/L R.J.Bennell	E/A damaged	Melun A/D	0044
85 Sqn Mosq FC S/L E.D.Crew	FW190 destroyed	25m NW Hardelot	0415~

23rd May 1943

1 Sqn Typh FC F/S W.H.Ramsay	FW190 destroyed	29m S Rye	1310~

23/24th May 1943

151 Sqn Mosq FC P/O J.D.Humphries	Ju88 damaged	Vechta	0300~
409 Sqn Beau FC S/L G.Bower	Do217 destroyed	6m E Tynemouth	0307
409 Sqn Beau FC Sgt D.M.Hildebrand	Ju88 damaged	30-40m E Tynemouth	0330

25th May 1943

91 Sqn Spit FC P/O D.H.Davy	FW190 destroyed	Dover Straits	2200~
S/L R.H.Harries	FW190 destroyed	Dover Straits	2200~
S/L R.H.Harries	FW190 destroyed	Dover Straits	2200~
F/O J.A.Maridor	FW190 destroyed	Folkestone-Griz Nez	2200~
P/O J.A.Round	FW190 destroyed	Dover Straits	2200~
486 Sqn Typh FC S/L D.J.Scott	FW190 destroyed	20-30m S Brighton	1335

25/26th May 1943

418 Sqn Mosq FC Sgt S.B.James	E/A damaged	Etampes A/D	0154

27th May 1943

331 Sqn Spit FC 2/Lt K.Bache	FW190 destroyed	Bruges-Ghent	1725
2/Lt O.Djonne	FW190 destroyed	Bruges-Ghent	1725

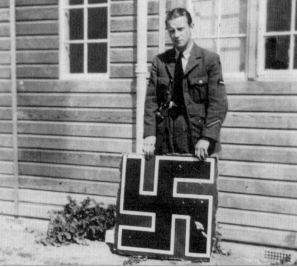

Left: Squadron Leader J.R.Gaynor and Flight Lieutenant G.T.Williams of 68 Squadron pictured at Coltishall. Their unit was to operate Beaufighters until July 1944. Right: A trophy taken from the fin of an unidentified Ju88. Such battle trophies were highly prized by the squadrons concerned.

(ww2images.com)

28th May 1943

331 Sqn	Spit	FC	Lt M.Y.Gran	FW190 damaged	Dunkirk	1750

29th May 1943

616 Sqn	Spit	FC	Sgt J.L.J.Croquet	FW190 damaged	S Poole	1320~
			P/O J.Joubert des Ouches	FW190 damaged	S Poole	1320~

29/30th May 1943

85 Sqn	Mosq	FC	F/O J.P.M.Lintott	Ju88 destroyed	N Lewes	0150
605 Sqn	Mosq	FC	Sgt A.T.Linn	Do217 destroyed	St Trond	0230~

30th May 1943

257 Sqn	Typh	FC	F/S B.C.J.Calnan	FW190 destroyed	Guernsey	1520~
341 Sqn	Spit	FC	S/Lt P.L.Laurent	FW190 destroyed	5m N Deauville	1602
			S/Lt P.L.Laurent	FW190 destroyed	5m N Deauville	1602
611 Sqn	Spit	FC	F/L J.M.Checketts	FW190 destroyed	5-8m SE Trouville	1600~
			Sgt V.A.Lancaster	FW190 destroyed	10m SE Trouville	1600~
			Lt R.T.Tradin	FW190 destroyed	Pont l'Evecque	1600~

31st May 1843

402 Sqn	Spit	FC	S/L L.V.Chadburn	FW190 damaged	Ostend-N Foreland	1748
403 Sqn	Spit	FC	Sgt D.Small*	FW190 destroyed	3m off Nieuport	1750

* Shared with 421 Squadron.

	F/O N.R.Fowlow	FW190 destroyed	Off Nieuport	1747-49
421 Sqn Spit FC	P/O J.W.E.Harten*	FW190 destroyed	3m off Nieuport	1750
	P/O R.W.Isbister	- shared -		

Also shared with 403 Squadron.

	S/L J.D.Hall	FW190 damaged	2m off Nieuport	1749
	F/L W.S.Quint	FW190 damaged	2m off Nieuport	1749

1st June 1943

331 Sqn Spit FC	Lt S.Heglund	FW190 destroyed	Le Touquet-St Omer	1220
	Lt S.Heglund	FW190 destroyed	Le Touquet-St Omer	1220
	Lt N.K.Jorstad	Bf109 prob.dest	Le Touquet-St Omer	1220
332 Sqn Spit FC	Lt E.Westly	Bf109 destroyed	E Boulogne	1220
403 Sqn Spit FC	W/O A.V.Hargreaves	Bf109 prob.dest	Doullens-St Pol	1212
	Squadron claim	Bf109F destroyed	Doullens-St Pol	1212
	F/O R.D.Bowen*	Bf109 destroyed	Somme estuary	1228

* Shared with Kenley Wing.*

609 Sqn Typh FC	F/O I.J.Davies	FW190 destroyed	Lyddon	1310
	F/O I.J.Davies	FW190 destroyed	Off Broadstairs	1310~
	F/O I.J.Davies	FW190 destroyed	Off Broadstairs	1310~
	F/L J.C.Wells	FW190 destroyed	Off Broadstairs	1310~
	F/L J.C.Wells	FW190 destroyed	Off Broadstairs	1310~
Ken Wg Spit FC	W/C J.E.Johnson*	Bf109 destroyed	Somme estuary	1228

* Shared with 403 Squadron.*

4th June 1943

41 Sqn Spit FC	F/O D.H.Smith	FW190 damaged	S Eastbourne	1125
	F/O J.Solak	FW190 destroyed	Eastbourne	1125
453 Sqn Spit FC	F/L D.G.Andrews	FW190 damaged	Somme estuary	1200
	S/L K.M.Barclay	FW190 damaged	Somme estuary	1200
	F/L D.H.Smith	FW190 damaged	Somme estuary	1200
Hch Wg Spit FC	W/C J.R.Ratten	FW190 destroyed	Near Somme estuary	1244

6th June 1943

91 Sqn Spit FC	P/O D.H.Davy	FW190 destroyed	6m off le Treport	1400~
	Sgt J.Watterson	- shared -		

10th June 1943

167 Sqn Spit FC	Sgt C.A.Joseph	FW190 damaged	Eekloo	1845~
302 Sqn Spit FC	P/O J.Krajewski	FW190 destroyed	S Knocke-Ostend	1840
	Sgt J.Kryzstofinski	FW190 destroyed	S Knocke-Ostend	1840
	F/O C.Sniec	FW190 destroyed	S Knocke-Ostend	1840

Made in Germany, but finished in England. This Ju88, 3E+LK of 2./KG 6, was lost on 12/13th June during an attack on Plymouth. It was shot down by Flying Officer D.R.MacLachlin of 125 Squadron and crashed at Stoke, Devon, narrowly missing a WRNS hostel.

			Sgt E.Lucyszyn	FW190 damaged	N Ghent	1845
			F/L B.M.Gladych	FW190 destroyed	S Knocke-Ostend	1840-50
			F/O B.Kaczmarek	FW190 prob.dest	N Ghent	1840-50
332 Sqn	Spit	FC	Capt W.Christie	FW190 damaged	Eekloo	1850
485 Sqn	Spit	FC	F/L M.R.D.Hume	FW190 damaged	Eekloo	1835
			F/S L.S.McQ.White	- shared -		
611 Sqn	Spit	FC	F/L F.F.Colloredo -Mansfeld	FW190 destroyed	NW Ghent	1845~
BH Wg	Spit	FC	W/C A.C.Deere	FW190 damaged	NW Ghent	1845~

11th June 1943

25 Sqn	Mosq	FC	F/O J.E.Wootton	Ju88 damaged	Biscay	1615~
25 Sqn	Mosq	FC	F/L J.Singleton	Ju88 destroyed	Biscay	1615~
316 Sqn	Spit	FC	F/O M.M.Maciejowski	Bf109G destroyed	10m N Beauvais	1650-55
421 Sqn	Spit	FC	S/L J.D.Hall	Bf109 destroyed	NE Poix	1750
			S/L J.D.Hall	Bf109 damaged	NE Poix	1750
			F/L A.H.Sager	Bf109 damaged	NE Poix	1750
456 Sqn	Mosq	FC	P/O J.W.Newell	Ju88 damaged	Biscay	1617
			P/O J.W.Newell	Ju88 damaged	Biscay	1617
611 Sqn	Spit	FC	F/L J.M.Checketts	FW190 destroyed	NE St Pol	1640

11/12th June 1943

256 Sqn	Mosq	FC	P/O C.V.Bennett	Do217 destroyed	SE Ford	2350~
605 Sqn	Mosq	FC	F/O A.G.Woods	E/A destroyed	Gilze-Rijn	0130~

During WW2, NCO pilots were the 'backbone' of the RAF. (l to r) Sergeants Coates, Cohen, Ferguson, Evans, Gray, Chapin and Lewis, all from 401 Squadron at Kenley.

12th June 1943

41 Sqn	Spit	FC	F/O R.G.Middlemiss	Bf109 damaged	Near Caudebec	1948
403 Sqn	Spit	FC	F/O N.R.Fowlow	Bf109 destroyed	Caudebec	1948
412 Sqn	Spit	FC	F/L G.C.Keefer	FW190 damaged	15m NW Ile de Batz	0935-40
			P/O R.N.Earle	FW190 prob.dest	15m NW Ile de Batz	0935-40

12/13th June 1943

125 Sqn	Beau	FC	S/L P.L.Caldwell	Do217 damaged	S Plymouth	0300~
125 Sqn	Beau	FC	W/C R.F.H.Clerke	Ju88 destroyed	25m S Start Pt	0100~
125 Sqn	Beau	FC	P/O G.S.Irving	Do217 damaged	S Plymouth	u/k
125 Sqn	Beau	FC	F/O D.R.McLachlin	Ju88 destroyed	S Plymouth	0052
125 Sqn	Beau	FC	Sgt W.H.Miller	Do217 destroyed	20m SE Plymouth	u/k
			Sgt W.H.Miller	Ju88 destroyed	SE Plymouth	0045
604 Sqn	Beau	FC	F/O J.N.Howard-Williams	Ju88 damaged	Off Yarmouth	2300~
605 Sqn	Mosq	FC	F/O R.R.Smart	E/A damaged	Twente	u/k

13th June 1943

124 Sqn	Spit	FC	W/O G.L.Nowell DFM	FW190 destroyed	Off Ramsgate	0840~
151 Sqn	Mosq	FC	F/O L.A.D.Boyle (shared) P/O J.D.Humphries	FW200 destroyed - shared -	Biscay	1100~
264 Sqn	Mosq	FC	F/S W.Kent	FW190 damaged	60m SW Scilly Isles	1600~
402 Sqn	Spit	FC	Sgt L.A.Moore	FW190 prob.dest	Flushing-Bradwell	0915
			Squadron claim	FW190 prob.dest	Flushing-Bradwell	0915
Dig Wg	Spit	FC	W/C L.V.Chadburn	FW190 damaged	Flushing-Bradwell	0915

The first day of June brought two victories for Lieutenant Svein Heglund of 331 Squadron, while Wing Commander Johnnie Johnson shared one with Flying Officer Bob Bowen of 403 Squadron. After a 'rest' with a transport unit in 1944, Heglund returned to combat, this time as a long-range Mosquito intruder pilot, adding three more kills to his impressive total of eleven.

13/14th June 1943

68 Sqn	Beau FC	F/O D.B.Wills *	He177 destroyed	10m E Flamboro' Hd	0400~

* On attachment to 604 Sqn.

85 Sqn	Mosq FC	W/C J.Cunningham	FW190 destroyed	Wrotham	0050

0014/15th June 1943

141 Sqn	Beau FC	W/C J.R.D.Braham	Bf110 destroyed	N Stavoren	0300~

15th June 1943

402 Sqn	Spit FC	F/O R.D.Bowen	FW190 damaged	Yvetot area	0827
		S/L H.C.Godefroy	FW190 destroyed	Yvetot area	0827
		F/L H.D.MacDonald	FW190 prob.dest	Near Caudebec	0827
Ken Wg	Spit FC	W/C J.E.Johnson	FW190 destroyed	Yvetot area	0827
		W/C J.E.Johnson	FW190 destroyed	Yvetot area	0827

15/16th June 1943

137 Sqn	Whir FC	W/C J.B.Wray	FW190 damaged	Cayeux	0100~
605 Sqn	Mosq FC	F/O R RSmart	He177 destroyed	Aalborg	0130~

16th June 1943

1 Sqn	Typh FC	P/O S.P.Dennis	FW190 damaged	W Douai	0535
91 Sqn	Spit FC	F/O R.S.Nash	FW190 damaged	16m SE Dover	0710

F/O R.S.Nash	FW190 damaged	16m SE Dover	0710
P/O V.P.Seydel	FW190 damaged	16m SE Dover	0710

16/17th June 1943

141 Sqn Beau FC	W/C J.R.D.Braham	Ju88 damaged	Schouwen Island	0300~
141 Sqn Beau FC	F/O R.C.MacAndrew	Bf110 damaged	S Eindhoven	0300~
605 Sqn Mosq FC	F/S Irving	E/A destroyed	Venlo	u/k
	F/S Irving	E/A damaged	Venlo	u/k

17th June 1943

316 Sqn Spit FC	F/O A.F.Prochnicki	FW190 damaged	Bruges	0945
331 Sqn Spit FC	Capt S.Heglund	FW190 prob.dest	NE Flushing	0945
	F/S R.H.Olsen	FW190 destroyed	NE Flushing	0945
	Sgt P.Thulin	FW190 damaged	NE Flushing	0945
332 Sqn Spit FC	Capt R.From Sgt B.Aarflot	FW190 destroyed - shared -	NE Flushing	0945
	Capt W.Christie	FW190 damaged	NE Flushing	0945
	Capt R.From	FW190 prob.dest	NE Flushing	0945
	Sgt O.Gabrielson	FW190 destroyed	NE Flushing	0945
	Maj H.O.Mehre	FW190 destroyed	NE Flushing	0945
	Maj H.O.Mehre	FW190 damaged	NE Flushing	0945
	Sgt H.Odman	FW190 prob.dest	NE Flushing	0945
	Sgt H.Odman	FW190 damaged	NE Flushing	0945
	Maj F.Thorsager Sgt S.Sandvik	FW190 destroyed - shared -	NE Flushing	0945
	Maj F.Thorsager	FW190 damaged	NE Flushing	0945
403 Sqn Spit FC	F/S G.M.Shouldice	FW190 destroyed	N St Omer	1544
421 Sqn Spit FC	S/L P.L.I.Archer*	FW190 destroyed	Ypres-St Omer	1537
	F/O J.E.McNamara	FW190 damaged	Ypres-St Omer	1537

Phil Archer failed to return and was found dead in his aircraft. Although credited with a victory, no official documentation has been traced and no Combat Report (Form F) appears to have been submitted.

453 Sqn Spit FC	F/L D.G.Andrews	FW190 prob.dest	Axel-Hulst	1537
	F/O F.B.McDermott	FW190 damaged	Axel-Hulst	1537
Ken Wg Spit FC	W/C J.E.Johnson	FW190 destroyed	Ypres-St Omer	1537

17/18th June 1943

85 Sqn Mosq FC	Lt J.Raad	FW190 damaged	Tonbridge	0100~

19th June 1943

151 Sqn Mosq FC	S/L H.G.Bodien	Ju88 destroyed	Biscay	1900

On the night of 20th June, Massy Beveridge of 418 Squadron (left) claimed a Do217 'probable' over France. On 22nd, both Ola Aanjesen of 332 Squadron and Ray Hesselyn of 277 Squadron fought FW190s, the latter flying an Air Sea Rescue Spitfire.

	F/O A.D.Boyle	Ju88 damaged	Biscay	1900
	Unnamed crew	Ju88 damaged	Biscay	1900
264 Sqn Mosq FC	F/O E.A.Turner	Ju88 damaged	65m W Raz Point	1640~
307 Sqn Mosq FC	F/L J.Bienkowski*	BV138 destroyed	W Bordeaux	1223
	F/O J.Pelka	- shared -		
	S/L S.Szablowski	- shared -		

* Also shared with 410 Squadron.

410 Sqn Mosq FC	F/O E.A.Murray*	BV138 destroyed	W Bordeaux	1223

* Shared with 307 Squadron.

456 Sqn Mosq FC	W/O G.F.Gatenby	Ju88 damaged	Biscay	2000~
605 Sqn Mosq FC	F/O K.F.Dacre	Do217 destroyed	Compeigne	0200~
	F/O K.F.Dacre	Bf110 destroyed	St Dizier	0200~

20th June 1943

264 Sqn Mosq FC	F/O F.W.Moncur	Ju88 prob.dest	2m S Ushant	1700~
421 Sqn Spit FC	S/L R.W.McNair	FW190 destroyed	Mear Doullens	1318
	F/O F.J.Sherlock	FW190 prob.dest	Mear Doullens	1318

20/21st June 1943

264 Sqn Mosq FC	W/C W.J.Alington (shared)	BV138 destroyed	Biscarosse	2330~
	S/L L.T.Bryant-Fenn	- shared -		
	F/O J.L.Mason	- shared -		
	F/O E.E.Pudsey	- shared -		
	W/C W.J.Alington (shared)	BV138 destroyed	Near Biscarosse	2330~
	F/O J.L.Mason	- shared -		
	F/O F.W.Moncur	Ju88 prob.dest	2m S Ushant	2330~
418 Sqn Mosq FC	F/L M.W.Beveridge	Do217 prob.dest	Nr Colommieres A/D	0040

21/22nd June 1943

85 Sqn	Mosq	FC	F/L W.H.Maguire	FW190 destroyed	Strood	0030
85 Sqn	Mosq	FC	P/O R.L.T.Robb	FW190 damaged	Dungeness	0120~
141 Sqn	Beau	FC	S/L C.V.Winn	Ju88 destroyed	Weert	0230~

22nd June 1943

118 Sqn	Spit	FC	P/O E.A.McKinley	FW190 damaged	Unknown	1810~

* Not claimed by McKinley, but credited by squadron.

222 Sqn	Spit	FC	F/L P.V.K.Tripe	FW190 damaged	Sliedrecht	1021
277 Sqn	Spit	FC	F/L R.B.Hesselyn	FW190 damaged	E Orfordness	2100~
332 Sqn	Spit	FC	Capt R.From	FW190 prob.dest	SW Rotterdam	0835
			Capt R.From	FW190 damaged	W Schouwen	0835
			Sgt O.G.Aanjesen	FW190 prob.dest	W Schouwen	0855
341 Sqn	Spit	FC	Cdt B.Duperier	FW190 damaged	40m E North Foreland	1015
453 Sqn	Spit	FC	S/L K.M.Barclay	FW190 damaged	Tholen, S Rotterdam	1023
610 Sqn	Spit	FC	Sgt H.Fallon	Bf109 damaged	Dutch coast	1020~
			F/O R.Wood	FW190 damaged	Dutch coast	1020~

22/23rd June 1943

141 Sqn	Beau	FC	F/O H.C.Kelsey	Bf110 destroyed	Rijssen	0200~
605 Sqn	Mosq	FC	Sgt A.T.Linn	Me210 destroyed	Venlo	0300~

23rd June 1943

118 Sqn	Spit	FC	2/Lt S.K.Liby	FW190 destroyed	Near Abbeville	1800-10
			2/Lt S.K.Liby	FW190 damaged	Near Abbeville	1800-10
			F/L R.A.Newbery	FW190 damaged	Near Abbeville	1800-10
416 Sqn	Spit	FC	Squadron claim	FW190 destroyed	Somme estuary	1802
611 Sqn	Spit	FC	S/L E.F.J.Charles	FW190 destroyed	nr Meaulte	1810~
BH Wg	Spit	FC	W/C A.C.Deere	FW190 destroyed	3m N Rue	1810~

24th June 1943

302 Sqn	Spit	FC	F/O S.Brzeski	FW190 prob.dest	NE Brest	1644
			F/S W.Gretkierewicz	FW190 prob.dest	NE Brest	1644
303 Sqn	Spit	FC	F/L A.Kolubinski	FW190 damaged	Nieuport	0858
			Unknown pilot	FW190 prob.dest	Nieuport	0858
310 Sqn	Spit	FC	Sgt A.Sveceny	FW190 damaged	N Guipavas	1642-52
			F/O K.Zouhar	FW190 damaged	15-20m N Brest	1642-52
316 Sqn	Spit	FC	Sgt C.Bartlomiejczyk	FW190 destroyed	Nieuport	0900~
			F/O J.Sobolewski	FW190 damaged	Nieuport	0900~
317 Sqn	Spit	FC	F/O J.Walawski	FW190 damaged	10m N Brest	1645-50

Left: Geoff Northcott claimed his second solo kill, a Bf109G, on 27th June leading 402 Squadron. He would end the war as Wing Leader of 126 Wing, having scored eight solo kills and having been awarded a DSO and two DFCs. Right: 'Bob' Braham led 141 Squadron in 1943, pioneering the use of the 'Serrate' radar homer to hunt German nightfighters. On 24/25th June his score reached fifteen when he caught a Bf110 near Gilze-Rijn. He would end the war as the most decorated RAF pilot, with three DSOs and three DFCs

		F/O M.Ciach	FW190 damaged	40m N Brest		1654-59
		F/O J.Walawski	FW190 damaged	40m N Brest		1654-59
331 Sqn	Spit	FC	2/Lt F.A.S.Fearnley	FW190 damaged	SE St Omer	1205-10
		Lt M.Y.Gran	FW190 prob.dest	SE St Omer		1205-10
		Lt N.K.Jorstad	FW190 destroyed	SE St Omer		1205-10
		Lt K.Nyerrod	FW190 damaged	SE St Omer		1205-10
332 Sqn	Spit	FC	Maj F.Thorsager	FW190 damaged	SE St Omer	1205-10
		Maj F.Thorsager	FW190 damaged	SE St Omer		1205-10
		Lt E.Westly	FW190 destroyed	SE St Omer		1205-10
		Lt E.Westly	FW190 damaged	SE St Omer		1205-10
		Lt E.Westly	FW190 damaged	SE St Omer		1205-10
403 Sqn	Spit	FC	F/L H.D.MacDonald	FW190 destroyed	SE St Omer	1220
421 Sqn	Spit	FC	S/L R.W.McNair	FW190 destroyed	S Fecamp	1750
486 Sqn	Typh	FC	S/L D.J.Scott	FW190 destroyed	5-10m NE Somme mouth	1445-50
		F/L A.E.Umbers	FW190 destroyed	5-10m NE Somme mouth		1445-50
Ken Wg	Spit	FC	W/C J.E.Johnson	FW190 destroyed	S Fecamp	1750

24/25th June 1943

141 Sqn	Beau FC	W/C J.R.D.Braham	Bf110 destroyed	SW Gilze-Rijn	0200~
418 Sqn	Mosq FC	F/S J.H.Kingsbury	E/A damaged	Nantes/Gassicourt	0126

25/26th June 1943

141 Sqn	Beau FC	F/O H.C.Kelsey	Bf110 destroye	Hardenburg	0200~

26th June 1943

264 Sqn	Mosq FC	F/O E.A.Turner Sgt R.Wilkie	Ju88 damaged - shared -	Biscay	0830~

26/27th June 1943

418 Sqn	Mosq FC	F/S C.D.Ball	E/A damaged	Bretigny	0130
418 Sqn	Mosq FC	S/L C.C.Moran	He111 destroyed	Avord	0105
		S/L C.C.Moran	Ju88 destroyed	Avord	0110

27th June 1943

64 Sqn	Spit FC	S/L W.V.Crawford -Compton	Bf109 destroyed	Audricq	1050
118 Sqn	Spit FC	F/L R.A.Acworth	FW190 damaged	Off The Hague	1505-10
		F/S J.Hollingsworth	FW190 damaged	Near The Hague	1505-10
		F/L R.A.Newbery	FW190 destroyed	Den Helder	1505-10
124 Sqn	Spit FC	W/O G.L.Nowell	FW190 destroyed	38m E N Foreland	0640~
402 Sqn	Spit FC	S/L G.W.Northcott	Bf109 destroyed	8m off The Hague	1505
416 Sqn	Spit FC	P/O R.D.Phillip F/L J.A.Rae	FW190 destroyed - shared -	8m off The Hague	1305
453 Sqn	Spit FC	S/L K.M.Barclay	Bf109 damaged	Near Bethune	1047
		P/O J.H.Ferguson	Bf109 destroyed	Near Bethune	1047
Dig Wg	Spit FC	W/C L.V.Chadburn	FW190 damaged	8-10m off The Hague	1305
Ken Wg	Spit FC	W/C J.E.Johnson	FW190 destroyed	W St Omer	1053
NW Wg	Spit FC	Maj H.O.Mehre	FW190 destroyed	Near Flushing	0945
		Maj H.O.Mehre	FW190 damaged	Near Flushing	0945

28/29th June 1943

418 Sqn	Mosq FC	F/S J.H.Kingsbury	FW190 damaged	St Trond A/D	0232

29th June 1943

65 Sqn	Spit FC	S/L J.A.Storrar DFC	FW190 prob.dest	Off Le Havre	2120~
AFDU	Must FC	S/L J.A.F.Maclachlan F/L A.G.Page	Ju88 destroyed - shared -	Rambouillet	1045~
		S/L J.A.F.Maclachlan F/L A.G.Page	Ju88 destroyed - shared -	Rambouillet	1045~

S/L J.A.F.Maclachlan	Hs126 destroyed	Rambouillet	1045~
F/L A.G.Page	- shared -		
S/L J.A.F.Maclachlan	Hs126 destroyed	Rambouillet	1045~
F/L A.G.Page	- shared -		
S/L J.A.F.Maclachlan	Hs126 destroyed	Rambouillet	1045~
F/L A.G.Page	- shared -		
S/L J.A.F.Maclachlan	Hs126 destroyed	Rambouillet	1045~
F/L A.G.Page	- shared -